Deploying Cisco Wide Area Application Services

Zach Seils, CCIE No. 7861
Joel Christner, CCIE No. 15311

Cisco Press

Cisco Press
800 East 96th Street
Indianapolis, Indiana 46240 USA

Deploying Cisco Wide Area Application Services

Zach Seils, Joel Christner

Copyright © 2008 Cisco Systems, Inc.

Published by:
Cisco Press
800 East 96th Street
Indianapolis, IN 46240 USA

Printed in the United States of America

First Printing   May 2008

Library of Congress Cataloging-in-Publication Data

Seils, Zach.
  Deploying Cisco Wide area application services / Zach Seils, Joel
Christner.
     p. cm.
  ISBN 978-1-58705-494-5 (hardcover)
  1. Wide area networks (Computer networks) 2. Application software I.
Christner, Joel. II. Cisco Systems, Inc. III. Title.

  TK5105.87.S35 2008
  004.67--dc22

2008011639
ISBN-13: 978-1-58705-494-5
ISBN-10: 1-58705-494-9

Warning and Disclaimer

This book is designed to provide information about deploying Cisco Wide Area Application Services (WAAS), a powerful solution that enables IT infrastructure consolidation while ensuring remote users fast access to centralized resources. Every effort has been made to make this book as complete and as accurate as possible, but no warranty or fitness is implied.

The information is provided on an "as is" basis. The authors, Cisco Press, and Cisco Systems, Inc. shall have neither liability nor responsibility to any person or entity with respect to any loss or damages arising from the information contained in this book or from the use of the discs or programs that may accompany it.

The opinions expressed in this book belong to the author and are not necessarily those of Cisco Systems, Inc.

Trademark Acknowledgments

All terms mentioned in this book that are known to be trademarks or service marks have been appropriately capitalized. Cisco Press or Cisco Systems, Inc., cannot attest to the accuracy of this information. Use of a term in this book should not be regarded as affecting the validity of any trademark or service mark.

Corporate and Government Sales

The publisher offers excellent discounts on this book when ordered in quantity for bulk purchases or special sales, which may include electronic versions and/or custom covers and content particular to your business, training goals, marketing focus, and branding interests. For more information, please contact: **U.S. Corporate and Government Sales** 1-800-382-3419 corpsales@pearsontechgroup.com

For sales outside the United States please contact: **International Sales** international@pearsoned.com

Feedback Information

At Cisco Press, our goal is to create in-depth technical books of the highest quality and value. Each book is crafted with care and precision, undergoing rigorous development that involves the unique expertise of members from the professional technical community.

Readers' feedback is a natural continuation of this process. If you have any comments regarding how we could improve the quality of this book, or otherwise alter it to better suit your needs, you can contact us through e-mail at feedback@ciscopress.com. Please make sure to include the book title and ISBN in your message.

We greatly appreciate your assistance.

Publisher	Paul Boger
Associate Publisher	Dave Dusthimer
Cisco Representative	Anthony Wolfenden
Cisco Press Program Manager	Jeff Brady
Editor-in-Chief	Karen Gettman
Managing Editor	Patrick Kanouse
Senior Development Editor	Christopher Cleveland
Senior Project Editor	San Dee Phillips
Copy Editor	Bill McManus
Technical Editors	Mani Ramaswamy, Etai Lev Ran
Editorial Assistant	Romny French
Cover and Book Designer	Louisa Adair
Composition	Octal Publishing, Inc.
Indexer	Publishing Works
Proofreader	Sheri Cain

Americas Headquarters	Asia Pacific Headquarters	Europe Headquarters
Cisco Systems, Inc.	Cisco Systems, Inc.	Cisco Systems International BV
170 West Tasman Drive	168 Robinson Road	Haarlerbergpark
San Jose, CA 95134-1706	#28-01 Capital Tower	Haarlerbergweg 13-19
USA	Singapore 068912	1101 CH Amsterdam
www.cisco.com	www.cisco.com	The Netherlands
Tel: 408 526-4000	Tel: +65 6317 7777	www-europe.cisco.com
800 553-NETS (6387)	Fax: +65 6317 7799	Tel: +31 0 800 020 0791
Fax: 408 527-0883		Fax: +31 0 20 357 1100

Cisco has more than 200 offices worldwide. Addresses, phone numbers, and fax numbers are listed on the Cisco Website at **www.cisco.com/go/offices.**

About the Authors

Zach Seils, CCIE No. 7861, is a technical leader in the Cisco Advanced Services Data Center Networking Practice. Zach's focus is the design, deployment, and troubleshooting of data center and branch application services solutions for Cisco's largest enterprise and service provider customers. Zach is frequently engaged with partners and internal Cisco engineers worldwide to advise on the design, implementation, and troubleshooting of Cisco WAAS. In addition to working closely with partners and customers, Zach collaborates with various Cisco business units on product enhancements, testing, and application services architectures. Prior to joining Cisco, Zach spent six years in various senior technical roles at a managed service provider.

Joel Christner, CCIE No. 15311, is the director of product management for Reconnex Corporation, the industry leader in data loss prevention (DLP) solutions. At Reconnex, Joel drives the product strategy and direction for a comprehensive portfolio of solutions for protecting corporate sensitive information and ensuring compliance with industry and government regulation.

Prior to joining Reconnex, Joel was the senior manager of technical marketing for the Application Delivery Business Unit (ADBU) at Cisco Systems, Inc. Joel led the technical marketing engineering team and helped drive product strategy as a lead contributor to the product management organization. Along with product strategy, Joel and his team were responsible for global sales enablement, including technical whitepapers, product presentations, transfer of information, and competitive leadership. Joel is co-author of the book *Application Acceleration and WAN Optimization Fundamentals* (Cisco Press), which outlines architecture and relevance for WAN optimization and application acceleration technologies in today's dynamic I/T organizations.

Joel was previously a senior technical marketing engineer within ADBU, and was also part of the data center and storage networking advanced technology team within Cisco prior to joining ADBU. Joel's background and experience includes information security, content, data center networking and security, storage networking, and application networking services.

Joel is presently an MS Computer Science student at Columbia University in New York, NY, and holds a BS in Electronics Engineering Technology. Joel is co-author of *Application Acceleration and WAN Optimization Fundamentals* (Cisco Press), which outlines architecture and relevance for WAN optimization and application acceleration technologies in today's dynamic IT organizations.

Dedications

This book is dedicated to my three boys, Rowan, Evan, and Jeeper. Thanks for your patience while I spend endless hours on the computer. I love you.

—Zach Seils

This book is dedicated to my beautiful wife Christina, our family, and to our Lord and Savior Jesus Christ, through Him all things are possible.

—Joel Christner

Acknowledgments

From Zach Seils: I'd like to give special thanks to my peers and the management team of the Advanced Services Data Center Networking Practice. The DCN team has been my home since I joined Cisco, and I can't imagine a better team to be a part of.

I owe a significant debt of gratitude to the technical reviewers, Etai Lev Ran and Mani Ramaswamy. Thanks for not only lending your precious time to review this book, but also answering my constant queries about the minute engineering details of the WAAS solution.

To my co-author Joel, thanks for making this project happen and your guidance throughout the writing process. I was selfishly sad to see you leave Cisco, but know that our paths will cross again one day.

Thanks to the Cisco Press team—Romny French, Karen Gettman, Christopher Cleveland, San Dee Phillips—for agreeing to take on this project, and for the assistance in getting things done on time and with quality.

And finally, I'd like to thank my parents, who always supported me, my brother, who has always inspired me to think, and my wife, Margaret—I love you.

From Joel Christner: To Christina, my beautiful, loving, and patient wife—thank you. I promise I won't write another book for a little while.

I'd like to express my deepest appreciation to you, the reader, for taking the time to read this book. Zach and I are honored to have been given the opportunity to earn a spot in your personal library, and look forward to your feedback.

To Zach, for being such a great co-author and a good friend. Your expertise and ability to clearly articulate complex technical concepts is amazing, and I'm thankful to have been given the opportunity to collaborate with you. Numerous thanks to Etai Lev Ran and Mani Ramaswamy, our technical reviewers. Your attention to detail and focus helped keep our material accurate and concise. It was a pleasure working with you on this book—and at Cisco.

A tremendous thank you to the team at Cisco Press—Romny French, Karen Gettman, Christopher Cleveland—your guidance has been great, and Zach and I both appreciate you keeping us on track and focused.

This Book Is Safari Enabled

The Safari® Enabled icon on the cover of your favorite technology book means the book is available through Safari Bookshelf. When you buy this book, you get free access to the online edition for 45 days.

Safari Bookshelf is an electronic reference library that lets you easily search thousands of technical books, find code samples, download chapters, and access technical information whenever and wherever you need it.

To gain 45-day Safari Enabled access to this book:

- Go to http://www.ciscopress.com/safarienabled.

- Complete the brief registration form.

- Enter the coupon code CZGA-KEHE-VK9A-8CEB-RXX8.

If you have difficulty registering on Safari Bookshelf or accessing the online edition, please e-mail customer-service@safaribooksonline.com.

Contents at a Glance

Foreword   xvi

Introduction   xvii

Chapter 1   Introduction to Cisco Wide Area Application Services (WAAS)   3

Chapter 2   Cisco Wide Area Application Engine (WAE) Family   33

Chapter 3   Planning, Discovery, and Analysis   51

Chapter 4   Network Integration and Interception   75

Chapter 5   Branch Office Network Integration   117

Chapter 6   Data Center Network Integration   165

Chapter 7   System and Device Management   207

Chapter 8   Configuring WAN Optimization   247

Chapter 9   Configuring Application Acceleration   285

Chapter 10   Case Studies   325

Index   359

Contents

Foreword xvi

Introduction xvii

Chapter 1 Introduction to Cisco Wide Area Application Services (WAAS) 3

Understanding Application Performance Barriers 3
Layer 4 Through Layer 7 4
Latency 6
Bandwidth Inefficiencies 7
Network Infrastructure 8
Bandwidth Constraints 9
Network Latency 11
Loss and Congestion 14

Introduction to Cisco WAAS 15
WAN Optimization 17
Data Redundancy Elimination 18
Persistent LZ Compression 21
Transport Flow Optimization 22
Application Acceleration 23
Object and Metadata Caching 25
Prepositioning 27
Read-Ahead 27
Write-Behind 28
Multiplexing 29
Other Features 29

Summary 31

Chapter 2 Cisco Wide Area Application Engine (WAE) Family 33

Cisco WAE Product Architecture 33
Disk Encryption 34
Central Management Subsystem 35
Interface Manager 35
Reporting Facilities 35
Network Interception and Bypass Manager 36
Application Traffic Policy Engine 36

Hardware Family 38
Router-Integrated Network Modules 38
NME-WAE Model 302 39
NME-WAE Model 502 39
NME-WAE Model 522 40

    Appliances   40

        WAE Model 512   41

        WAE Model 612   41

        WAE Model 7326   41

        WAE Model 7341   41

        WAE Model 7371   42

    Licensing   42

    Performance and Scalability Metrics   42

        Device Memory   43

        Disk Capacity   44

        Number of Optimized TCP Connections   46

        WAN Bandwidth and LAN Throughput   46

        Number of Peers and Fan-Out   47

        Number of Devices Managed   48

    Summary   49

Chapter 3   Planning, Discovery, and Analysis   51

    Planning Overview   51

        Planning Overview Checklist   52

    Requirements Collection and Analysis   52

    Site Information   54

        Site Types   54

        User Population   55

        Physical Environment   55

        Site Information Checklist   56

    Network Infrastructure   56

        WAN Topology   56

        Remote Office Topology   59

        Data Center Topology   60

        Traffic Flows   62

        Network Infrastructure Checklist   64

    Application Characteristics   64

        Application Requirements Checklist   65

    File Services Requirements   65

        Advanced Features   66

        File Services Utilization   66

        File Services Requirements Checklist   67

Platform Requirements   67
  Platform Requirements Checklist   67

Scalability Requirements   67
  Scalability Requirements Checklist   67

Availability Requirements   68
  Availability Checklist   68

Management Requirements   68
  SNMP Trap/Inform Routing   69
  SNMP Community Strings   69
  Syslog Servers   70
  Management Requirements Checklist   70

Security Requirements   70
  Security Requirements Checklist   72

Summary   73

Chapter 4   Network Integration and Interception   75

Interface Connectivity   75
  Link Aggregation Using EtherChannel   78
    EtherChannel Configuration   79
  Using the Standby Interface Feature   82
    Standby Interface Configuration   84

Interception Techniques and Protocols   86
  Web Cache Communication Protocol   86
    WCCP Overview   87
    Service Groups   87
    Forwarding and Return Methods   90
    Load Distribution   92
    Failure Detection   94
    Flow Protection   95
    Graceful Shutdown   95
    Scalability   95
    Redirect Lists   96
    Service Group Placement   97
    WCCP Configuration   98
    Hardware-based Platforms   102
  Policy-Based Routing   103
  Inline Interception   105
  Content Switching   109
    Application Control Engine   109

Egress Methods for Intercepted Connections   111

Network Integration Best Practices   114

Summary   115

Chapter 5   Branch Office Network Integration   117

In-Path Deployment   117
   Nonredundant Branch Office   118
   Redundant Branch Office   122
   Serial Clustering   125

Off-Path Deployment   127
   Small to Medium-Sized Nonredundant Branch Office   127
      Enhanced Network Module (NME-WAE)   131
      Two-Arm Deployment   132
   Large Nonredundant Branch Office   134
   Off-Path Redundant Topology   141
      Small to Medium-Sized Redundant Branch Office   141
      Large Redundant Branch Office   149
   Policy-Based Routing Interception   158
   Cisco IOS Firewall Integration   161

Summary   163

Chapter 6   Data Center Network Integration   165

Data Center Placement   165

Deployment Solutions   174
   WCCP   175
   Content Switching   186

Scaling Transparent Interception   192
   WCCP Scalability   192
   Application Control Engine Scalability   198

Firewall Integration   199

Summary   205

Chapter 7   System and Device Management   207

System and Device Management Overview   207
   Initial Setup Script and Device Setup   208
   Command-Line Interface   212
   Central Manager Overview   213
   Centralized Management System Service   216

Device Registration and Groups   219
    Device Activation   220
    Device Groups   222

Provisioned Management   224
    Role-Based Access Control   224
    Integration with Centralized Authentication   227

Device Configuration, Monitoring, and Management   229
    Device Homepage   229
    Status and Health Monitoring   232
    Software Upgrade and Downgrade   235

Reporting and Logging   239

Backup and Restore of Central Manager   241

Summary   244

Chapter 8   Configuring WAN Optimization   247

Cisco WAAS WAN Optimization Capabilities   247
    Transport Flow Optimization   247
    Data Redundancy Elimination   249
    Persistent LZ Compression   251
    Automatic Discovery   251
    Enabling and Disabling Features   253
    TFO Blacklist Operation   255
    Tuning TFO Buffers   257

Application Traffic Policy   261
    Application Groups   262
    Traffic Classifiers   264
    Policy Maps   266
    Negotiating Policies   269
    EndPoint Mapper Classification   270

Reporting   274
    Automatic Discovery Statistics   274
    Connection Statistics and Details   276
    WAN Optimization Statistics   279

Summary   283

Chapter 9   Configuring Application Acceleration   285

Application Acceleration Overview   285
    Core Services   287
    Edge Services   288

Connectivity Directives   289
Interaction with WAN Optimization   289

Configuring CIFS Acceleration   291
Configuring Core Services   291
Creating a WAFS Core Cluster   291
Enabling Core Services   292
Configuring Edge Services   294
Configuring Connectivity Directives   297
Examining CIFS Acceleration Traffic Policies   300
Verifying CIFS Acceleration   301

CIFS Preposition   304
CIFS Preposition Architecture   304
Configuring CIFS Preposition   306
Examining Preposition Statistics   311

Disconnected Mode of Operation   313
Domain Integration   314
Configuring System Time   315
Defining Domain-Related Parameters   317
Joining an Active Directory Domain   318
Configuring Disconnected Mode of Operation   320

Summary   322

Chapter 10   Case Studies   325

Common Requirements   325

Existing WAN Topology   325

Remote Site Profile A   327
Profile A Site Requirements   327
Site Network Topology   327
WAE Placement and Interception   328
WAE Configuration Details   329
WAN Router Configuration Details   330
LAN Switch Configuration Details   331

Remote Site Profile B   333
Profile B Site Requirements   333
Site Network Topology   333
WAE Placement and Interception   334
WAE Configuration Details   334
WAN Router Configuration Details   336

Remote Site Profile C   337
Profile C Site Requirements   338
Site Network Topology   338
WAE Placement and Interception   338
WAE Configuration Details   340
WAN Router 1 Configuration Details   341
WAN Router 2 Configuration Details   343

Data Center Profile   345
Data Center Site Requirements   345
Site Network Topology   345
WAE Placement and Interception   346
WAE Configuration Details   348
Data Center Switch 1 Configuration Details   349
Data Center Switch 2 Configuration Details   352

Application Traffic Policy   355

Summary   357

Index   359

Icons Used in This Book

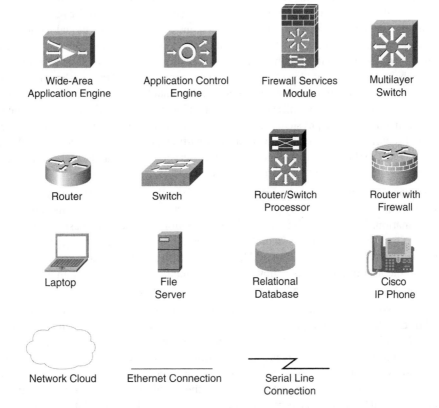

Wide-Area Application Engine

Application Control Engine

Firewall Services Module

Multilayer Switch

Router

Switch

Router/Switch Processor

Router with Firewall

Laptop

File Server

Relational Database

Cisco IP Phone

Network Cloud

Ethernet Connection

Serial Line Connection

Command Syntax Conventions

The conventions used to present command syntax in this book are the same conventions used in the *IOS Command Reference*, which describes these conventions as follows:

- **Boldface** indicates commands and keywords that are entered literally as shown. In actual configuration examples and output (not general command syntax), boldface indicates commands that are manually input by the user (such as a **show** command).
- *Italics* indicate arguments for which you supply actual values.
- Vertical bars (|) separate alternative, mutually exclusive elements.
- Square brackets [ ] indicate optional elements.
- Braces { } indicate a required choice.
- Braces within brackets [{ }] indicate a required choice within an optional element.

Foreword

Several important and pervasive trends are driving the rapid adoption of WAN optimization technologies. The globalization of business has driven the need to provide reliable 24x7 information access to the extended enterprise of suppliers, distributors, customers, and employees. The global nature of business has driven steady growth in the number of branch offices, as corporations have relentlessly tried to put a local, customer-intimate face to their global brands and operations. This, for example, is the case in retail banking where new forms of "lean branches" have emerged in storefronts, shopping malls, and other locations, bringing the "branch to the customer" rather than "the customer to the branch." Deploying a traditional "heavy" application infrastructure to such locations is simply impossible due to constraints of space, manpower, and physical security. Furthermore, additional pressures of cost, regulatory compliance, and security have driven the need for IT departments to seriously evaluate further global consolidation of their application infrastructures, such as servers, storage and backup, and network equipment, and even to consider a "software-as-a-service" application model.

WAN optimization technology offers the promise to transform the way corporations do business, by enabling collaboration and teamwork by providing cost-effective, responsive, anytime, anywhere access to critical information. At the same time, as WAN optimization "crosses the chasm" to mainstream adoption, we at Cisco believe that it is important to integrate these technologies closely with the network and the operating services on the WAN, such as security, routing, and so on. Not only is this nondisruptive to the network, but it also allows customers the flexibility to evolve their network, network services, and application architectures with the needs of the business.

I have known the two authors for several years and can vouch for their qualifications to write such a book. Each brings extensive and respected practitioner's experience in the development, design, and deployment of Cisco's award-winning WAN optimization technology solutions to more than 2000 customers. The authors have provided many of our customers counsel on the successful design of their solutions and have given our engineering team direction for important new capabilities being built into our products. Each brings both a deep understanding of the broad range of wide-area networking technologies and a practical bent to the successful integration of these technologies into a systematic solution.

I strongly recommend that you read this book if you are interested in WAN optimization technologies or are considering deploying such technology; it will serve you well.

George Kurian
Vice President and General Manager
Application Delivery Business Unit
Cisco Systems, Inc.

Introduction

IT organizations are realizing the benefits of infrastructure consolidation and virtualization—cost savings, operational savings, better posture toward disaster recovery—and the challenges associated. Consolidating infrastructure increases the distance between the remote office worker and the tools they need to ensure productivity—applications, servers, content, and more. Application acceleration and WAN optimization solutions such as Cisco Wide Area Application Services (WAAS) bridge the divide between consolidation and performance to enable a high-performance consolidated infrastructure.

Goals and Methods

The goal of this book is to familiarize you with the concepts and fundamentals of sizing and deploying Cisco WAAS in your environment. This book provides a technical introduction to the product, followed by deployment sizing guidelines, through integration techniques, and configuration of major components and subsystems. This book provides you with 95 percent or more of the knowledge that you need to ensure a successful deployment of Cisco WAAS in your environment, including configuration tips, pointers, and notes that will guide you through the process.

Who Should Read This Book?

This book is written for anyone who is responsible for the design and deployment of Cisco WAAS in their network environment. The text assumes the reader has a basic knowledge of data networking, specifically TCP/IP and basic routing and switching technologies.

As the WAAS technology continues to evolve, the content in this book will provide a solid framework to build on. Mastering the topics in this book will ensure that you can approach any WAAS design project with confidence.

How This Book Is Organized

Although this book could be read cover to cover, it is designed to be flexible and allow you to easily move between chapters and sections of chapters to cover just the material that you need more work with. While each of the chapters builds upon the foundation laid by previous chapters, enough background information is provided in each chapter to allow it to be a standalone reference work in and of itself. Chapter 1 provides a technical examination of the Cisco WAAS product and its core capabilities, along with use cases and the "why you care" about each of the solution components. Chapters 2 through 9 are the core chapters and, although they can be covered in any order, it is recommended that they be covered sequentially for continuity. Chapter 10 provides a series of use cases for the Cisco WAAS product family, which can also provide insight into how other customers are using this technology to meet their business infrastructure requirements.

- **Chapter 1, "Introduction to Cisco Wide Area Application Services":** This chapter provides a technical examination and overview of Cisco WAAS and its core components.

- **Chapter 2, "Cisco Wide Area Application Engine (WAE) Family":** This chapter discusses the Cisco WAE appliance and router-integrated network module hardware family, positioning of each of the platforms, and system specifications that impact the design of a solution relative to the performance and scalability of each component.

- **Chapter 3, "Planning, Discovery, and Analysis":** Planning is a critical part to any successful WAAS deployment. Spending ample time at the beginning of the project to understand the requirements, including those imposed by the existing network environment, is critical for a successful deployment. Chapter 3 gives you a head start by outlining the key topic areas that should be taken into consideration as you are planning your WAAS deployment.

- **Chapter 4, "Network Integration and Interception":** This chapter provides an in-depth review of the network integration and interception capabilities of Cisco WAAS. The topics discussed in Chapter 4 form the foundation for the design discussions in subsequent chapters.

- **Chapter 5, "Branch Office Network Integration":** This chapter provides a detailed discussion of the different design options for deploying Cisco WAAS in the branch office environment. Several design options are discussed, including detailed configuration examples.

- **Chapter 6, "Data Center Network Integration":** This chapter examines the key design considerations for deploying WAAS in the data center. Sample design models and configuration examples are provided throughout the chapter. Best practices recommendations for scaling to support hundreds or thousands of remote sites are also included.

- **Chapter 7, "System and Device Management":** This chapter walks you through the initial deployment of the Central Manager and each of the accelerator WAEs, including the setup script, registration, activation, and use of management techniques such as device groups. This chapter also provides you with a series of helpful sections on commonly used configuration items, such as syslog and SNMP.

- **Chapter 8, "Configuring WAN Optimization":** This chapter guides you through the WAN optimization framework provided by Cisco WAAS, including each of the optimization techniques and the Application Traffic Policy manager. This chapter also examines the configuration of optimization policies, verification that policies are applied correctly, and an examination of statistics and reports.

- **Chapter 9, "Configuring Application Acceleration":** This chapter focuses on the application acceleration components of Cisco WAAS, including configuration, verification, and how the components interact. This chapter also looks closely at how these components leverage the underlying WAN optimization framework, and how they are managed.

- **Chapter 10, "Case Studies":** This chapter brings together various topics discussed in the previous chapters through several case studies. The case studies presented focus on real-world deployment examples, discussing the key design considerations, options, and final device-level configurations.

CHAPTER 1

Introduction to Cisco Wide Area Application Services (WAAS)

IT organizations are struggling with two opposing challenges: to provide high levels of application performance for an increasingly distributed workforce, and to consolidate costly infrastructure to streamline management, improve data protection, and contain costs. Separating the growing remote workforce from the location that IT desires to deploy infrastructure is the wide-area network (WAN), which introduces tremendous delay, packet loss, congestion, and bandwidth limitations, all of which can impede a user's ability to interact with applications in a high-performance manner.

Cisco Wide Area Application Services (WAAS) is a solution designed to bridge the divide between application performance and infrastructure consolidation in WAN environments. By employing robust optimizations at multiple layers, Cisco WAAS is able to ensure high-performance access to distant application infrastructure, including file services, e-mail, intranet, portal applications, and data protection. By mitigating the performance-limiting factors of the WAN, Cisco WAAS not only improves performance, but also positions IT organizations to better consolidate distributed infrastructure to better control costs and ensure a stronger position toward data protection and compliance.

The purpose of this book is to discuss the Cisco WAAS solution in depth, including a thorough examination of how to design and deploy Cisco WAAS solutions. This chapter provides an introduction to the performance barriers that are created by the WAN, and a technical introduction to Cisco WAAS. This chapter also examines the software architecture of Cisco WAAS, and outlines how each of the fundamental optimization components overcomes those application performance barriers. The chapter ends with a discussion of how Cisco WAAS fits into a network-based architecture of optimization technologies, and how these technologies can be deployed in conjunction with Cisco WAAS to provide a holistic solution for improving application performance over the WAN.

Understanding Application Performance Barriers

Before examining how Cisco WAAS overcomes performance challenges created by network conditions in the WAN, it is important to have an understanding of how those conditions in the WAN impact application performance. Applications today are becoming increasingly robust and complex compared to applications ten years ago, and it is expected that this trend will continue. Many enterprise applications are multitiered, having a presentation layer (commonly comprised of web services), which in turn accesses an application tier of servers, which interacts with a database tier (commonly referred to as an n-tier architecture). Each of these distinct layers commonly interacts with one another using middleware, which is a subsystem that connects disparate software components or architectures. As of this writing, the majority of applications in use today are client/server, involving only a single tier on the server side (for instance, a simple file server). However, n-tier application infrastructures are becoming increasingly popular.

Layer 4 Through Layer 7

Server application instances, whether single-tier or n-tier, primarily interact with user application instances at the application layer of the Open Systems Interconnection (OSI) model. At this layer, application layer control and data messages are exchanged to perform functions based on the business process or transaction being performed. For instance, a user may 'GET' an object stored on a web server using HTTP. Interaction at this layer is complex, as the number of operations that can be performed over a proprietary protocol or even a standards-based protocol can be literally in the hundreds or thousands. Between the application layers on a given pair of nodes exists a hierarchical structure of layers between the server application instance and user application instance, which also adds complexity—and performance constraints.

For instance, data that is to be transmitted between application instances might pass through a shared (and prenegotiated) presentation layer. This layer may or may not be present depending on the application, as many applications have built-in semantics around data representation. This layer is responsible for ensuring that the data conforms to a specific structure, such as ASCII or Extensible Markup Language (XML).

From the presentation layer, the data might be delivered to a session layer, which is responsible for establishing an overlay session between two endpoints. Session layer protocols provide applications with the capability to manage checkpoints and recovery of atomic upper-layer protocol (ULP) exchanges, which occur at a transactional or procedural layer as compared to the transport of raw segments (provided by the Transmission Control Protocol, discussed later). Similar to the presentation layer, many applications may have built-in semantics around session management and may not use a discrete session layer. However, some applications, commonly those that use remote procedure calls (RPC), do require a discrete session layer.

Whether the data to be exchanged between a user application instance and server application instance requires the use of a presentation layer or session layer, data to be transmitted across an internetwork will be handled by a transport protocol. The transport protocol is primarily responsible for data multiplexing—that is, ensuring that data transmitted by a node is able to be processed by the appropriate application process on the recipient node. Commonly used transport layer protocols include the Transmission Control Protocol (TCP), User Datagram Protocol (UDP), and Stream Control Transmission Protocol (SCTP). The transport protocol is commonly responsible for providing guaranteed delivery and adaptation to changing network conditions, such as bandwidth changes or congestion. Some transport protocols, such as UDP, do not provide such capabilities. Applications that leverage UDP either implement their own means of guaranteed delivery or congestion control, or these capabilities simply are not required for the application.

The components mentioned previously, including transport, session, presentation, and application layers, represent a grouping of services that dictate how application data is exchanged between disparate nodes. These components are commonly called Layer 4 through Layer 7 services, or L4–7 services, or application networking services (ANS). L4–7 services rely on the packet routing and forwarding services provided by lower layers, including the network, data link, and physical layers, to move segments of application data in network packets between nodes that are communicating. With the exception of network latency caused by distance and the speed of light, L4–7 services generally add the largest amount of operational latency to the performance of an application. This is due to the tremendous amount of processing that must take place to move data into and out of buffers (transport layer), maintain long-lived sessions between nodes (session layer), ensure data conforms to representation requirements (presentation layer), and exchange application control and data messages based on the task being performed (application layer).

Figure 1-1 shows an example of how L4–7 presents application performance challenges.

Figure 1-1 *L4–7 Performance Challenges*

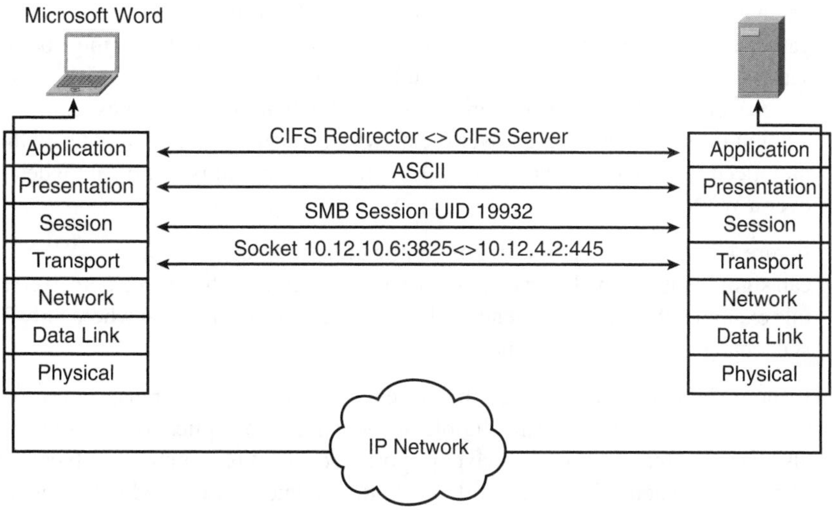

The performance challenges caused by L4–7 can generally be classified into the following categories: latency, bandwidth inefficiencies, and throughput. These are examined in the following three sections.

Latency

L4–7 latency is a culmination of the latency components added by each of the four layers involved: application, presentation, session, and transport. Given that presentation layer, session layer, and transport layer latency are typically low and have minimal impact on overall performance, this section focuses on latency that is incurred at the application layer. It should be noted that, although significant, the latency added by L4–7 processing in the node itself is typically minimal compared to latency found in the network itself, and far less than the performance impact of application layer latency caused by protocol chatter over a high-latency network.

Application layer latency is defined as the operational latency of an application protocol and is generally exhibited when applications or protocols have a "send-and-wait" type of behavior. An example of application layer latency can be observed when accessing a file on a file server using the Common Internet File System (CIFS) protocol, which is predominant in environments using Windows clients and Windows servers, or network-attached storage (NAS) devices that are being accessed by Windows clients. In such a case, the client and server must exchange a series of "administrative" messages prior to any data being sent to a user.

For instance, the client must first establish the session to the server, and establishment of this session involves validation of user authenticity against an authority such as a domain controller. Then, the client must establish a connection to the specific share (or named pipe), which requires that client authorization be examined. Once the user is authenticated and authorized, a series of messages is exchanged to traverse the directory structure and gather metadata. After the file is identified, a series of lock requests must be sent in series (based on file type), and then file I/O requests (such as read, write, or seek) can be exchanged between the user and the server. Each of these messages requires that a small amount of data be exchanged over the network, causing operational latency that may be unnoticed in a local-area network (LAN) environment but is significant when operating over a WAN.

Figure 1-2 shows an example of how application layer latency alone in a WAN environment can significantly impede the response time and overall performance perceived by a user. In this example, the one-way latency is 100 ms, leading to a situation where only 3 KB of data is exchanged in 600 ms of time.

It should be noted that although the presentation, session, and transport layers do indeed add latency, it is commonly negligible in comparison to application layer latency. It should also be noted that the transport layer performance itself is commonly subject to the amount of perceived latency in the network due to the slowness associated with relieving transmission windows and other factors. The impact of network latency on application performance is examined in the next section, "Network Infrastructure."

Figure 1-2   *Latency-Sensitive Application Example*

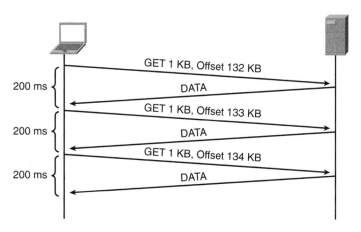

Bandwidth Inefficiencies

The lack of available network bandwidth (discussed in the section, "Network Infrastructure") coupled with application layer inefficiencies in the realm of data transfer creates an application performance barrier. This performance barrier is manifest when an application is inefficient in the way information is exchanged between two communicating nodes. For instance, assume that ten users are in a remote office that is connected to the corporate campus network by way of a T1 (1.544 Mbps). If these users use an e-mail server (such as Microsoft Exchange) in the corporate campus network, and an e-mail message with a 1-MB attachment is sent to each of these users, the e-mail message needs to be transferred once for each user, or ten times. Such scenarios can massively congest enterprise WANs, and similarities can be found across many different applications:

- Redundant e-mail attachments being downloaded over the WAN multiple times by multiple users

- Multiple copies of the same file stored on distant file servers being accessed over the WAN by multiple users

- Multiple copies of the same web object stored on distant intranet portals or application servers being accessed over the WAN by multiple users

In many cases, the data contained in objects being accessed across the gamut of applications used by remote office users will likely contain a significant amount of redundancy. For instance, one user might send an e-mail attachment to another user over the corporate WAN, while another user accesses that same file (or a different version of that file) using a file server protocol over the WAN. The packet network itself has historically been independent of the application network, meaning that characteristics of data were generally not considered, examined, or leveraged when routing information throughout the corporate network.

Some applications and protocols have since added semantics that help to minimize the bandwidth inefficiencies of applications operating in WAN environments. For instance, the web browsers of today have built-in client-side caching capabilities. Objects from Internet sites and intranet applications that are transferred over the WAN have metadata included in the protocol header that provides information to the client browser, thus allowing the browser to make a determination of whether or not caching should be used for the object. By employing a client-side cache in such applications, the repeated transmission of objects can be mitigated when the same user requests the object using the same application. Although this improves performance for that particular user, this information goes completely unused when a different user attempts to access that same object, as the application cache is wholly contained on each individual client and not shared across multiple users. Application-level caching is isolated not only to the user that cached the object, but also to the application within that user's workstation. This means that while the user's browser has a particular file cached, a different application has no means of leveraging that cached object. Some applications require that software upgrades be added to provide caching functionality.

Although the previous two sections focused primarily on latency and bandwidth utilization as application layer performance challenges, the items discussed in the next section, "Network Infrastucture," also impact application layer performance. The next section focuses primarily on the network infrastructure aspects that impact end-to-end performance, and also discusses how these challenges have a direct impact on L4–7 and end-to-end performance.

Network Infrastructure

The network itself also creates a tremendous number of application performance barriers. In many cases, the challenges found in L4–7 are exacerbated by the challenges that are manifest in the network infrastructure itself. For instance, the impact of application layer latency is amplified when network infrastructure latency is high. The impact of application layer bandwidth inefficiencies are amplified when the amount of available bandwidth in the network is not sufficient. Packet loss has an adverse effect on application performance, generally indirectly, as transport protocols react to loss events to normalize connection throughput around the available network capacity. This section focuses specifically on the issues that are present in the network infrastructure that negatively impact application performance, and also examines how these issues impact the L4–7 challenges discussed previously. These issues include bandwidth constraints, network latency, and loss and congestion.

Bandwidth Constraints

Network bandwidth can create performance constraints related to application performance. Bandwidth found in the LAN has evolved over the years from Fast Ethernet (100 Mbps), to Gigabit Ethernet (1 Gbps), to 10-Gigabit Ethernet (10 Gbps), and eventually 100-Gigabit Ethernet (100 Gbps) will begin to be deployed. Generally speaking, the bandwidth capacity on the LAN is not a limitation from an application performance perspective. WAN bandwidth, on the other hand, is not increasing as rapidly as LAN bandwidth, and the price per megabit of bandwidth is significantly higher than it is on the LAN. This is largely due to the fact that WAN bandwidth is commonly provided as a service from a carrier or service provider, and the connections must traverse a "cloud" of network locations to connect two geographically distant networks. Most carriers have done a substantial amount of research into what levels of oversubscription in the core network are tolerable to their customers, with the exception being dedicated circuits where the bandwidth is guaranteed.

Nevertheless, WAN bandwidth is far more costly than LAN bandwidth, and the most common WAN circuits found today are an order of magnitude smaller in bandwidth than what can be deployed in a LAN. The most common WAN link found in today's remote office and branch office environment is the T1 (1.544 Mbps), which is roughly 1/64 the capacity of a Fast Ethernet connection, which is in today's network environments being phased out in favor of Gigabit Ethernet.

When examining application performance in WAN environments, it is important to note the bandwidth disparity that exists between LAN and WAN environments, as the WAN is what connects the many geographically distributed locations. Such a bandwidth disparity makes environments where nodes are on disparate LANs and separated by a WAN susceptible to a tremendous amount of oversubscription. In these cases, the amount of bandwidth that is able to be used for service is tremendously smaller than the amount of bandwidth capacity found on either of the LAN segments connecting the devices that are attempting to communicate. This problem is exacerbated by the fact that there are commonly tens, hundreds, or even in some cases thousands of nodes that are trying to compete for this precious WAN bandwidth.

Figure 1-3 provides an example of the oversubscription found in a simple WAN environment with two locations, each with multiple nodes attached to the LAN via Fast Ethernet (100 Mbps), contending for available bandwidth on a T1. In this example, the location with the server is also connected to the WAN via a T1, and the potential for exceeding 500:1 oversubscription is realized.

Figure 1-3 *Network Oversubscription in a WAN Environment*

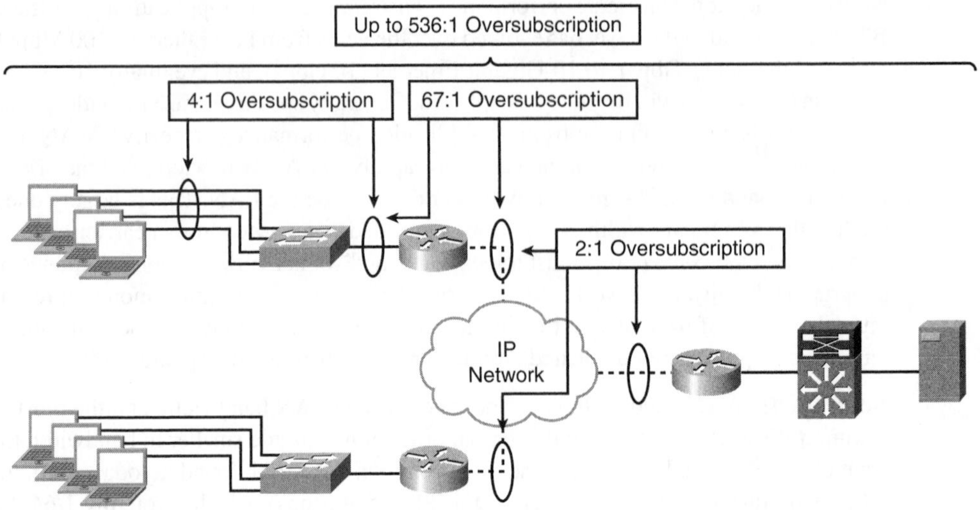

When oversubscription is encountered, traffic that is competing for available WAN bandwidth must be queued to the extent allowed by the intermediary network devices. The queuing and scheduling disciplines applied can be dictated by a configured policy for control and bandwidth allocation (such as quality of service, or QoS) on the intermediary network elements. In any case, if queues become exhausted, packets must be dropped, as there is no memory available in the oversubscribed network device to store the data for service. Loss of packets will likely impact the application's ability to achieve higher levels of throughput and, in the case of a connection-oriented transport protocol, likely cause the communicating nodes to adjust their rate of transmission to a level that allows them to use only their fair share of the available bandwidth.

As an example, consider a user transmitting a file by way of the File Transfer Protocol (FTP). The user is attached to a Fast Ethernet LAN, as is the server, but a T1 WAN separates the two locations. The maximum achievable throughput would be limited by the T1, as it is the slowest link in the path of communication. Thus, the application throughput (assuming 100 percent efficiency and no packet loss) would be limited to roughly 1.544 Mbps (megabits per second), or 193 kBps (kilobytes per second). Given that packet loss is imminent, and no transport protocol is 100 percent efficient, it is likely that the user would see approximately 90 percent of line-rate in terms of application throughput, or roughly 1.39 Mbps (174 kBps).

Taking the example one step further, if two users were performing the same test (FTP transfer over a T1), the router queues (assuming no QoS policy favoring one user over the other) would quickly become exhausted as the connections began discovering available bandwidth. As packets begin to get dropped by the router, the transport protocol would react to the loss and adjust throughput accordingly. The net result is that both nodes would rapidly converge to a point where they were sharing the bandwidth fairly, and connection throughput would oscillate around this point of convergence (roughly 50 percent of 1.39 Mbps, or 695 kbps, which equals 86.8 kBps). This example is simplistic in that it assumes there is no packet loss or latency found in the WAN. The impact of transport protocols will be examined as part of the discussions on network latency, loss, and congestion.

Network Latency

The example at the end of the previous section did not take into account network latency. *Network latency* is the amount of time taken for data to traverse a network in between two communicating devices. Network latency is considered the "silent killer" of application performance, as most network administrators have simply tried (and failed) to circumvent application performance problems by adding bandwidth to the network. Put simply, network latency can have a significant effect on the amount of network capacity that can be consumed by two communicating nodes.

In a campus LAN, latency is generally under 1 ms, meaning the amount of time for data transmitted by a node to be received by the recipient is less than 1 ms. This number may of course increase based on how geographically dispersed the campus LAN is, and also on what levels of utilization and oversubscription are encountered. In a WAN, latency is generally measured in tens or hundreds of milliseconds, much higher than what is found in the LAN. Latency is caused by the propagation delay of light or electrons, which is generally 66 percent of the speed of light (or 2×10^8 meters per second). Although this seems extremely fast on the surface, when stretched over a great distance, the latency can be quite noticeable. For instance, in a network that spans 3000 miles (4.8 million meters), the distance between New York and San Francisco, it would take roughly 24.1 ms in one direction for a packet to traverse the network from one end to the other. This of course assumes no serialization delays, loss, or congestion in the network, and that the most direct route is chosen through the network with little to no deviation in distance. It would therefore take at least 52.8 ms for a transmitting node to receive an acknowledgment for a segment that was sent, assuming no time was required for the recipient to process that the data was received.

Figure 1-4 shows how latency in its simplest form can impact the performance of a telephone conversation, which is analogous to two nodes communicating over an internetwork with 1 second of one-way latency.

Figure 1-4 *Challenges of Network Latency*

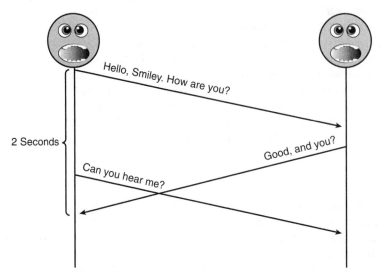

The reason network latency has an impact on application performance is two-fold. First, network latency introduces delays that impact mechanisms that control rate of transmission. For instance, connection-oriented, guaranteed-delivery transport protocols such as TCP use a sliding-window mechanism to track what transmitted data has been successfully received by a peer and how much additional data can be sent. As data is received, acknowledgments are generated, which not only notify the sender that the data is received, but also relieves window capacity so more data can be transmitted if available. Transport protocol control messages are exchanged between nodes on the network, so any latency found in the network will also impact the rate at which these control messages can be exchanged. Overall, this impacts the rate at which data can be drained from a sender's transmission buffer into the network. This has a cascading effect, which causes the second impact on application performance for those applications that rely on transport protocols that are susceptible to performance barriers caused by latency. This second impact is discussed later in this section.

Latency not only delays the receipt of data and the subsequent receipt of the acknowledgment for that data, but also can be so large that it actually renders a node unable to leverage all of the available bandwidth capacity. This problem is encountered when the capacity of the network, which is the amount of data that can be in flight at any one given time, is greater than the sliding-window capacity of the sender. For instance, a DS3 (45 Mbps, or roughly 5.63 MBps) with 100 ms of latency can have up to 563 KB (5.63 MBps × .1) of data in flight and traversing the link at any point in time (assuming the link is 100 percent utilized). This "network capacity" is called the *bandwidth delay product (BDP)*, and is calculated by multiplying the network bandwidth (after conversion to bytes) by the amount of latency. Given that many computers today have only a small amount of memory allocated for each TCP connection (64 KB, unless window scaling is used), if the network BDP exceeds 64 KB, the transmitting node will not be able to successfully "fill the pipe." This is primarily due to the fact that the window is not relieved quickly enough because of the latency, and the buffer is not big enough to keep the link full. This also assumes that the recipient has large enough buffers on the distant end to allow the sender to continue transmission without delay.

Figure 1-5 shows an example of how latency and small buffers render the transmitter unable to fully capitalize on the available bandwidth capacity.

Figure 1-5   *Latency and Small Transmission Buffers*

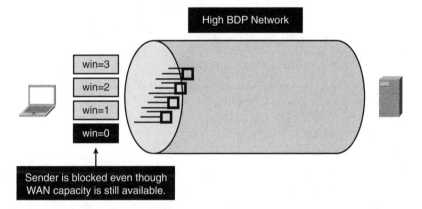

The second impact on application performance is related to application-specific messages that must be exchanged using latency-sensitive transport protocols. Most applications today are very robust and require that a series of messages be exchanged between nodes before any real "work" is done. In many cases, these control messages are exchanged in a serial fashion, where each builds upon the last until ultimately small pieces of usable data are exchanged. This type of behavior, where applications exhibit send-and-wait behavior, is also known as "application ping-pong," because many messages must be exchanged in sequence and in order before any actual usable data is exchanged. In many cases, these same applications exchange only a small amount of data, and each small piece of data is followed by yet another series of control messages leading up to the next small piece of data.

As this section has shown, latency has an impact on the transmitting node's transport protocol and its ability to effectively utilize available WAN capacity. Furthermore, applications that exhibit "ping-pong" behavior are impacted even further due to the latency encountered when exchanging application layer messages over the impacted transport protocol. The next section examines the impact of packet loss and congestion on throughput and application performance.

Loss and Congestion

Packet loss and congestion also have a negative impact on application throughput. Although packet loss can be caused by anything from signal degradation to faulty hardware, it is most commonly the result of either of the following two scenarios:

- Internal oversubscription of allocated connection memory within a transmitting node
- Oversubscribed intermediary network device queues

Packet loss is not generally a scenario that can be proactively reported to a transmitter; that is, a router that drops a particular packet cannot notify a transmitting node that a specific packet has been dropped due to a congested queue. Packet loss is generally handled reactively by a transmitting node based on the acknowledgments that are received from the recipient or the lack thereof. For instance, in the case of a connection-oriented transport protocol, if 5 KB of data is sent in five unique 1-KB sequences, an acknowledgment of only four of the five segments would cause the transmitter to retransmit the missing segment. This behavior varies among transport protocols and is also dependent upon the extensions to the transport protocol that are being used, but the general behavior remains consistent: an unacknowledged segment is likely a segment that was contained in a packet that was lost, not received correctly (due to signal degradation or errors), or oversubscription of the recipient buffer. Double and triple acknowledgments may also be used to indicate the window position of a segment that was not successfully received, to specify what the transmitter should resend.

In the case of TCP, the lack of an acknowledgment causes the transmitter not only to resend, but also to re-evaluate the rate at which it was sending data. A loss of a segment causes TCP to adjust its window capacity to a lower value to cover scenarios where too much data was being sent—either too much data for the network to deliver (due to oversubscription of the network) or too much data for the recipient to receive (due to congested receive buffers). The net effect is that, upon encountering packet loss and subsequently having to retransmit data, the transmitter will decrease the overall throughput of the connection to try and find a rate that will not oversubscribe the network or the recipient. This behavior is called *congestion avoidance*, as TCP adjusts its rate to match the available capacity in the network and the recipient.

The most common TCP implementation found today, TCP Reno, reduces the congestion window by 50 percent upon encountering packet loss. Although reducing the congestion window by 50 percent does not necessarily correlate to a 50 percent decrease in connection throughput, this reduction can certainly constrain a connection's ability to saturate the link. During the congestion avoidance phase with TCP Reno, each successful transmission (signaled by receipt of an acknowledgment) causes the congestion window to increase by one segment size. The purpose of the congestion window is to allow TCP to first react to packet loss, which ensures throughput is adjusted to available capacity, and secondly to continue to try and find additional available capacity as a result of continually increasing the congestion window for each successful transmission.

Figure 1-6 shows an example of how packet loss impacts the TCP congestion window, which impacts overall application throughput.

Figure 1-6 *Impact of Packet Loss on Throughput*

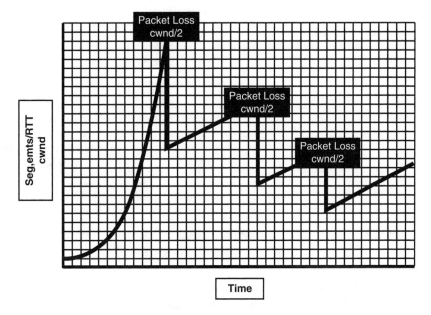

This "backoff" behavior not only helps TCP normalize around the available network capacity and available capacity in the recipient buffer, but also helps to ensure fairness among nodes that are competing for the available WAN bandwidth.

Introduction to Cisco WAAS

The previous sections examined the most common causes of application performance challenges found in WAN environments. Although the previous sections certainly did not cover every possible performance barrier, they summarized and briefly examined the largest of these problems. With this fundamental understanding of what contributes to application performance challenges, one might ask, "How are they solved?" Each application performance challenge has an appropriate solution, and these solutions must be implemented in a hierarchical manner with the appropriate solution in the appropriate point within the network, as shown in Table 1-1.

Table 1-1 *Solutions to Application Performance Barriers Found in the WAN*

Performance Barrier	Technology Solution
Application layer latency	Application layer optimization, including parallelization of serial tasks, prefetching, message prediction, local response handling, and object prepositioning
Application layer bandwidth consumption	Application layer object caching with local delivery at the edge of the network near the requesting user
Network bandwidth consumption and congestion	Compression, data suppression, QoS, application layer object caching
Packet loss sensitivity	Optimized transport protocol implementation with advanced congestion avoidance algorithms, TCP proxy architectures, rate-based transmission protocols, or forward error correction (FEC)
Network throughput	Optimized transport protocol implementation with advanced congestion avoidance algorithms, large transmit and receive buffers, window scaling
Prioritization and resource allocation	End-to-end QoS, including basic classification, deep packet inspection, prequeuing operations, hierarchical queuing and scheduling, post-queuing optimization

Cisco WAAS provides a solution to the performance barriers presented by the WAN by employing a series of application-agnostic optimizations, also known as WAN optimization, in conjunction with a series of application-specific optimizations, also known as application acceleration. WAN optimization refers to employing techniques at the network or transport protocol that apply across any application protocol using that network or transport protocol. Application acceleration refers to employing optimizations directly against an application or an application protocol that it uses. WAN optimization has broad applicability, whereas application acceleration has focused applicability.

Cisco WAAS is a solution that is transparent in three domains:

- **Client nodes:** No changes are needed on a client node to benefit from the optimization provided by Cisco WAAS.

- **Servers:** No changes are needed on a server node to benefit from Cisco WAAS.

- **Network:** Cisco WAAS provides the strongest levels of interoperability with technologies deployed in the network, including QoS, NetFlow, IP service-level agreements (IP SLA), access control lists (ACL), firewall policies, and more. Transparency in the network is unique to Cisco WAAS.

This unique combination of three domains of transparency allows Cisco WAAS the least disruptive introduction into the enterprise IT infrastructure of any WAN optimization or application acceleration solution.

The following sections examine the WAN optimization and application acceleration components of Cisco WAAS in detail.

WAN Optimization

Cisco WAAS implements a number of WAN optimization capabilities to help overcome challenges encountered in the WAN. These optimizations include a foundational set of three key elements:

- **Data Redundancy Elimination (DRE):** DRE is an advanced compression mechanism that uses disk and memory. DRE minimizes the amount of redundant data found on the WAN by utilizing a loosely synchronized compression history on Wide Area Application Engine (WAE) peers. When redundant data is identified, the WAE will send a signature referencing that data to the peer as opposed to sending the original data, thereby providing potentially very high levels of compression. Data that is nonredundant is added to the compression history on both peers and is sent across the WAN with newly generated signatures.

- **Persistent LZ Compression (PLZ):** PLZ is a variant of the Lempel-Ziv (LZ) compression algorithm. The WAE uses a persistent session history to extend the compression capabilities of basic LZ, which helps minimize bandwidth consumption for data traversing the WAN. PLZ is helpful for data that is identified as nonredundant by DRE, and can also compress signatures that are sent by DRE on behalf of redundant chunks of data.

- **Transport Flow Optimization (TFO):** TFO is a series of TCP optimizations that helps mitigate performance barriers associated with TCP. TFO includes large initial windows, selective acknowledgment and extensions, window scaling, and an advanced congestion avoidance algorithm that helps "fill the pipe" while preserving fairness among optimized and unoptimized connections.

Determining which optimization to apply is a function of the Application Traffic Policy (ATP), which can be managed discretely per WAAS device or within the Cisco WAAS Central Manager console, and is also dependent upon the optimization negotiation that occurs between WAAS devices during automatic discovery (discussed later in this chapter in "Other Features").

The data path for optimization within the Cisco WAAS device is the TCP proxy, which is used for each connection that is being optimized by Cisco WAAS. The TCP proxy allows Cisco WAAS to transparently insert itself as a TCP-compliant intermediary. In this way, Cisco WAAS devices can receive and temporarily buffer data sent from a host and locally acknowledge data segments when appropriate. By employing a TCP proxy, Cisco WAAS can also send larger blocks of data to the optimization software components, which permits higher levels of compression to be realized when compared to per-packet architectures in which the compression domain may be limited by the size of the packets being received.

Data in the TCP proxy is then passed through the associated optimization components based on the configured policy, and the optimized traffic is transmitted across the WAN using the optimized TCP implementation. By implementing a TCP proxy, Cisco WAAS can shield communicating nodes from unruly WAN conditions such as packet loss or congestion. Should the loss of a segment be encountered, Cisco WAAS devices can extract the segment from the TCP proxy retransmission queue and retransmit the optimized segment, thereby removing the need for the original transmitting node to retransmit the data that was lost in transit. Transmitting nodes enjoy the benefits of having LAN-like TCP performance, exhibiting the characteristics of minimal packet loss and rapid acknowledgment. By using a TCP proxy, Cisco WAAS allows data to be drained from the transmitting nodes more quickly and nearly eliminates the propagation of performance-limiting challenges encountered in the WAN.

Figure 1-7 shows the Cisco WAAS TCP proxy architecture and how it provides a buffer that prevents WAN performance from impacting transmitting nodes.

Figure 1-7   *Cisco WAAS TCP Proxy Architecture*

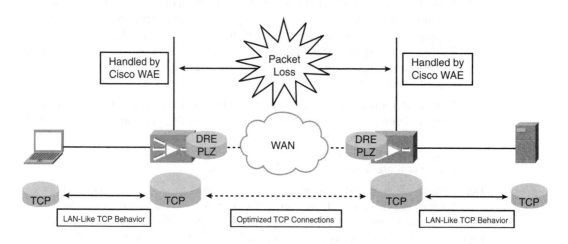

The following sections examine each of these optimizations in more detail.

Data Redundancy Elimination

DRE is an advanced, lossless compression algorithm that leverages both memory (high throughput and high I/O rates) and disk (persistent and large compression history). DRE examines data in-flight for redundant patterns (patterns that have been previously identified). As redundant patterns are identified, they are replaced with a signature that references the redundant pattern within the peer WAAS device compression history. As these signatures are only 5 or 6 bytes in size (depending on the breakpoints identified within the data), and the redundant pattern identified could potentially be tens or hundreds of kilobytes, DRE can provide significant levels of compression for flows containing data that has been previously identified, which helps minimize bandwidth consumption on the WAN.

DRE is bidirectional, meaning patterns identified during one direction of traffic flow can be leveraged for traffic flowing in the opposite direction. DRE is also application agnostic in that patterns identified within a flow for one application can be leveraged to optimize flows for a different application. An example of the bidirectional and application-agnostic characteristics of DRE is as follows. Assume two users are located in the same remote office, which is connected to the corporate campus by way of a T1 WAN. Both the remote office and the corporate campus have Cisco WAAS devices installed. Should the first user download an e-mail containing an attachment, the compression history on each of the WAAS devices in the connection path would be updated with the relevant data patterns contained within the flow. Should the second user have a copy of that file, or a file containing similarities, and upload that file by way of another application such as FTP, the compression history that was previously built from the e-mail transfer could be leveraged to provide tremendous levels of compression for the FTP upload.

Hierarchical Chunking and Pattern Matching

As data from a connection configured for DRE optimization enters the TCP proxy, it is buffered for a short period of time. After data builds up in the buffer, the large block of buffered data is passed to DRE to enter a process known as encoding. Encoding is the process of taking transmitted data in from a transmitting node, eliminating redundancy, updating the compression library with any new data, and transmitting compressed messages.

DRE encoding calculates a message validity signature over the original block of data. This message is used by the decoding process on the peer WAE to ensure correctness when rebuilding the message based on the signatures contained in the encoded message. A sliding window is used over the block of data to be compressed, which employs a CPU-efficient calculation to identify breakpoints within the data based on the actual data being transferred, which is also known as *content-based chunking*. Content-based chunking relies on the actual data itself to identify breakpoints within the data and, as such, is less sensitive to slight changes (additions, removals, changes) upon subsequent transfers of the same or similar data. With content-based chunking, if a small amount of data is inserted into a chunk during the next transmission, the chunk boundaries shift with the insertion of data, allowing DRE better isolation of new data, which helps retain high levels of compression as the other chunks remain valid.

Chunks are identified at multiple layers, and aggregate chunks referencing smaller, lower-layer chunks can be identified. Due to this multi-layer approach to chunking, DRE is hierarchical in that one chunk may reference a number of smaller, lower-layer chunks. If higher-layer chunks are identified as redundant, a single signature can be used to reference a larger number of lower-layer chunks in aggregate form. In essence, DRE aggregation provides a multiresolution view of the same data using chunks of different sizes and levels.

Each chunk that is identified is assigned a 5-byte signature. This signature is used as the point of reference on each Cisco WAAS device for that particular chunk of data. As DRE is encoding data, if any chunk of data is found within the DRE compression history, it is considered redundant, and the signature is transmitted instead of the chunk. For instance, if a 32-KB chunk was found to be redundant and was replaced with the associated signature, an effective compression ratio of over 500:1 would be realized for that particular chunk of data. If any chunk of data is not found in the DRE compression history, it is added to the local compression history for later use. In this case, both the chunk and the signature are transmitted to allow the peer to update its DRE compression history.

Figure 1-8 illustrates the encoding process.

Figure 1-8 *Data Redundancy Elimination Encoding*

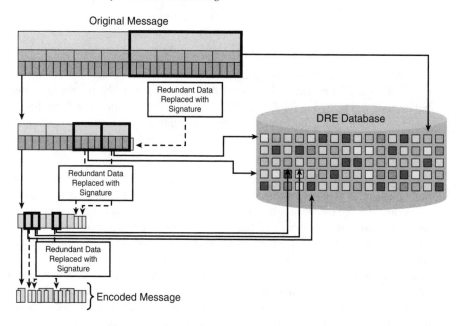

After the encoding process is complete, the encoding WAE transmits the encoded message with the message validity signature that was calculated for the original block of data. Aside from the message validity signature, the encoded message contains signatures for data patterns that are recognized as redundant, and signatures and data for data patterns that are identified as nonredundant.

Message Validation

DRE uses two means of verifying that encoded messages can be properly rebuilt and match the original data being transmitted. As the decoding WAAS device (closest to the recipient) receives an encoded message, it begins to parse the encoded messages to separate signatures that were sent without an associated chunk of data (redundant data that should exist in the compression history) and signatures that were sent with an accompanying chunk of data (nonredundant data that should be added to the compression history).

As the decoding WAE receives an encoded message, each signature identifying redundant data is used to search the DRE compression history and is replaced with the appropriate chunk of data if found. If the signature and associated chunk of data are not found, a synchronous nonacknowledgment is sent to the encoding WAE to request that the signature and chunk of data both be re-sent. This allows the WAE to rebuild the message with the missing chunk while also updating its local compression history. For chunks of data that are sent with an accompanying signature, the local compression history is updated, and the signature is removed from the message so that only the data remains.

Once the decoding WAAS device has rebuilt the original message based on the encoded data and chunks from the compression history, it then generates a new message validity signature. This message validity signature, which is calculated over the rebuilt message, is compared against the original message validity signature generated by the encoding WAAS device. If the two signatures match, the decoding WAAS device knows that the message has been rebuilt correctly, and the message is returned to the TCP proxy for transmission to the recipient. If the two signatures do not match, the decoding WAAS device sends a synchronous nonacknowledgment over the entire message, requesting that the encoding WAAS device send all of the signatures and data chunks associated with the message that failed decoding. This allows the decoding WAAS device to update its compression history and transmit the message as intended.

Persistent LZ Compression

Cisco WAAS can also employ Persistent LZ Compression, or PLZ, as an optimization based on configured policy. PLZ is a lossless compression algorithm that uses an extended compression history to achieve higher levels of compression than standard LZ variants can achieve. PLZ is helpful for data that has not been identified as redundant by DRE, and can even provide additional compression for DRE-encoded messages, as the DRE signatures are compressible. PLZ is similar in operation to DRE in that it uses a sliding window to analyze data patterns for redundancy, but the compression history is based in memory only and is far smaller than that found in DRE.

Transport Flow Optimization

Cisco WAAS TFO is a series of optimizations that is leveraged for connections that are configured for optimization. By employing TFO, communicating nodes are shielded from performance-limiting WAN conditions such as packet loss and latency. Furthermore, TFO allows nodes to more efficiently use available network capacity and minimize the impact of retransmission. TFO provides the following suite of optimizations:

- **Large initial windows:** Large initial windows, found in RFC 3390, allows TFO to mitigate the latency associated with connection setup, as the initial congestion window is increased. This allows the connection to more quickly identify the bandwidth ceiling during slow-start and enter congestion avoidance at a more rapid pace.

- **Selective acknowledgment (SACK) and extensions:** SACK, found in RFCs 2018 and 2883, allows a recipient node to explicitly notify the transmitting node what ranges of data have been received within the current window. With SACK, if a block of data goes unacknowledged, the transmitting node need only retransmit the block of data that was not acknowledged. SACK helps minimize the bandwidth consumed upon retransmission of a lost segment.

- **Window scaling:** Window scaling, found in RFC 1323, allows communicating nodes to have an enlarged window. This allows for larger amounts of data to be outstanding and unacknowledged in the network at any given time, which allows end nodes to better utilize available WAN bandwidth.

- **Large buffers:** Large TCP buffers on the WAAS device provide the memory capacity necessary to keep high-BDP WAN connections full of data. This helps mitigate the negative impact of high-bandwidth networks that also have high latency.

- **Advanced congestion avoidance:** Cisco WAAS employs an advanced congestion avoidance algorithm that provides bandwidth scalability (fill the pipe, used in conjunction with window scaling and large buffers) without compromising on cross-connection fairness. Unlike standard TCP implementations that use linear congestion avoidance, TFO leverages the history of packet loss for each connection to dynamically adjust the rate of congestion window increase when loss is not being encountered. TFO also uses a less-conservative backoff algorithm should packet loss be encountered (decreasing the congestion window by 12.5 percent as opposed to 50 percent), which allows the connection to retain higher levels of throughput in the presence of packet loss. Cisco WAAS TFO is based on Binary Increase Congestion (BIC) TCP.

Figure 1-9 shows a comparison between typical TCP implementations and TFO. Notice how TFO is more quickly able to realize available network capacity and begin leveraging it. When congestion is encountered, TFO is able to more intelligently adjust its throughput to accommodate other connections while preserving bandwidth scalability.

Figure 1-9   *Comparison of TCP Reno and Cisco WAAS TFO*

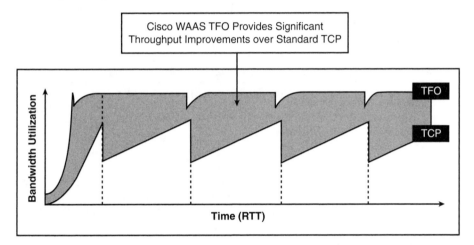

Whereas this section focused on the WAN optimization components of Cisco WAAS, the next section focuses on the application acceleration components of Cisco WAAS.

Application Acceleration

Application acceleration refers to employing optimizations directly against applications or the application protocols that they use. Whereas WAN optimization refers to techniques employed generally against a network layer or transport layer protocol (Cisco WAAS employs them against the transport layer), application acceleration is employed at higher layers. The optimizations found in application acceleration are in many ways common across applications and application protocols, but because they must be specific to each application or application protocol, these optimizations may be implemented differently.

Ensuring application correctness (don't break the application), data integrity (don't corrupt the data), and data coherency (don't serve stale data) is of paramount importance in any application acceleration solution. With WAN optimization components, ensuring these items is generally easy, as the optimizations employed are done against a lower layer with well-defined semantics for operation. With application acceleration, however, ensuring these items is more difficult, as applications and application protocols are more diverse, complex, and finicky with respect to how they must be handled.

Table 1-2 lists the high-level application acceleration techniques that can be found within Cisco WAAS. Note that this list is not all-inclusive, and focuses on the techniques that are commonly applied to accelerated applications, but others certainly exist.

Table 1-2   *Cisco WAAS Application Acceleration Techniques*

Acceleration Technique	Functional Description and Value
Object caching	Object caching allows Cisco WAAS to, when safe, store copies of previously accessed objects (files, other content) to be reused by subsequent users. This only occurs when the application state permits caching, and cached objects are served to users only if application state requirements are met and the object has been validated against the origin server as having not changed. Caching mitigates latency (objects served locally), saves WAN bandwidth (does not have to be transferred over the WAN), minimizes server workload (does not have to be transferred from the server), and improves application performance.
Local response handling	By employing stateful optimization, Cisco WAAS can locally respond to certain message types on behalf of the server. This only occurs when the application state permits such behavior, and can help minimize the perceived latency as fewer messages are required to traverse the WAN. As with object caching, this helps reduce the workload encountered on the server while also improving application performance.
Prepositioning	Prepositioning is used to allow an administrator to specify what content should be proactively copied to a remote Cisco WAAS object cache. This helps improve first-user performance by better ensuring a "cache hit," and can also be used to populate the DRE compression history. Population of the DRE compression history is helpful in environments where the object being prepositioned may be written back from the remote location with some changes applied, which is common in software development and CAD/CAM environments.
Read-ahead	Read-ahead allows Cisco WAAS to, when safe, increase read request sizes on behalf of users, or initiate subsequent read requests on behalf of users, to have the origin server transmit data ahead of the user request. This allows the data to reach the edge device in a more timely fashion, which in turn means the requesting user is served more quickly. Read-ahead is helpful in cache-miss scenarios, or in cases where the object is not fully cached. Read-ahead minimizes the WAN latency penalty by prefetching information.

Table 1-2   *Cisco WAAS Application Acceleration Techniques (Continued)*

Acceleration Technique	Functional Description and Value
Write-behind	Write-behind allows Cisco WAAS to, when safe, locally acknowledge write requests from a user application. This allows Cisco WAAS to streamline the transfer of data over the WAN, minimizing the impact of WAN latency.
Multiplexing	Multiplexing refers to a group of optimizations that can be applied independently of one another or in tandem. These include fast connection setup, TCP connection reuse, and message parallelization. Multiplexing helps overcome WAN latency associated with TCP connections or application layer messages, thereby improving performance.

The application of each of these optimizations is determined dynamically for each connection or user session. Because Cisco WAAS is strategically placed in between two communicating nodes, it is in a unique position not only to examine application messages being exchanged to determine what the state of the connection or session is, but also to leverage state messages being exchanged between communicating nodes to determine what level of optimization can safely be applied.

As of Cisco WAAS v4.0.13, Cisco WAAS employs these optimizations against the CIFS protocol and certain MS-RPC operations. WAAS also provides a local print services infrastructure for the remote office, which helps keep print traffic off of the WAN if the local file and print server have been consolidated. Releases beyond v4.0.13 will add additional application protocols to this list.

The following sections provide an example of each of the application acceleration techniques provided by Cisco WAAS. It is important to note that Cisco WAAS employs application layer acceleration capabilities only when safe to do so. The determination on "safety" is made based on state information and metadata exchanged between the two communicating nodes. In any circumstance where it is not safe to perform an optimization, Cisco WAAS dynamically adjusts its level of acceleration to ensure compliance with protocol semantics, data integrity, and data coherency.

Object and Metadata Caching

Object and metadata caching are techniques employed by Cisco WAAS to allow an edge device to retain a history of previously accessed objects and their metadata. Unlike DRE, which maintains a history of previously seen data on the network (with no correlation to the upper-layer application), object and metadata caching are specific to the application being used, and the cache is built with pieces of an object or the entire object, along with its associated metadata. With caching, if a user attempts to access an object, directory listing, or file attributes that are stored in the cache, such as a file previously accessed from a particular file server, the file can be safely served from the edge device, assuming the user has successfully completed authorization and authentication and the object has been validated (verified that it has not changed). Caching requires that the origin server notify the client that caching is permitted through the use of opportunistic locks or other state propagation mechanisms.

Object caching provides numerous benefits, including:

- **LAN-like access to cached objects:** Objects that can be safely served out of cache are served at LAN speeds by the WAE adjacent to the requester.
- **WAN bandwidth savings:** Object caching minimizes the transfer of redundant objects over the network, thereby minimizing overall WAN bandwidth consumption.
- **Server offload:** Object caching minimizes the amount of workload that must be managed by the server being accessed. By safely offloading work from the server, IT organizations may be in a position to minimize the number of servers necessary to support an application.

Figure 1-10 shows an example of object caching and a cache hit as compared to a cache miss.

Figure 1-10 *Examining Cache Hit and Cache Miss Scenarios*

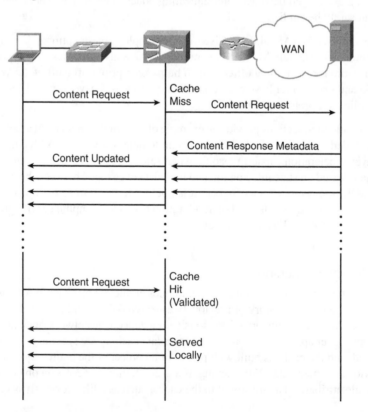

As shown in Figure 1-10, when a cache hit occurs, object transfers are done on the LAN adjacent to the requesting node, which minimizes WAN bandwidth consumption and improves performance. When a cache miss occurs, the object is fetched from the origin server in an optimized fashion and, if applicable, the data read from the origin server is used to build the cache to improve performance for subsequent users. This is often referred to as the "first-user penalty" for caching.

Prepositioning

Prepositioning is a function by which an administrator can specify which objects should be proactively placed in the cache of a specific edge device or group of edge devices. By using prepositioning, an administrator can ensure high-performance access to an object for the first requesting user (assuming caching is safe to be used for the user's session), eliminating the first-user penalty. Prepositioning is helpful in environments where large object transfers are necessary. For instance, CAD/CAM, medical imaging, software distribution, software development all require the movement of large files, and prepositioning can help improve performance for remote users while also offloading the WAN and servers in the data center. Prepositioning can also be used as a means of prepopulating the DRE compression history.

Read-Ahead

Read-ahead is a technique that is useful both in application scenarios where caching can be applied and in scenarios where caching cannot be applied. With read-ahead, a Cisco WAAS device may, when applicable, increment the size of the application layer read request on behalf of the user, or generate additional read requests on behalf of the user. The goal of read-ahead is two-fold:

- When used in a cache-miss scenario, provide near-LAN response times to overcome the first-user penalty. Read-ahead, in this scenario, allows the WAE to begin immediate and aggressive population of the edge cache.

- When used in a scenario where caching is not permitted, aggressively fetch data on behalf of the user to mitigate network latency. Read-ahead, in this scenario, is not used to populate a cache with the object, but rather to proactively fetch data that a user may request. Data prefetched in this manner is only briefly cached to satisfy immediate read requests that are for blocks of data that have been read ahead.

Figure 1-11 shows an example of how read-ahead can allow data to begin transmission more quickly over the WAN, thereby minimizing the performance impact of WAN latency.

Figure 1-11 *Read-Ahead in Caching and Noncaching Scenarios*

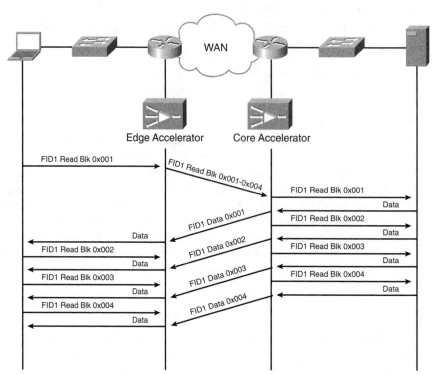

Write-Behind

Write-behind is an optimization that is complementary to read-ahead optimization. Whereas read-ahead focuses on getting the information to the edge more quickly, write-behind focuses on getting the information to the core more quickly—at least from the perspective of the transmitting node. In reality, write-behind is a technique by which a Cisco WAAS device can positively acknowledge receipt of an application layer write request, when safe, to allow the transmitting node to continue to write data. This optimization is commonly employed against application protocols that exhibit high degrees of ping-pong, especially as data is written back to the origin server.

As an optimization that positively acknowledges write requests that have not yet been received by the server being written to, write-behind is only employed against protocols that support information recovery in the event of disconnection (for instance, through temporary files) and is only employed when safe to do so. For applications that do not support information recovery in the event of loss, this optimization cannot be safely applied.

Multiplexing

Multiplexing is a term that refers to any process where multiple message signals are combined into a single message signal. Multiplexing, as it relates to Cisco WAAS, refers to the following optimizations:

- **TCP connection reuse:** By reusing existing established connections rather than creating new connections, TCP setup latency can be mitigated, thereby improving performance. TCP connection reuse is applied only on subsequent connections between the same client and server pair over the same destination port.

- **Message parallelization:** For protocols that support batch requests, Cisco WAAS can parallelize otherwise serial tasks into batch requests. This helps minimize the latency penalty, as it is amortized across a series of batched messages as opposed to being experienced on a per-message basis. For protocols that do not support batch requests, Cisco WAAS may "predict" subsequent messages and presubmit those messages on behalf of the user in an attempt to mitigate latency.

This section focused on the application-specific acceleration components of Cisco WAAS, including caching, prepositioning, read-ahead, write-behind, and multiplexing. The next section focuses on the integration aspects of Cisco WAAS as it relates to the ecosystem that is the enterprise IT infrastructure, as well as additional value-added features that are part of the Cisco WAAS solution.

Other Features

Cisco WAAS is a unique application acceleration and WAN optimization solution in that it is the only solution that not only provides the most seamless interoperability with existing network features, but also integrates physically into the Cisco Integrated Services Router (ISR). With the Cisco ISR, customers can deploy enterprise edge connectivity to the WAN, switching, wireless, voice, data, WAN optimization, and security in a single platform for the branch office. (The router modules and the appliance platforms are examined in the next chapter.) The following are some of the additional features that are provided with the Cisco WAAS solution:

- **Network transparency:** Cisco WAAS is fundamentally transparent in three domains—client transparency, server transparency (no software installation or configuration changes required on clients or servers), and network transparency. Network transparency allows Cisco WAAS to interoperate with existing networking and security functions such as firewall policies, optimized routing, QoS, and end-to-end performance monitoring.

- **Enterprise-class scalability:** Cisco WAAS can scale to tens of gigabits of optimized throughput and tens of millions of optimized TCP connections using the Cisco Application Control Engine (ACE), which is an external load-balancer and is discussed in detail in Chapter 6, "Data Center Network Integration." Without external load balancing, Cisco WAAS can scale to tens of gigabits of optimized throughput and over one million TCP connections using the Web Cache Coordination Protocol version 2 (WCCPv2), which is discussed in both Chapter 4, "Network Integration and Interception," and Chapter 6.

- **Trusted WAN optimization:** Cisco WAAS is a trusted WAN optimization and application acceleration solution in that it integrates seamlessly with many existing security infrastructure components such as firewalls, intrusion detection systems (IDS), intrusion prevention systems (IPS), and virtual private network (VPN) solutions. Integration work has been done on not only Cisco WAAS but adjacent Cisco security products to ensure that security posture is not compromised when Cisco WAAS is deployed. Cisco WAAS also supports disk encryption (using AES-256 encryption) with centrally managed keys. This mitigates the risk of data loss or data leakage if a WAE is compromised or stolen.

- **Automatic discovery:** Cisco WAAS devices can automatically discover one another during the establishment of a TCP connection and negotiate a policy to employ. This eliminates the need to configure complex and tedious overlay networks. By mitigating the need for overlay topologies, Cisco WAAS permits optimization without requiring that administrators manage the optimization domain and topology separate from the routing domain.

- **Scalable, secure central management:** Cisco WAAS devices are managed and monitored by the Cisco WAAS Central Manager. The Central Manager can be deployed in a highly available fashion using two Cisco WAAS devices. The Central Manager is secure in that any exchange of data between the Central Manager and a managed Cisco WAAS device is done using SSL, and management access to the Central Manager is encrypted using HTTPS for web browser access or SSH for console access (Telnet is also available). The Central Manager provides a simplified means of configuring a system of devices through device groups, and provides role-based access control (RBAC) to enable segregation of management and monitoring. The Central Manager is discussed in more detail in Chapter 7, "System and Device Management."

Summary

IT organizations are challenged with the need to provide high levels of application performance for an increasingly distributed workforce. Additionally, they are faced with an opposing challenge to consolidate costly infrastructure to contain capital and operational expenditures. Organizations find themselves caught between two conflicting realities: to distribute costly infrastructure to remote offices in order to solve performance requirements of a growingly distributed workforce, and to consolidate costly infrastructure from those same remote offices to control capital and operational costs and complexity. Cisco WAAS is a solution that employs a series of WAN optimization and application acceleration techniques to overcome the fundamental performance limitations of WAN environments to allow remote users to enjoy near-LAN performance when working with centralized application infrastructure and content.

CHAPTER 2

Cisco Wide Area Application Engine (WAE) Family

Chapter 1 introduced the performance challenges created by the WAN and how they are addressed by the Cisco Wide Area Application Services (WAAS) solution. Cisco WAAS is a software component that is resident on a hardware device deployed at each location with users and servers. This hardware device, which can be deployed as a router-integrated network module for the Integrated Services Router (ISR) or as an appliance, is called the Cisco Wide Area Application Engine (WAE). This chapter provides an introduction to the Cisco WAE family, along with an in-depth examination of the hardware and software architecture. This chapter also looks at the licensing options for Cisco WAAS, positioning for each of the WAE platforms, and performance and scalability metrics for each of the platforms.

Cisco WAE Product Architecture

The Cisco WAE product family consists of a series of appliances and router-integrated network modules that are based on an Intel x86 hardware architecture. The product family scales from 512 MB of memory to 24 GB of memory, utilizing single-processor subsystems up to dual quad-core processor subsystems. Each Cisco WAE device, regardless of form factor, is configured with some amount of hard disk storage and a compact flash card. The compact flash card is used for boot-time operation and configuration files, whereas the hard disk storage is used for optimization data, swap space, and as a repository for spawning the operating system. Having a compact flash card allows the WAE device to remain accessible on the network even in the face of an entire hard disk subsystem failure. Also, by using the compact flash card in this way, a WAE device can successfully boot and become accessible on the network if no disks are available.

The foundational layer of the Cisco WAAS software is the underlying Cisco Linux platform. The Cisco Linux platform is hardened to ensure that rogue services are not installed, and secured such that third-party software or other changes cannot be made to the kernel. The Cisco Linux platform hosts a command-line interface (CLI) similar to that of Cisco IOS, which, along with the Central Manager and other interfaces, is the primary means of configuring, managing, and troubleshooting a device or system. All relevant configuration, management, monitoring, and troubleshooting subsystems are made accessible directly through this CLI as opposed to exposing the Linux shell.

The Cisco Linux platform hosts a variety of services for WAAS runtime operation. These include disk encryption, Central Management Subsystem (CMS), interface manager, reporting facilities, network interception and bypass, and Application Traffic Policy (ATP) engine, as shown in Figure 2-1.

Figure 2-1   *Cisco WAAS Hardware and Software Architecture*

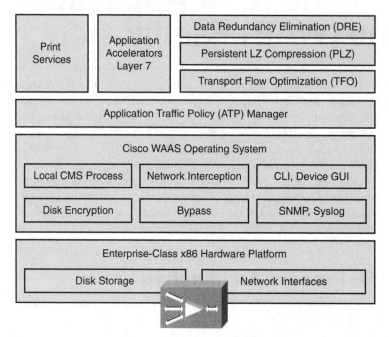

The following sections examine each of the Cisco WAE and Cisco Linux architecture items in turn. Cisco WAAS optimization components, including Data Redundancy Elimination (DRE), Persistent LZ Compression (PLZ), Transport Flow Optimization (TFO), and application acceleration, are discussed in detail in Chapter 1, and thus are not discussed in this chapter.

Disk Encryption

Cisco WAE devices can be configured to encrypt the data, swap, and spool partitions on the hard disk drives using encryption keys that are stored on and retrieved from the Central Manager. The disk encryption feature uses AES-256 encryption, the strongest commercially available encryption, and keys are only stored in the WAE memory. Should a WAE be physically compromised or a disk stolen, power is removed from the device, which destroys the copy of the key in memory. This renders data on the disk useless. Keys are stored in the Central Manager database and synchronized among Central Manager WAEs for high availability. If a WAE device is not able to retrieve its key from the Central Manager during boot time, it remains in pass-through mode until connectivity is restored or disk encryption is administratively bypassed.

Central Management Subsystem

CMS is a process that runs on each WAE device, including accelerators and Central Managers. This process manages the configuration and monitoring components of a WAE and ensures that each WAE is synchronized with the Central Manager based on a scheduler known as the Local Central Manager (LCM) cycle. The LCM cycle is responsible for synchronizing the Central Manager CMS process with the remote WAE CMS process to exchange configuration data, fetch health and status information, and gather monitoring and reporting data. The CMS process is also tied to the available management interfaces. For instance, the CMS process on the Central Manager must be running before the secure web user interface is made available (if it weren't, there wouldn't be much to show).

Interface Manager

The Cisco WAE interface manager manages the physical and logical interfaces that are available to the WAE. Each WAE includes two integrated Gigabit Ethernet interfaces (including the WAE network modules, one interface is internal, the other is external). Each WAE appliance has expansion slots to support one or more additional feature cards, such as the inline bypass adapter, which has two two-port fail-to-wire pairs. The interface manager also provides management over logical interfaces that can be configured over physical interfaces. Logical interfaces include active/standby interfaces, where one physical interface is used as a primary interface and a second interface is used as a backup in the event the primary interface fails. Another logical interface is the PortChannel interface, which can be used to team WAE interfaces together for the purposes of high availability and load balancing. It should be noted that active/standby interfaces are used when WAE interfaces connect to separate switches, whereas PortChannel interfaces are used when the WAE interfaces connect to the same switch.

Reporting Facilities

Cisco Linux provides an interface for the Cisco WAAS software to use for purposes of reporting and generating alarms. Cisco Linux supports the Simple Network Management Protocol (SNMP) versions 1, 2c, and 3, as well as definition of up to four syslog servers.

Network Interception and Bypass Manager

The network interception and bypass manager is used by the Cisco WAE to establish relationships with intercepting devices where necessary and ensure low-latency bypass of traffic that the WAE is not intended to handle. The Web Cache Coordination Protocol version 2 (WCCPv2) is a protocol managed by the network interception and bypass manager to allow the WAE to successfully join a WCCPv2 service group with one or more adjacent routers, switches, or other WCCPv2-capable server devices. WCCPv2 is discussed in more detail in Chapter 4, "Network Integration and Interception." Other network interception options, which are also discussed in Chapter 4, include policy-based routing (PBR), physical inline interception, and Application Control Engine (ACE). As flows are intercepted by the WAE and determined to be optimization candidates, they are handed to the Application Traffic Policy (ATP) engine, which is discussed in the next section.

Application Traffic Policy Engine

While the foundational platform component of Cisco WAAS is Cisco Linux, the foundational optimization layer of the Cisco WAAS software (which is as much a component of the Cisco Linux platform as it is the software) is the ATP engine. The ATP is responsible for examining details of each incoming flow (after being handled by the interception and bypass mechanisms) in an attempt to identify the application or protocol associated with the flow. This association is done by comparing the packet headers against a set of predefined or administratively configured classifiers, each with its own set of one or more match conditions. Flows that do not have a match with an existing classifier are considered "other" traffic and are handled according to the policy defined for other traffic.

When a classifier match is found, the ATP examines the policy configuration for that classifier to determine how to optimize the flow. The ATP also notes the application group that the classifier belongs to in order to route statistics gathered to the appropriate application group for proper reporting. The configured policy dictates which optimization subsystems are enacted upon the flow. The list of optimization actions that can be configured within a policy include the following:

- **Pass-through:** This traffic should not be optimized by Cisco WAAS.
- **TFO only:** Apply only TCP optimization.
- **TFO+LZ:** Apply TCP optimization in conjunction with PLZ.
- **TFO+DRE:** Apply TCP optimization in conjunction with DRE.
- **Full optimization:** Apply TCP optimization, PLZ, and DRE.
- **Accelerator:** First route the flow through a specific application acceleration component for latency optimization and other techniques. This policy is applicable for traffic using a protocol that has an associated application accelerator, such as Common Internet File System (CIFS). This list will be extended in releases beyond v4.0.13.

Policies from the preceding list can be employed in conjunction with one another. For instance, the CIFS policy is, by default, configured to leverage the CIFS accelerator prior to leveraging the "full optimization" (DRE, PLZ, TFO) capabilities of the underlying WAN optimization layer. This is defined in a single policy, thereby simplifying overall system policy management. Classifiers within the ATP can be defined based on source or destination IP addresses or TCP port numbers, or ranges of these values. The ATP is examined during the establishment of a new connection when a TCP synchronize (SYN) packet is seen. By making a comparison against the ATP using the SYN packet of the connection being established, the ATP does not need to be consulted for traffic flowing in the reverse direction. Classification performed by the ATP is done once against the SYN packet and is applicable for both directions of traffic flow. In this way, classification does not need to be performed for traffic flowing in the reverse direction.

Figure 2-2 shows how the ATP engine interacts with a flow and a particular policy.

Figure 2-2   *Connection Interaction with Application Traffic Policy*

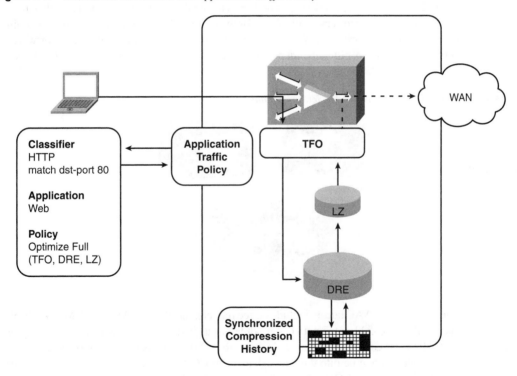

Hardware Family

The Cisco WAE hardware family consists of five appliances and three router-integrated network modules. With such a diverse hardware portfolio, Cisco WAAS can be deployed in each location with the appropriate amount of optimization capacity for the needs of the users or servers in that particular location. This section examines the specifics of each of the hardware platforms and positioning of each. Performance and scalability metrics for each are examined later in this chapter.

Router-Integrated Network Modules

The Cisco WAE router-integrated network modules are designed to provide optimization services for the remote branch office or enterprise edge. These modules, which are single-processor systems based on the Network Module Enhanced (NME) hardware, can occupy an open NME-capable slot in a Cisco Integrated Services Router (ISR), including models 2811, 2821, 2851, 3825, and 3845. The ISR is an ideal platform for the branch office in that it provides a converged service platform for the remote office, including routing, switching, wireless, voice, security, and WAN optimization in a single chassis (platform, software version, and slot capacity dependent). Figure 2-3 shows a picture of the Cisco NME-WAE family and the ISR family.

Figure 2-3 *Cisco ISR Family and WAAS Network Modules*

The Cisco NME-WAE family includes three models: the NME-WAE-302, NME-WAE-502, and NME-WAE-522. Each network module has a single hard disk with capacity ranging from 80 to 160 GB. With only a single drive, the NME-WAE is not capable of RAID. NME-WAE devices integrate into the network using WCCPv2 as a means of interception (PBR can also be used, but WCCPv2 is preferred). Each NME-WAE has two network interfaces—one internal (connected to the ISR backplane) and one external (accessible through the front of the module). Figure 2-4 shows the architecture of the NME, internal and external interfaces, and intersection points between the NME and the ISR.

Figure 2-4   *Cisco WAAS Network Module Architecture*

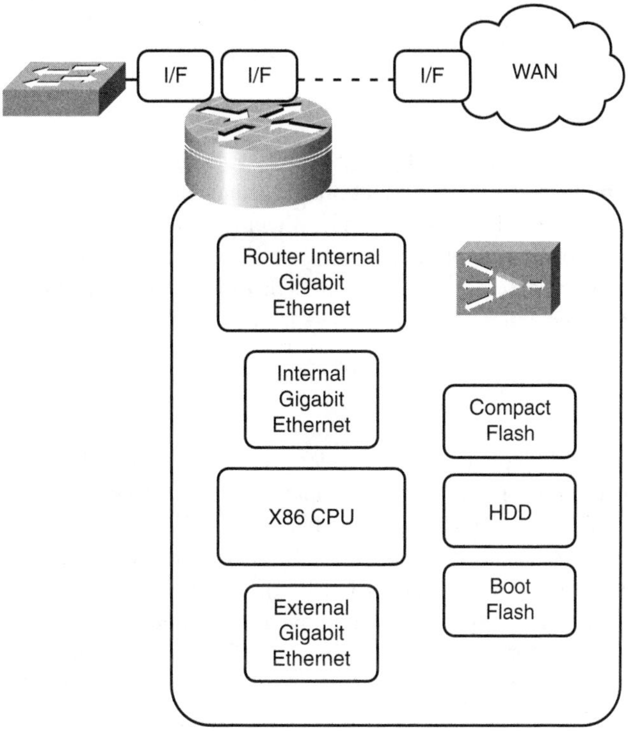

NME-WAE Model 302

The Cisco NME-WAE model 302 (NME-WAE-302) is designed for customers that want to employ only basic WAN optimization capabilities, which are permitted through the use of the Transport license (licensing is discussed later in this chapter). These capabilities include the ATP engine, DRE, PLZ, and TFO. This module is not capable of running the advanced services enabled by the Enterprise license (discussed later in the chapter), including application layer acceleration or disk encryption. The NME-WAE-302 is a single-processor system with 512 MB of RAM and a single 80-GB hard disk.

NME-WAE Model 502

The Cisco NME-WAE model 502 (NME-WAE-502) is designed for customers that want to employ WAN optimization capabilities and some of the Enterprise license features for an enterprise edge location. The NME-WAE-502 can be configured with the Enterprise license, providing full WAN optimization functionality and all edge application acceleration functionality. The NME-WAE-502 is a single-processor system with 1 GB of RAM and a single 120-GB hard disk. The NME-WAE-502 is capable of supporting a larger number of users than the NME-WAE-302, as discussed in the "Performance and Scalability Metrics" section later in this chapter.

NME-WAE Model 522

The Cisco NME-WAE model 522 (NME-WAE-522) is designed for customers that want to employ appliance-equivalent functionality to an enterprise edge location. The NME-WAE-522 supports the full suite of Enterprise license features, including all WAN optimization and application acceleration capabilities as either a core or edge device. The NME-WAE-522 is a single-processor system with 2 GB of RAM and a 160-GB hard disk, serving as the most powerful network module available as of this writing.

Appliances

The Cisco WAE appliance family is designed to be deployed in a location of any size, including the small branch office, campus networks, or the largest of enterprise data center networks. The Cisco WAE appliance family includes models 512, 612, 7326, 7341, and 7371. Each WAE appliance has externally accessible hard disk drives and RAID (some models support hot-swappable disk drives). The WAE appliance has two built-in Gigabit Ethernet interfaces, which can be deployed independently of one another or as a pair in either an active/standby configuration or PortChannel configuration. Such interface configurations are discussed in Chapter 5, "Branch Office Network Integration," and Chapter 6, "Data Center Network Integration." The WAE appliance family also has one or more PCI expansion slots that support installation of additional feature cards, such as the in-path card. Each WAE appliance can be deployed using a variety of network interception techniques, including physical inline interception, WCCPv2, PBR, and ACE (all of which are described in Chapter 4). Any appliance model can be used as a core or edge device. Figure 2-5 shows an image of the Cisco WAE appliance family.

Figure 2-5   *Cisco WAAS Appliance Family*

WAE Model 512

The Cisco WAE model 512 (WAE-512) is a single-processor system that is designed for deployment in small and medium-sized branch office locations or small data center locations. The WAE-512 can be configured with 1 or 2 GB of RAM. In a 1-GB RAM configuration, the WAE-512 can provide full WAN optimization, edge application acceleration, and advanced services capabilities, whereas with 2 GB of RAM, the WAE-512 can be configured with any feature. Regardless of memory configuration, the WAE-512 can be configured with the Transport or Enterprise license. The WAE-512 supports two 250-GB SATA2 hard disk drives, which are configured automatically for software RAID-1.

WAE Model 612

The Cisco WAE model 612 (WAE-612) is a dual-core processor system that is designed for deployment in medium-sized branch office locations or medium-sized data center locations. The WAE-612 can be configured with 2 GB or 4 GB of RAM and, in any configuration, supports the full breadth of features and capabilities offered by any available Cisco WAAS license. The WAE-612 supports two 300-GB or 750-GB SAS hard disk drives, which are configured automatically for software RAID-1.

WAE Model 7326

The Cisco WAE model 7326 (WAE-7326) is a dual processor system that is designed for deployment in large branch office locations or large data center locations. The WAE-7326 includes 4 GB of RAM and up to six 300-GB SAS hard disk drives, which are configured automatically for software RAID-1. Each pair of drives is configured in a RAID-1 mirror, totaling three RAID-1 pairs when the WAE-7326 is fully populated with disk drives. The WAE-7326 supports the full breadth of features and capabilities offered by any available Cisco WAAS license.

WAE Model 7341

The Cisco WAE model 7341 (WAE-7341) is a quad-core system (four processors) that is designed for deployment in large to enterprise data centers. The WAE-7341 includes 12 GB of RAM and four 300-GB SAS hard disk drives, which are configured automatically for hardware RAID-5. The WAE-7341 supports the full breadth of features and capabilities offered by any available Cisco WAAS license.

WAE Model 7371

The Cisco WAE model 7371 (WAE-7371) is a dual quad-core system (eight processors) that is designed for deployment in the largest of enterprise data centers and under the most demanding conditions. The WAE-7371 includes 24 GB of RAM and six 300-GB SAS hard disk drives, which are configured automatically for hardware RAID-5. The WAE-7371 supports the full breadth of features and capabilities offered by any of the available Cisco WAAS licenses.

Licensing

Each Cisco WAE device, whether it is an appliance or a router-integrated network module, must be configured with a license. This license dictates what features are permitted to be configured on a WAE device. Three licenses exist for Cisco WAAS:

- **Transport license:** Allows a WAE to apply only basic WAN optimization capabilities to a particular flow. It supports use of TFO, DRE, and PLZ. WAE devices configured with the Transport license cannot provide application-acceleration capabilities or disk encryption. WAE devices configured with the Transport license can, however, register with and be managed and monitored by a Central Manager WAE.

- **Enterprise license:** Allows a WAE to apply all of the WAN optimization provided by the Transport license and all of the application acceleration functionality and disk encryption. Like the Transport license, WAE devices configured with the Enterprise license can register with and be managed and monitored by a Central Manager WAE.

- **Central Manager license:** Allows a WAE to be configured as a Central Manager WAE. A WAE configured as a Central Manager acts as the owner and manager for configuration and monitoring data, and for disk encryption keys. Although most Central Manager deployments involve two WAE devices (one active and one standby), multiple standby Central Manager WAEs can be deployed in a given Cisco WAAS network.

Performance and Scalability Metrics

Design of a Cisco WAAS solution involves many factors, but the cornerstone of the solution design is based on the performance and scalability metrics required for the solution as a whole and for each individual location. Every component in an end-to-end system has a series of static and dynamic system limits. For instance, a server may be limited in terms of the number of connections it can support, disk I/O throughput, or network throughput. Likewise, each Cisco WAE device has static and dynamic system limits that dictate how and when a particular WAE device is selected for a location within an end-to-end design. This section examines the performance and scalability metrics of the Cisco WAE family, and provides a definition of what each item is and how it is relevant to a localized (per location) design and an end-to-end system design.

Each Cisco WAE device has a series of associated static and dynamic limits. These limits are used as a means of identifying which device is best suited to provide services to a particular location in the network. The device may be deployed as an edge device, where it connects to potentially many peer devices in one or more data center locations, or as a core device, where it serves as an aggregation point for many connected edges. WAEs can also be deployed as devices to optimize links between data center locations, where each side is realistically a core device. A fundamental understanding of the performance and scalability metrics is paramount in ensuring a sound design. This section examines each of the performance and scalability system limits, both static and dynamic, that should be considered. These include device memory, disk capacity, number of optimized TCP connections, WAN bandwidth and LAN throughput, number of peers and fan-out, and number of devices managed.

Device Memory

The amount of memory installed in a device dictates the level of performance and scalability the device can provide. As the memory capacity increases, the ability of a WAE to handle a larger number of connections or a larger addressable index space for compression also increases. Having larger amounts of memory also enables the WAE to run additional services, such as application acceleration or disk encryption, and positions the device to accept additional features that may be introduced in future software releases.

The NME-WAE family members all have fixed memory capacity and cannot be upgraded. From the WAE appliance family, the WAE-7326, 7341, and 7371 have fixed memory configurations. The WAE-512 and WAE-612, however, have configurable memory options, in that the WAE-512 can be configured with 1 GB or 2 GB of memory, and the WAE-612 can be configured with 2 GB or 4 GB of memory.

The amount of installed memory directly impacts what license is supported on each of the WAE models. The Transport license can be configured on any WAE model that has 512 MB of memory or more, which includes the entire product family. WAE models that have 1 GB of memory or more can be configured with the Enterprise license, which allows the WAE to operate some or all of the Enterprise license features. 1-GB WAE models configured with the Enterprise license (that is, NME-WAE-502 and WAE-512-1GB) can use disk encryption and perform application acceleration for CIFS as an edge device but not as a core device, but can terminate WAN optimized connections as a core device. WAE models with 2 GB or more (including the NME-WAE-522, WAE-512-2GB, WAE-612, WAE-7326, WAE-7341, and WAE-7371) can run the full suite of Enterprise license features as either a core or edge device.

Disk Capacity

Optimization services within the Cisco WAE leverage both memory and disk. From a disk perspective, the larger the amount of available capacity, the larger the amount of optimization history that can be leveraged by the WAE during run-time operation. For instance, a WAE-502 has 120 GB of physical disk capacity, of which 47 GB is available for use by DRE for compression history. With 47 GB of compression history, one can estimate the length of the compression history given WAN conditions, expected network utilization, and assumed redundancy levels.

Table 2-1 shows how the length of the compression history can be calculated for a particular WAE device, along with an example. This example assumes a T1 WAN that is 75 percent utilized during business hours (8 hours per day) and 50 percent utilized during nonbusiness hours (16 hours per day), and assumes that data traversing the network is 75 percent redundant. This table also assumes an NME-WAE-502 with 50 GB of allocated capacity for DRE compression history.

Table 2-1   *Calculating Compression History*

Step	Action	Example Result
1	Convert WAN capacity to bytes (divide by 8)	(T1 = 1.544 Mbps) / 8 = 193 KB/sec
2	Identify maximum WAN throughput for a given day	193 KB/sec × 60 sec/min 11.58 MB/min × 60 min/hr 694.8 MB/hr × 24 hr/day Total 16.68 GB/day
3	Identify WAN throughput given utilization	(694.8 MB/hr × 8 hours) × 75% utilization = 4.168 GB (694.8 MB/hr × 16 hours) × 50% utilization = 5.56 GB Total = 9.72 GB/day
4	Identify WAN throughput given utilization and expected redundancy	9.72 GB/day × .25 (as .75 is 75% redundancy) = 2.43 GB/day
5	Calculate compression history	Storage capacity of unit divided by daily throughput 47 GB / 2.43 GB/day = 19.3 days of history

It is generally recommended that at minimum ten days of compression history be available in a WAE device. In the example in Table 2-1, the NME-WAE-502 contains enough storage capacity to provide an effective compression history of almost three weeks.

The disk capacity available to a WAE device is split among four major components:

- **DRE compression history:** This capacity is used for storing DRE chunk data and signatures.

- **CIFS acceleration:** This capacity is preallocated on all devices, and used when a WAE is configured as a CIFS edge device (requires Enterprise license).

- **Print services:** This capacity is preallocated for print spool capacity. Print services require that the Enterprise license be configured and that CIFS edge services be configured.

- **Platform services:** This capacity is preallocated for operating system image storage, log files, and swap space.

Table 2-2 shows the storage allocation for each WAE device for each of these components.

Table 2-2   *Disk Capacity Allocation per Platform*

Platform	Total Capacity (Usable Capacity)	DRE	CIFS	Print	Platform
Network Modules					
302	80 GB (79 GB)	55 GB	0 GB	1 GB	23 GB
502	120 GB (118 GB)	47 GB	47 GB	1 GB	23 GB
522	160 GB (158 GB)	67 GB	67 GB	1 GB	23 GB
Appliances					
512-1GB	250 GB (209 GB) RAID-1	75 GB	110 GB	1 GB	23 GB
512-2GB	250 GB (244 GB) RAID-1	110 GB	110 GB	1 GB	23 GB
612-2GB	300 GB (284 GB) RAID-1	130 GB	130 GB	1 GB	23 GB
612-4GB	300 GB (284 GB) RAID-1	130 GB	130 GB	1 GB	23 GB
7326	900 GB (704 GB) RAID-1	380 GB	300 GB	1 GB	23 GB
7341	900 GB (824 GB) RAID-5	500 GB	300 GB	1 GB	23 GB
7371	1500 GB (1324 GB) RAID-5	1 TB	300 GB	1 GB	23 GB

Number of Optimized TCP Connections

Each WAE device has a static number of TCP connections that can be optimized concurrently. Each TCP connection is allocated resources within the system, and if the concurrently optimized TCP connection static limit is met, additional connections are handled in a pass-through fashion. The TCP connection limit of each WAE can be roughly correlated to the number of users supported by a given WAE model, but note that the number of TCP connections open on a particular node may vary based on user productivity, application behavior, time of day, and other factors. It is commonly assumed that a user will have 5 to 15 connections open at any given time, with roughly 4 to 7 of those connections requiring optimization. If necessary, policies can be adjusted on the WAAS Central Manager to pass through certain applications that may realize only a small amount of benefit from WAAS. This type of change could potentially help increase the number of users that can be supported by a particular WAE device.

Table 2-3 shows the optimized TCP connection capacity per Cisco WAE model.

Table 2-3   *Optimized TCP Connection Capacity per Platform*

Network Module	Connection Capacity	Appliance	Connection Capacity
302	250	512-1GB	750
502	500	512-2GB	1500
522	800	612-2GB	2000
		612-4GB	6000
		7326	7500
		7341	12,000
		7371	50,000

WAN Bandwidth and LAN Throughput

WAE devices are not restricted in software or hardware in terms of the amount of WAN bandwidth or LAN throughput supported. However, recommendations are in place to specify which WAE should be considered for a specific WAN environment. WAN bandwidth is defined as the amount of WAN capacity that the WAE can fully utilize when employing the full suite of optimization capabilities (this includes DRE and PLZ). LAN throughput is defined as the maximum amount of application layer throughput (precompression) that can be achieved with the particular WAE model and an equivalent or more-powerful peer deployed in the path.

Another factor is for deployments where the WAE is providing TCP optimization only. Cisco WAAS TFO provides a powerful suite of optimizations to better allow communicating nodes to "fill the pipe" (that is, fully leverage available WAN bandwidth capacity) when the application protocol is not restricting throughput due to application-induced latency. Each Cisco WAE has a TFO-only throughput capacity that can be considered when WAEs are deployed strictly for TCP optimization only (compression and other optimizations are not being applied).

Table 2-4 shows the WAN bandwidth supported by each WAE model and the maximum LAN-side throughput and TFO-only throughput capacity.

Table 2-4 *WAN Bandwidth and LAN Throughput Capacity per WAE*

WAE Model	WAN Supported	LAN Throughput Maximum	TFO-Only Throughput Maximum
NME-WAE-302	4 Mbps	90 Mbps	100 Mbps
NME-WAE-502	4 Mbps	150 Mbps	150 Mbps
NME-WAE-522	8 Mbps	150 Mbps	250 Mbps
WAE-512-1GB	8 Mbps	100 Mbps	350 Mbps
WAE-512-2GB	20 Mbps	150 Mbps	400 Mbps
WAE-612-2GB	45 Mbps	250 Mbps	450 Mbps
WAE-612-4GB	90 Mbps	350 Mbps	500 Mbps
WAE-7326	155 Mbps	450 Mbps	600 Mbps
WAE-7341	310 Mbps	600 Mbps	800 Mbps
WAE-7371	1 Gbps	>1 Gbps	>1 Gbps

Number of Peers and Fan-Out

Each Cisco WAE has a static system limit in terms of the number of concurrent peers it can actively communicate with at any one given time. When designing for a particular location where the number of peers exceeds the maximum capacity of an individual device, multiple devices can be deployed, assuming an interception mechanism that uses load balancing is employed (such as WCCPv2 or ACE; these are discussed in Chapter 4). In cases where load balancing is used, TCP connections are distributed according to the interception configuration, thereby allowing for near-linear scalability increases in connection count, peer count, and WAN bandwidth, as devices are added to the pool.

Peer relationships time out after 10 minutes of inactivity (that is, no active connections are established between two peers for 10 minutes). When the peer relationship is timed out, it becomes reusable by another peer. Data stored in the DRE compression history remains intact even if a peer becomes disconnected due to inactivity, unless the DRE compression history becomes full. In cases where the DRE compression history becomes full, an eviction process is initiated to remove the oldest set of data in the DRE compression history to make room for new data.

Table 2-5 shows the maximum number of concurrent peers supported per WAE platform. If peers are connected beyond the allocated limit, the WAE permits the connections to be established and gracefully degrades performance as needed. Connections associated with peers in excess of the maximum fan-out ratio are able to use the existing compression history but will not be able to add new chunks of data to it. The end result is lower effective compression ratios for the connections using peers that are in excess of the specified fan-out ratio.

Table 2-5 *Maximum Supported Peers per WAE*

Network Module	Concurrent Peers	Appliance	Concurrent Peers
302	5	512-1GB	15
502	15	512-2GB	40
522	40	612-2GB	40
		612-4GB	96
		7326	96
		7341	200
		7371	400

Number of Devices Managed

Each Cisco WAAS deployment must have a Central Manager. The Central Manager is responsible for system-wide policy definition, synchronization of configuration, device monitoring, and reporting. The Central Manager can be deployed only on appliances, and may be deployed in an active/standby fashion. When a certain WAE device is configured as a Central Manager, it is able to, based on the hardware platform selected for the Central Manager, manage a maximum number of WAEs within the topology. Only WAE appliances can be configured as Central Manager WAEs, and in high-availability configurations, each Central Manager WAE should be of the same hardware configuration. While hardware disparity between Central Manager WAEs will work, it is not a recommended practice given the difference in the number of devices that can be managed among the WAE hardware models.

Table 2-6 shows the maximum number of managed nodes that can be supported by each WAE appliance when configured as a Central Manager.

Table 2-6   *Central Manager Scalability*

Appliance	Managed Nodes
WAE-512-1GB	500
WAE-512-2GB	1000
WAE-612-2GB	2000
WAE-612-4GB	2500
WAE-7326	2500

Summary

The Cisco WAE family includes three network modules for the ISR and five appliance models. This provides customers with the flexibility necessary to allocate the right platform for each network location where WAN optimization and application acceleration capabilities are needed. Three licenses are available for Cisco WAAS, including the Transport license (WAN optimization capabilities only), Enterprise license (all product features), and Central Manager license (to manage a network of Cisco WAE devices). Sizing of a Cisco WAAS solution requires consideration of a number of factors, including network conditions, number of users and concurrent TCP connections, disk capacity, memory, and fan-out. By following the recommended guidelines for performance and scalability, a robust Cisco WAAS design can be realized, thereby allowing administrators to deploy the solution confidently.

CHAPTER 3

Planning, Discovery, and Analysis

Proper planning is a critical step to any successful WAAS deployment. Understanding the business goals, project goals, expected results, and technical requirements when deploying WAAS helps to ensure that the proposed solution and design can meet those goals. Most problems encountered during the deployment of a WAAS solution stem from not having a complete understanding of the environment in which the solution is being deployed. Treating the existing infrastructure and its characteristics as part of the requirements for the solution will help prevent issues during the deployment phase of the project.

This chapter outlines the project content and critical requirements that you should collect as part of the WAAS design discovery and analysis process. The following sections cover the various different types of requirements, from user communities to IT infrastructure, which will help you define the final WAAS solution design.

Planning Overview

There are many different aspects of an infrastructure that you need to take into consideration when planning a Cisco WAAS deployment. Oftentimes, the planning process involves resources from multiple technology teams. Although Cisco WAAS is a network-integrated technology, it is not uncommon for the application, server, and storage teams to become involved in the project as stakeholders. In some cases, these teams are driving the project and deployment of the WAAS solution.

The level of involvement from the various teams depends on the business or project purpose for deploying the solution. For example, if the primary (initial) driver behind deploying Cisco WAAS is to enable the consolidation of remote branch office file servers, storage, and data, then the file server and storage teams might be heavily involved in the project. In contrast, if the primary driver for the project is reducing WAN bandwidth consumption in an effort to delay/prevent upgrading circuits, then the solution might involve only the network engineering teams and leverage only the application-agnostic features of the solution. The point is that the first thing you should always understand is what is driving the need for the solution.

In addition to understanding the reason(s) for deploying the WAAS solution, you should also have a keen understanding of the project timelines. The amount of time allocated for the project impacts how detailed you can be in your requirements collection and analysis activities. The more complex an infrastructure, the more time that should be allocated for the planning stages of the project. It also helps to have an understanding of the change control processes that will be affected by your design recommendation. For example, if you know that the Cisco IOS version on all of the branch office routers needs to be upgraded to support WCCP for transparent interception, you may want to make that recommendation as soon as possible to allow for adequate time for scheduling and change control.

The remaining sections of this chapter discuss the specific types of requirements that you should collect, why it is important to collect those requirements, and which aspects of the WAAS design they influence.

Planning Overview Checklist

The planning overview checklist includes a list of items that help you understand what business reasons are driving the project, and which groups within the organization have a vested interest.

☐ Understand the business drivers

☐ Understand the project scope and goals

☐ Identify the resources and teams that need to be involved

☐ Identify the processes and procedures you need to follow or update

Requirements Collection and Analysis

There are many different types of requirements, ranging from business requirements to specific technical requirements, such as the WAN characteristics of the existing network infrastructure.

Requirements can be collected using a variety of interactive techniques, including interviews and workshops, and noninteractive techniques, such as questionnaires and requests for static forms to be completed. Static information, such as WAN characteristics (bandwidth and latency), device models, and software versions can be collected using standard templates, which typically does not require much interaction. However, interactive discussion is beneficial for collecting other types of requirements, such as network topology, traffic flows, and application use cases. Basically, an interactive requirements collection session should be used for any type of requirement for which the answer to a question will generate more questions from you. Do not underestimate the value of involving the end user early in the process. A significant part of your design validation testing should include user and application-specific use cases.

Wherever possible, you should develop requirements based on templates or "models." For example, instead of collecting requirements from every single site where you plan to deploy WAAS, you should identify a handful of representative sites. This may include some sites that are not the most obvious choice for deploying WAAS. The key is to make sure that your sample represents all of the significant variations within your environment. This type of categorization greatly speeds the design process. Figure 3-1 shows an example of grouping like sites into a small number of groups.

Figure 3-1   *Grouping Similar Sites into Representative Groups*

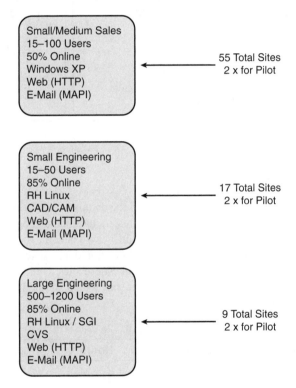

This technique can also carry over into your design development process. You can create different deployment models based on the specific requirements of the sites. For example, you may have one deployment model you use for all of your small and medium-sized sales offices, and another model you use for all of your large engineering facilities. Figure 3-2 shows an example of scaling your design using standardized deployment models.

Figure 3-2 *Scalable Design Deployment Models*

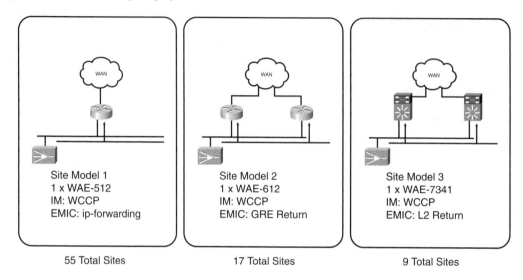

Site Information

First and foremost, you need to understand the details of the locations where WAAS will be deployed. Start by composing a list of sites, including the geographic location, site type, hours of operation, and number of users. This list will become the foundation on which you build deployment models for your design. You should also note sites that do not fall into a standard configuration or deployment model. These sites need to be addressed on a case-by-case basis as part of the design. You can start with a simple list of sites, such as the example in Table 3-1.

Table 3-1 *Key Information Sites*

Site Name	Site Type	Hours	Users/Concurrent
Austin, TX	Remote Sales	8–5, M–F	25/15

Site Types

The site type refers to the primary business function performed at the site. For example, your site list may include sales offices, manufacturing locations, engineering facilities, and multipurpose campuses. Identifying the type of site is useful because it enables you to classify the types of users and other characteristics about the site. You may have an existing standard for the types of networking equipment that is deployed to a given type of site. Also, users at different types of sites usually require different sets of applications, which place different loads on the network infrastructure. Identifying all of these attributes helps you to understand the sizing requirements for a site, which in turn helps you to size the overall WAAS solution and develop different models for deployment.

User Population

There are different types of users, or populations, in every customer environment. Understanding the users that will be affected by deploying Cisco WAAS helps with solution sizing and test use case development. The types of information that you should collect about the user community include:

- Location of users
- Location(s) of resources accessed by users
- Types of users
- Client systems (traditional desktop/laptop, handheld devices, etc.)
- Common/critical applications

You should also try to determine the percentage of users concurrently online at any given point in time. You typically see that anywhere from 60 to 80 percent of the total number of users at a site are online and actively working. This helps you understand the total load that will be placed on the WAAS infrastructure.

Document each unique community of users for easy reference. These user community profiles will help you when determining which sites should be considered for pilot testing and deployment.

Physical Environment

The WAAS solution will have a physical footprint at each location where it is deployed. It is important not to overlook the physical requirements of the solution, particularly cabling. In some cases, it may be necessary to perform a physical site assessment as part of the planning and design process. The site assessment checklist should address the following areas:

- Determine whether the site has adequate power and cooling for the required number and type of Wide Area Application Engine (WAE) appliances. This should include available network module slots in routers when deploying the NME-WAE.

- Determine whether the site has available rack space for the number and type of WAE appliances. Note that the WAE-73xx Series appliances require a four-post rack for installation.

- Identify a physically secure location for installation of the WAE hardware.
- Determine whether there available interfaces and cabling for the LAN and console interfaces of each WAE.

The physical requirements for each WAE appliance can be found on Cisco.com at the following location:

http://cisco.com/en/US/products/ps6474/products_data_sheets_list.html

Site Information Checklist

☐ Create a list of basic site information

☐ Develop user community profiles

☐ Validate physical infrastructure through site assessments

Network Infrastructure

The network infrastructure is one of the most important areas to focus on when designing a Cisco WAAS solution. This is where you will spend the majority of your time from a requirements collection, analysis, and design perspective. Because WAAS is a network-integrated WAN optimization and application acceleration solution, having an in-depth understanding of the network infrastructure is required for a successful deployment. For example, the differences in the WAN characteristics of a low-bandwidth, high-latency satellite network and a high-speed, low-latency MPLS-based WAN are significant. These differences impact not only how the solution is sized and the configuration is tuned, but also the expectations that should be set for the amount of performance gain to be expected.

WAN Topology

You should develop a high-level WAN topology, specifically focusing on the portions of the WAN where WAAS will be deployed. The topology should show all major network nodes, identify critical routing and switching device types, service providers, and network link types. This information will give you a "big picture" view of the network infrastructure, which helps you understand how the users and resources identified in the previous section are tied together. Figure 3-3 shows a sample high-level topology diagram.

Figure 3-3   *Sample High-Level WAN Topology*

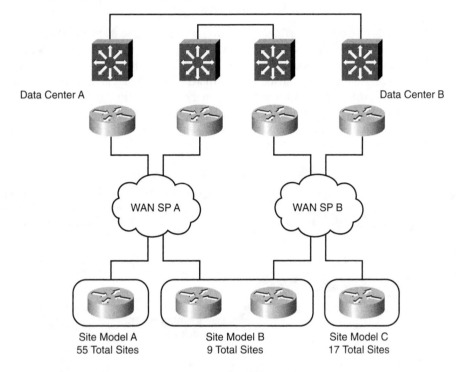

If you are dealing with a large WAN infrastructure, you only need to represent the different site types in your topology diagram. In Figure 3-3 the different site types are represented, with an indication of how many actual sites of that type exist.

An important aspect of understanding the WAN infrastructure is collecting information about the bandwidth, latency, and loss characteristics. This information is used for sizing the hardware for each location and for tuning the configuration once the solution is deployed. For each site type, you should document the following:

- Number and type of WAN links
- WAN bandwidth
- Round-trip time (RTT) latency
- Loss (as a percentage)

Configuration tuning for different types of WAN environments is discussed in detail in Chapter 8, "Configuring WAN Optimization."

You should also collect existing WAN utilization statistics so that you can compare a before and after picture of deploying Cisco WAAS. There are a number of methods for collecting WAN utilization and application performance statistics. Per-application statistics can be collected using NetFlow from the existing routers and switches in the network infrastructure. NetFlow statistics show WAN utilization on a per-application basis, which allows you to see which types of applications can potentially benefit the most from deploying Cisco WAAS. Figure 3-4 shows an example WAN utilization graph generated by NetQoS ReporterAnalyzer from NetFlow data.

Figure 3-4 *Per-Application Link Utilization Using NetQoS ReporterAnalyzer*

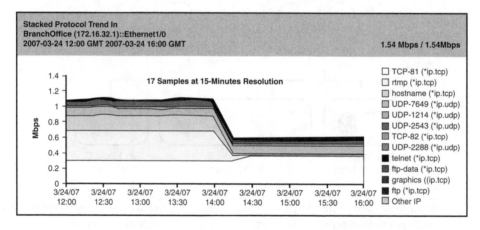

Per-application response time statistics can also be useful when assessing the need for Cisco WAAS. Version 4.0.13 of Cisco WAAS includes a component called FlowAgent, which allows each WAE to export application response time statistics to a NetQoS SuperAgent. The SuperAgent Aggregator is then able to compile the end-to-end response characteristics of each application. When SuperAgent is deployed prior to Cisco WAAS, existing application response time statistics are available to show the benefit on application performance of Cisco WAAS. Figure 3-5 shows an example NetQoS SuperAgent application response time report.

Figure 3-5 *NetQoS SuperAgent Application Response Time Report*

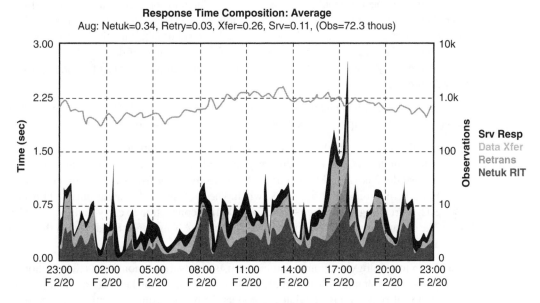

NOTE   More information on using Cisco WAAS with NetQos SuperAgent is available on
Cisco.com at the following location:

http://www.cisco.com/en/US/prod/collateral/contnetw/ps5680/ps6870/prod_white_
paper0900aecd80693006.html

Remote Office Topology

Once you have established a high-level overview of the WAN network topology, you can
then dive down into the site-level network infrastructure details. For each type of site
identified, a site-level analysis should include the physical and logical network topology,
the make and model of networking equipment, and the associated software versions. It is
important to remember the LAN infrastructure as well, because the WAEs will physically
integrate with the LAN environment.

As with the site information requirements, you should generate a set of remote office models. It is not necessary to generate a topology diagram for every single remote office, but rather create a template based on your site information templates. The network topology and equipment information should provide another level of detail for the site topology templates. Make sure to inquire about the use of firewalls or other deep packet inspection technologies, as you will need to consider integration with these types of technologies in your design.

A short description for each remote office type should be provided. The following example provides a brief description of the key characteristics of the topology:

> For Site Model 2, the WAN access router terminates multiple physical circuits, each with a single PVC back to a different headend data center. The WAN bandwidth for Site Model 2 is 1.536 Mbps. For LAN connectivity, the WAN access router has a FastEthernet connection to a LAN switch. The LAN switch functions purely at Layer 2. 802.1q trunking is used across the FastEthernet connection to carry multiple VLANs. The default gateway for devices is the physical LAN interface IP address of the WAN access router.

In addition to topology diagrams, equipment lists, software versions, and a description of the topology, you should collect sample configurations from the key network components as well. It is also recommended that you collect the output from the routing table on each device. The configuration and routing table output will help you validate your understanding of the site and identify any additional features or configuration items of interest.

Data Center Topology

After you have collected the requirements for the various types of remote offices, you can then address each data center. Even though in recent years there has been a push for standardization in the data center, it is still very common for organizations to have multiple data centers deployed using different topologies and different types of networking equipment. It is also quite normal for data centers in different geographical locations to leverage different WAN transport providers, each one with varying service levels and capabilities. And finally, data centers can be designed for different purposes altogether. For example, some data centers may host internal applications and services, while other data centers may be built to support external Internet commerce. It is recommended that you address WAAS data center integration on a data center by data center basis.

As with the remote offices, you need a detailed topology diagram for each data center, including equipment models, software versions, sample configuration, and so forth. Figure 3-6 shows a sample data center topology diagram.

Figure 3-6   *Sample Data Center Topology*

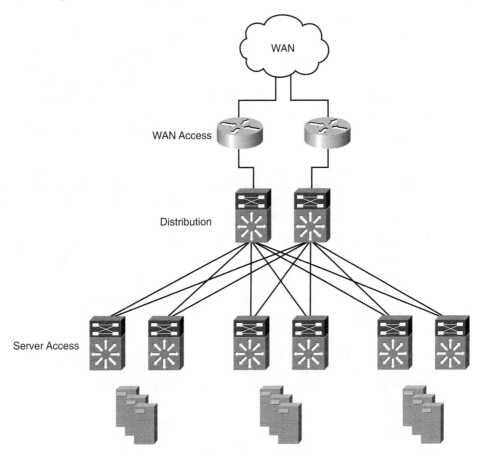

Another area to pay close attention to in the data center is the use and placement of other intelligent network technologies. This includes items such as firewalls, IDS/IPS, content switches, Network-Based Application Recognition (NBAR), content caching devices, and any other device that interacts with Layer 4 through Layer 7 or can directly manipulate the flow of traffic. Any other technology that validates, manipulates, examines, or otherwise relies on information in the transport and application areas of network traffic should be well documented. Because WAAS also interprets and manipulates TCP traffic for optimization purposes, you need to address integration with these technologies as part of your WAAS design. Chapters 5 and 6 provide a detailed discussion of placement considerations and integration with other intelligent network technologies.

Traffic Flows

Understanding traffic flows, both within a single site and between multiple sites, is extremely important. WAAS relies on in-path and off-path interception techniques to receive traffic for optimization. Regardless of the interception mechanisms chosen for the design, the underlying assumption is that WAAS must be inserted into the data path between the client and server on both sides of a network link and for both directions of traffic flow. This means that you have to understand how traffic flows between clients and servers over the existing network infrastructure. For each site profile that is created, you should map the various different traffic flow patterns over the network topology. You should make sure to explicitly call out the following characteristics:

- Default gateway selection: How do host systems at each location select a default gateway? Are default gateway redundancy techniques such as Hot Standby Router Protocol (HSRP), Virtual Router Redundancy Protocol (VRRP), or Gateway Load Balancing Protocol (GLBP) used?

- Which paths are preferred when multiple entry and exit points exist for a site?

- How do traffic flows change when there is a failure in the network? What is the expectation of the WAAS solution during each type of failure?

You should document each major type of flow with a source and destination site, and the capacity and performance requirements of the flow. Figure 3-7 shows the sample WAN topology with the major flow types.

Figure 3-7 shows three different flow types: client-to-server, client-to-client, and server-to-server. Each type of flow likely has different capacity and performance requirements as well. Table 3-2 shows some common characteristics for different types of flow.

Table 3-2   *Flow Type Characteristics*

Flow Type	Characteristics
Client-to-server	Many-to-few relationship
	Upload capacity requirements are low
	Download capacity requirements are relatively high
	Example: Remote file access or web browsing
Client-to-client	Many-to-many relationship
	Upload and download capacity requirements are usually equal
	Example: Peer-to-peer file sharing or VoIP
Server-to-server	Few-to-few relationship
	Asynchronous or synchronous flows
	Very high capacity requirements
	Example: Server replication or n-tier application architectures

Figure 3-7 *WAN Topology with Flow Types*

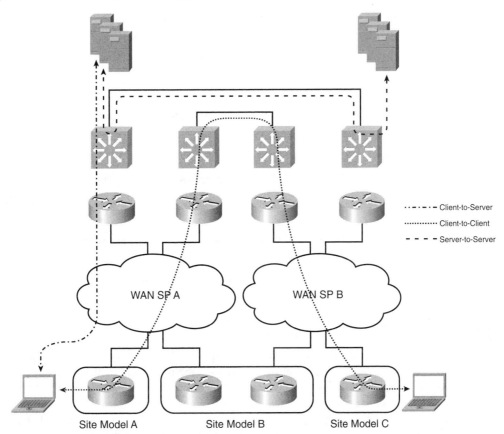

In addition to the source and destination of the flows, you should also have an understanding of the number of concurrent flows. This is most commonly derived from the number of users at a site and the percentage of concurrently online users. In general, most enterprise uses have between five and ten concurrent TCP connections that require optimization. This is only a general observation that should be validated in your environment. This number can also vary by the type of user. For example, an engineer who is frequently working on collaborative projects with many colleagues around the world might have more concurrent connections than does a graphic designer who is working mostly with local files.

The importance of understanding how traffic flows over the network infrastructure cannot be overstated. Understanding the various flows will help you determine where within the network infrastructure WAEs should be placed, and which interception options are available. Each identified flow pattern should be tested to ensure that the proposed design performs as expected.

Network Infrastructure Checklist

☐ Identify the physical and logical network topologies

☐ Identify the existing and planned IP addressing schemes

☐ Identify the hardware models of all relevant network equipment (routers and switches)

☐ Identify the standard IOS versions in use

☐ Identify the WAN characteristics for all sites where WAAS will be deploted

☐ Identify the transport technologies in use

☐ Identify the WAN and LAN bandwidth for all sites where WAAS will be deployed

☐ Identify the RTT latency for all sites where WAAS will be deployed

☐ Identify the packet loss percentage (if any) for all links that optimized traffic will traverse

☐ Collect sample device configurations for all relevant network devices

☐ Identify the existing routing policy

☐ Document traffic flows across the existing network topology

Application Characteristics

It is common for enterprises to have hundreds, if not thousands, of different applications running across the network. Your requirements gathering should focus on the key applications used by the business. Consider collecting information for the top *n* applications, where *n* is some reasonable number such as 5. In many cases, the WAAS solution may be targeted at improving the performance of a specific application or set of applications. Understanding these applications in depth is important, because they will have the biggest impact on the design, and may be the driving force behind the funding of the project. You need to understand the network characteristics of the critical applications in your environment. This may require involving the specific application team who supports the application, in order to understand how it was deployed. This can include information such as whether or not the application is performing compression or encryption. You should collect the following key pieces of information about each application:

- Application name
- Vendor
- Version, including patches/service packs
- Locations deployed
- Protocols/ports used
- Network capacity and performance requirements

The network capacity and performance requirements are from the perspective of the application. For example, what are the throughput and response time requirements for a given application? Understanding the performance requirements of the applications helps you to identify which WAAS optimizations (such as compression) will provide the most benefit.

Additional requirements are also collected for applications for which WAAS provides application-specific acceleration, such as Wide Area File Services (WAFS).

Application Requirements Checklist

☐ Identify the top *n* applications that are critical to the success of the project

☐ Evaluate the network characteristics of critical applications

☐ Develop application-specific use cases for lab validation and pilot testing

☐ Define minimum network capacity and performance requirements

☐ Review existing baseline performance statistics

File Services Requirements

The Wide Area File Services Application Optimizer (WAFS AO) in Cisco WAAS requires the collection and analysis of additional information by the designer. This additional information is used for configuring advanced features and functionality, such as content prepositioning, disconnected mode of operation, and dynamic shares. Because the WAFS AO provides application-specific acceleration, it is also important to understand which vendor implementations you are dealing with. The level of accelerations the WAFS AO is able to provide depends on the behavior of the specific CIFS implementation being used. Areas that you should address as part of the file services requirements include:

- What client operating system versions are being used, including the service pack level?
- What types of file servers will be accelerated using the WAFS AO?
- What type of content will be served from the file servers?
- Which CIFS ports are allowed/supported?
- What is the namespace used for the file services environment? This should include not only global namespace technologies, such as DFS, but also whether or not a file server name maps to multiple IP addresses/interfaces.

The amount of data hosted by the origin file servers also has an impact on the WAE sizing of the WAAS solution. WAAS has a separate CIFS object cache used by the WAFS AO for serving local copies of previously cached content. The CIFS object cache is typically sized to hold what is considered the active working set for a site. The active working set of data is the amount of data that is currently being accessed and updated by users at a site. The active working set is typically up to 10 percent of the total data footprint for a site.

Advanced Features

There are several advanced features used in file services environments today, some of which you need to take into consideration when deploying Cisco WAAS. You should document the use and implementation details of the following advanced features as part of your requirements collection:

- **Microsoft Volume Shadow Copy Services (VSS):** Provides a mechanism for creating point-in-time copies of data

- **Microsoft Access-Based Enumeration (ABE):** Filters the folders visible to a user based on the user's access rights

- **Dynamic shares:** Dynamically associate users with a specific share based on the user's credentials

- **SMB signing (aka digital signatures):** Cryptographic integrity mechanism used for validating CIFS message integrity between two host systems

File Services Utilization

For each file server that will be accelerated using the WAFS AO, you need to know the peak number of concurrent CIFS sessions used by that file server. This information is used for solution sizing. On a Microsoft Windows file server, this information can be collected using the Microsoft Performance Monitor (Perfmon) utility, shown in Figure 3-8.

Figure 3-8 *Microsoft Perfmon*

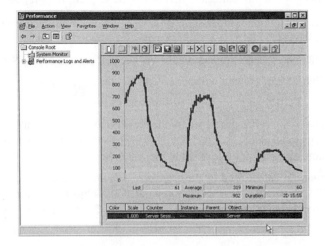

File Services Requirements Checklist

☐ Identify the client OS versions being used

☐ Identify the type of file servers and OS versions being used

☐ Identify the size of the active data set for cache sizing

☐ Understand the namespace and client use cases

☐ Baseline the existing file server performance for concurrent sessions and open files

Platform Requirements

Platform requirements address the basic information required for configuration of the WAE devices. This includes information such as hostname standards, DNS domain membership, NTP server IP addresses, IP addressing schemes, and so forth. This type of information can be collected using standard request forms and templates.

Platform Requirements Checklist

☐ Identify the IP addresses for that will be used for each WAE

☐ Identify the DNS domain name(s) that will be configured on the WAEs (up to three)

☐ Identify the DNS server IP addresses that will be configured on the WAEs

☐ Identify the NTP server IP addresses that will be configured on the WAEs

Scalability Requirements

The overall scalability of your WAAS design will be determined by the WAE hardware you deploy and the network interception mechanisms you choose. Chapter 2 provides the capabilities of each WAE platform. It is important to understand the scalability limitations of your design. The scalability requirements you identify will help define which choices you make as part of the design development process. As you size the WAAS solution, make sure you allow some room for organic growth of the solution.

Scalability Requirements Checklist

☐ Determine how many concurrent users the design should scale to handle

☐ Determine how many sites the design should scale to handle

☐ Determine how many additional users per site the design should scale to handle

☐ Determine how many new sites the design should scale to handle

Availability Requirements

Availability requirements influence the design and configuration by determining how much redundancy is built into the individual components and the design as a whole. Availability requirements can also influence the hardware selection and solution sizing decisions. Availability requirements should address the following areas:

- Acceptable levels of service loss
- Acceptable levels of capacity loss
- Expected failure detection and response times
- Automatic or manual recovery expectations

Availability requirements are also a good place to document various failure test cases. These test cases can be used to validate the resiliency of the proposed design through lab validation and testing.

Availability Checklist

- ☐ Identify any loss of service and capacity requirements
- ☐ Identify the failure detection and response time requirements
- ☐ Identify the device component availability requirements
- ☐ Identify the device availability requirements

Management Requirements

The requirements for management of the WAAS solution are sometimes overlooked. "Management" is a somewhat general term that can be interpreted in many different ways. From a design and configuration perspective, the management requirements deal with integrating the individual WAEs into existing network management systems and operational processes and procedures. What you are mostly interested in determining here is which NMS platform the WAAS solution will need to integrate with, and which protocol interfaces will be used. WAAS 4.0.13 supports the following management protocols:

- WAAS Central Manager
- SNMP v1/2c/3
- Syslog
- SMTP (limited to the WAFS AO)
- FlowAgent (limited to NetQoS SuperAgent)

Once you understand the systems and protocol interfaces required, you can collect some more practical information for the device-specific configurations.

SNMP Trap/Inform Routing

SNMP traps/informs generated by Cisco WAAS can be routed to various NMS devices. Up to four trap/inform destinations can be specified. Table 3-3 can be used for collecting SNMP trap/inform types and destinations.

Table 3-3 *SNMP Trap/Inform Routing*

Device Name	IP Address	Community String
zas01.cisco.com	10.88.88.88	notsopublic

SNMP Community Strings

Cisco WAAS support read-only SNMP objects for querying the status of each WAE and collecting utilization statistics. The following SNMP MIBs are supported by Cisco WAAS:

- ACTONA-ACTASTOR-MIB
- CISCO-CDP-MIB
- CISCO-CONFIG-MAN-MIB
- CISCO-CONTENT-ENGINE-MIB
- CISCO-ENTITY-ASSET-MIB
- CISCO-SMI
- CISCO-TC
- ENTITY-MIB
- EVENT-MIB
- HOST-RESOURCES-MIB
- MIB-II
- SNMP-COMMUNITY-MIB
- SNMP-FRAMEWORK-MIB
- SNMP-NOTIFICATION-MIB
- SNMP-TARGET-MIB
- SNMP-USM-MIB
- SNMPV2-MIB
- SNMP-VCAM-MIB

One of the important pieces of information exposed through SNMP is the WAAS Alarm Book, which provides an explanation for all types of alarms generated by WAAS, and is accessed using SNMP using the CISCO-CONTENT-ENGINE-MIB. The WAAS Alarm Book is available on Cisco.com at the following location:

http://www.cisco.com/cgi-bin/tablebuild.pl/waas40

Table 3-4 can be used for collecting SNMP community string information.

Table 3-4   *SNMP Community Strings*

Community	Notes
notsopublic	Traps only

Syslog Servers

Syslog messages generated by Cisco WAAS can be routed to various NMS devices. Up to four syslog destinations can be specified. The WAAS Error Message Book contains an explanation and proposed action for the syslog messages generated by WAAS. The Error Message Book is available on Cisco.com at the following location:

http://www.cisco.com/cgi-bin/tablebuild.pl/waas40

Table 3-5 can be used for collecting syslog server information.

Table 3-5   *Syslog Routing*

Log Level	Server Name	IP Address
7 (debug)	sys01.cisco.com	10.44.72.189

Management Requirements Checklist

☐ Understand which management systems you are required to integrate with

☐ Identify the specific management protocols you need to configure

☐ Collect the information required to configure support for the various management protocols

Security Requirements

There are two primary aspects to the security of the WAAS solution: data encryption and management access control.

Starting in WAAS 4.0.13, administrators can choose to encrypt the cached content on a WAE configured as an application accelerator. The disk encryption feature is configurable on a device-by-device basis. From a requirements perspective, all you need to do is identify the sites where disk encryption should be enabled, which is generally only remote offices. In most cases, WAEs deployed in campus or data center locations are physically secured, thus removing the need to encrypt the disk drives.

Cisco WAAS supports multiple methods for authenticating administrative users, including TACACS, RADIUS, and Windows Authentication. AAA Accounting is also supported using TACACS. WAAS also supports RBAC, which allows you to further limit what administrative functions a user can perform, and which WAEs (or groups of WAEs) they can be performed on. RBAC is based on the following two concepts:

- **Roles:** Defines a set of objects (configuration pages) in the Central Manager GUI that a user can access
- **Domains:** Defines a set of devices (WAEs) or device groups that a user can access

A user account can be assigned to one or more roles and domains. When no roles or domains are assigned to a user account, the built-in "default" role is applied, which provides the user with no access to any of the Central Manager objects. Figure 3-9 shows the Central Manager roles configuration page.

Figure 3-9 *Configuring Central Manager Roles*

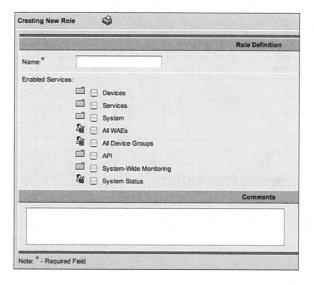

The requirements you need to collect/define fall into three primary areas:

- Security server information
- Role definitions
- Domain definitions

The security server information includes information such as IP addresses and shared encryption keys. For example, you can define up to three TACACS servers or up to five RADIUS servers for authentication.

For roles definitions, you need to define different classes of users, and which portions of the Central Manager GUI they should have access to. Table 3-6 provides a format for defining this information.

Table 3-6 *Central Manager Role Definitions*

Role Name	Description	CM Pages Required
NA-Admins	North America Admins	Devices
		Services > File
		Services > Acceleration
		System Status

Similar to the role definitions, you also need to define the domain a user will belong to. By default, a user has access to all of the WAEs registered to the Central Manager. If you have a requirement to limit which WAEs a user (or group of users) can access, you need to create one or more domain. Table 3-7 provides a format for defining this information.

Table 3-7 *Central Manager Domain Definitions*

Domain Name	Entry Type	Description	WAE/DeviceGroup
NorthAmerica	Device Groups	All WAEs in NA	NAEastCoast
			NACentral
			NAWestCoast

Security Requirements Checklist

☐ Identify the authentication, authorization, and accounting method you will use

☐ Collect the AAA server information (IP addresses, encryption keys, etc.)

☐ Determine which users need access to the WAAS infrastructure

☐ Develop roles and domains based on the type and scope of administrative access required

Summary

This chapter reviewed the key requirements that you should collect and analyze as part of developing a Cisco WAAS solution design. The approach outlined in this chapter treats everything as a requirement, whether it is a new requirement for a specific feature in the WAAS solution, or a requirement imposed by the existing network infrastructure. Although it is important to define as many of the requirements up front, you should not let the collection of requirements impede the overall progress of the project. You have to find a balance between the level of detail you need to move forward and the amount of time allocated for the discovery and analysis process. Requirements will likely change over the course of the project, and you are almost always certain to discover new requirements during lab validation and pilot deployment.

CHAPTER 4

Network Integration and Interception

This chapter provides an in-depth review of the network integration and interception capabilities of Cisco WAAS. The chapter begins by describing the options for basic connectivity, including link aggregation and NIC teaming. This is followed by a discussion of the interception methods available for redirecting traffic to a WAAS device for optimization. The techniques and methods discussed in this chapter form the foundation of the design and deployment solutions presented in subsequent chapters of this book.

Interface Connectivity

Each Cisco Wide Area Application Engine (WAE) has two 10/100/1000BASE-T Ethernet interfaces. In a typical deployment, each WAE is connected using a single interface to a LAN switch or router. By default, WAE interfaces auto-negotiate their speed and duplex. You can optionally configure the interface speed to 10 or 100 Mbps. In order for the interface speed to run at 1000 Mbps, it must be configured for auto-negotiation. The duplex of the interface is also configurable.

CAUTION Do not configure WAE interfaces for half-duplex operation. The collision and retransmission behavior of half-duplex Ethernet has a negative effect on WAE performance.

The router-integrated network module (NME-WAE) is also equipped with two Ethernet interfaces, but only one interface is accessible externally. The other interface connects directly to the internal router PCI bus at 1 Gbps and is configured in a similar manner as an external interface would be configured on a WAE appliance. Unlike a WAE appliance configuration, the WAE interface IP address and default gateway are configured as part of the Cisco IOS interface configuration where the NME-WAE is installed. Figure 4-1 shows the physical interface layout on the router-integrated NME-WAE.

Figure 4-1 *NME-WAE Physical Interface Connectivity*

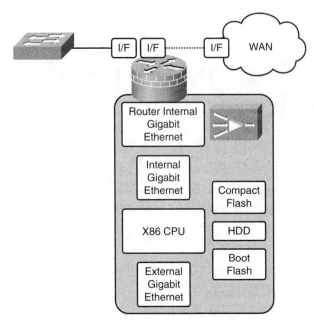

The WAE interface configuration options are similar to the Cisco IOS configuration options, both in terms of function and CLI commands. Example 4-1 shows the interface configuration options available on a WAE.

Example 4-1 *WAE Interface Configuration Options*

```
WAE-612(config)# interface gigabitEthernet 1/0
WAE-612(config-if)# ?
  autosense      Interface autosense
  bandwidth      Interface bandwidth
  cdp            Cisco Discovery Protocol Interface Config commands
  channel-group  Configure EtherChannel group
  description    Interface specific description
  exit           Exit from this submode
  full-duplex    Interface fullduplex
  half-duplex    Interface halfduplex
  ip             Interface Internet Protocol Config commands
  mtu            Set the interface Maximum Transmission Unit (MTU)
  no             Negate a command or set its defaults
  shutdown       Shutdown the specific interface
  standby        Standby interface config commands
WAE-612(config-if)#
```

One of the interface configuration commands that behaves differently in WAAS versus IOS is the **bandwidth** command. The **bandwidth** interface configuration command in WAAS is used to specify the speed of the interface when auto-negotiation is disabled. The way in which the **standby** interface command is used is another important difference between WAAS and IOS. In IOS, the **standby** interface command is used for configuring the Hot Standby Router Protocol (HSRP) feature, while in WAAS it is used to configure the standby interface feature, described in the next section. You can see from the output in Example 4-1 that the remaining WAAS interface configuration commands are similar to the corresponding IOS interface configuration commands.

You can explicitly configure the interface with an IP address and subnet mask, or the WAE can acquire an IP address using DHCP. Each WAE interface can also be configured with multiple secondary IP addresses. It is also possible for the same interface to acquire an IP address through DHCP, and have multiple secondary IP addresses statically configured. By default, the interfaces on a WAE are administratively disabled, and are automatically enabled when a valid IP address is configured.

Each WAE interface is primarily referenced using the standard Cisco IOS interface naming scheme:

<interface-name> <slot/port>

This is how WAE interfaces are referred to during configuration through the CLI or GUI. The interfaces also have an internal name by which the Linux operating system knows them. Table 4-1 shows the mapping between the internal and external interface names.

Table 4-1   *WAE External and Internal Interface Names*

IOS Name	Internal Name
gigabitEthernet 1/0	eth0
gigabitEthernet 2/0	eth1

Understanding the internal name of an interface is useful for understanding system log messages and using internal operating system tools, such as Ethereal or Tcpdump, which are useful for capturing traffic for offline analysis.

Just like the interface configuration, the outputs of interface **show** commands in WAAS are similar to Cisco IOS. Example 4-2 shows the output from the **show interface** command in WAAS.

Example 4-2   *WAE **show interface** Command Output*

```
AST6-CCO-02# show interface gigabitEthernet 1/0
Type:Ethernet
Ethernet address:00:11:25:AB:43:28
Internet address:10.88.81.2
```

continues

Example 4-2 *WAE* **show interface** *Command Output (Continued)*

```
Broadcast address:10.88.81.15
Netmask:255.255.255.240
Maximum Transfer Unit Size:1500
Metric:1
Packets Received: 966044
Input Errors: 0
Input Packets Dropped: 0
Input Packets Overruns: 0
Input Packets Frames: 0
Packet Sent: 1046794
Output Errors: 0
Output Packets Dropped: 0
Output Packets Overruns: 0
Output Packets Carrier: 0
Output Queue Length:1000
Collisions: 0
Base address:0x2000
Flags:UP BROADCAST RUNNING MULTICAST
Mode: autoselect, full-duplex, 100baseTX
AST6-CCO-02#
```

In addition to the normal interface information, such as IP address, Ethernet address, and counters, each interface also has a set of flags. These flags are the same flags that can be seen in the output of the **ifconfig** command in Linux. The two most important flags are UP and RUNNING. The presence of the UP flag indicates that the interface is administratively enabled. The presence of the RUNNING flag indicates that line protocol on the interface is operational.

Link Aggregation Using EtherChannel

To increase the available interface bandwidth for a WAE, Cisco WAAS supports EtherChannel. EtherChannel allows for the grouping of multiple physical interfaces to create a single "virtual" interface. The virtual interface, which functions as a single interface, has the aggregate bandwidth of the available physical interfaces in the channel group. EtherChannel is useful when the output from a single WAE exceeds the physical limitations of a single interface. For example, some remote sites may only have 100-Mbps LAN connections available, whereas the traffic from a single WAE can easily exceed 100 Mbps. In these situations, using EtherChannel to group both physical WAE interfaces together provides 200 Mbps of usable interface bandwidth.

In addition to increasing the available interface bandwidth, the EtherChannel has automatic failure and recovery detection based on the link state of each individual interface. In the event of a single interface failure, traffic continues to pass over the remaining interface in the channel group. The EtherChannel interface uses the MAC address from one of the physical interfaces in the group. The same MAC address is used persistently for the EtherChannel interface, even if the physical interface associated with that MAC address goes down. The formation of an EtherChannel in WAAS is based purely on device configuration. WAAS does not support Cisco Port Aggregation Protocol (PAgP) or 802.3ad Link Aggregation Control Protocol (LACP). When configuring EtherChannel between a WAE and a LAN switch, the channel mode on the LAN switch should be set to On for the WAE EtherChannel.

By default, the WAE load balances packets across all available interfaces in the channel group using a round-robin algorithm. WAAS also supports load balancing using destination IP address or destination MAC address.

Figure 4-2 shows a WAE connected to a single LAN switch using EtherChannel.

Figure 4-2   *WAE Connected Using EtherChannel Feature*

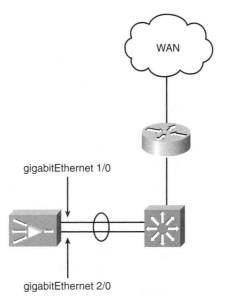

EtherChannel Configuration

Configuring EtherChannel in WAAS involves the following steps:

Step 1   Create a virtual PortChannel interface.

Step 2   Configure an IP address and subnet mask for the PortChannel interface.

Step 3   Assign the physical interfaces to the PortChannel.

Example 4-3 shows a basic EtherChannel configuration.

Example 4-3 *WAE EtherChannel Configuration*

```
!
interface PortChannel 1
 description ** EtherChannel Link to Switch ABC ***
 ip address 10.10.10.5 255.255.255.0
 exit
!
interface GigabitEthernet 1/0
 channel-group 1
 exit
interface GigabitEthernet 2/0
 channel-group 1
 exit
!
```

You should observe the following limitations when configuring EtherChannel in WAAS:

- Both interfaces in the channel group must run at the same speed.

- Access control lists (ACL) are still applied to each physical interface.

The load-balancing algorithm used for distributing traffic across the EtherChannel is configured using the following command:

port-channel load-balance *dst-ip* | *dst-mac* | **round-robin**

The command is configured globally and applies to all PortChannels on the WAE.

To check the status of the PortChannel interface, use the **show interface PortChannel** *channel-number* command. Example 4-4 demonstrates the output of this command.

Example 4-4 *WAAS* **show interface PortChannel** *Output*

```
AST6-CCO-01# show interface PortChannel 1
Interface PortChannel 1 (2 physical interface(s)):
        GigabitEthernet 1/0 (active)
        GigabitEthernet 2/0 (active)
--------------------
Type:Ethernet
Ethernet address:00:11:25:AB:43:32
Internet address:10.88.80.130
Broadcast address:10.88.80.255
Netmask:255.255.255.128
Maximum Transfer Unit Size:1500
Metric:1
Packets Received: 815996
Input Errors: 0
Input Packets Dropped: 0
Input Packets Overruns: 0
Input Packets Frames: 0
```

Example 4-4   *WAAS* **show interface PortChannel** *Output (Continued)*

```
Packet Sent: 321842
Output Errors: 0
Output Packets Dropped: 0
Output Packets Overruns: 0
Output Packets Carrier: 0
Output Queue Length:0
Collisions: 0
Flags:UP BROADCAST RUNNING MASTER MULTICAST
AST6-CCO-01#
```

Each member of the channel group, along with the status of the interface, is shown at the beginning of the output. The MASTER flag in the example output indicates that this is the virtual EtherChannel interface. Also notice the Ethernet address, which is taken from one of the physical interfaces in the channel group. Example 4-5 demonstrates the same command for each physical interface in the channel group.

Example 4-5   *Channel Group Member Interface Output*

```
AST6-CCO-01# show interface gigabitEthernet 1/0
Type:Ethernet
Ethernet address:00:11:25:AB:43:32
Internet address:10.88.80.130
Broadcast address:10.88.80.255
Netmask:255.255.255.128
Maximum Transfer Unit Size:1500
Metric:1
Packets Received: 816176
Input Errors: 0
Input Packets Dropped: 0
Input Packets Overruns: 0
Input Packets Frames: 0
Packet Sent: 321880
Output Errors: 0
Output Packets Dropped: 0
Output Packets Overruns: 0
Output Packets Carrier: 0
Output Queue Length:1000
Collisions: 0
Base address:0x2000
Flags:UP BROADCAST RUNNING SLAVE MULTICAST
Mode: full-duplex, 100baseTX
AST6-CCO-01#
AST6-CCO-01# show interface gigabitEthernet 2/0
Type:Ethernet
Ethernet address:00:11:25:AB:43:32
Internet address:10.88.80.130
Broadcast address:10.88.80.255
Netmask:255.255.255.128
```

continues

Example 4-5   *Channel Group Member Interface Output (Continued)*

```
Maximum Transfer Unit Size:1500
Metric:1
Packets Received: 0
Input Errors: 0
Input Packets Dropped: 0
Input Packets Overruns: 0
Input Packets Frames: 0
Packet Sent: 0
Output Errors: 0
Output Packets Dropped: 0
Output Packets Overruns: 0
Output Packets Carrier: 0
Output Queue Length:1000
Collisions: 0
Base address:0x3400
Flags:UP BROADCAST SLAVE MULTICAST
Mode: autoselect
AST6-CCO-01#
```

The command output for each physical interface is the same as it is without EtherChannel configured, with the following exceptions:

- The SLAVE flag is set, indicating that the interface is part of an EtherChannel group.

- The Ethernet address for each interface is the same, and matches the MAC address used by the virtual EtherChannel interface.

Using the Standby Interface Feature

When you do not require increased interface bandwidth but desire interface redundancy, you can use the standby interface feature. The standby interface feature configures both physical interfaces on the WAE in an active/standby failover pair. At any point in time, only one of the interfaces is active and passing traffic. The second interface, or standby interface, is passively waiting to take over in the event that the active interface fails. When the active interface fails, the standby interface takes over the active role. When the previously active interface recovers, it assumes the standby role. The interface with the highest priority is preferred as the active interface. The priority is configurable.

The standby interface feature has become a popular choice for deployments because the WAE can be physically connected to two different LAN switches. This prevents the failure of a single LAN switch or switchport from disrupting the operation of the WAE. Figure 4-3 shows an example of a WAE connected using the standby interface feature.

Figure 4-3 *WAE Connected Using Standby Interface Feature*

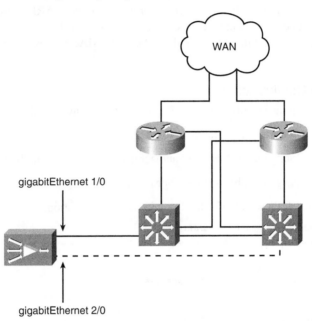

The failure of the active interface in the standby group is detected using three different methods. The first method monitors the link state of the active interface. Line protocol is up when the RUNNING flag is present on the Ethernet interface. If line protocol fails on the active interface, the interface is marked as down.

The second method uses an ICMP ping to check availability of the default gateway configured on the WAE. An ICMP echo request is sent once every 10 seconds to the configured default gateway. If there is a response to the echo request, the interface is considered up. If there is no response to the echo request, five more echo requests are sent. If at least three responses are received, the interface is considered up. Otherwise, the interface is considered failed, and the interface is marked as down.

The final method available for monitoring the health of the active interface uses the interface error count to determine if an unacceptable number of errors have been seen on the interface. The error count is the absolute number of transmit and receive errors on the active interface. This check is disabled by default, but can be enabled using the following command:

errors *1-2147483647*

The interface state and error counts (when configured) are checked once every 10 seconds. If the active link fails or the error count threshold is exceeded, the interface with the next highest priority is activated. When the failed interface recovers, it becomes the standby interface for the group. The standby interface does not have a preempt capability. When a new interface is activated, the WAE generates a gratuitous ARP to update the MAC address for the shared IP on all other devices on the same subnet. This prevents devices from sending traffic to the shared IP address on the WAE to the MAC address of the failed WAE interface.

Standby Interface Configuration

Configuring the standby interface feature in WAAS involves the following steps:

Step 1 Create a virtual standby interface.

Step 2 Configure an IP address and subnet mask for the standby interface.

Step 3 Assign the physical interfaces to the standby group.

Example 4-6 shows a basic standby interface configuration.

Example 4-6 *WAE Standby Interface Configuration*

```
!
interface Standby 1
 ip address 10.88.80.130 255.255.255.128
 exit
!
interface GigabitEthernet 1/0
 standby 1 priority 105
 exit
interface GigabitEthernet 2/0
 standby 1
 exit
!
```

You should observe the following limitations when configuring the standby interface feature within WAAS:

* The physical interfaces in the standby group do not require IP addresses.

* The standby interface feature does not have a preempt capability.

Each physical interface can be assigned a numeric priority between 1 and 2,147,483,647. The default standby priority for an interface is 100. The virtual standby interface uses the MAC address of the active interface. When the active interface fails and the standby interface takes over, the WAE generates a gratuitous ARP request to update the adjacent devices with the new MAC address associated with the WAE IP address.

To check the status of the standby interface, use the **show interface Standby** *standby-interface-number* command. Example 4-7 shows the output of this command.

Example 4-7 *WAAS* **show interface Standby** *Interface Output*

```
AST6-CCO-01# show interface Standby 1
Standby Group: 1
        IP address: 10.88.80.130, netmask: 255.255.255.128
        Member interfaces:
                GigabitEthernet 1/0     priority: 105
                GigabitEthernet 2/0     priority: 100
        Active interface: GigabitEthernet 1/0
AST6-CCO-01#
```

Each member of the standby group, as well as the status of the interface, is shown in the output. The current active interface is also displayed. The output for each physical interface is shown in Example 4-8.

Example 4-8 *Standby Group Member Interface Output*

```
AST6-CCO-01# show interface gigabitEthernet 1/0
Type:Ethernet
Ethernet address:00:11:25:AB:43:32
Internet address (secondary): 10.88.80.130 Netmask: 255.255.255.128
Maximum Transfer Unit Size:1500
Metric:1
Packets Received: 819025
Input Errors: 0
Input Packets Dropped: 0
Input Packets Overruns: 0
Input Packets Frames: 0
Packet Sent: 322492
Output Errors: 0
Output Packets Dropped: 0
Output Packets Overruns: 0
Output Packets Carrier: 0
Output Queue Length:1000
Collisions: 0
Base address:0x2000
Flags:UP BROADCAST RUNNING MULTICAST
Mode: full-duplex, 100baseTX
AST6-CCO-01#
AST6-CCO-01# show interface gigabitEthernet 2/0
Type:Ethernet
Ethernet address:00:11:25:AB:43:33
Maximum Transfer Unit Size:1500
Metric:1
Packets Received: 0
Input Errors: 0
Input Packets Dropped: 0
```

continues

Example 4-8 *Standby Group Member Interface Output (Continued)*

```
Input Packets Overruns: 0
Input Packets Frames: 0
Packet Sent: 0
Output Errors: 0
Output Packets Dropped: 0
Output Packets Overruns: 0
Output Packets Carrier: 0
Output Queue Length:1000
Collisions: 0
Base address:0x3400
Flags:UP BROADCAST MULTICAST
Mode: autoselect
AST6-CCO-01#
```

In this output, the only indication that the interface is a member of a standby group is the secondary IP address, which matches the IP address configured on the virtual standby interface.

Interception Techniques and Protocols

There are two approaches for leveraging the network infrastructure to intercept and redirect traffic to WAAS for optimization. The first method relies on interception protocols or routing configuration used by the networking components (routers and switches) to selectively intercept traffic and redirect it to the WAAS infrastructure. This method is referred to as off-path interception. The most common method for off-path network interception is the Web Cache Communication Protocol, or WCCPv2.

The second method places the WAE physically inline between two network elements, most commonly a router and LAN switch. All traffic between the two network elements is passed through the WAE, which can then selectively intercept traffic for optimization. This method is referred to as *in-path interception*, because the WAE is physically placed in the data path between the clients and servers.

This section discusses both off-path (WCCPv2) and in-path interception in detail. It also discusses other interception options for specific use cases, such as policy-based routing (PBR) and content switching. These additional interception options add to the flexibility with which WAAS can be integrated into existing network infrastructures of all sizes.

Web Cache Communication Protocol

This section does not provide an exhaustive reference for the WCCPv2 protocol. Rather, it provides enough information about the protocol background and concepts to enable you to understand the WCCPv2 implementation in Cisco WAAS. For an in-depth understanding of the WCCPv2 protocol, you are encouraged to read the WCCPv2 protocol draft. The full WCCPv2 IETF draft is available online at http://www.wrec.org/Drafts/draft-wilson-wrec-wccp-v2-00.txt.

WCCP Overview

WCCP is a transparent interception protocol first developed by Cisco Systems, Inc. in 1997. WCCP is a control plane protocol that runs between devices running Cisco IOS and WCCP "clients" such as WAAS. The protocol enables the network infrastructure to selectively intercept traffic based on IP protocol and port numbers, and redirect that traffic to a WCCP client. WCCP is considered transparent, because it allows for local interception and redirection of traffic without any configuration changes to the clients or servers. WCCP has built-in load-balancing, scalability, fault-tolerance, and service assurance (fail open) mechanisms. Figure 4-4 shows the basic functions of WCCP.

Figure 4-4 *Basic WCCP Functionality*

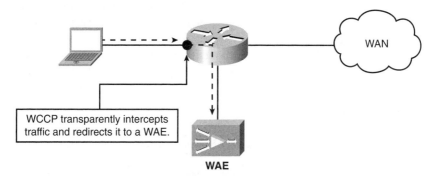

The current version, WCCPv2, is used by Cisco WAAS to transparently intercept and redirect all TCP traffic, regardless of port. The following section describes the basic WCCPv2 concepts and how they are specifically used by Cisco WAAS.

Service Groups

The routers and WAEs participating in the same service constitute a service group. A service group defines a set of characteristics about what types of traffic should be intercepted, as well as how the intercepted traffic should be handled. There are two types of service groups:

- Well-known services
- Dynamic services

Well-known services, also referred to as static services, have a fixed set of characteristics that are known by both IOS and WCCPv2 client devices. There is currently a single well-known service called web-cache. This service redirects all TCP traffic with a destination port of 80. The characteristics of a dynamic service are initially only known to the WCCPv2 clients within the service group. The characteristics of the service group are communicated to the IOS devices by the first WCCPv2 client device to join the service group.

A unique service ID identifies service groups, which is a number from 0 to 255. Service IDs 0 to 50 are reserved for well-known services.

The WCCPv2 implementation in WAAS supports a single dynamic WCCPv2 service, the tcp-promiscuous service. Although referred to in WAAS as a single service, the tcp-promiscuous service is in fact two different services. The two service IDs enabled with the tcp-promiscuous service are 61 and 62. These are the two service group IDs that are configured in IOS when using WCCPv2 with WAAS. Two different service groups are used because both directions (client-to-server and server-to-client) of a TCP connection must be transparently intercepted. To optimize a connection, WAAS must see both directions of the connection on the same WAE. Not only does WAAS intercept the connection in both directions, but it also intercepts the connection on both sides of the WAN link. Because the packet Layer 3 and Layer 4 headers are preserved, transparent interception is used on both sides of the WAN in both directions to redirect connections to the WAAS infrastructure for optimization. Figure 4-5 shows a basic topology with WCCPv2 interception configured for WAAS.

Figure 4-5 *Basic Network Topology with WCCP*

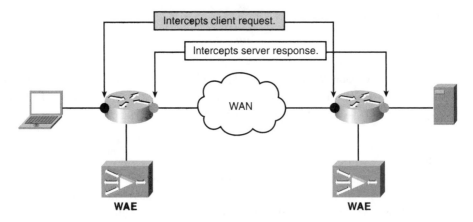

What is the difference between services 61 and 62? You can view the service attributes using CLI commands in both WAAS and IOS. Example 4-9 shows the attributes of services 61 and 62 using the IOS CLI.

Example 4-9   *WCCP Service Group Attributes*

```
AST6-RTR-02# show ip wccp 61 service
WCCP service information definition:
        Type:           Dynamic
        Id:             61
        Priority:       34
        Protocol:       6
        Options:        0x00000501
        . . . . . . . . .
            Hash:       SrcIP
            Alt Hash:   SrcIP SrcPort
            Ports:      -none-

AST6-RTR-02#
AST6-RTR-02# show ip wccp 62 service
WCCP service information definition:
        Type:           Dynamic
        Id:             62
        Priority:       34
        Protocol:       6
        Options:        0x00000502
        . . . . . . . . .
            Hash:       DstIP
            Alt Hash:   SrcIP SrcPort
            Ports:      -none-

AST6-RTR-02#
```

A description of each value is provided in Table 4-2.

Table 4-2   *WCCP Service Group Attributes*

Value	Description
Type	Well-known or dynamic service.
Id	The numeric service ID for the group.
Priority	The priority for the service group. When multiple service groups are configured on the same interface in the same direction, they are evaluated in descending priority order.
Protocol	The IP protocol number defined by the service group.
Options	Flags field indicating further service characteristics.
Hash	The value(s) in the redirected packet used as the hash key.
Alternate Hash	The value(s) in the redirected packet used as the alternate hash key.
Ports	The Layer 4 port numbers defined by the service group.

The command output shows that the only difference between services 61 and 62 is the value from the packet used as the hash key. By default, service group 61 hashes on the source IP address and service group 62 hashes on the destination IP address. Later, this chapter discusses the significance of the hash key used in each service group. By default, the **spoof-client-ip** feature is enabled for both services. This is the WCCPv2 feature that allows WAAS to handle optimized traffic transparently. Traffic forwarded to the WAE uses the same source and destination IP addresses and TCP ports as when it entered the WAE.

The tcp-promiscuous services define TCP as the protocol and do not define any ports. By not defining any ports as part of the service groups, this causes interception and redirection of all TCP traffic. When traffic passes through an interface in the IOS device with WCCPv2 redirection configured, it is evaluated against the protocol and port combination defined by the service to determine whether or not the packet should be redirected. By default this is the only criteria that is used to determine whether or not a packet is redirected. It is important to note that the IOS WCCPv2 implementation is not stateful. This means that IOS WCCPv2 is only dealing with redirected traffic on a packet-by-packet basis. It does not keep track of TCP connection state for redirected traffic. On the other hand, the WCCPv2 implementation in WAAS is stateful. WAAS tracks each connection as a flow throughout the life of the connection.

Forwarding and Return Methods

WCCPv2 supports different methods for forwarding redirected traffic to a WAE, and for the WAE to return traffic to the router for forwarding. These methods are referred to as the *forwarding* and *return* methods and are negotiated between IOS and the WAE when a WAE joins the service group.

The forwarding method defines how traffic that is being redirected from IOS to the WAE is transmitted across the network. The first method, GRE forwarding, encapsulates the original packet in an IP GRE header with the destination IP address set to the target WAE and the source IP address set to the WCCPv2 router ID of the redirecting router. When the WAE receives the GRE-encapsulated packet, the GRE header is removed, and the packet is processed. Figure 4-6 shows an example of GRE forwarding.

The second forwarding method, L2 forwarding, simply rewrites the destination MAC address of the packet being redirected to equal the MAC address of the target WAE. This forwarding method assumes that the WAE is Layer 2 adjacent to the redirecting router. L2 forwarding was originally developed for the WCCPv2 implementation on hardware-based platforms, such as the Catalyst 6500. Figure 4-7 shows an example of L2 forwarding.

Figure 4-6 *WCCP Redirection Using GRE Forwarding*

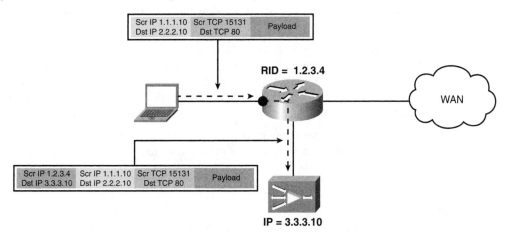

Figure 4-7 *WCCP Redirection Using L2 Forwarding*

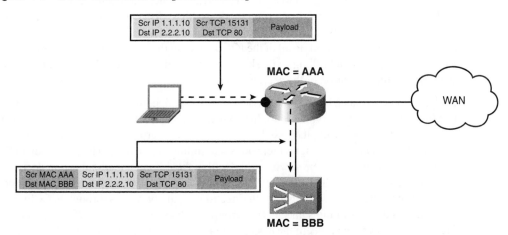

One of the benefits of L2 forwarding is that it allows for the WCCPv2 redirection to occur in hardware on Cisco Catalyst Series switches. In fact, on the Catalyst 3560/3750 and 4500/4948 series switches, the only forwarding method supported by WCCPv2 is L2 forwarding. Additional information about the configuration requirements for deploying WCCPv2 on Cisco Catalyst switches is provided in the "WCCP Configuration" section.

The return method defines how traffic should be returned from the WAE to the redirecting router for normal forwarding. Like the forwarding method, there are two different return methods:

- **GRE return:** Egress traffic from the WAE using GRE return are encapsulated using IP GRE, with a destination IP address of the WCCPv2 router ID and a source IP address of the WAE itself. When the WCCPv2-enabled router receives the returned packet, the IP GRE header is removed and the packet is forwarded normally. WCCPv2 in IOS knows not to re-intercept traffic returned to it using GRE return.

- **L2 return:** The L2 return method returns traffic to the WCCPv2-enabled router by rewriting the destination MAC address of the packet to equal the MAC address of the WCCPv2-enabled router.

Load Distribution

When multiple WAEs exist in a service group, WCCPv2 automatically distributes redirected traffic across all WAEs in the service group. When traffic passes through an IOS device with WCCPv2 redirection configured, the IOS device assigns traffic for that connection to a bucket. Each bucket is assigned to a specific WAE. The method that determines to which bucket traffic is assigned, which determines how traffic is distributed across multiple WAEs within a service group, is called the assignment method. The bucket assignments are communicated from the lead WAE to all of the IOS devices in the service group. The assignment method can use either a hashing or masking scheme, and is negotiated between IOS and WAE during the formation of the service group.

Hash assignment, which is the default assignment method, performs a bitwise hash on a key identified as part of the service group. In WAAS, the hash key used for service group 61 is the source IP address, while the hash key used for service group 62 is the destination IP address. The hash is not configurable, and is deterministic in nature. This means that all of the routers within the same service group will make the same load-balancing decision given the same hash key. This deterministic behavior is what allows WCCPv2 to support asymmetric traffic flows, so long as both directions of the flow pass through WCCPv2-enabled IOS devices in the same service group. Hash assignment uses 256 buckets. Figure 4-8 shows an example of the hash assignment method and bucket-based distribution model used by WCCPv2.

The second assignment method is called mask assignment. With mask assignment, the source IP address, destination IP address, source port, and destination port are concatenated and ANDed with a 96-bit mask to yield a value. The resulting 96-bit value is compared to a list of mask/value pairs. Each mask/value pair is associated with a bucket, and each bucket is in turn assigned to a WAE. Unlike hash assignment, the number of buckets used with mask assignment depends on the number of bits used in the mask. By default, WAAS uses a mask of 0x1741. This results in 2^6 buckets that can be assigned across the WAEs in a service group. With current Catalyst WCCPv2 implementations, up to 7 bits can be defined for the mask. Figure 4-9 shows an example of the mask assignment method and bucket-based distribution model used by WCCPv2.

Figure 4-8 *WCCP Redirection Using Hash Assignment*

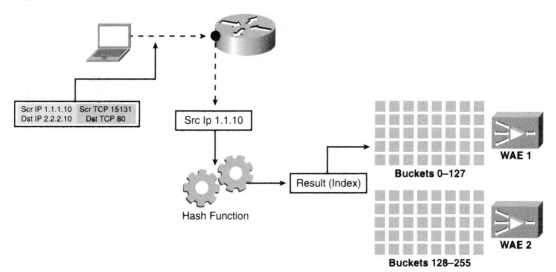

Figure 4-9 *WCCP Redirection Using Mask Assignment*

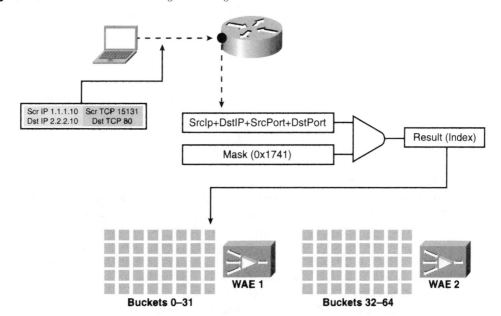

Failure Detection

Once a WAE has successfully joined a service group, a periodic keepalive packet is sent every 10 seconds from the WAE to each router in the service group. The keepalive mechanism occurs independently for each configured service group. If a router in the service group has not received a keepalive packet from the WAE in 25 seconds, the router unicasts a Removal Query message to that WAE requesting that it immediately respond. If no response is received within 5 seconds, for a total of 30 seconds since the last keepalive message from the WAE, the WAE is considered offline and is removed from the service group. Figure 4-10 illustrates this behavior.

Figure 4-10 *WCCP Keepalive Timeout*

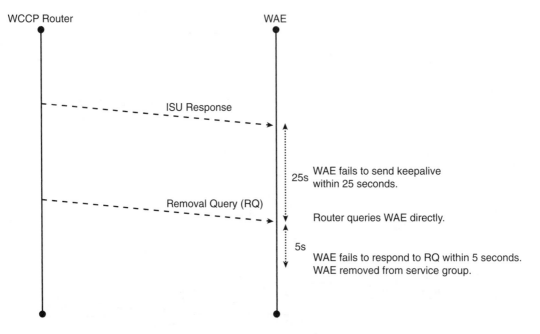

When the WAE is removed from the service group, it is reflected in the Router View advertised from each router in the service group. When the lead WAE determines that a WAE has been removed from the service group, it generates a Redirect Assignment message to each router in the service group. The Redirect Assignment message instructs the routers how to reallocate the buckets across the remaining WAEs in the service group. The length of time required to calculate the new assignments might very depending upon when the group of WAEs becomes stable. The WAE waits a minimum of 9 seconds. The maximum length of time depends on when the IOS device sends an update message without any changes indicated, typically between 19 and 39 seconds.

Flow Protection

When a WAE (re)joins the service group, a new Redirect Assignment message is generated by the lead WAE. When the new WAE begins receiving redirected traffic from the routers in the service group, it does one of two things, depending on whether or not the redirected traffic is for a new connection or part of an existing connection. Traffic associated with newly established connections is evaluated against the Application Traffic Policy (ATP) and processed normally by the WAE. Traffic associated with existing connections is forwarded directly to the WAE that previously owned the bucket for that connection. This WCCPv2 mechanism is called flow protection and is enabled by default. Flow protection allows for existing connections to continue to be optimized even when the traffic assignments for the WAEs in a service group change.

Graceful Shutdown

After the **no wccp ver 2** command is issued, WCCPv2 checks whether any connections are being served by the WAE. If zero connections are being served, the shutdown is immediately carried out. If there are more than zero connections being served, WCCPv2 waits for the user-configured **wccp shutdown max-wait** *XX* time.

During this time, if the connection count goes down to zero, shutdown is immediately done. At the end of the max-wait time, if the connection count has decreased but is still non-zero, the shutdown count waits another 60 seconds, in the hope that if the connection count has decreased other connections may complete too. At the end of the max-wait time, if the connection count has not decreased, shutdown is immediately done. During the 60-second incremental wait, if the connection count becomes zero, shutdown is done. At the end of the 60-second incremental wait, if the connection count has not reduced, the shutdown is done. At the end of the 60-second incremental wait, if the count has further reduced but is still non-zero, another 60-second incremental wait is done.

Unless the user interrupts the wait period, the code waits first for the configured length of time. If it thinks that connections are reducing, it waits a little longer in the hope that more connections can be completed. However, if it realizes that the connection count has not decreased, it discontinues waiting and shuts down.

Scalability

With WCCPv2, each service group can support up to 32 routers and 32 WAEs. This means that a single service group can support $N \times 32$ concurrent optimized TCP connections, where N is the number of concurrent optimized TCP connections supported by the largest WAE model. Each WAE in the service group is manually configured with the IP address of each router in the service group. The WAE then uses unicast packets to exchange WCCPv2 messages with each router. It is not required that the routers in the service are manually configured with the IP address of each WAE in the service group. Each router listens passively for WCCPv2 messages from the WAEs in the service group and responds only as a result of receiving those messages.

The WAE in the service group with the lowest IP address is elected as the "lead" WAE. The lead WAE is responsible for communicating the list, or view, of the routers in the service group to the service group routers. The lead WAE is also responsible for informing the routers how traffic should be distributed across WAEs in the service group. Upon receiving the view of the routers in the service group from the lead WAE, each router responds individually with a Router View. The Router View contains a list of each WAE that the router is currently communicating with. What is implied is that the routers in the service group do not communicate directly with each other; they learn about each other through the Router View advertised by the WAE. Likewise, the WAEs in a service group do not communicate directly with each; they learn about each other from the WAE View advertised by the routers.

Redirect Lists

For deployments where you may want to limit redirection to specific types of traffic, you can use a WCCPv2 redirect list. A WCCPv2 redirect list is a standard or extended IOS access list that is associated with a WCCPv2 service. Traffic passing through an interface on the router with WCCPv2 redirection configured must match not only the protocol/port specified as part of the service group, but also a permit entry in the redirect list. Packets that match the service group protocol/port criteria but do not match a permit entry in the redirect list are forwarded normally. Example 4-10 demonstrates the use of a WCCPv2 redirect list.

Example 4-10 *WCCP Redirection Using a Redirect List*

```
!
access-list 100 permit ip 10.10.10.0 0.0.0.255 any
access-list 100 permit ip any 10.0.0.0 0.0.0.255
access-list 100 deny ip any any
!
ip wccp 61 redirect-list 100
ip wccp 62 redirect-list 100
!
```

In this example, TCP traffic sourced from or destined to subnet 10.10.10.0/24 will be intercepted and redirected by WCCPv2. Another option is to use a redirect list to specify a subset of TCP ports for redirection. Example 4-11 shows how this could be done.

Example 4-11 *WCCP Redirect List Using Application Ports*

```
!
access-list 101 permit tcp any any eq 25
access-list 101 permit tcp any eq 25 any
access-list 101 deny ip any any
!
ip wccp 61 redirect-list 101
ip wccp 62 redirect-list 101
!
```

This example uses a redirect list to allow WCCPv2 to intercept and redirect SMTP traffic only on port 25.

Service Group Placement

The placement of service groups 61 and 62 should not be overlooked in your deployment. The placement refers to which IOS interfaces are configured with service group 61 and which interfaces are configured with service group 62. In most environments, service group 61 should be configured on the client-facing interfaces. For example, when deploying WCCPv2 on a remote-office WAN router, service group 61 is configured to intercept a client request. Configuring group 61 inbound on the router's LAN interface or outbound on the router's WAN interface accomplishes this. Figure 4-11 shows an example of configuring service group 61 inbound on the router's LAN interface.

Figure 4-11 *WCCP Service Group 61 Placement*

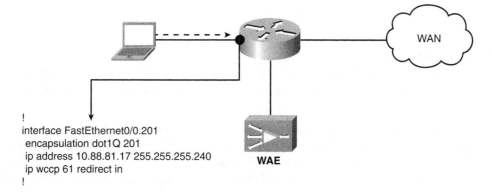

```
!
interface FastEthernet0/0.201
  encapsulation dot1Q 201
  ip address 10.88.81.17 255.255.255.240
  ip wccp 61 redirect in
!
```

For the reverse direction of the connection, service group 62 is used. Service group 62 will be configured in the opposite direction of service group 61. Using the same example shown in Figure 4-11, Figure 4-12 shows service group 62 configured inbound on the router's WAN interface. The following figure shows the complete placement and configuration using both service groups.

Figure 4-12 *WCCP Service Group 61 and 62 Placement*

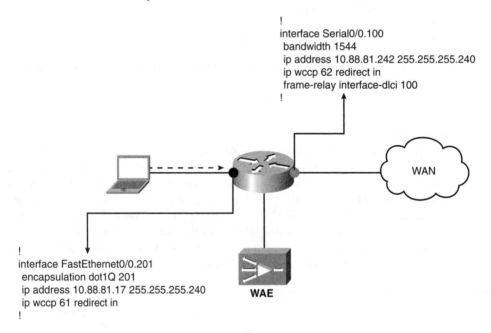

```
!
interface Serial0/0.100
  bandwidth 1544
  ip address 10.88.81.242 255.255.255.240
  ip wccp 62 redirect in
  frame-relay interface-dlci 100
!
```

```
!
interface FastEthernet0/0.201
  encapsulation dot1Q 201
  ip address 10.88.81.17 255.255.255.240
  ip wccp 61 redirect in
!
```

WCCP Configuration

This section provides a basic overview of configuring WCCPv2 within both IOS and WAAS. Detailed WCCPv2 configurations specific to various design options are presented in Chapters 5 and 6.

There are three primary steps involved when configuring WCCPv2 in WAAS. First, you must define which routers the WAE will establish WCCPv2 communication with. WCCPv2 can be configured to use either unicast or multicast for communication. Unicast is the most commonly deployed configuration. For unicast communication, you must define the IP address of each router in the service group that the WAE will communicate with. This is done using a router list. A router list is configured using the following syntax:

```
wccp router-list 1-4 ip_addr...
```

Example 4-12 shows a basic WCCP router list configuration.

Example 4-12 *WAAS WCCP Router List Configuration*

```
wccp router-list 1 10.10.10.1
```

Up to six IP addresses may be defined per line. For deployments where there are more than six routers in the service group, additional router IP addresses can be defined by configuring a second line using the same router list number. Example 4-13 shows a WCCPv2 router list configured with ten IP addresses.

Example 4-13 *WCCP Router List Using Multiple IP Addresses*

```
wccp router-list 1 10.10.10.1 10.10.10.2 10.10.10.3 10.10.10.4 10.10.10.5
10.10.10.10.6
wccp router-list 1 10.10.10.7 10.10.10.8 10.10.10.9 10.10.10.10
```

CAUTION   Do not use virtual IP (VIP) addresses, such as an HSRP virtual IP address, in the WCCPv2 router list. The router list should contain only interface IP addresses. When the WAE is L2 adjacent to the WCCP-enabled router(s), the IP address(es) used in the WCCP router list should be the directly connected interface IP addresses. In cases where the WAE is not L2 adjacent to the WCCP-enabled router(s) (that is, the WAE is multiple L3 hops away from the WCCP-enabled router or routers), a loopback interface IP address should be used in the router list configuration. Using a loopback interface IP address improves the reliability of the WCCP service group, because the loopback interface IP address is not tied to the availability of any single physical interface.

For the second step, the WCCPv2 tcp-promiscuous service is configured and associated with the router list created in the first step. The following command syntax is used:

```
wccp tcp-promiscuous router-list-num 1
```

The final configuration step is to enable WCCPv2 using the command **wccp version 2**. This command starts the WCCPv2 negotiation with any IOS devices configured in the router list. Example 4-14 shows a complete WCCPv2 configuration in Cisco WAAS.

Example 4-14 *Complete WAAS WCCP Configuration*

```
!
wccp router-list 1 10.10.20.1
wccp tcp-promiscuous router-list-num 1
wccp version 2
!
```

The IOS WCCPv2 configuration involves two steps. First, the WCCPv2 services are configured in global configuration mode. The WCCPv2 services in IOS are configured using the numeric service ID, as opposed to the service name used on the WAAS configuration. Example 4-15 shows the tcp-promiscuous services configured in IOS.

Example 4-15 *Cisco IOS WCCP Global Configuration*

```
!
ip wccp 61
ip wccp 62
!
```

The second step involves configuring WCCPv2 redirection on each interface through which client and server data passes. Unless you are using the WCCPv2 negotiated return egress method discussed later in this chapter, WCCPv2 redirection should never be configured on the interface connecting to the WAE. Interception is configured in either the inbound or outbound direction. When using outbound redirection, the **ip wccp redirect exclude in** command must be configured in the interface connecting to the WAE. This prevents traffic coming into the WCCPv2 server (router) from being re-intercepted, which would cause a redirection loop. Example 4-16 demonstrates a complete IOS WCCPv2 configuration, including the use of the **ip wccp redirect exclude in** command.

Example 4-16 *Complete Cisco IOS WCCP Configuration*

```
!
ip wccp 61
ip wccp 62
!
ip cef
!
interface Serial0/0
 bandwidth 1536
 no ip address
 encapsulation frame-relay
!
interface Serial0/0.100
 ip add 10.88.80.18 255.255.255.252
 ip wccp 61 redirect out
 ip wccp 62 redirect in
 frame-relay interface-dlci 100
!
interface GigabitEthernet0/0
 no ip address
 duplex auto
 speed auto
!
interface GigabitEthernet0/0.1
 description ** Branch Client VLAN **
 encapsulation dot1q 10
```

Example 4-16 *Complete Cisco IOS WCCP Configuration (Continued)*

```
 ip address 10.10.10.1 255.255.255.0
 !
interface GigabitEthernet0/0.20
 description ** Branch WAE VLAN **
 ip address 10.10.20.1 255.255.255.0
 ip wccp redirect exclude in
 !
end
```

Note that the **ip wccp redirect exclude in** command is configured on the subinterface connecting to the WAE. This is required because outbound redirection is used on the serial interface connecting to the WAN. An alternative configuration is shown in Example 4-17.

Example 4-17 *Cisco IOS WCCP Configuration Using Inbound Redirection*

```
!
ip wccp 61
ip wccp 62
!
ip cef
!
interface Serial0/0
 bandwidth 1536
 no ip address
 encapsulation frame-relay
!
interface Serial0/0.100
 ip add 10.88.80.18 255.255.255.252
 ip wccp 62 redirect in
 frame-relay interface-dlci 100
!
interface GigabitEthernet0/0
 no ip address
 duplex auto
 speed auto
!
interface GigabitEthernet0/0.1
 description ** Branch Client VLAN **
 encapsulation dot1q 10
 ip address 10.10.10.1 255.255.255.0
 ip wccp 61 redirect in
!
interface GigabitEthernet0/0.20
 description ** Branch WAE VLAN **
 ip address 10.10.20.1 255.255.255.0
!
end
```

This example uses inbound redirection on the interface connecting to the client subnet and the serial interface connecting to the WAN. Because outbound redirection is not used, the **ip wccp redirect exclude in** command is not required on the interface connecting to the WAE.

Hardware-Based Platforms

In addition to running WCCPv2 on software-based IOS platforms such as the Cisco Integrated Services Router (ISR), WCCPv2 is supported on Cisco Catalyst Series switches. At the time of this writing, the Cisco Catalyst Series switches listed in Table 4-3 support WCCPv2 for use with Cisco WAAS.

Table 4-3 *Cisco Catalyst Platforms Supporting WCCPv2 with WAAS*

Catalyst 3560/3750
Catalyst 4500/4900
Catalyst 6500, Sup2
Catalyst 6500, Sup32
Catalyst 6500, Sup720

With the exception of the Catalyst 6500 with a Sup720, the hardware-based platforms require L2 forwarding and mask assignment for all of the redirection to happen in hardware. The Sup720 is capable of performing GRE forwarding in hardware, but still requires mask assignment for hardware acceleration. In addition to the requirements for forwarding and assignment methods, only inbound WCCPv2 redirection should be used on hardware-based platforms. In fact, the Catalyst 3560/3750 and 4500/4900 only support inbound redirection. While it is possible to configure outbound redirection on the Catalyst 6500 platform, it is not recommended because it causes the first packet for every redirected connection to be processed in software by the MSFC. Likewise, using the **ip wccp redirect exclude in** command on a Catalyst 6500 causes the first packet for every flow entering the interface to be processed by the MSFC and switched in software. However, because inbound redirection is the recommendation for hardware-based platforms, this command is not required.

The following configuration guidelines should be followed to ensure WCCPv2 redirection on hardware-based platforms is handled completely in hardware:

- Use L2 forwarding instead of GRE forwarding.
- Always use mask assignment.
- Only use inbound redirection.
- Do not use the **ip wccp redirect exclude in** command.

The L2 forwarding and mask assignment options are configured as part of the service definition in WAAS. These capabilities are advertised to the WCCPv2-enabled IOS devices when a WAE first joins the service group. Example 4-18 demonstrates the WAAS WCCPv2 configuration with the L2 forwarding and mask assignment options.

Example 4-18   *WCCP Configuration Using L2 Forwarding and Mask Assignment*

```
!
wccp router-list 1 10.10.20.1
wccp tcp-promiscuous router-list-num 1 l2-redirect mask-assign
wccp version 2
!
```

Unlike the hash algorithm used with hash assignment, the mask used for mask assignment is configurable. As mentioned previously in this chapter, the default mask used by WAAS is 0x1741. The default mask is applied to the source IP address for service group 61 and is applied to the destination IP address for service group 62. Depending on the IP addressing used in your environment, you may want to change the default mask to provide for better load distribution among the WAEs in a service group. The default mask is changed on the WAE using the following command syntax:

wccp tcp-promiscuous mask src-ip-mask *0-4261412864*

The configured mask is applied to service group 61. Service group 62 mirrors the configuration and cannot be configured separately. Example 4-19 shows using a non-default mask with WCCPv2.

Example 4-19   *Custom WCCP Mask*

```
!
wccp router-list 1 10.10.20.1
wccp tcp-promiscuous mask src-ip-mask 0xf
wccp tcp-promiscuous router-list-num 1 l2-redirect mask-assign
wccp version 2
!
```

Policy-Based Routing

Policy-based routing (PBR) provides another alternative for transparent interception with WAAS, although it is less commonly deployed than WCCPv2 and inline interception. PBR can be used in situations where customers are unable to run WCCPv2 or inline interception. PBR can also be used in conjunction with a content switch, such as the Cisco Application Control Engine (ACE), to provide transparent interception and load balancing for large-scale data center deployments. Deployment examples using PBR for transparent interception are provided in Chapters 5 and 6.

PBR functions in a similar manner to WCCPv2, in that a router/switch running Cisco IOS is configured to intercept interesting traffic and redirect it to a WAE. Unlike WCCPv2, no configuration is required on the WAE to support interception using PBR. The following configuration steps are required for a basic PBR configuration:

Step 1   Create an access list to define interesting traffic for redirection.

Step 2   Create a route map that matches the ACL created in Step 1 and sets an IP next-hop address of the target WAE.

Step 3   Apply the route map to interfaces through which client and server traffic traverses.

Example 4-20 demonstrates a basic PBR configuration used for redirecting all TCP traffic to a single WAE.

Example 4-20   *PBR Configuration*

```
!
ip cef
!
access-list 199 permit tcp any any
!
route-map WAAS-INTERCEPT 10
 match ip address 199
 set ip next-hop 10.10.20.5
!
interface Serial0/0
 bandwidth 1536
 no ip address
 encapsulation frame-relay
!
interface Serial0/0.100
 ip add 10.88.80.18 255.255.255.252
 ip policy route-map WAAS-INTERCEPT
 frame-relay interface-dlci 100
!
interface GigabitEthernet0/0
 no ip address
 duplex auto
 speed auto
!
interface GigabitEthernet0/0.1
 description ** Branch Client VLAN **
 encapsulation dot1q 10
 ip address 10.10.10.1 255.255.255.0
 ip policy route-map WAAS-INTERCEPT
!
interface GigabitEthernet0/0.20
 description ** Branch WAE VLAN **
```

Example 4-20 *PBR Configuration (Continued)*

```
  ip address 10.10.20.1 255.255.255.0
  !
end
```

Because PBR evaluates only traffic entering an interface, the route map entries are configured on both the client and server-facing interfaces. This is the equivalent of using only inbound redirection with WCCPv2. The **set ip next-hop** command in the route map is configured with the IP address of the WAE. By default, PBR does not validate to availability of the IP address specified as the next-hop address. As long as the next-hop address exists in the routing table, the route map entry will be applied. On software-based platforms (ISR, and so forth), Cisco Service Assurance Agent (SAA) can be used to track the availability of the next-hop IP address. If the next-hop address becomes unreachable, traffic matching the route map entry is forwarded normally using the routing table. However, this capability does not currently exist on hardware-based platforms.

Other difference between WCCPv2 and PBR is that PBR does not perform automatic load distribution and failover when multiple WAEs exist. The first next hop IP address configured in the route map is used until it becomes unavailable. Only at that point is traffic redirected to a secondary next hop IP address in the route map. Chapters 5 and 6 provide examples of PBR deployments that include next hop availability tracking using SAA and load distribution among multiple WAEs.

Inline Interception

An alternative to the various off-path interception mechanisms is to place the WAE physically inline between two network elements, such as a WAN access router and local-area network (LAN) switch. Figure 4-13 shows a basic topology with the WAE deployed physically inline.

Figure 4-13 *WAE Physical In-Path Deployment*

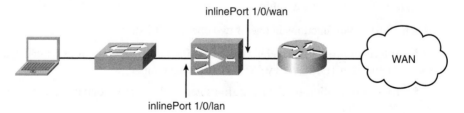

Physical inline interception is an attractive option for situations where it is not possible or ideal to run WCCPv2. It is also possible that the networking equipment at a site is provided and managed by a managed service provider (MSP). The MSP may not be able to configure or support a WCCPv2 solution on the managed devices.

To support physical inline interception, the WAE requires a separate inline module. The inline module is a 4-port, fail-to-wire NIC that supports two separate inline groups. Each inline group has a synchronous pair of inline ports that interconnect two network elements. Traffic entering one inline port is optimized by WAAS (when applicable) and switched out the opposite inline port in the same group. The inline group functions like a transparent Layer 2 bridge.

By providing two inline groups on a single module, the WAE can support designs where multiple paths out of a site exist for redundancy and load sharing. Each unique path is connected to the WAE through a separate inline group. Figure 4-14 shows a sample remote site topology with multiple WAN routers and a single WAE deployed with inline interception.

Figure 4-14   *Physical In-Path Deployment Using Multiple Routers*

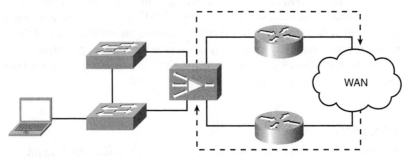

As the arrows in Figure 4-14 indicate, traffic can enter or leave the site through either router. Even though the same flow enters the site through one inline group and exits the site through another inline group, the connection will still be optimized. The optimized connection state is not tied to a physical interface, but is tracked for the WAE as a whole independent of the interfaces traversed by the traffic.

Each inline group functions in one of two operating modes:

- **Intercept operating mode:** Traffic entering the inline group is evaluated against the Application Traffic Policy (ATP) for optimization.

- **Bypass operating mode:** All traffic entering the inline group is bridged without any optimization.

The bypass operating mode is designed to allow the WAE to continue passing traffic if the WAE looses power. A keepalive mechanism between the network drivers and the inline module is used to determine if the WAE is functioning properly and can optimize connections.

The keepalive frequency is configurable between 1 and 10 seconds. The default failover timer is set to 3 seconds. The transition between intercept operating mode and bypass operating mode does cause a momentary loss of line protocol. If one or more of the inline ports are connected to a LAN switch, this transition in interface state can cause the Spanning Tree Protocol (STP) recalculation. To prevent the STP calculation from interrupting traffic forwarding, the switchport connected to the inline module on the WAE should have the STP PortFast feature enabled. Failure of a single inline port in the group is propagated to the other port in the group. For example, if the LAN0 port in InlineGroup 1/0 goes down, the WAE will take down line protocol on the WAN0 port in the same inline group. This propagation of interface state between the ports in the same inline group prevents situations where adjacent devices connected to an operational InlinePort believe the network path to be online and usable, when in reality the connection on the other side of the WAE is unavailable.

When a WAE is deployed physically inline, all traffic between the two network elements will be seen by the WAE. Non-TCP traffic is bridged through the inline module without modification. In addition, packets associated with a connection that was first seen on the opposite inline port in a group are bridged. This type of traffic flow is common when a WAE is deployed inline on a trunk between a router and LAN switch. If the router is providing routing for traffic going between VLANs locally, it is possible for traffic to traverse the inline module twice. Figure 4-15 shows an example of this type of traffic flow.

Figure 4-15   *Physical In-Path Deployment with One-Armed Routing*

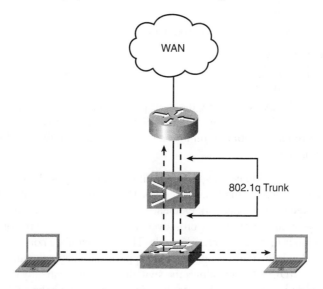

The inline module also supports 802.1Q trunk connections between the two network elements. An added benefit to using the inline module is the ability to define which VLANs are evaluated for interception. Traffic that is received by the inline module tagged with a

VLAN ID that is excluded from interception will be bridged without any optimization. This capability is supported only for tagged VLANs. Traffic received by the inline module on untagged VLANs will be intercepted and evaluated against the ATP for optimization and acceleration. By default, TCP traffic received on all VLANs is intercepted and evaluated against the ATP. VLANs can be excluded or included for interception using the following commands:

```
no inline vlan all
inline vlan 100
```

Example 4-21 shows the resulting InlineGroup configuration.

Example 4-21 *WAE InlineGroup Configuration*

```
!
interface InlineGroup 1/0
 inline vlan all
 no inline vlan native,0-99,101-4095
 exit
!
```

There are different sequences of the inline CLI command that will result in the same VLAN filter being applied. For example,

```
inline vlan all
no inline vlan 100
```

results in all VLANs except for 100 being intercepted. But so does the following:

```
inline vlan native
inline vlan 0-4095
no inline vlan 100-110
inline vlan 101-200
```

In terms of VLAN assignment, the most permissive command takes precedence. If the inline group is already configured with **inline vlan all**, then you need to selectively remove VLANs from interception or remove all VLANs and selectively add individual VLANs back for interception.

When an inline group is in bypass operating mode, a physical cross-connect is enabled between the two ports in the inline group. This behavior essentially creates a crossover cable between the two network elements. In cases where the two network elements are unable to communicate using a crossover cable, line protocol will not be restored when the inline group is in bypass operating mode. This is generally a nonissue when the switchport that the LAN InlinePort is connected to supports automatic medium-dependent interface crossover (MDIX). MDIX allows the switchport to automatically detect the pinouts of the cables used to connect two devices. In cases where the switchport does not support this capability, the cabling guidelines outlined in Table 4-4 should be followed.

Table 4-4   *WAE Inline Module Cabling Guidelines*

Connection	Required Cable
Switch to switch (no WAE)	Crossover
Switch to router (no WAE)	Straight-through
Router to router (no WAE)	Crossover
Switch to WAE	Straight-through
WAE to switch	Crossover
Switch to WAE	Straight-through
WAE to switch	Straight-through
Router to WAE	Straight-through
WAE to router	Straight-through
WAE to WAE	Crossover

Content Switching

Content switching is the final interception mechanism discussed in this chapter. Content switches have traditionally provided load-balancing services for servers, firewalls, and content caches. Within the context of WAAS, content switching provides dedicated hardware for intercepting and load balancing connections across a farm of WAEs. Using content switches for transparent interception with WAAS is useful for large data center deployments, complex topologies, and integration with other advanced features such as application protocol optimization and SSL-offload. In addition, customers with existing content switching deployments can leverage their experience and investments in content switches for transparent interception with WAAS. The Application Control Engine is the Cisco content switch that will be discussed in this section. Deployment and configuration examples for integrating ACE with Cisco WAAS are provided in Chapter 6.

Application Control Engine

The Cisco Application Control Engine (ACE) module is a service module for the Cisco Catalyst 6500 series switches and Catalyst 7600 series routers. ACE provides intelligent load balancing and security services for enterprise applications and network devices. ACE can be used in a large-scale data center environment to transparently intercept and load balance connections for WAAS. The following are some of the key performance characteristics of Cisco ACE:

- Up to 16 Gbps of throughput and 345,000 connections per second per module
- Up to 4 million concurrent connections

- Support for up to 250 virtual partitions, allowing customers to create virtual ACE modules using a single hardware module

- Up to 16,000 real servers, which when used with Cisco WAAS provides nearly infinite scalability

- High availability and scalability by using up to four ACE modules in the same Catalyst 6500 chassis or across multiple chassis

There are two common deployment models for integrating ACE into the network infrastructure: bridge mode and routed mode.

In bridge mode, ACE is used to merge two VLANs together. In order for traffic to pass between the two VLANs, it must pass through the ACE module. As traffic passes through the ACE module, it is evaluated against the configured service policies to determine whether or not it should be acted upon. The IP subnet used on the bridged VLAN is the same. Figure 4-16 shows an ACE module deployed using bridge mode.

Figure 4-16   *ACE Deployed Using Bridge Mode*

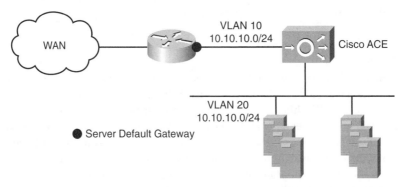

The WAN-facing VLAN in Figure 4-16 is referred to as the client-side VLAN. The VLAN facing the data center resources is referred to as the server-side VLAN. As traffic enters the client-side VLAN, it is evaluated against the configured service policy. Traffic matching the service policy is redirected to a WAE, which has a dedicated VLAN interface configured on the ACE module. Traffic egressing the WAE comes back into the ACE module, where it is switched out the server-side VLAN toward the origin server.

In contrast to bridge mode, deploying ACE in routed mode allows for traffic to be routed between two different IP subnets. Using this deployment model, the client and server-side VLANs are on different IP subnets. Because the ACE module is a Layer 3 hop, traffic must be directed to the ACE module through the routing configuration of the hosts or network infrastructure. Figure 4-17 shows an ACE module deployed using routed mode.

Figure 4-17   *ACE Deployed Using Routed Mode*

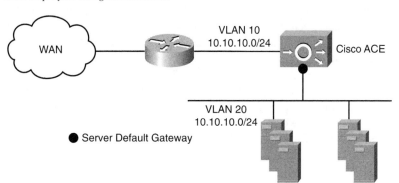

ACE is typically deployed in conjunction with WAAS using transparent, or directed, mode. This means that the ACE module does not perform any Network Address Translation (NAT) of traffic passing through it.

Egress Methods for Intercepted Connections

Cisco WAAS provides several options for handling egress traffic received on intercepted connections. These options allow for flexibility when determining where to integrate WAAS into the existing network infrastructure, and help preserve the original path selection for traffic flows. These deployment options, referred to as the egress methods for intercepted connections (EMIC), are discussed in detail in this section.

The first EMIC available in Cisco WAAS is IP forwarding. Egress traffic received on intercepted connections is forwarded based on the configuration of the local WAE routing table, which typically means that traffic is forwarded to the configured default gateway. In addition to supporting a single default gateway, WAAS supports up to 1024 static routes. Static routes are configured with a next hop IP address of a directly connected interface; recursive next hop IP addresses are not supported. Although it is possible to configure multiple static routes for the same destination, there is no support for equal-cost multipath (ECMP). Only a single route will be installed in the routing table at a time. It should be noted that traffic originating from the WAE itself will also use IP forwarding, regardless of the EMIC configuration. The IP forwarding EMIC is suited for very basic topologies where only a single egress path for traffic exists, or in situations where other EMICs are not supported.

For more complex topologies, the IP forwarding EMIC can lead to undesirable forwarding of traffic for intercepted connections. Take for example the topology shown in Figure 4-18. This example shows a remote office with multiple WAN routers connecting to diverse circuits. Traffic can enter or leave the site through either router. When multiple paths exist for traffic leaving a site, it is common for either HSRP or the Gateway Load Balancing

Protocol (GLBP) to be used for default gateway redundancy. HSRP provides an active/ standby configuration based on a virtual IP (VIP) address. At any given point in time, a single VIP address is "active" on one of the routers. Hosts are configured with the HSRP VIP address as their default gateway, causing all traffic from those hosts to be forwarded to one of the two routers. In the case of GLBP, either router can be selected as the outbound path for a host, depending on the specific GLBP configuration. Because GLBP operates based on MAC addresses, a WAE running Cisco WAAS appears as a single host. This means that traffic egressing a WAE will also select one of the two routers to forward outbound traffic to. For deployments that use GLBP for default-gateway redundancy, the issue with IP forwarding is the most pronounced.

Figure 4-18 *Branch Topology with Multiple Entry and Exit Points*

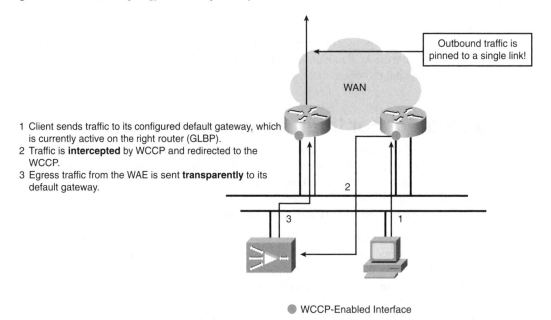

You can see in the previous example how all egress traffic from the WAE is "pinned" to a single router. This can defeat the purpose of deploying GLBP in the first place, which is to distribute outbound traffic across both routers.

There are several options with WAAS for preserving the network path affinity originally chosen by the host system or network elements. The first two options leverage the WCCPv2 return mechanism. You'll recall from earlier in this chapter that the WCCPv2 return mechanism is used by WCCPv2 clients to handle bypass traffic by sending it back to the WCCPv2-enabled router that redirected it. Cisco WAAS has the ability to leverage the return method negotiated between the router and WAE for forwarding egress traffic from the WAE. The following CLI command changes the default EMIC from IP forwarding to negotiated return:

```
egress-method negotiated-return intercept-method wccp
```

If GRE is the return method negotiated between the WAE and IOS, traffic received on optimized connections is encapsulated in a GRE header with a destination IP address of the WCCPv2 router ID and a source IP address of the WAE. When the WCCPv2-enabled IOS device receives the GRE-encapsulated packet, it removes the GRE header and forwards the packet normally. Because the GRE header uses a source IP address of the WAE, the IOS WCCPv2 process knows not to re-intercept the packet. This capability to return traffic to the IOS device that redirected it allows for the preservation of the original path selection made by the host or network infrastructure.

Another benefit of the GRE return method is that the WAE can reside on the same IP subnet with clients or servers that it optimizes connections for. This greatly simplifies branch deployments by removing the requirement for a separate subnet dedicated to the WAE. Figure 4-19 shows the same topology as Figure 4-18, except using the negotiated return EMIC instead of IP forwarding.

Figure 4-19 *Branch Topology Using GRE Return EMIC*

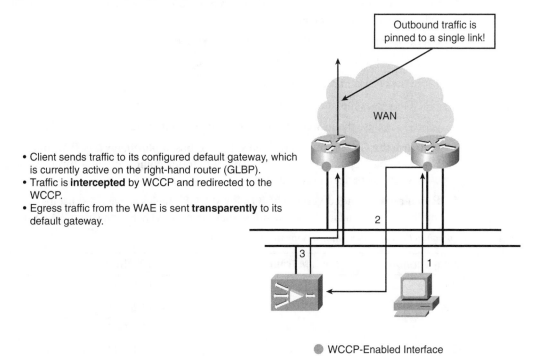

Network Integration Best Practices

The following network integration best practices are recommended for most WAAS deployments:

- **Leave the physical WAE interfaces set to auto-sense:** Because it is possible that some of your WAEs will be able to run at 1-Gbps speed, leaving all of the WAEs deployed set to auto-sense simplifies the configuration and deployment. In addition, an alarm will be raised in the Central Manager if an interface negotiates to half duplex.

- **Use EtherChannel for interface redundancy when both physical WAE interfaces connect to the same LAN switch:** Improve performance by providing 2X the available LAN bandwidth.

- **Use a standby interface for interface redundancy when both physical WAE interfaces connect to different LAN switches:** Increase WAE availability in the event of a problem with the primary interface or connected LAN switch.

- **Always configure a MD5 password for WCCP service groups:** Protect the integrity of the service group members by making sure that only authorized devices can join the service group.

- **Stick to inbound WCCP redirection:** Even on software-based platforms, inbound redirection is more efficient.

- **On hardware-based platforms, configure WCCP using the following guidelines:**
  - Use L2 forwarding instead of GRE forwarding.
  - Always use mask assignment.
  - Only use inbound redirection.
  - Do not use the **ip wccp redirect exclude in** command.

- **Only use the GRE return EMIC on software-based platforms (i.e. ISR routers):** Hardware-based platforms process GRE return traffic completely in software, which causes serious performance issues.

- **Run a recommended version of IOS for WCCP:** Tables 4-5 and 4-6 list the minimum recommended IOS versions when running WCCP with Cisco WAAS.

Table 4-5 *Minimum IOS Recommendations: Software-Based Platforms*

Major Version	M Train	T Train
12.1	12.1(14)	12.1(3)T
12.2	12.2(26)	12.2(14)T
12.3	12.3(13)	12.3(14)T5
12.4	12.4(10)	12.4(9)T1

Table 4-6   *Minimum IOS Recommendations: Hardware-based Platforms*

Platform	Version
Catalyst 3560/3750	12.2(37)SE
Catalyst 4500/4900	12.2(31)SG
Catalyst 6500, Sup2	12.2(18)SXF13
Catalyst 6500, Sup32	CatOS 8.5/12.2(18)SXF13
Catalyst 6500, Sup720 (Native)	12.2(18)SXF13
Catalyst 6500, Sup720 (Hybrid)	CatOS 8.5/12.2(18)SXF13

Summary

This chapter provided a detailed examination of the various methods for integrating WAAS into the network infrastructure. The chapter reviewed the various techniques for physical connectivity, including options for increased interface bandwidth and high availability. The chapter also previewed the network interception techniques that are used to transparently redirect traffic to the WAAS infrastructure for optimization. Particular focus was given to WCCPv2 and inline interception, which are the two most common interception methods. The interception method you choose is a site-local decision. For example, you can use WCCPv2 at some locations and inline at other locations. Finally, the chapter discussed the different egress methods available in WAAS, which provide control over how traffic on intercepted connections is reinserted into the network after redirection to a WAE. You should now have a good feel for the flexibility of the WAAS solution when it comes to network integration. The techniques available allow Cisco WAAS to integrate into network infrastructures of any size and complexity. The next chapter begins to put these various techniques to use, as you look at specific deployment models for the branch office environment.

CHAPTER 5

Branch Office Network Integration

This chapter provides a detailed discussion of the different methods for integrating Cisco WAAS into the branch office network infrastructure. It examines both in-path and off-path integration options, applying them to small, medium-sized, and large branch office topologies of various configurations. In-path deployments leverage the inline module available for the WAE appliance models. Off-path deployments in the branch can use WCCP or PBR. The preferred interception method in the branch office environment is WCCP, followed by inline. PBR is limited in the areas of load distribution and failover, and should be considered for interception only as a last resort. Detailed device configurations are provided for each scenario, leveraging current Cisco best practices. This chapter also discusses different deployment scenarios when integrating with Cisco IOS Firewall (IOS FW).

In-Path Deployment

Deploying WAAS in-path means that the WAE is physically placed between two network components, typically a WAN router and LAN switch. Inline deployments are intended for branch office environments, as opposed to the data center. Each WAE supports one 4-port inline network interface card, which allows a single WAE to support interception on two physical paths. The in-path deployment model is typically used in branch office environments where the network topology is less complex than the data center infrastructure. In-path deployments are attractive for branch offices in the following cases:

- The WAN access router is unable to sustain the increased traffic throughput enabled by Cisco WAAS. For example, 1 Mbps of compressed traffic from the WAN can decode into tens or hundreds of megabits-per-second worth of uncompressed traffic between the local WAE and clients. Some branch office routers are not suitable for such high levels of throughput. As a general rule, Cisco recommends that branch offices using routers other than the Cisco 1800, 2800, 3700, 3800, and 7200 Series leverage an in-path deployment model.

- The IOS routers or switches do not support WCCP or it is not feasible to upgrade the IOS version to a release that is recommended with WCCP. In these cases, an in-path deployment may provide an alternate method for interception that does not require software or configuration changes to the existing branch office network infrastructure.

- The IOS router or switches are not under the administrative control of the group deploying WAAS. This is sometimes the case when the network equipment in a branch office is provided and managed by a service provider. In other cases, the team responsible for deploying WAAS might not have administrative access to the network devices, and therefore might not be comfortable depending on another team for operational support of the solution.

In all of these cases, deploying WAAS in-path provides an alternative to off-path deployment models. The following sections describe the in-path integration options for various reference topologies.

Nonredundant Branch Office

A very basic branch office topology includes a single WAN router and LAN switch. The router is used for connecting the branch office to the WAN and routing traffic between local users and remote resources across the WAN. The site may have multiple VLANs, with the WAN router responsible for routing traffic locally between the VLANs. The reference topology has two existing VLANs, one for data traffic and one for VoIP traffic. This topology will allow demonstration of the per-VLAN interception capabilities of the inline module. Figure 5-1 shows the nonredundant reference branch office topology discussed in this section.

Figure 5-1 *Nonredundant Reference Topology*

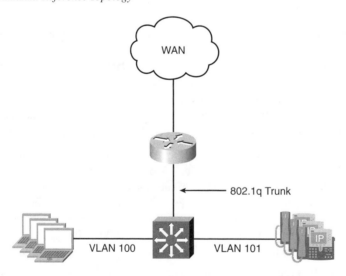

In this scenario, the goal is to optimize traffic from clients on the data VLAN accessing resources at other locations across the WAN. Traffic from the VoIP VLAN should be passed through without optimization. Because an in-path deployment model is being used, a WAE with an inline module installed is physically placed in the network path between the WAN router and the LAN switch. Figure 5-2 shows the branch office topology with a WAE deployed in-path between the WAN router and LAN switch.

Figure 5-2   *Nonredundant In-Path Branch Office Topology*

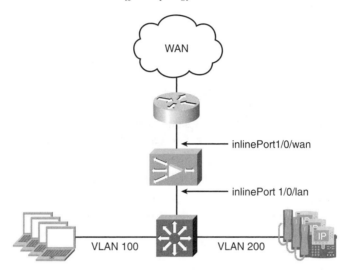

The WAN0 port of inlineGroup 1/0 is connected to the LAN interface of the WAN router, and the LAN0 port of inlineGroup 1/0 is connected to a switchport on the LAN switch. No configuration changes are required on the WAN router or LAN switch to accommodate an in-path deployment.

The switchport connecting to the LAN0 port of the WAE inline module should have the **PortFast** feature enabled. This enables faster recovery of traffic forwarding when the inlineGroup transitions between intercept and bypass operating mode.

Because VLAN 200 is carrying the VoIP traffic, any packets with this VLAN ID are excluded from interception. Packets tagged with VLAN ID 200 will be bridged through the inline module without any optimization. TCP traffic on all other VLANs, including any untagged VLANs, is intercepted and optimized (based on policy configuration). Example 5-1 shows the inlineGroup configuration of the WAE.

Example 5-1   *WAE inlineGroup Configuration*

```
!
interface InlineGroup 1/0
 inline vlan all
 no inline vlan 200
 no autosense
```

continues

Example 5-1 *WAE inlineGroup Configuration (Continued)*

```
  bandwidth 100
  full-duplex
  exit
 interface InlineGroup 1/1
  inline vlan all
  shutdown
  exit
 !
```

In Example 5-1, the speed and duplex of the inlineGroup are manually set to 100 Mbps, full-duplex. Note that the speed and duplex configuration settings are applied to the inlineGroup. This ensures that the same interface settings are applied consistently to both ports in the inlineGroup, which is required for proper operation during bypass operating mode.

Example 5-2 shows the full WAE configuration that is used for this deployment scenario.

Example 5-2 *Small to Medium-Sized Branch Office In-Path WAE Configuration*

```
 !
 device mode application-accelerator
 !
 hostname AUSTIN-WAE
 !
 ip domain-name cisco.com
 !
 primary-interface GigabitEthernet 1/0
 !
 interface GigabitEthernet 1/0
  ip address 10.88.80.137 255.255.255.128
  exit
 interface GigabitEthernet 2/0
  shutdown
  exit
 !
 interface InlineGroup 1/0
  inline vlan all
  no inline vlan 200
  no autosense
  bandwidth 100
  full-duplex
  exit
 interface InlineGroup 1/1
  inline vlan all
  shutdown
  exit
 !
 ip default-gateway 10.88.80.129
 !
 no auto-register enable
```

Example 5-2 *Small to Medium-Sized Branch Office In-Path WAE Configuration (Continued)*

```
!
ip name-server 10.88.80.53
!
authentication login local enable primary
authentication configuration local enable primary
!
central-manager address cm.cisco.com
cms enable
!
no adapter epm enable
!
<default ATP removed>
!
! End of WAAS configuration
```

Note that interface GigabitEthernet 1/0 is configured with an IP address and specified as the primary interface. In this example, one of the built-in Ethernet interfaces is used for management traffic to and from the WAE. The default gateway specified in the configuration is used only for traffic sourced from the WAE itself. Alternatively, you can configure an IP address on the inlineGroup interface, which allows you to deploy the WAE without using one of the built-in Ethernet interfaces for management. Example 5-3 shows the inlineGroup configured with a management IP address.

Example 5-3 *Management IP Address on inlineGroup*

```
!
primary-interface InlineGroup 1/0
!
interface GigabitEthernet 1/0
 shutdown
 exit
interface GigabitEthernet 2/0
 shutdown
 exit
!
interface InlineGroup 1/0
 ip address 10.88.80.137 255.255.255.128
 inline vlan all
 no inline vlan 200
 no autosense
 bandwidth 100
 full-duplex
 exit
interface InlineGroup 1/1
 inline vlan all
 shutdown
 exit
!
ip default-gateway 10.88.80.129
!
```

The IP address associated with the inlineGroup is applied to the WAN0 interface. Also note that the primary interface has been configured as inlineGroup 1/0.

Redundant Branch Office

Large branch offices typically have multiple WAN routers and LAN switches for increased capacity and improved availability of the WAN resources. The links between the WAN routers and LAN switches can be configured either as Layer 2 trunks, as in the previous scenario, or as point-to-point routed links. The reference topology is configured with routed links between the WAN routers and LAN switches. The LAN switches handle local routing between VLANs. Figure 5-3 shows the redundant reference branch office topology discussed in this section.

Figure 5-3 *Redundant Branch Office Reference Topology*

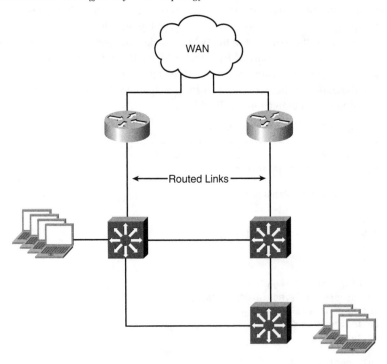

In this scenario, the goal is to optimize traffic from clients accessing resources at other locations across the WAN. Because the links between the WAN routers and LAN switches do not carry all of the VLANs for the site, all TCP traffic will be intercepted and optimized (based on policy configuration).

Traffic can be excluded from optimization by creating a policy in the Application Traffic Policy (ATP) that instructs the WAE to handle certain IP addresses or ranges of IP addresses as pass-through. See Chapter 8, "Configuring WAN Optimization," for more information on configuring custom traffic policies.

A WAE with an inline module installed is physically placed in the network path between the WAN router and the LAN switch. The in-path deployment model for the redundant reference topology leverages both inline groups in a single module to intercept traffic on two physical paths. Traffic can traverse either inlineGroup when entering or existing the site. Figure 5-4 shows the large redundant branch office topology with a WAE deployed in-path between the WAN routers and LAN switches.

Figure 5-4   *Redundant In-Path Branch Office Deployment*

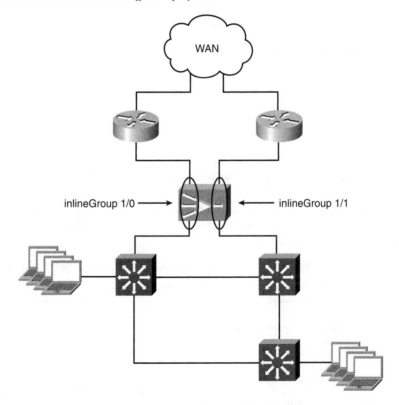

The WAN0 port of each inlineGroup is connected to the LAN interface of one of the WAN routers. The LAN0 port of each inlineGroup is connected to a switchport in the LAN infrastructure. In this reference topology, the LAN port for each inlineGroup is connected to separate switches, but these could just as well be connected to the same switch. Again, there is no special configuration required on the WAN router LAN interfaces or LAN switchports to support the in-path deployment model.

TIP   The switchport connecting to the LAN0 ports of the WAE inline module should have the **PortFast** feature enabled. This enables faster recovery of traffic forwarding when the inlineGroup transitions between intercept and bypass operating mode.

Example 5-4 shows the inlineGroup configuration of the WAE.

Example 5-4   *Redundant Branch Office inlineGroup Configuration*

```
!
interface InlineGroup 1/0
 inline vlan all
 exit
interface InlineGroup 1/1
 inline vlan all
 exit
!
```

Because this reference topology represents a large branch office, both inline groups are configured with the default setting to autosense the speed and duplex of the individual ports, which allows them to negotiate to 1 Gbps. Example 5-4 also specifies the **inline vlan all** command, which instructs the WAE to intercept all TCP-based traffic, regardless of the VLAN it is associated with.

Example 5-5 shows the full WAE configuration that is used for this deployment model.

Example 5-5   *Redundant Branch Office In-Path WAE Configuration*

```
!
device mode application-accelerator
!
hostname AUSTIN-WAE
!
ip domain-name cisco.com
!
primary-interface GigabitEthernet 1/0
!
interface GigabitEthernet 1/0
 ip address 10.88.80.137 255.255.255.128
 exit
```

Example 5-5   *Redundant Branch Office In-Path WAE Configuration (Continued)*

```
interface GigabitEthernet 2/0
 shutdown
 exit
!
interface InlineGroup 1/0
 inline vlan all
 exit
interface InlineGroup 1/1
 inline vlan all
 exit
!
ip default-gateway 10.88.80.129
!
no auto-register enable
!
ip name-server 10.88.80.53
!
authentication login local enable primary
authentication configuration local enable primary
!
central-manager address cm.cisco.com
cms enable
!
no adapter epm enable
!
<default ATP removed>
!
! End of WAAS configuration
```

Serial Clustering

In both the nonredundant and redundant topologies, you can serially connect multiple WAEs in a back-to-back configuration for high availability. Cisco supports clustering up to two WAEs in this fashion. Figure 5-5 shows two WAEs serially clustered for high availability.

Unlike the off-path integration models discussed later in this chapter, serial clustering does not provide any active/active load sharing across the clustered WAEs. The first WAE in the cluster to receive the TCP SYN packet initiates optimization for that connection. When a peer WAE is discovered across the WAN, the second WAE in the cluster determines through the TFO auto-discovery process that it is in the middle of two other WAEs. This causes the intermediate WAE to handle the connections as pass-through. If one of the WAEs in the cluster becomes overloaded or unavailable, the remaining WAE in the cluster begins optimizing new connections. Existing connections are seen as "In Progress" and handled as pass-through. Figure 5-6 shows the behavior of the clustered WAEs when the first WAE exceeds its maximum optimized connection limit.

Figure 5-5 *Clustering Multiple WAEs for High Availability*

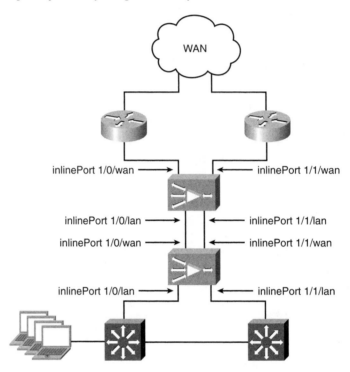

Figure 5-6 *Serial Clustering Overload Connection Handling*

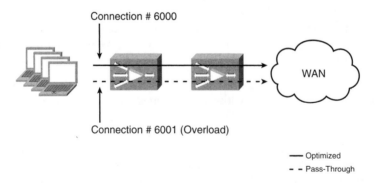

Off-Path Deployment

Off-path deployments involve leveraging intelligence within the network infrastructure to intercept and redirect traffic to WAAS. With off-path deployments, the WAE is logically inline, as opposed to physically inline as with in-path deployments. Common off-path deployment techniques include WCCP, policy-based routing (PBR), and content switching. This chapter focuses on deployments using WCCP and PBR in the branch office. WCCP is the preferred transparent interception mechanism for off-path deployments. Content switching is discussed as one of the data center network integration options in Chapter 6, "Data Center Network Integration."

Small to Medium-Sized Nonredundant Branch Office

The branch office topology discussed in this section includes a single WAN router and LAN switch. The router is used for connecting the branch office to the WAN and routing traffic between local users and remote resources across the WAN. The WAN router is a software-based platform, such as the Cisco 1800, 2800, or 3800 Series Integrated Services Router (ISR). The site has a single existing VLAN upon which clients are located. Figure 5-7 shows the nonredundant reference branch office topology discussed in this section.

Figure 5-7   *Small to Medium-Sized Nonredundant Reference Topology*

VLAN 100
10.10.100.0/24

In this scenario, the goal is to optimize traffic from clients accessing resources at other locations across the WAN. For an off-path deployment, the WAE is connected to the network through one of the built-in Ethernet interfaces. WCCP is configured on the WAN router to intercept all TCP traffic and redirect it to the WAE.

Because this topology has only a single existing VLAN, and the link between the WAN access router and the LAN switch is not configured as a trunk, adding a VLAN subnet for the WAE is not desirable. In these cases, the WAE is deployed on the existing VLAN with the hosts it is optimizing connections for. Figure 5-8 shows the branch office topology for this scenario.

Figure 5-8 *Small to Medium-Sized Nonredundant Branch Office Deployment*

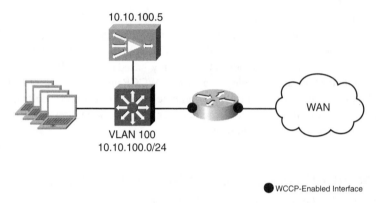

10.10.100.5

VLAN 100
10.10.100.0/24

WAN

● WCCP-Enabled Interface

When the WAE is located on the same VLAN with hosts it is optimizing connections for, the router needs some way to differentiate between traffic sourced from a host and traffic coming from the WAE. To accomplish this, the WAE is configured to use WCCP GRE return as the egress method. This causes the WAE to return egress traffic to the intercepting router encapsulated in a WCCP GRE header. The WCCP GRE header uses the WAE IP address as the source IP address and the intercepting router as the destination IP address. By definition of the protocol, WCCP will not intercept GRE-encapsulated traffic sourced from the WAE registered in a service group defined on the router. Figure 5-9 shows the traffic flow between the WAE and intercepting router when WCCP GRE return is configured as the egress method.

Figure 5-9 *WCCP GRE Return Traffic Flow*

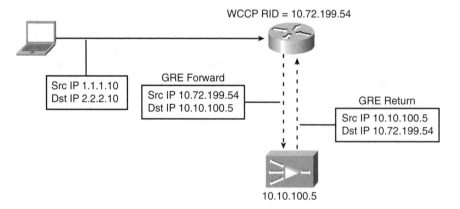

WCCP RID = 10.72.199.54

Src IP 1.1.1.10
Dst IP 2.2.2.10

GRE Forward
Src IP 10.72.199.54
Dst IP 10.10.100.5

GRE Return
Src IP 10.10.100.5
Dst IP 10.72.199.54

10.10.100.5

The WCCP configuration of the WAN router is shown in Example 5-6.

Example 5-6 *Small to Medium-Sized Nonredundant Branch Office WCCP Configuration*

```
!
hostname WR-01
!
ip wccp 61 password cisco
ip wccp 62 password cisco
!
interface FastEthernet0/0
 ip address 10.10.100.1 255.255.255.0
 ip wccp 61 redirect in
!
interface Serial0/0
 description ** Link to WAN **
 ip address 10.72.199.54 255.255.255.252
 ip wccp 62 redirect in
!
```

Remember that Cisco WAAS uses two WCCP service groups, 61 and 62, for interception on the WAN router. It is important to pay attention to which interfaces you apply each service group. In a branch office, where you have a high concentration of clients, service group 61 is configured on the client-facing interface. In Example 5-6, this is interface FastEthernet0/0. This means that service group 61 will intercept requests coming into the router from clients on interface FastEthernet0/0. Service group 62 is configured on the server-facing interface, in this example Serial0/0. This ensures that service group 62 intercepts responses from the remote servers coming in from the WAN. When there are multiple WAEs deployed at a branch office, this placement of the two service groups causes WCCP to perform load distribution based on the client IP addresses.

The configuration of the WAE in this deployment scenario is shown in Example 5-7.

Example 5-7 *Small to Medium-Sized Nonredundant Branch Office WAE Configuration*

```
!
device mode application-accelerator
!
hostname AUSTIN-WAE
!
ip domain-name cisco.com
!
primary-interface GigabitEthernet 1/0
!
interface GigabitEthernet 1/0
 ip address 10.10.100.5 255.255.255.0
 exit
```

continues

Example 5-7 *Small to Medium-Sized Nonredundant Branch Office WAE Configuration (Continued)*

```
interface GigabitEthernet 2/0
 shutdown
 exit
!
ip default-gateway 10.10.100.1
!
wccp router-list 1 10.10.100.1
wccp tcp-promiscuous router-list-num 1 password cisco
wccp version 2
!
egress-method negotiated-return intercept-method wccp
!
no auto-register enable
!
ip name-server 10.88.80.53
!
authentication login local enable primary
authentication configuration local enable primary
!
central-manager address cm.cisco.com
cms enable
!
no adapter epm enable
!
<default ATP removed>
!
! End of WAAS configuration
```

When a WAE is deployed on the same VLAN with hosts that it is optimizing connections for, the egress method must be configured for WCCP GRE return. Note the **egress-method** command in Example 5-7. This tells the WAE to use the return method negotiated via WCCP to handle traffic for connections received using WCCP.

CAUTION   At the time of this writing, Cisco WAAS only supports WCCP GRE return and IP forwarding as egress methods. If the egress method is configured for negotiated return and the WAE has negotiated L2 return with the intercepting router, the WAE will fall back to IP forwarding as the egress method.

Also note that a default gateway is still configured. The default gateway is used for forwarding traffic sourced from the WAE itself, regardless of the egress method configured.

Enhanced Network Module (NME-WAE)

The Network Module Enhanced WAE (NME-WAE) provides a router-integrated network module capable of running Cisco WAAS. When deploying the NME-WAE, WCCP is required as the interception mechanism. Traffic entering the router is intercepted by WCCP and redirected over an internal GigabitEthernet interface to the NME-WAE. Figure 5-10 shows a remote branch topology using a router-integrated NME-WAE.

Figure 5-10 *Branch Deployment Model Using NME-WAE*

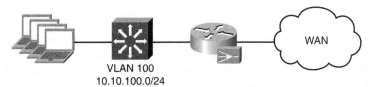

VLAN 100
10.10.100.0/24

The internal GigabitEthernet interface available on the NME-WAE is exposed in the router IOS configuration as an interface named **IntegratedServicesEngine***slot/port*. This interface is configured in a similar manner to any other IOS interface, with the following exceptions:

- The IP address of the WAE is configured on the IntegratedServicesEngine interface using the command **service-module ip address** *addr mask*.

- The default gateway of the WAE is configured on the IntegratedServicesEngine interface using the command **service-module ip default-gateway** *addr*.

Example 5-8 shows the full configuration of the IntegratedServicesEngine interface in IOS.

Example 5-8 *IOS NME-WAE IOS Interface Configuration*

```
!
interface Integrated-Service-Engine1/0
 ip address 10.88.81.17 255.255.255.240
 ip wccp redirect exclude in
 service-module ip address 10.88.81.18 255.255.255.240
 service-module ip default-gateway 10.88.81.17
 no keepalive
!
```

Note that the **ip wccp redirect exclude in** command is configured on the IntegratedServicesEngine interface. This ensures that the WCCP process running on the router does not re-intercept any traffic coming into the router from the NME-WAE. Once the required interface configuration is complete in the router, the WAE can be accessed and managed just like an external WAE appliance. Because the NME-WAE does not have an external console interface for out-of-band management, additional CLI commands are available in IOS for managing the NME-WAE.

Two-Arm Deployment

At small to medium-sized sites where an off-path deployment is used with a low-end router, the WAE can be deployed in a two-arm mode to help offload decoded traffic directly to the local client subnet. The two-arm deployment model is intended for small to medium-sized branch offices that have a single host subnet. The two-arm deployment model still leverages WCCP to transparently intercept and redirect traffic to the primary interface of the WAE. The primary interface of the WAE resides on a dedicated subnet, separate from the hosts it is optimizing connections for. The difference with this deployment model is that the second built-in Ethernet interface on the WAE is directly connected to the same subnet as the local hosts. Figure 5-11 shows an example of this topology.

Figure 5-11   *Two-Arm WAE Deployment*

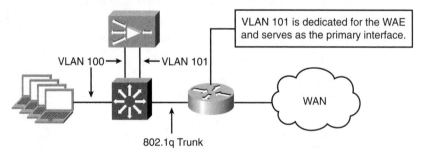

The primary interface of the WAE is used for receiving traffic intercepted using WCCP, and serves as the interface through which the default gateway is configured. The egress method used in this deployment model is IP forwarding. The second WAE interface is configured with an IP address in the local host subnet. This allows optimized traffic that is received across the WAN to be decoded in the WAE and then sent directly to the local destination host systems, bypassing the need to return through the WAN access router. Bypassing the WAN access router reduces the increased levels of throughput that can cause performance problems for legacy routers when WAAS is deployed. Figure 5-12 shows the traffic flow in a two-arm deployment model.

Figure 5-12   *Two-Arm Deployment Traffic Flow*

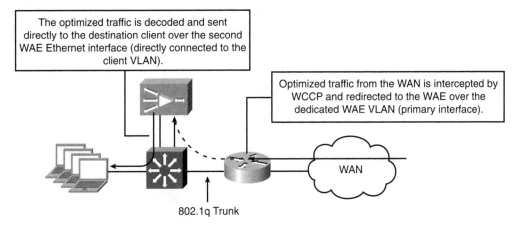

The WCCP configuration of the WAN router is shown in Example 5-9.

Example 5-9   *Two-Arm Deployment WAN Router Configuration*

```
!
hostname WR-01
!
ip wccp 61 password cisco
ip wccp 62 password cisco
!
interface FastEthernet0/0
 no ip address
 duplex full
 speed 100
!
interface FastEthernet0/0.201
 description ** Branch Client Subnet **
 encapsulation dot1Q 201
 ip address 10.88.81.17 255.255.255.240
 ip wccp 61 redirect in
!
interface FastEthernet0/0.202
 description ** Branch WAE Subnet **
 encapsulation dot1Q 202
 ip address 10.88.81.1 255.255.255.240
 ip wccp redirect exclude in
!
interface Serial0/0
 description ** Link to WAN **
 ip address 10.88.81.254 255.255.255.252
 ip wccp 62 redirect in
!
```

Example 5-10 shows the WAE configuration that is used for this deployment model.

Example 5-10   *Two-Arm Deployment WAE Configuration*

```
!
device mode application-accelerator
!
hostname AUSTIN-WAE
!
ip domain-name cisco.com
!
primary-interface GigabitEthernet 1/0
!
interface GigabitEthernet 1/0
 ip address 10.88.81.2 255.255.255.240
 exit
interface GigabitEthernet 2/0
 ip address 10.88.81.18 255.255.255.240
 exit
!
ip default-gateway 10.88.81.1
!
wccp router-list 1 10.88.81.1
wccp tcp-promiscuous router-list-num 1 password cisco
wccp version 2
!
no auto-register enable
!
ip name-server 10.88.80.53
!
authentication login local enable primary
authentication configuration local enable primary
!
central-manager address cm.cisco.com
cms enable
!
no adapter epm enable
!
<default ATP removed>
!
! End of WAAS configuration
```

Large Nonredundant Branch Office

The large nonredundant branch office topology has a similar topology as the small to medium-sized branch. The primary differences are the number of LAN switches and the routing configuration. At larger branch locations, it is also possible for the WAN router to be a hardware-based platform, such as a Cisco 7600 Series router or a Catalyst 6500 Series switch with a FlexWAN module. Large branch offices have clients on multiple VLANs, which are not only accessing resources across the WAN, but are also communicating between each other locally. In these cases, it is most common for the LAN switches to provide IP routing capabilities. Figure 5-13 shows the large nonredundant reference branch office topology discussed in this section.

Figure 5-13   *Large Nonredundant Reference Topology*

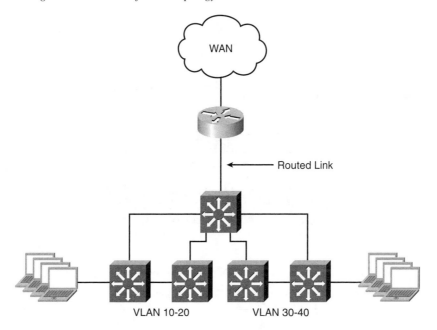

Here the link between the WAN access router and the LAN switch is a point-to-point routed link. The goal is to optimize traffic from clients going across the WAN. Because there are multiple existing VLANs, and maintaining the proximity of the WAE to the WAN access layer is desired, it makes sense to create a new VLAN on the top-level LAN switch dedicated for the WAE(s) that will be deployed in this branch. WCCP is still configured on the WAN router to intercept all TCP traffic and redirect it to the WAE. Figure 5-14 shows the branch office topology for this deployment model.

Unlike the small to medium-sized topology, the LAN switch performs routing for the subnet the WAE resides on. Because WCCP interception is still configured on the WAN access router, the WAE is multiple Layer 3 hops away from the intercepting router. This scenario requires that WCCP be configured to use both GRE forwarding and GRE return, because the intercepted traffic must traverse an intermediate Layer 3 hop between the intercepting router and the WAE.

Figure 5-14 *Large Nonredundant Deployment*

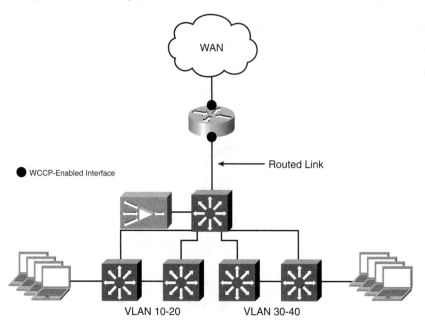

The WCCP configuration of the WAN router is shown in Example 5-11.

Example 5-11 *Large Nonredundant Deployment WAN Router Configuration*

```
!
hostname WR-01
!
ip wccp 61 password cisco
ip wccp 62 password cisco
!
interface Loopback0
 ip address 10.32.77.66 255.255.255.255
!
interface FastEthernet0/0
 ip address 10.88.80.1 255.255.255.252
 ip wccp 61 redirect in
 duplex full
 speed 100
!
interface Serial0/0
 description ** Link to WAN **
 ip address 10.88.81.254 255.255.255.252
 ip wccp 62 redirect in
!
```

Example 5-12 shows the configuration of the LAN switch in this deployment scenario.

Example 5-12 *Large Nonredundant Deployment LAN Switch Configuration*

```
!
interface GigabitEthernet1/0/1
 ip address 10.88.80.2 255.255.255.252
!
<removed for brevity>
!
interface Vlan196
 ip address 10.88.81.17 255.255.255.240
!
ip route 0.0.0.0 0.0.0.0 10.88.80.1
ip classless
!
end
```

The configuration of the WAE in this deployment scenario is shown in Example 5-13.

Example 5-13 *Large Nonredundant Deployment WAE Configuration*

```
!
device mode application-accelerator
!
hostname AUSTIN-WAE
!
ip domain-name cisco.com
!
primary-interface GigabitEthernet 1/0
!
interface GigabitEthernet 1/0
 ip address 10.88.81.18 255.255.255.128
 exit
interface GigabitEthernet 2/0
 shutdown
 exit
!
ip default-gateway 10.88.81.17
!
wccp router-list 1 10.32.77.66
wccp tcp-promiscuous router-list-num 1 password cisco
wccp version 2
!
egress-method negotiated-return intercept-method wccp
!
no auto-register enable
!
ip name-server 10.88.80.53
!
authentication login local enable primary
```

continues

Example 5-13 *Large Nonredundant Deployment WAE Configuration (Continued)*

```
authentication configuration local enable primary
!
central-manager address cm.cisco.com
cms enable
!
no adapter epm enable
!
<default ATP removed>
!
! End of WAAS configuration
```

The default gateway of the WAE is configured as the SVI interface on the LAN switch where the WAE subnet is located. However, because the WAE is multiple Layer 3 hops away from the intercepting router, the IP address configured in the WCCP router list is the Loopback0 interface address on the intercepting router. This is recommended to provide stability to the WCCP process on the intercepting router, and allow for WCCP to continue operating if there are multiple paths available between the WAE and the intercepting router. Another example of this configuration will be provided for the redundant branch office topology.

Another option in this scenario is to move the WCCP interception functionality to the LAN switch. This is useful in cases where you may not have administrative access to the WAN access router or you want to leverage the performance of the LAN switch to perform WCCP interception in hardware. Figure 5-15 shows the branch office topology for this deployment model.

Figure 5-15 *WCCP Interception on LAN Switch*

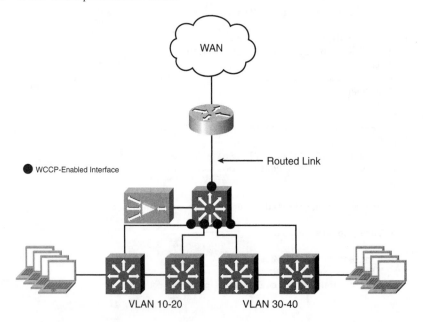

This topology configures WCCP interception on the Cisco Catalyst LAN switch. The LAN switch in this case handles routing for the subnet the WAE resides on. No configuration changes are required on the WAN access router.

The IOS configuration of the LAN switch in this deployment scenario is shown in Example 5-14.

Example 5-14 *WCCP on LAN Switch Configuration*

```
!
ip wccp 61 password cisco
ip wccp 62 password cisco
!
interface GigabitEthernet1/0/1
 ip address 10.88.80.2 255.255.255.252
 ip wccp 62 redirect in
!
<removed for brevity>
!
interface Vlan100
 ip address 10.88.81.1 255.255.255.240
 ip wccp 61 redirect in
!
interface Vlan196
 ip address 10.88.81.17 255.255.255.240
!
ip route 0.0.0.0 0.0.0.0 10.88.80.1
ip classless
!
end
```

WCCP is configured on interface GigabitEthernet1/0/1, which is the physical routed interface connecting to the WAN router at the site. WCCP interception is also enabled on all of the client-facing SVI interfaces.

CAUTION Do not use the command **ip wccp redirect exclude in** on hardware-based (that is, Catalyst) platforms.

TIP When configuring WCCP on a hardware-based platform, always use inbound redirection to ensure full hardware acceleration.

The configuration of the WAE in this deployment scenario is shown in Example 5-15.

Example 5-15 *WCCP on LAN Switch Deployment WAE Configuration*

```
!
device mode application-accelerator
!
hostname AUSTIN-WAE
!
ip domain-name cisco.com
!
primary-interface GigabitEthernet 1/0
!
interface GigabitEthernet 1/0
 ip address 10.88.80.137 255.255.255.128
 exit
interface GigabitEthernet 2/0
 shutdown
 exit
!
ip default-gateway 10.88.81.17
!
wccp router-list 1 10.88.81.17
wccp tcp-promiscuous router-list-num 1 l2-redirect mask-assign password cisco
wccp version 2
!
no auto-register enable
!
ip name-server 10.88.80.53
!
authentication login local enable primary
authentication configuration local enable primary
!
central-manager address cm.cisco.com
cms enable
!
no adapter epm enable
!
<default ATP removed>
!
! End of WAAS configuration
```

Because WCCP is running on a hardware-based platform in this configuration, there are two additional WCCP options configured on the WAE: **l2-redirect** and **mask-assign**. The **l2-redirect** option tells the Catalyst 3750 to redirect traffic to the WAE by rewriting the destination MAC address of redirected traffic to equal the MAC address of the target WAE (as opposed to encapsulating the packet in a WCCP GRE header). The **mask-assign** option is an alternative to the default hash assignment, which is optimized for use in hardware-based platforms. Both of these options are required to ensure that WCCP redirection is handled completely in hardware.

Off-Path Redundant Topology

Redundant branch office network topologies present additional challenges in that there are multiple paths traffic can traverse within the site and when entering and existing the WAN. It is common for the traffic load from the site to be distributed across multiple WAN links for increased capacity/performance, and to minimize the impact of a single WAN link outage. When deploying WAAS in redundant branch office topologies, one of the design goals is to preserve the original path selection, or outbound load distribution, of traffic across multiple WAN links. The following sections explore various placement and interception configuration options for off-path integration in redundant branch office topologies.

Small to Medium-Sized Redundant Branch Office

Small/medium redundant branch offices have multiple WAN routers and one or more LAN switches. The site may have multiple VLANs, with the WAN router responsible for routing traffic locally between the VLANs. The reference topology has a single existing VLAN. Figure 5-16 shows the redundant reference branch office topology discussed in this section.

Figure 5-16   *Small to Medium-Sized Redundant Reference Topology*

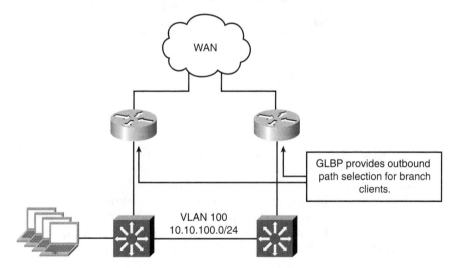

In this scenario, all IP routing for the branch is handled by the WAN routers (that is, the LAN switches function only at Layer 2). The WAN access routers are configured with GLBP on the LAN interfaces to provide default gateway redundancy for the local host systems. Traffic can enter or exit the site through either WAN router. Because there is only a single existing VLAN, and the links between the WAN access routers and the LAN switches are not configured as trunks, adding a dedicated VLAN for the WAE is not desirable. In these cases, the WAE is deployed on the existing VLAN with the hosts it is optimizing connections for. Figure 5-17 shows the branch office topology for this deployment model.

Figure 5-17 *Small to Medium-Sized Branch Office Redundant Deployment*

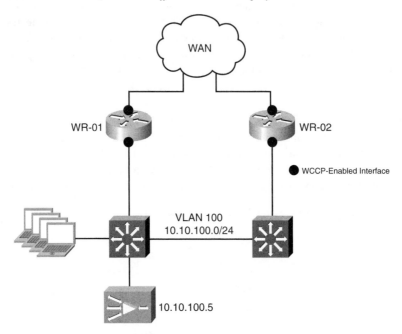

Both WAN access routers are configured with WCCP for transparent interception. Because both WAN access routers are members of the same WCCP service group, traffic can enter or exit the remote office through either router. The deterministic behavior of WCCP will ensure that traffic is redirected to the correct WAE in both directions. Egress traffic from the WAEs is returned directly to the intercepting routers' real interface IP addresses (as opposed to the GLBP virtual IP addresses) using WCCP GRE return as the egress method. In addition to allowing the WAE to reside on the same VLAN with client systems, this configuration preserves the original WAN router selection for intercepted traffic.

| TIP | The use of WCCP GRE return as an egress method is only intended for software-based platforms (ISR, 7200, and so on). If a hardware-based platform is being used as the WAN access routers (in other words, Cisco Catalyst switch), IP forwarding should be used as the egress method. |

As traffic is redirected to the WAE, the WAE records the source IP address (from the WCCP GRE header) of the intercepting router that redirected the traffic to it. This allows the WAE to return the traffic to the intercepting router it came from once processing is complete. This stateful behavior is performed on a connection-by-connection basis, and is a key feature that allows for the existing WAN router selection to be preserved. The configuration of the WAN routers is shown in Example 5-16.

Example 5-16   *Small to Medium-Sized Redundant Deployment WAN Router Configuration*

```
!
hostname WR-01
!
ip wccp 61 password cisco
ip wccp 62 password cisco
!
interface FastEthernet0/0
 ip address 10.10.100.2 255.255.255.0
 ip wccp 61 redirect in
 speed 100
 full-duplex
 glbp 1 ip 10.10.100.1
 glbp 1 priority 105
 glbp 1 preempt delay minimum 60
 glbp 1 load-balancing host-dependent
 glbp 1 authentication text cisco
!
interface Serial0/0
 description ** Link to WAN **
 ip address 10.88.81.254 255.255.255.252
 ip wccp 62 redirect in
!

!
hostname WR-02
!
ip wccp 61 password cisco
ip wccp 62 password cisco
!
interface FastEthernet0/0
 ip address 10.10.100.3 255.255.255.0
 ip wccp 61 redirect in
 speed 100
 full-duplex
 glbp 1 ip 10.10.100.1
 glbp 1 priority 100
 glbp 1 preempt delay minimum 60
 glbp 1 load-balancing host-dependent
 glbp 1 authentication text cisco
```

continues

Example 5-16 *Small to Medium-Sized Redundant Deployment WAN Router Configuration (Continued)*

```
!
interface Serial0/0
 description ** Link to WAN **
 ip address 10.88.81.250 255.255.255.252
 ip wccp 62 redirect in
!
```

Example 5-17 shows the WAE configuration that is used for this deployment model.

Example 5-17 *Small to Medium-Sized Redundant Deployment WAE Configuration*

```
!
device mode application-accelerator
!
hostname AUSTIN-WAE
!
ip domain-name cisco.com
!
primary-interface GigabitEthernet 1/0
!
interface GigabitEthernet 1/0
 ip address 10.10.100.5 255.255.255.0
 exit
interface GigabitEthernet 2/0
 shutdown
 exit
!
ip default-gateway 10.10.100.1
!
wccp router-list 1 10.10.100.2 10.10.100.3
wccp tcp-promiscuous router-list-num 1 password cisco
wccp version 2
!
egress-method negotiated-return intercept-method wccp
!
no auto-register enable
!
ip name-server 10.88.80.53
!
authentication login local enable primary
authentication configuration local enable primary
!
central-manager address cm.cisco.com
cms enable
!
no adapter epm enable
!
<default ATP removed>
!
! End of WAAS configuration
```

It is important to analyze the current routing configuration and traffic flows at sites with redundant topologies. It is possible even when deploying the WAEs on a dedicated subnet to experience a redirection loop for traffic that transits between routers on host subnets. Figure 5-18 shows an example of how a redirection loop can be created when traffic passes between WAN access routers on host VLANs.

Figure 5-18   *Redirection Loop with WCCP Interception on Transit Paths*

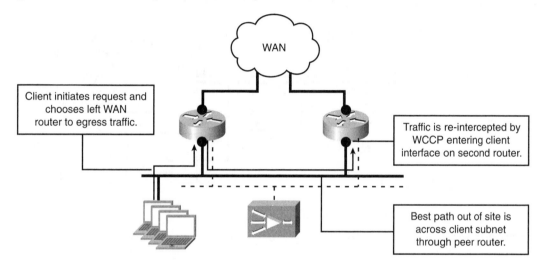

The solution is to prevent traffic from transiting between routers over the existing host subnets, and make the newly created WAE subnet the transit path between the WAN access routers. If the host subnets are not a transit path between the WAN access routers, it is possible to deploy the WAEs on an existing host subnet. If any of the current host subnets are serving as transit paths between the WAN access routers, the WAEs should be deployed on a dedicated subnet that can also serve as the new transit path. Figure 5-19 shows the modified traffic flow with the WAE subnet serving as the transit path between the WAN access routers.

Figure 5-19 *Dedicated WAE Subnet as Transit Path*

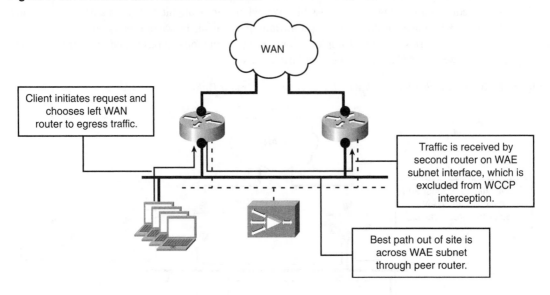

Example 5-18 shows the configuration of the WAN routers.

Example 5-18 *Small to Medium-Sized Redundant Deployment WAN Router Configuration*

```
!
hostname WR-01
!
ip wccp 61 password cisco
ip wccp 62 password cisco
!
interface FastEthernet0/0
 no ip address
 duplex full
 speed 100
!
interface FastEthernet0/0.201
 ip address 10.10.100.2 255.255.255.0
 ip wccp 61 redirect in
 speed 100
 full-duplex
 glbp 1 ip 10.10.100.1
 glbp 1 priority 105
 glbp 1 preempt delay minimum 60
 glbp 1 load-balancing host-dependent
 glbp 1 authentication text cisco
!
interface FastEthernet0/0.202
 ip address 10.88.81.2 255.255.255.240
 ip wccp redirect exclude in
```

Example 5-18 *Small to Medium-Sized Redundant Deployment WAN Router Configuration (Continued)*

```
 speed 100
 full-duplex
 glbp 2 ip 10.88.81.1
 glbp 2 priority 105
 glbp 2 preempt delay minimum 60
 glbp 2 load-balancing host-dependent
 glbp 2 authentication text cisco

!
interface Serial0/0
 description ** Link to WAN **
 ip address 10.88.81.254 255.255.255.252
 ip wccp 62 redirect in
!
router ospf 100
 passive-interface FastEthernet0/0.201
 network 10.10.100.0 0.0.0.255 area 0
 network 10.88.81.0 0.0.0.15 area 0
 network 10.88.81.252 0.0.0.3 area 0
!
```

```
!
hostname WR-02
!
ip wccp 61 password cisco
ip wccp 62 password cisco
!
interface FastEthernet0/0
 no ip address
 duplex full
 speed 100
!
interface FastEthernet0/0.201
 ip address 10.10.100.3 255.255.255.0
 ip wccp 61 redirect in
 speed 100
 full-duplex
 glbp 1 ip 10.10.100.1
 glbp 1 priority 100
 glbp 1 preempt delay minimum 60
 glbp 1 load-balancing host-dependent
 glbp 1 authentication text cisco
!
interface FastEthernet0/0.202
 ip address 10.88.81.3 255.255.255.240
 ip wccp redirect exclude in
 speed 100
 full-duplex
 glbp 2 ip 10.88.81.1
 glbp 2 priority 100
```

continues

Example 5-18 *Small to Medium-Sized Redundant Deployment WAN Router Configuration (Continued)*

```
 glbp 2 preempt delay minimum 60
 glbp 2 load-balancing host-dependent
 glbp 2 authentication text cisco
!
interface Serial0/0
 description ** Link to WAN **
 ip address 10.88.81.250 255.255.255.252
 ip wccp 62 redirect in
!
router ospf 100
 passive-interface FastEthernet0/0.201
 network 10.10.100.0 0.0.0.255 area 0
 network 10.88.81.0 0.0.0.15 area 0
 network 10.88.81.248 0.0.0.3 area 0
!
```

In Example 5-18, the interface connecting to the client subnet is set as passive under the OSPF process. This prevents a routing protocol adjacency from forming across the client subnet, which prevents it from becoming a transit path.

NOTE   Make sure that any static routes that are configured with a next-hop address across a client subnet are changed to use the WAE subnet as the transit path.

Example 5-19 shows the WAE configuration that is used for this deployment model.

Example 5-19 *Dedicated WAE Subnet WAE Configuration*

```
!
device mode application-accelerator
!
hostname AUSTIN-WAE
!
ip domain-name cisco.com
!
primary-interface GigabitEthernet 1/0
!
interface GigabitEthernet 1/0
 ip address 10.88.81.5 255.255.255.240
 exit
interface GigabitEthernet 2/0
 shutdown
 exit
!
ip default-gateway 10.88.81.1
```

Example 5-19   *Dedicated WAE Subnet WAE Configuration (Continued)*

```
!
wccp router-list 1 10.88.81.2 10.88.81.3
wccp tcp-promiscuous router-list-num 1 password cisco
wccp version 2
!
egress-method negotiated-return intercept-method wccp
!
no auto-register enable
!
ip name-server 10.88.80.53
!
authentication login local enable primary
authentication configuration local enable primary
!
central-manager address cm.cisco.com
cms enable
!
no adapter epm enable
!
<default ATP removed>
!
! End of WAAS configuration
```

Large Redundant Branch Office

Large branch offices are much more likely to implement a multilayer Core, Distribution, and Access topology. It is also common for the WAN routers at large branch offices to be hardware-based platforms, such as Catalyst 6500 Series switches or 7600 Series routers. With a more extensive network infrastructure in large branch offices comes more options for where to configure interception. Figure 5-20 shows the large redundant reference branch office topology discussed in this section.

All of the switch links in the reference topology are routed links. Traffic load is distributed across both WAN routers as it leaves the site. We want to preserve this routing behavior after WAAS is deployed. Although we want to maintain the proximity of the WAEs to the WAN access layer, we need to consider how egress traffic from the WAEs will be handled. Because this topology uses hardware-based WAN routers, using WCCP GRE return as the egress method is not recommended. Instead, configure WCCP one hop away from the WAN routers on the LAN distribution switches. By moving down into the branch office infrastructure, we can take advantage of the dynamic IGP routing between the WAN routers and the LAN distribution layer switches. With the WAEs using IP forwarding as the egress method, and the LAN distribution switches configured as the default gateway of the WAEs, the routing protocol can handle outbound load distribution to the WAN routers. Figure 5-21 shows the branch office topology for this deployment model.

Figure 5-20 *Large Redundant Reference Topology*

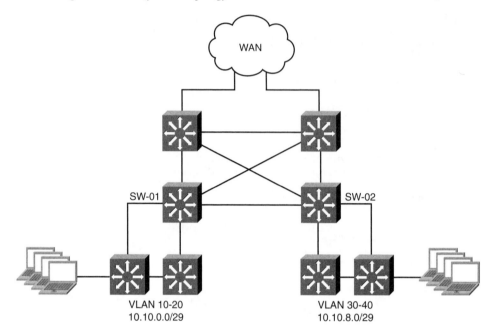

Figure 5-21 *Large Redundant Off-Path Deployment*

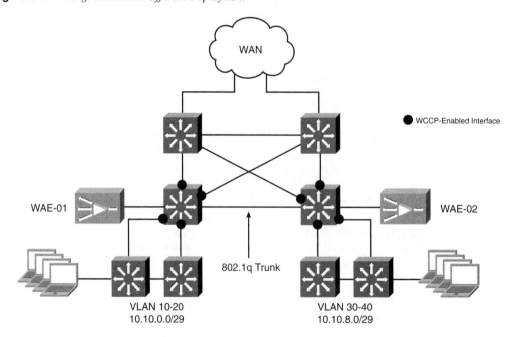

A dedicated VLAN is created for the WAEs on the LAN distribution switches. To facilitate WCCP L2 forwarding, the WAE VLAN is trunked between the two LAN distribution switches. This allows traffic to be intercepted on either LAN distribution switch and get redirected to the correct WAE. HSRP is configured on the WAE VLAN to provide default gateway redundancy.

The IOS configuration of both LAN distribution switches is shown in Example 5-20.

Example 5-20 *Large Redundant Off-Path Deployment LAN Switch Configuration*

```
!
hostname SW-01
!
ip wccp 61 redirect-list NO-LOCAL-TRAFFIC password cisco
ip wccp 62 redirect-list NO-LOCAL-TRAFFIC password cisco
!
interface Port-channel1
 switchport
 switchport trunk encapsulation dot1q
 switchport trunk allowed vlan 10-40,100
 switchport mode trunk
 no ip address
!
interface GigabitEthernet1/0
 description ** Link to WAN Router **
 ip address 10.88.81.250 255.255.255.252
 ip wccp 62 redirect in
!
interface GigabitEthernet1/1
 description ** Link to LAN Access Switch **
 ip address 10.88.81.246 255.255.255.252
 ip wccp 61 redirect in
!
interface GigabitEthernet1/2
 switchport
 switchport trunk encapsulation dot1q
 switchport trunk allowed vlan 10-40,100
 switchport mode trunk
 no ip address
 channel-group 1 mode desirable
!
interface GigabitEthernet1/3
 description ** WAE-01 **
 switchport
 switchport access vlan 100
 switchport mode access
 no ip address
 spanning-tree portfast
!
interface GigabitEthernet2/0
 description ** Link to WAN Router **
```

continues

Example 5-20 *Large Redundant Off-Path Deployment LAN Switch Configuration (Continued)*

```
 ip address 10.88.81.254 255.255.255.252
 ip wccp 62 redirect in
!
interface GigabitEthernet2/1
 description ** Link to LAN Access Switch **
 ip address 10.88.81.242 255.255.255.252
 ip wccp 61 redirect in
!
interface GigabitEthernet2/2
 switchport
 switchport trunk encapsulation dot1q
 switchport trunk allowed vlan 10-40,100
 switchport mode trunk
 no ip address
 channel-group 1 mode desirable
!
<removed for brevity>
!
interface Vlan100
 description ** WAAS WAE VLAN **
 ip address 10.88.81.2 255.255.255.240
 standby 1 ip 10.88.81.1
 standby 1 priority 105
 standby 1 password cisco
!
ip access-list extended NO-LOCAL-TRAFFIC
 deny ip 10.10.0.0 0.0.15.255 10.10.0.0 0.0.15.255
 permit ip any any
!
end
```

```
!
hostname SW-02
!
ip wccp 61 redirect-list NO-LOCAL-TRAFFIC password cisco
ip wccp 62 redirect-list NO-LOCAL-TRAFFIC password cisco
!
interface Port-channel1
 switchport
 switchport trunk encapsulation dot1q
 switchport trunk allowed vlan 10-40,100
 switchport mode trunk
 no ip address
!
interface GigabitEthernet1/0
 description ** Link to WAN Router **
 ip address 10.88.81.238 255.255.255.252
 ip wccp 62 redirect in
!
interface GigabitEthernet1/1
 description ** Link to LAN Access Switch **
 ip address 10.88.81.234 255.255.255.252
```

Example 5-20 *Large Redundant Off-Path Deployment LAN Switch Configuration (Continued)*

```
 ip wccp 61 redirect in
!
interface GigabitEthernet1/2
 switchport
 switchport trunk encapsulation dot1q
 switchport trunk allowed vlan 10-40,100
 switchport mode trunk
 no ip address
 channel-group 1 mode desirable
!
interface GigabitEthernet1/3
 description ** WAE-02 **
 switchport
 switchport access vlan 100
 switchport mode access
 no ip address
 spanning-tree portfast
!
interface GigabitEthernet2/0
 description ** Link to WAN Router **
 ip address 10.88.81.230 255.255.255.252
 ip wccp 62 redirect in
!
interface GigabitEthernet2/1
 description ** Link to LAN Access Switch **
 ip address 10.88.81.226 255.255.255.252
 ip wccp 61 redirect in
!
interface GigabitEthernet2/2
 switchport
 switchport trunk encapsulation dot1q
 switchport trunk allowed vlan 10-40,100
 switchport mode trunk
 no ip address
 channel-group 1 mode desirable
!
<removed for brevity>
!
interface Vlan100
 description ** WAAS WAE VLAN **
 ip address 10.88.81.3 255.255.255.240
 standby 1 ip 10.88.81.1
 standby 1 priority 100
 standby 1 password cisco
!
ip access-list extended NO-LOCAL-TRAFFIC
 deny ip 10.10.0.0 0.0.15.255 10.10.0.0 0.0.15.255
 permit ip any any
!
end
```

The configuration of the WAEs in this deployment scenario is shown in Example 5-21.

Example 5-21 *Large Redundant Off-Path Deployment WAE Configuration*

```
!
device mode application-accelerator
!
hostname WAE-01
!
ip domain-name cisco.com
!
primary-interface GigabitEthernet 1/0
!
interface GigabitEthernet 1/0
 ip address 10.88.81.5 255.255.255.240
 exit
interface GigabitEthernet 2/0
 shutdown
 exit
!
ip default-gateway 10.88.81.1
!
wccp router-list 1 10.88.81.2 10.88.81.3
wccp tcp-promiscuous router-list-num 1 l2-redirect mask-assign password cisco
wccp version 2
!
no auto-register enable
!
ip name-server 10.88.80.53
!
authentication login local enable primary
authentication configuration local enable primary
!
central-manager address cm.cisco.com
cms enable
!
no adapter epm enable
!
<default ATP removed>
!
! End of WAAS configuration
```

Both WAE configurations are the same, except for the WAE IP address itself. Because WCCP is running on a hardware-based platform in this configuration, there are two additional WCCP options configured on the WAE: **l2-redirect** and **mask-assign**. The **l2-redirect** option tells the Catalyst 3750 to redirect traffic to the WAE by rewriting the destination MAC address of redirected traffic to equal the MAC address of the target WAE (as opposed to encapsulating the packet in a WCCP GRE header). The **mask-assign** option is an alternative to the default hash assignment, which is optimized for use in hardware-based platforms. Both of these options are required to ensure that WCCP redirection is handled completely in hardware. The default gateway of the WAE is configured as the HSRP VIP. In the WCCP router list, the IP address of the directly connected WAE VLAN interface is configured.

CAUTION   Do not use the HSRP VIP in the WCCP router list on the WAE.

Inbound WCCP interception is configured on the interfaces connecting to the WAN routers and the interfaces connecting to the LAN access switches.

CAUTION   Do not use the command **ip wccp redirect exclude in** on hardware-based (that is, Catalyst) platforms.

TIP   When configuring WCCP on a hardware-based platform, always use inbound redirection to ensure full hardware acceleration.

As an alternative to a single HSRP virtual IP (VIP) address that the WAEs use a default gateway, Multigroup HSRP (MHSRP) can be configured on the WAE VLAN. With this configuration, each WAE can use a different VIP for its default gateway, which accomplishes a manual form of load distribution. Example 5-22 shows an MHSRP configuration on the WAE VLAN interface configuration on the LAN distribution switches.

Example 5-22   *MHSRP Configuration for WAE VLAN*

```
!
hostname SW-01
!
interface Vlan100
 description ** WAAS WAE VLAN **
 ip address 10.88.81.3 255.255.255.240
 standby 1 ip 10.88.81.1
 standby 1 priority 105
 standby 1 password cisco
 standby 2 ip 10.88.81.2
```

continues

Example 5-22 *MHSRP Configuration for WAE VLAN (Continued)*

```
 standby 2 priority 105
 standby 2 password cisco
!

!
hostname SW-02
!
interface Vlan100
 description ** WAAS WAE VLAN **
 ip address 10.88.81.4 255.255.255.240
 standby 1 ip 10.88.81.1
 standby 1 priority 100
 standby 1 password cisco
 standby 2 ip 10.88.81.2
 standby 2 priority 100
 standby 2 password cisco
!
```

Example 5-23 shows the configurations of the WAEs in this deployment scenario.

Example 5-23 *WAE Configuration Using MHSRP*

```
!
device mode application-accelerator
!
hostname WAE-01
!
ip domain-name cisco.com
!
primary-interface GigabitEthernet 1/0
!
interface GigabitEthernet 1/0
 ip address 10.88.81.5 255.255.255.240
 exit
interface GigabitEthernet 2/0
 shutdown
 exit
!
ip default-gateway 10.88.81.1
!
wccp router-list 1 10.88.81.3 10.88.81.4
wccp tcp-promiscuous router-list-num 1 l2-redirect mask-assign password cisco
wccp version 2
!
no auto-register enable
!
ip name-server 10.88.80.53
!
authentication login local enable primary
authentication configuration local enable primary
```

Example 5-23   *WAE Configuration Using MHSRP (Continued)*

```
!
central-manager address cm.cisco.com
cms enable
!
no adapter epm enable
!
<default ATP removed>
!
! End of WAAS configuration
```

```
!
device mode application-accelerator
!
hostname WAE-02
!
ip domain-name cisco.com
!
primary-interface GigabitEthernet 1/0
!
interface GigabitEthernet 1/0
 ip address 10.88.81.6 255.255.255.240
 exit
interface GigabitEthernet 2/0
 shutdown
 exit
!
ip default-gateway 10.88.81.2
!
wccp router-list 1 10.88.81.3 10.88.81.4
wccp tcp-promiscuous router-list-num 1 l2-redirect mask-assign password cisco
wccp version 2
!
no auto-register enable
!
ip name-server 10.88.80.53
!
authentication login local enable primary
authentication configuration local enable primary
!
central-manager address cm.cisco.com
cms enable
!
no adapter epm enable
!
<default ATP removed>
!
! End of WAAS configuration
```

Policy-Based Routing Interception

Policy-based routing (PBR) is another transparent interception option for off-path deployments. PBR is configured on the same routers and switches where you would normally configure WCCP. You should take into account the following items when considering PBR for transparent interception:

- PBR requires more configuration steps in IOS than does WCCP.

- The only egress method supported with PBR is IP forwarding. This means that the WAEs cannot be deployed multiple L3 hops away from the intercepting routers.

- By default, PBR does not provide load distribution among multiple WAEs at a site.

- By default, PBR does not track the availability of the WAE to receive traffic (requires the IOS IP SLA feature).

Based on these limitations, PBR is recommended over WCCP only as a last resort. The remainder of this section provides sample configurations for using PBR for transparent interception with WAAS.

The following example shows the configuration steps required to use PBR for WAAS interception:

Step 1   Configure an access list to match the traffic you want to redirect to WAAS:

```
!
access-list 100 permit tcp any any
access-list 100 deny ip any any
!
```

Step 2   Create a route map that references the access list, and sets a next-hop IP address of the WAE:

```
!
route-map WAAS permit 10
    match ip address 100
    set ip next-hop 10.88.81.2
!
```

Step 3   Apply PBR to the individual interfaces:

```
!
interface FastEthernet0/0
 no ip address
 duplex full
 speed 100
!
interface FastEthernet0/0.201
 description ** Branch Client Subnet **
 encapsulation dot1Q 201
```

```
    ip address 10.88.81.17 255.255.255.240
    ip policy route-map WAAS
   !
   interface FastEthernet0/0.202
    description ** Branch WAE Subnet **
    encapsulation dot1Q 202
    ip address 10.88.81.1 255.255.255.240
   !
   interface Serial0/0
    description ** Link to WAN **
    ip address 10.88.81.254 255.255.255.252
    ip policy route-map WAAS
```

By default, PBR does not verify that the IP next-hop address specified in the route map is reachable. This can lead to a situation where traffic is being redirected to a WAE that is down. You can configure IOS devices to check the availability of IP next-hop address(es) using a combination of IP SLA features and the **set ip next-hop verify-availability** route map command.

Example 5-24 shows how to configure the WAN router to verify that the **IP next-hop** address specified in the route map is up and reachable.

Example 5-24 *Verifying IP Next Hop Address Using IP SLA*

```
!
hostname WR-01
!
ip sla monitor 10
 type echo protocol ipIcmpEcho 10.88.81.2
 frequency 10
ip sla monitor schedule 10 life forever start-time now
!
track 10 rtr 10 reachability
!
route-map WAAS permit 10
 match ip address 100
 set ip next-hop verify-availability 10.88.81.2 10 track 10
!
```

If the IP next-hop address becomes unavailable, the WAN router will start forwarding traffic natively across the WAN using the entries in the routing table as opposed to the policy route.

Another limitation of PBR is scenarios where multiple WAEs are deployed at a single site. Multiple WAEs can be deployed at a single site for scalability, redundancy, or both. The route map command **set ip next-hop** allows you to define multiple IP addresses. Example 5-25 shows a router-map with multiple next-hop addresses configured.

Example 5-25 *Multiple IP Next Hop Addresses*

```
!
route-map WAAS permit 10
      match ip address 100
      set ip next-hop 10.88.81.2 10.88.81.3
  !
```

In Example 5-25, the IP addresses of both WAEs are configured as "IP next hop" addresses. The problem with this configuration is that the second IP address, 10.88.81.3, will be used only if the first IP address becomes unavailable. When the failover occurs to the second WAE, all traffic associated with existing TCP connections will be forwarded unoptimized. As new TCP connections are established, they will be optimized. So at any given time, only a single WAE will be receiving traffic. A potential workaround for this would be to use multiple route map entries to manually distribute traffic to each WAE. In Example 5-26, the LAN subnet at the location is using IP subnet 10.10.10.0/24. PBR is configured to send even-numbered hosts to the first WAE, and odd-numbered hosts to the second WAE. Each route map entry would be configured with the IP addresses of both WAEs, so if one fails, traffic will be rerouted to the other WAE.

Example 5-26 *Traffic Distribution with PBR*

```
!
hostname WR-01
!
ip sla monitor 10
 type echo protocol ipIcmpEcho 10.88.81.2
 frequency 10
ip sla monitor schedule 10 life forever start-time now
ip sla monitor 20
 type echo protocol ipIcmpEcho 10.88.81.3
 frequency 10
ip sla monitor schedule 20 life forever start-time now
!
track 10 rtr 10 reachability
!
track 20 rtr 20 reachability
!
access-list 100 permit tcp 10.10.10.1 0.0.0.254 any
access-list 100 permit tcp any 10.10.10.1 0.0.0.254
access-list 101 permit tcp 10.10.10.0 0.0.0.254 any
access-list 101 permit tcp any 10.10.10.1 0.0.0.254
!
route-map WAAS permit 10
 match ip address 100
 set ip next-hop verify-availability 10.88.81.2 10 track 10
 set ip next-hop verify-availability 10.88.81.3 20 track 20
```

Example 5-26   *Traffic Distribution with PBR (Continued)*

```
!
route-map WAAS permit 20
 match ip address 101
 set ip next-hop verify-availability 10.88.81.3 10 track 20
 set ip next-hop verify-availability 10.88.81.2 20 track 10
 !
```

Cisco IOS Firewall Integration

Cisco IOS Firewall (IOS FW) is a fundamental part of the integrated threat-control solution available on Cisco low- and midrange routing platforms. An enhancement in Cisco IOS Release 12.4(11)T2 allows Cisco IOS FW and Cisco IOS IPS to recognize traffic being optimized by Cisco WAAS. With this enhancement, Cisco IOS FW observes the TCP options used in WAAS automatic discovery. If Cisco IOS FW notices that a connection has successfully completed WAAS automatic discovery, it permits the initial sequence number shift for the connection and maintains the Layer 4 state on the optimized connection.

NOTE   The capability of Cisco WAAS to interoperate with Cisco IOS FW and Cisco IOS IPS applies only to the Cisco IOS Zone-Based Policy Firewall starting from Release 12.4(11)T2. Cisco IOS Classic Firewall does not incorporate the Cisco WAAS interoperability enhancement.

In a branch office deployment, it is common to have security features, such as Cisco IOS FW, Cisco IOS IPS, or IPsec VPN, deployed on an ISR router. Cisco WAAS has three different deployment options:

- **Cisco WAAS deployed with an NME-WAE on the same router as Cisco IOS FW and IOS IPS, using WCCP redirect for traffic interception:** This scenario supports IPsec VPN, along with IOS FW and IOS IPS features.

- **Cisco WAAS deployed as an off-path, standalone appliance, using WCCP redirection for traffic interception:** This scenario also supports IPsec VPN, along with IOS FW and IOS IPS features,. The configuration for this option is the same as for the previous option.

- **Cisco WAAS deployed as an inline appliance, in front of the ISR router:** This scenario supports IPsec VPN, along with IOS FW. In this case, because IOS FW and IOS IPS will receive WAAS optimized packets, Layer 7 inspection on the client side is not supported. The IOS IPS feature is partially supported because traffic is uncompressed during the first few RTTs, and IOS IPS will work if a signature is matched at the beginning of a connection.

An edge Cisco WAAS with Cisco IOS FW or Cisco IOS IPS is applied at branch office sites that must inspect traffic moving to and from a WAN connection and may use VPN connectivity. Cisco IOS FW monitors traffic for optimization indicators (TCP options and subsequent TCP sequence number changes) and allows optimized traffic to pass, while still applying Layer 4 stateful inspection and deep packet inspection to all traffic, maintaining security while accommodating Cisco WAAS optimization advantages.

Example 5-27 shows a configuration with IOS FW and WCCP interception configured on the same router.

Example 5-27 *IOS Firewall and WCCP Interception*

```
!
ip wccp 61
ip wccp 62
!
ip inspect WAAS enable
class-map type inspect match-any most-traffic
 match protocol icmp
 match protocol ftp
 match protocol tcp
 match protocol udp
!
policy-map type inspect p1
 class type inspect most-traffic
  inspect
 class class-default
zone security inside
zone security outside
zone-pair security in-out source inside destination outside
 service-policy type inspect p1
zone-pair security out-in source outside destination inside
 service-policy type inspect p1
!
interface GigabitEthernet0/0
 description Trusted interface
 ip address 10.70.0.1 255.255.255.0
 ip wccp 61 redirect in
 zone-member security inside
!
interface GigabitEthernet0/1
 description Untrusted interface
 ip address 10.72.2.3 255.255.255.0
 ip wccp 62 redirect in
 zone-member security outside
!
interface Integrated-Service-Engine1/0
 ip address 10.70.100.1 255.255.255.252
 ip wccp redirect exclude in
 zone-member security inside
 service-module ip address 10.70.100.2 255.255.255.252
 service-module ip default-gateway 10.70.100.1
 !
```

Summary

This chapter explored various options for integrating Cisco WAAS into the branch office network infrastructure. Different topology and configuration scenarios were discussed, including both in-path and off-path interception options. As a point of reference, configuration examples for using PBR for transparent interception were provided. Finally, integration with Cisco IOS FW was reviewed, including deployment options and the associated device configurations. The material in this chapter provides the reader with a solid set of options for integrating WAAS into a common branch office network topologies.

CHAPTER 6

Data Center Network Integration

Data center network integration is a key component to a successful Cisco WAAS deployment. This chapter examines the key design considerations for deploying WAAS in the data center environment, including considerations for environments with multiple data centers. Sample design models and configurations are provided throughout this chapter, including the latest recommendations for integrating with Cisco firewall solutions commonly found in data center environments. This chapter also provides best practice recommendations for data center deployments that can scale to support hundreds or thousands of remote sites.

Data Center Placement

Determining where to deploy WAAS within the data center infrastructure requires careful consideration and planning. Data center environments are generally made up of complex network infrastructures, multiple layers of devices, diverse paths over which traffic can flow, and numerous types of systems performing various functions. This section focuses on where WAAS should be deployed within the data center, irrespective of the interception method used. Subsequent sections in this chapter provide design recommendations and sample configurations for network interception in the data center. Figure 6-1 shows the sample data center topology that will be used as a reference for discussing where within a data center WAAS should be deployed.

Starting from the top of the topology shown in Figure 6-1, traffic enters the data center through any of several Cisco routers located at the WAN edge. All of the WAN edge routers are aggregated into a pair of Cisco Catalyst 6500 Series switches. From there, traffic passes through another pair of Cisco Catalyst 6500 Series switches, which act as the core of the data center network infrastructure. Connecting to the core switches are multiple pairs of distribution switches, each providing connectivity for a different block of resources within the data center. For example, one resource block hosts multiple server farms, while another block provides connectivity to multiple Internet service providers (ISP) for corporate Internet connectivity, and another block could be present, connecting to downstream access layer infrastructure to support campus users.

Figure 6-1 *Reference Data Center Topology*

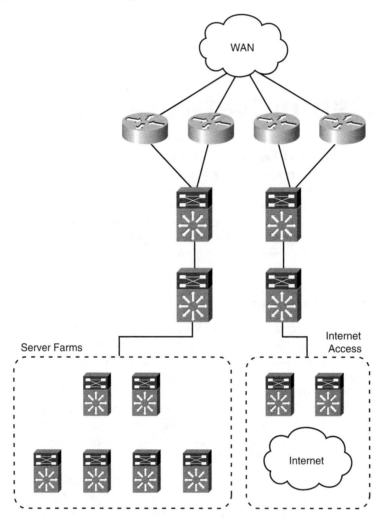

The first logical location within the data center to consider deploying WAAS is the WAN edge, or the point where traffic from remote branch offices first enters the data center. The benefits to deploying WAAS at this location include:

- The WAN edge is a natural aggregation point for traffic destined to or sourced from a remote branch office, and that is a good candidate for optimization. This is an important point, because passing intra-data center traffic through WAAS unnecessarily consumes resources and can potentially constrain throughput.

- The WAN edge layer in the data center is less likely to contain other application-aware components, such as firewalls, IDS/IPS, and content switches that require visibility into multiple layers of the traffic flows.

- The configuration required to support this deployment model is kept simple, because transparent interception needs to be configured and maintained only in a single location.

Deploying WAAS at a single aggregation point also provides the best hardware resource utilization, because a single cluster of WAEs can handle optimization and acceleration services for all WAN traffic. Figure 6-2 shows the reference data center topology with WAEs deployed at the WAN edge.

Figure 6-2   *WAN Edge WAAS Placement*

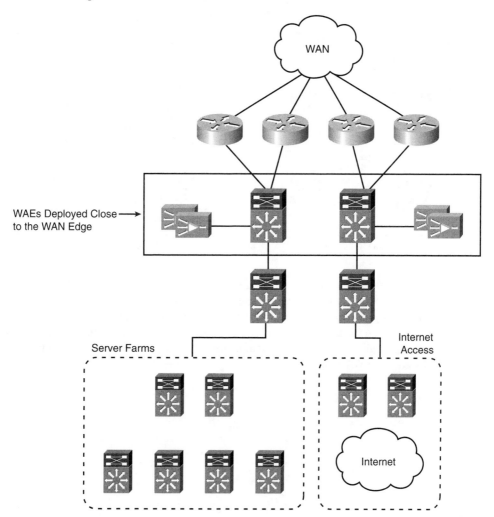

There are, however, reasons that can lead you to deploy WAAS deeper in the data center, that is, farther away from the WAN edge and closer to the server farm or host system. Take for example the topology in Figure 6-3, which shows a sample topology with multiple interconnected data centers.

Figure 6-3 *Multi-Data Center Reference Topology*

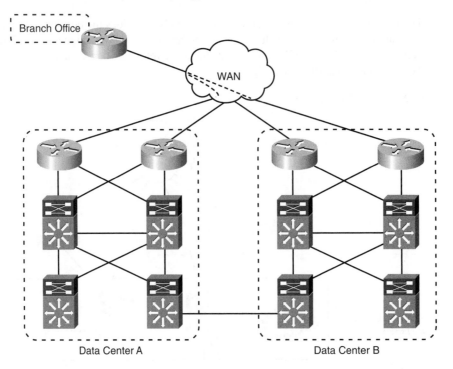

In this example, each remote branch office has WAN connectivity to both data centers. Users in the branch offices access resources in both data centers simultaneously. If the routing policy is such that users always take the most direct path to each data center, then deploying WAAS at the WAN edge in each data center will allow traffic to either data center to be optimized. Figure 6-4 shows sample traffic flows to each data center with WAAS deployed at the WAN edge.

Figure 6-4 *Dual Data Center with Symmetric Routing*

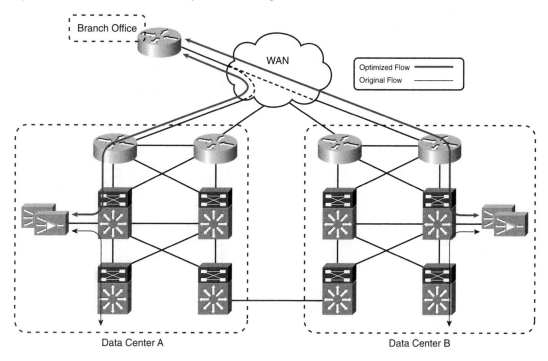

Data Center A   Data Center B

Figure 6-4 shows that, in a steady state, traffic from the remote branch office to either data center is optimized. However, in cases where traffic flows asymmetrically between the remote branch office and the data centers, the WAN edge might not be the best location to deploy WAAS in the data center. Asymmetric traffic flows can be the result of a WAN failure—for example, if the WAN link between the remote branch office and Data Center A in Figure 6-4 were to fail. Asymmetric traffic flows can also be caused by deliberate design; for example, if the routing policy dictates that both WAN links in the branch office are equal cost paths (that is, traffic can enter or leave over either WAN link, regardless of the final destination), all traffic from the branch office to Data Center A will flow across the WAN link to Data Center B, and then across the link between Data Center B and Data Center A. Figure 6-5 shows the traffic flow during a WAN link failure between the branch office and Data Center A.

Figure 6-5 *WAN Failure Causes Asymmetric Traffic Flows*

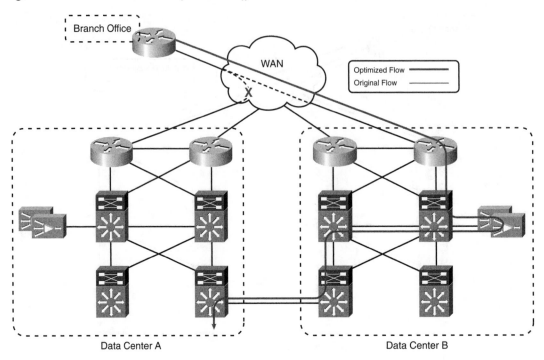

Data Center A   Data Center B

At the time of the failure, connections that were being optimized between the branch office WAE and the WAEs at the WAN edge in Data Center A would be reset, because the WAEs in Data Center A would no longer see the traffic. Connections between the branch office and Data Center B would continue to be optimized. As users reconnect to resources in Data Center A, the WAEs located in Data Center B would intercept the connections and begin optimization. This same behavior would happen again when the WAN link between the branch office and Data Center A was restored. Connections between hosts in the branch office and Data Center A would begin flowing over the direct connection between the two sites. Because the connections are no longer seen by the WAEs in Data Center B, those connections will be reset. As the connections are reestablished, they will be optimized between the branch office WAE and the WAEs in Data Center A.

TIP   As a general recommendation, when the network topology provides multiple paths over which traffic can flow, the WAAS design should assume that traffic will flow asymmetrically over both paths, even if the current design intends for traffic to flow symmetrically.

There are two design approaches to handle cases where traffic flows asymmetrically between multiple sites and the WAN edge is not the ideal location to deploy WAAS. The first approach stretches the transparent interception logic across the WAN edge layers in both data centers. This approach ensures that traffic entering or leaving either data center WAN edge is redirected to the same WAE in both directions. The design approach is easily accomplished with WCCP, by configuring a single WCCP service group that spans the WAN edge layer of both data centers. Figure 6-6 shows the use of a single WCCP service group to encompass the WAN edge layer of both data centers.

Figure 6-6   *Single WCCP Service Group Spanning Multiple Data Centers*

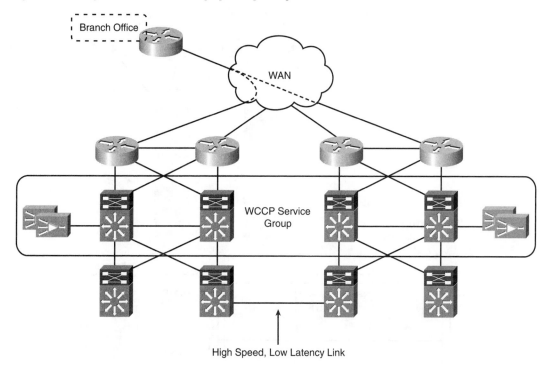

This design approach assumes that the data centers are "well connected"—that is, the connectivity between data centers is high bandwidth (>100 Mbps) and low latency (<10 msec). In essence, the WAEs in both data centers act as a single logical cluster. This design and the associated configurations are discussed in more detail later in this chapter.

The second design approach involves moving the location where WAAS is deployed closer toward the host resources and away from the WAN edge. In this topology, WAAS should be deployed behind the point in the data center topology where the two data centers are interconnected. Moving the WAEs and interception configuration behind the point of connectivity between the data centers eliminates the potential for traffic to only be seen in a single direction by the data center WAEs. Figure 6-7 shows the reference topology with WAAS deployed behind the point of asymmetric traffic flows.

Figure 6-7 *Server Farm Distribution WAAS Placement*

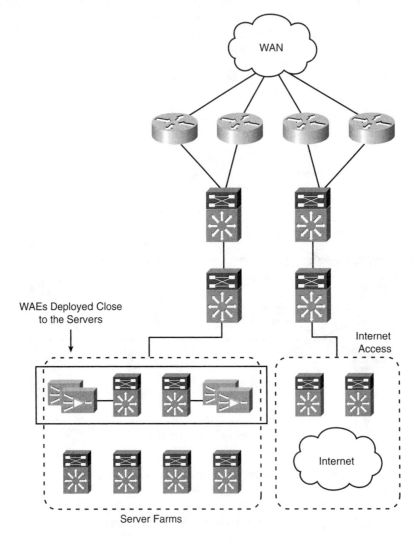

As you consider moving WAAS away from the WAN edge and deeper into the data center, you need to take into consideration other components in the data center that rely on access to various pieces of information in the traffic flow. These other components can include firewalls, IDS/IPS, and content switches, just to name a few. Understanding the traffic visibility requirements of these devices is required as part of the design process.

Consider the example of a content switch, such as the Application Control Engine (ACE). If ACE intercepts traffic for load balancing before it is intercepted by WAAS, there is the potential that information within the packet that ACE relies on to make a load-balancing decision will be obscured. Because this example is dealing with HTTP traffic, the default policy action in WAAS is Full Optimization (TFO+DRE+LZ). This means that the payload of the TCP segment will be compressed, and will not be readable by the load-balancing functions in ACE. If ACE is configured to make a load-balancing decision based on content in the Layer 7 HTTP header, it will not have access to that information. In this case, the WAEs need to be deployed in front of the ACE modules, so that the optimized connections are terminated prior to being intercepted by ACE for load balancing. This is just one example of how other application-aware components in the data center can potentially conflict with the optimizations provided by WAAS. Understanding the capabilities of these components, and their architectural placement within the data center, is a key design consideration.

Another key consideration as you look at deploying WAAS closer to the server farm is the impact on sizing—that is, the number of WAEs required in the data center to support the solution deployment. When WAAS devices are deployed at a common aggregation point for all traffic, a single cluster of WAEs can be used. If you move WAAS closer to the server farm infrastructure, and, due to the network topology, end up configuring interception at multiple locations in the data center, the number of WAEs required to support the design could increase. Figure 6-8 shows an example topology where WAAS has been deployed in multiple server farm distribution blocks.

The impact on sizing of splitting the design into multiple clusters within the data center is two-fold:

- Redundancy for each cluster must be accounted for separately. Data center deployments generally use $n+1$ sizing, where n is the number of WAEs required to support the expected load. The "+1" provides an additional WAE, which allows for the failure of a single WAE in the cluster without losing any cluster resource capacity. When you have multiple WAE clusters in the data center, having the same redundancy requirements means that each cluster is sized for $n+1$. This increases the number of WAEs required in the data center by the number separate WAE clusters that are deployed.

- Depending on what is driving the number of WAEs required in the data center, you could end up having to replicate the same number of WAEs in each separate cluster. For example, in a large deployment with 1000 remote branch offices, it is possible that the number of peer WAEs is the determining factor in how many WAEs are deployed in the data center. If the data center design calls for two separate clusters of WAEs, one for each server farm, and all of the remote branches are talking to resources in both server farms concurrently, then each cluster will need the same number of WAEs to support the fan-out ratio.

The following section discusses the specific network interception design options and associated configurations for the data center environment.

Figure 6-8 *Multiple WAAS Clusters*

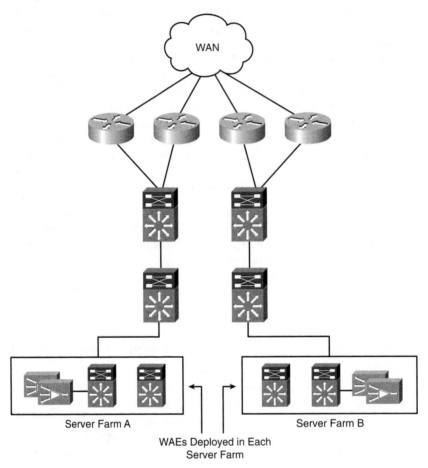

Deployment Solutions

This section provides the design and configuration details for deploying WAAS with transparent interception in the data center. The two transparent interception methods discussed are WCCP and content switching. The content switching design includes the Application Control Engine (ACE) from Cisco.

WCCP

WCCP provides a scalable and transparent interception method suitable for both the remote branch office and data center environments. Figure 6-9 shows the reference data center topology with WCCP enabled on the WAN edge routers.

Figure 6-9 *WCCP Enabled on WAN Edge Routers*

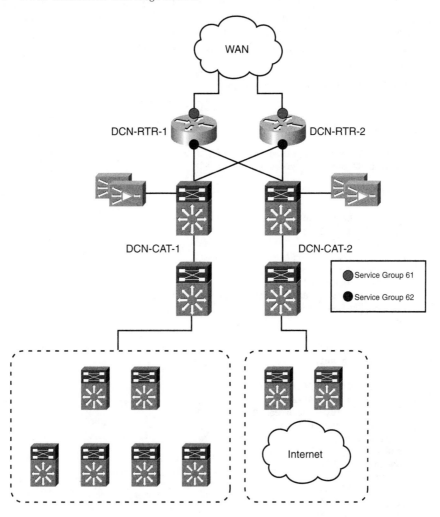

This case assumes that traffic flows symmetrically through the WAN edge in a single data center. Note that the placement of service groups 61 and 62 in the configuration is reversed from the branch office configuration. In the data center, service group 61 is configured on the WAN-facing interfaces, while service group 62 is configured on the LAN-facing interfaces.

This ensures that the load-distribution decision is based on the client IP address end-to-end. This is discussed in more detail in the section, "Scaling Transparent Interception" later in this chapter.

In Figure 6-9, WCCP is enabled on the Cisco WAN edge routers. The WAEs are connected to the WAN distribution switches on their own VLAN. WCCP is configured for GRE forwarding and hash assignment. To preserve the original path selection, and prevent the possibility of a redirection loop, the egress method is configured for negotiated return. This ensures that egress traffic from the WAEs is returned to the intercepting router after processing. Example 6-1 shows the relevant portions of each WAN edge router configuration for this deployment model.

Example 6-1 *WAN Edge Router WCCP Configuration*

```
!
hostname DCN-RTR-1
!
ip wccp 61 password cisco
ip wccp 62 password cisco
!
ip cef
!
interface Loopback0
 ip address 10.88.81.1 255.255.255.255
 no ip unreachables
!
interface GigabitEthernet0/1
 ** Link to DCN-CAT-1 **
 ip address 10.88.80.1 255.255.255.252
 ip wccp 62 redirect in
 duplex auto
 speed auto
 media-type gbic
 negotiation auto
!
interface GigabitEthernet0/2
 ** Link to DCN-CAT-2 **
 ip address 10.88.80.5 255.255.255.252
 ip wccp 62 redirect in
 duplex auto
 speed auto
 media-type gbic
 negotiation auto
!
interface ATM1/0
 no ip address
 load-interval 30
 no atm scrambling sts-stream
 no atm ilmi-keepalive
!
interface ATM1/0.55 point-to-point
 description ** 45 Mbps PVC to MPLS Service **
```

Example 6-1 *WAN Edge Router WCCP Configuration (Continued)*

```
 bandwidth 45000
 ip address 10.19.176.5 255.255.255.252
 ip wccp 61 redirect in
 no snmp trap link-status
 pvc 1/55
  vbr-nrt 44209 44209
  broadcast
  encapsulation aal5snap
 !
!
!
hostname DCN-RTR-2
!
ip wccp 61 password cisco
ip wccp 62 password cisco
!
ip cef
!
interface Loopback0
 ip address 10.88.81.2 255.255.255.255
 no ip unreachables
!
interface GigabitEthernet0/1
 ** Link to DCN-CAT-2 **
 ip address 10.88.80.9 255.255.255.252
 ip wccp 62 redirect in
 duplex auto
 speed auto
 media-type gbic
 negotiation auto
!
interface GigabitEthernet0/2
 ** Link to DCN-CAT-1 **
 ip address 10.88.80.13 255.255.255.252
 ip wccp 62 redirect in
 duplex auto
 speed auto
 media-type gbic
 negotiation auto
!
interface ATM1/0
 no ip address
 load-interval 30
 no atm scrambling sts-stream
 no atm ilmi-keepalive
!
interface ATM1/0.55 point-to-point
 description ** 45 Mbps PVC to MPLS Service **
 bandwidth 45000
 ip address 10.19.176.9 255.255.255.252
 ip wccp 61 redirect in
```

continues

Example 6-1 *WAN Edge Router WCCP Configuration (Continued)*

```
no snmp trap link-status
pvc 1/55
 vbr-nrt 44209 44209
 broadcast
 encapsulation aal5snap
 !
!
```

Example 6-2 shows a sample configuration for a WAE in this deployment model.

Example 6-2 *WCCP in WAN Edge Routers WAE Configuration*

```
!
device mode application-accelerator
!
hostname DCN-WAE-1
!
ip domain-name asdcnp-waas.cisco.com
!
primary-interface GigabitEthernet 1/0
!
interface GigabitEthernet 1/0
 ip address 10.74.155.11 255.255.255.0
 exit
interface GigabitEthernet 2/0
 shutdown
 exit
!
ip default-gateway 10.74.155.1
!
no auto-register enable
!
! ip path-mtu-discovery is disabled in WAAS by default
!
ip name-server 10.88.80.53
!
ntp server 10.88.121.253
!
wccp router-list 1 10.88.81.1 10.88.81.2
wccp tcp-promiscuous router-list-num 1 password cisco
wccp version 2
!
egress-method negotiated-return intercept-method wccp
!
authentication login local enable primary
authentication configuration local enable primary
!
central-manager address 10.88.80.133
cms enable
!
```

Example 6-2   *WCCP in WAN Edge Routers WAE Configuration (Continued)*

```
no adapter epm enable
!
<ATP Configuration Removed>
!
! End of WAAS configuration
```

To take advantage of hardware-accelerated interception, WCCP can be configured on the WAN distribution switches instead of the WAN edge routers. Figure 6-10 shows the reference data center topology with WCCP enabled on the WAN distribution switches.

Figure 6-10   *WCCP Enabled on WAN Distribution Switches*

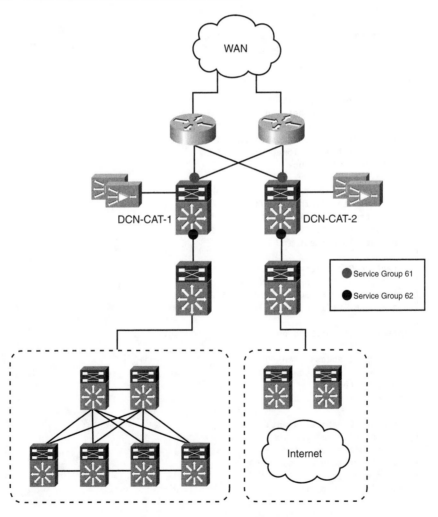

WCCP is enabled on the Cisco WAN distribution switches. The WAEs are directly connected to the WAN distribution switches on a dedicated VLAN, which is trunked between the two switches. This ensures that there is a Layer 2 adjacency between both switches and all WAEs in the service group. WCCP is configured for L2 forwarding and mask assignment. For performance reasons, the egress method is configured for IP forwarding. To distribute load across both WAN distribution switches, Multigroup HRSP is configured on the WAE VLAN. The default gateway configured on the WAEs in the cluster is balanced between the two HSRP VIPs. Example 6-3 shows the relevant portions of each WAN distribution switch configuration for this deployment model.

Example 6-3 *WAN Distribution Switch WCCP Configuration*

```
!
hostname DCN-CAT-1
!
ip wccp 61 password cisco accelerated
ip wccp 62 password cisco accelerated
!
vlan 65
!
interface Port-channel50
 description ** PC between CAT-1 to CAT-2 **
 switchport
 switchport trunk encapsulation dot1q
 switchport trunk allowed vlan 1,65
 switchport mode trunk
 no ip address
!
interface GigabitEthernet1/1
 description ** Link to DCN-RTR-1 **
 ip address 10.88.80.2 255.255.255.252
 ip wccp 61 redirect in
!
interface GigabitEthernet1/2
 description ** Link to DCN-RTR-2 **
 ip address 10.88.80.6 255.255.255.252
 ip wccp 61 redirect in
!
interface GigabitEthernet1/3
 switchport
 switchport access vlan 65
 switchport mode access
 no ip address
 spanning-tree portfast
!
interface GigabitEthernet1/4
 switchport
 switchport access vlan 65
 switchport mode access
 no ip address
 spanning-tree portfast
```

Example 6-3 *WAN Distribution Switch WCCP Configuration (Continued)*

```
!
interface GigabitEthernet1/5
 switchport
 switchport access vlan 65
 switchport mode access
 no ip address
 spanning-tree portfast
!
interface GigabitEthernet1/6
 switchport
 switchport access vlan 65
 switchport mode access
 no ip address
 spanning-tree portfast
!
interface GigabitEthernet1/41
 description ** Link to DCN-CORE-1 **
 ip address 10.88.80.17 255.255.255.252
 ip wccp 62 redirect in
!
interface GigabitEthernet1/42
 description ** Link to DCN-CORE-2 **
 ip address 10.88.80.21 255.255.255.252
 ip wccp 62 redirect in
!
interface GigabitEthernet1/47
 description CAT-1 to CAT-2 LINKS
 switchport
 switchport trunk encapsulation dot1q
 switchport trunk allowed vlan 1,65
 switchport mode trunk
 no ip address
 channel-group 50 mode desirable
!
interface GigabitEthernet1/48
 description CAT-1 to CAT-2 LINKS
 switchport
 switchport trunk encapsulation dot1q
 switchport trunk allowed vlan 1,65
 switchport mode trunk
 no ip address
 channel-group 50 mode desirable
!
interface Vlan1
 no ip address
 shutdown
!
interface Vlan65
 description ** WAAS WAE Vlan **
 ip address 10.74.155.3 255.255.255.0
```

continues

Example 6-3 *WAN Distribution Switch WCCP Configuration (Continued)*

```
 standby 1 ip 10.74.155.1
 standby 1 priority 105
 standby 1 preempt
 standby 2 ip 10.74.155.2
!
!
hostname DCN-CAT-2
!
ip wccp 61 password cisco accelerated
ip wccp 62 password cisco accelerated
!
vlan 65
!
interface Port-channel50
 description ** PC between CAT-2 to CAT-1 **
 switchport
 switchport trunk encapsulation dot1q
 switchport trunk allowed vlan 1,65
 switchport mode trunk
 no ip address
!
interface GigabitEthernet1/1
 description ** Link to DCN-RTR-2 **
 ip address 10.88.80.10 255.255.255.252
 ip wccp 61 redirect in
!
interface GigabitEthernet1/2
 description ** Link to DCN-RTR-1 **
 ip address 10.88.80.14 255.255.255.252
 ip wccp 61 redirect in
!
interface GigabitEthernet1/3
 switchport
 switchport access vlan 65
 switchport mode access
 no ip address
 spanning-tree portfast
!
interface GigabitEthernet1/4
 switchport
 switchport access vlan 65
 switchport mode access
 no ip address
 spanning-tree portfast
!
interface GigabitEthernet1/5
 switchport
 switchport access vlan 65
 switchport mode access
 no ip address
 spanning-tree portfast
```

Example 6-3   *WAN Distribution Switch WCCP Configuration (Continued)*

```
!
interface GigabitEthernet1/6
 switchport
 switchport access vlan 65
 switchport mode access
 no ip address
 spanning-tree portfast
!
interface GigabitEthernet1/41
 description ** Link to DCN-CORE-2 **
 ip address 10.88.80.25 255.255.255.252
 ip wccp 62 redirect in
!
interface GigabitEthernet1/42
 description ** Link to DCN-CORE-1 **
 ip address 10.88.80.29 255.255.255.252
 ip wccp 62 redirect in
!
interface GigabitEthernet1/47
 description CAT-2 to CAT-1 LINKS
 switchport
 switchport trunk encapsulation dot1q
 switchport trunk allowed vlan 1,65
 switchport mode trunk
 no ip address
 channel-group 50 mode desirable
!
interface GigabitEthernet1/48
 description CAT-1 to CAT-2 LINKS
 switchport
 switchport trunk encapsulation dot1q
 switchport trunk allowed vlan 1,65
 switchport mode trunk
 no ip address
 channel-group 50 mode desirable
!
interface Vlan1
 no ip address
 shutdown
!
interface Vlan65
 description ** WAAS WAE Vlan **
 ip address 10.74.155.4 255.255.255.0
 standby 1 ip 10.74.155.1
 standby 1 preempt
 standby 2 ip 10.74.155.2
 standby 2 priority 105
!
```

Example 6-4 shows a sample configuration for a WAE in this deployment model.

Example 6-4   *WCCP on WAN Distribution Switches WAE Configuration*

```
!
device mode application-accelerator
!
hostname DCN-WAE-1
!
ip domain-name asdcnp-waas.cisco.com
!
primary-interface GigabitEthernet 1/0
!
interface GigabitEthernet 1/0
 ip address 10.74.155.11 255.255.255.0
 exit
interface GigabitEthernet 2/0
 shutdown
 exit
!
ip default-gateway 10.74.155.1
!
no auto-register enable
!
! ip path-mtu-discovery is disabled in WAAS by default
!
ip name-server 10.88.80.53
!
ntp server 10.88.121.253
!
wccp router-list 1 10.74.155.3 10.74.155.4
wccp tcp-promiscuous router-list-num 1 l2-redirect mask-assign password cisco
wccp version 2
!
authentication login local enable primary
authentication configuration local enable primary
!
central-manager address 10.88.80.133
cms enable
!
no adapter epm enable
!
<ATP Configuration Removed>
!
! End of WAAS configuration
```

This same configuration could be used when deploying WAAS deeper in the data center, toward the server farms.

As discussed in the previous section, deploying WAAS in the WAN distribution layer when multiple data centers and asymmetric routing are involved requires that the WCCP service group span the WAN edge routers or switches in both data centers. Figure 6-11 shows a sample data center topology with a single WCCP service group that includes the WAN distribution switches in both data centers.

Figure 6-11 *Dual Data Center with Asymmetric Routing*

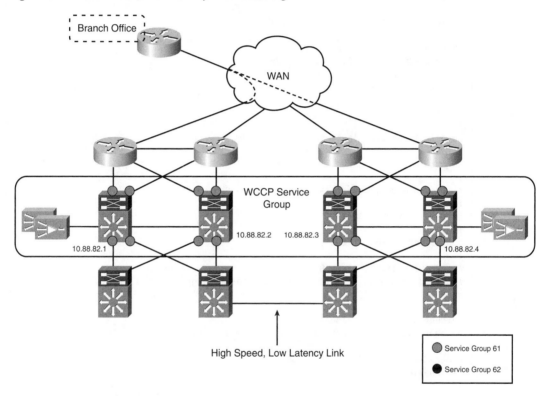

WCCP is enabled on the Cisco WAN distribution switches. The WAEs are directly connected to the WAN distribution switches on a dedicated VLAN, which is trunked between the two switches in the local data center. All of the WAEs in both data centers register with each pair of WAN distribution switches in both data centers. WCCP is configured for GRE forwarding and mask assignment. For performance reasons, the egress method is configured for IP forwarding. Each WAE uses the local WAN distribution switches as their default gateway. Example 6-5 shows a sample configuration for a WAE in this deployment model.

Example 6-5 *Dual Data Center WAE Configuration*

```
!
device mode application-accelerator
!
hostname DCN-WAE-1
!
ip domain-name asdcnp-waas.cisco.com
!
primary-interface GigabitEthernet 1/0
!
interface GigabitEthernet 1/0
 ip address 10.74.155.11 255.255.255.0
 exit
interface GigabitEthernet 2/0
 shutdown
 exit
!
ip default-gateway 10.74.155.1
!
no auto-register enable
!
! ip path-mtu-discovery is disabled in WAAS by default
!
ip name-server 10.88.80.53
!
ntp server 10.88.121.253
!
wccp router-list 1 10.88.82.1 10.88.82.2 10.88.82.3 10.88.82.4
wccp tcp-promiscuous router-list-num 1 mask-assign password cisco
wccp version 2
!
authentication login local enable primary
authentication configuration local enable primary
!
central-manager address 10.88.80.133
cms enable
!
no adapter epm enable
!
<ATP Configuration Removed>
!
! End of WAAS configuration
```

Content Switching

Using a content switch, such as ACE, provides an alternative to WCCP for transparent interception in the data center. ACE is best suited for designs where WCCP is unable to meet the scalability requirements of the deployment, or in data center designs where virtualization is used to provide logically separate infrastructures for different types of traffic. ACE can be deployed in either bridged mode or routed mode. Bridged mode is the equivalent of having ACE inline, as it bridges all traffic between VLANs. Routed mode requires that traffic be forwarded to ACE as a Layer 3 next hop. This is done by having traffic destined to a virtual IP address hosted on ACE, or using policy-based routing (PBR) to redirect traffic to ACE. Design and configuration examples of deploying ACE in bridged and routed mode for WAAS interception are provided in this section.

Figure 6-12 shows a topology where ACE is deployed in bridged mode at the server farm distribution layer.

Figure 6-12 *ACE Bridged Mode Deployment*

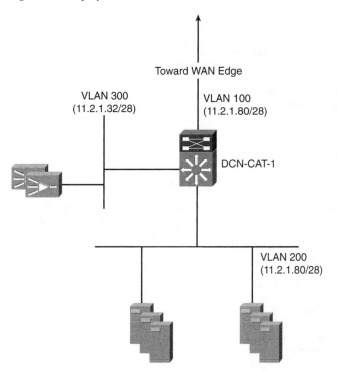

In this deployment model, ACE bridges all traffic between VLAN 100 and VLAN 200. All traffic flows through ACE, regardless of whether or not the traffic is intercepted and redirected to a WAE for optimization. When the packet arrives on VLAN 100 in the Catalyst 6500 switch, it is passed through to the ACE module. A service policy configured to intercept all TCP traffic redirects the packet to one of the WAEs in the WAAS cluster. The WAE selected by the ACE load-balancing algorithm records the packet TCP options, and returns the packet to its configured default gateway, which is the IP address configured on the WAAS VLAN in ACE. ACE forwards the packet based on the destination IP address and its routing configuration.

When a SYN-ACK response from the origin server arrives on VLAN 200, it is matched against the original flow created when the SYN packet was intercepted by ACE. Because the WAAS VLAN is configured with **mac-sticky**, the ACE returns the packet back to the WAE that handled the original SYN packet. The WAE matches the SYN-ACK with the original SYN packet and continues the TFO auto-discovery process. The packet is then returned to the ACE and routed back toward the WAN edge.

Example 6-6 shows the Catalyst 6500 and ACE configuration for this deployment model.

Example 6-6   *Catalyst 6500 and ACE Bridged Mode Configuration*

```
!
hostname DCN-CAT-1
!
svclc multiple-vlan-interfaces
svclc module 1 vlan-group 10
svclc vlan-group 10  100,200,300
!
interface Vlan100
 description ** Client-Side VLAN **
 ip address 11.2.1.81 255.255.255.240
!
!
hostname DCN-ACE-1
!
arp interval 15
!
access-list PERMIT-ALL line 10 extended permit ip any any
access-list PERMIT-ALL line 20 extended permit icmp any any
!
rserver host DCN-WAE-2
  ip address 11.2.1.34
  inservice
rserver host DCN-WAE-2
  ip address 11.2.1.35
  inservice
!
serverfarm host WAAS
  transparent
  predictor hash address source
  rserver DCN-WAE-1
    inservice
  rserver DCN-WAE-2
    inservice
!
class-map match-any ALL-TCP
  description ** Match all TCP traffic **
  10 match virtual-address 0.0.0.0 0.0.0.0 tcp any
!
class-map type management match-any ACE-MANAGEMENT
  2 match protocol telnet any
```

Example 6-6   *Catalyst 6500 and ACE Bridged Mode Configuration (Continued)*

```
   3 match protocol ssh any
   4 match protocol icmp any
class-map match-any TCP-ALL
  2 match virtual-address 0.0.0.0 0.0.0.0 tcp any
!
policy-map type management first-match ACE-MANAGEMENT
  class ACE-MANAGEMENT
    permit
policy-map type loadbalance first-match TCP-ALL
  class class-default
    serverfarm WAAS
policy-map multi-match WAAS-INTERCEPTION
  class TCP-ALL
    loadbalance vip inservice
    loadbalance policy TCP-ALL
!
service-policy input ACE-MANAGEMENT
!
interface vlan 300
  description ** WAAS WAE VLAN **
  ip address 11.2.1.40 255.255.255.240
  no normalization
  mac-sticky enable
  access-group input PERMIT-ALL
  access-group output PERMIT-ALL
  no shutdown
interface vlan 100
  description ** Client-Side VLAN **
  bridge-group 100
  no normalization
  access-group input PERMIT-ALL
  access-group output PERMIT-ALL
  service-policy input WAAS-INTERCEPT
  no shutdown
interface vlan 200
  description ** Server-Side VLAN **
  bridge-group 100
  no normalization
  access-group input PERMIT-ALL
  access-group output PERMIT-ALL
  service-policy input WAAS-INTERCEPT
  no shutdown
!
interface bvi 100
  ip address 11.2.1.83 255.255.255.240
  no shutdown
!
ip route 0.0.0.0 0.0.0.0 11.2.1.81
!
```

IP normalization is also disabled on the ACE VLAN interfaces with the command **no normalization**. This is required to allow the WAAS TFO auto-discovery process to function properly.

No special configuration is required on the WAE when ACE is used for interception. The default gateway configured on the WAE is the alias IP address of the WAE VLAN configured in ACE.

When ACE is deployed in routed mode, ACE must become a Layer 3 next hop for traffic in order for interception to take place. Because WAAS is transparent at Layer 3, traffic will not be destined to a VIP configured on ACE. For this deployment model, ACE is used in combination with PBR to intercept interesting traffic for optimization. PBR is configured in the network infrastructure devices, with a next-hop IP address of a VLAN interface on ACE.

The routed mode topology is similar to bridged mode, the primary difference being how traffic is intercepted by ACE. In the routed mode deployment, PBR is configured on the Catalyst 6500 switch to intercept TCP traffic that will be optimized by WAAS. The PBR configuration sets a next-hop address of an IP address configured on the ACE module. The WAEs are placed on a dedicated VLAN that is routed by the ACE module. Example 6-7 shows the ACE configuration for this deployment model.

Example 6-7   *Catalyst 6500 and ACE Routed Mode Configuration*

```
!
hostname DCN-CAT-1
!
vlan 500
!
interface Vlan100
 description ** Link to Data Center WAN Edge **
 ip address 10.88.81.6 255.255.255.252
 ip policy route-map PBR-TO-ACE
!
interface Vlan200
 ip address 172.16.0.1 255.255.254.0
 ip policy route-map PBR-TO-ACE
!
interface Vlan500
 description ** Lini to DCN-ACE-1 **
 ip address 30.30.5.4 255.255.255.0
!
ip access-list extended PBR-TO-ACE
 permit tcp any any
!
route-map PBR-TO-ACE permit 10
 match ip address PBR-TO-ACE
 set ip next-hop 30.30.5.1
!
!
hostname DCN-ACE-1
```

Example 6-7   *Catalyst 6500 and ACE Routed Mode Configuration (Continued)*

```
!
arp interval 15
!
access-list PERMIT-ALL line 10 extended permit ip any any
access-list PERMIT-ALL line 20 extended permit icmp any any
!
rserver host DCN-WAE-1
  ip address 30.30.51.10
  inservice
rserver host DCN-WAE-2
  ip address 30.30.51.11
  inservice
!
serverfarm host WAAS
  transparent
  rserver DCN-WAE-1
    inservice
  rserver DCN-WAE-2
    inservice
!
class-map type management match-any ACE-MANAGEMENT
  2 match protocol telnet any
  3 match protocol ssh any
  4 match protocol icmp any
class-map match-any TCP-ALL
  2 match virtual-address 0.0.0.0 0.0.0.0 tcp any
!
policy-map type management first-match ACE-MANAGEMENT
  class ACE-MANAGEMENT
    permit
policy-map type loadbalance first-match TCP-ALL
  class class-default
    serverfarm WAAS
policy-map multi-match WAAS-INTERCEPTION
  class TCP-ALL
    loadbalance vip inservice
    loadbalance policy TCP-ALL
!
service-policy input ACE-MANAGEMENT
!
interface vlan 500
  description ** Client-Side VLAN **
  ip address 30.30.5.1 255.255.255.0
  no normalization
  access-group input PERMIT-ALL
  access-group output PERMIT-ALL
  service-policy input WAAS-INTERCEPTION
  no shutdown
interface vlan 501
  description ** WAAS WAE VLAN **
  ip address 30.30.51.1 255.255.255.0
```

continues

Example 6-7 *Catalyst 6500 and ACE Routed Mode Configuration (Continued)*

```
  no normalization
  mac-sticky enable
  access-group input PERMIT-ALL
  access-group output PERMIT-ALL
  no shutdown
!
ip route 0.0.0.0 0.0.0.0 30.30.5.4
!
```

Again, no special configuration is required on the WAE when ACE is used for interception. The default gateway configured on the WAE is the IP address of the WAE VLAN configured in ACE.

Scaling Transparent Interception

As organizations continue to consolidate more and more IT resources into the data center, the data center becomes a natural aggregation point for traffic from the remote branch offices. Due to the high traffic volumes, diverse routing paths, and increasing number of data center resources accessed from remote branch offices, in-path deployment models are not considered a scalable solution for data center environments. The preferred transparent interception method in data center environments is either WCCP or ACE/CSM. Both of these interception methods provide the availability and scalability features required to support large-scale WAAS deployments. Each interception method, along with best practice recommendations and configuration examples, is discussed in turn in the following sections.

WCCP Scalability

The placement of services 61 and 62 in the router configuration plays an important role in the scalability of the WAAS solution. When multiple WAEs are deployed in the branch, the goal is to distribute load across the WAEs in the service group as evenly as possible. The TCP promiscuous services perform load distribution at IP address–level granularity. In most environments, the number of clients is far greater than the number of servers; therefore, performing load distribution based on the client IP address makes it statistically more likely that clients will be distributed more evenly across multiple WAEs. In contrast, if load is distributed based on server IP address, the effectiveness of DRE could potentially increase, because all content for a single server IP address would reside in a single WAE. However, using the server IP address does not allow for linear scalability of the solution. In addition, there is a potential for "hot spots," where in a cluster of WAEs only one or two WAEs are used for the majority of traffic. This can happen due to the limited number of server IP addresses, and the potential for virtual IP addresses, proxy addresses, and other heavily used destination IP addresses being pinned to a single WAE.

The hash function used by WCCP hash assignment is designed to distribute client load across all of the WAEs in a service group. Although this is appropriate for branch office deployments, load distribution in the data center must also take into consideration the fan-out ratio. Take for example a branch office with hosts using IP addresses in the 10.48.136.0/23 network. In the data center there are three WAEs deployed in a cluster. Example 6-8 shows the hash bucket distribution for each of the three WAEs.

Example 6-8   *Data Center WAE Hash Bucket Distribution*

```
AST6-RTR-02# show ip wccp 61 detail
WCCP Client information:
        WCCP Client ID:         10.88.81.2
        Protocol Version:       2.0
        State:                  Usable
        Initial Hash Info:      00000000000000000000000000000000
                                00000000000000000000000000000000
        Assigned Hash Info:     FFFFFFFFFFFFFFFFFFFFFFC0000000000
                                00000000000000000000000000000000
        Hash Allotment:         86 (33.59%)
        Packets s/w Redirected: 0
        Connect Time:           1d22h
        Bypassed Packets
          Process:              0
          Fast:                 0
          CEF:                  0
        WCCP Client ID:         10.88.80.138
        Protocol Version:       2.0
        State:                  Usable
        Initial Hash Info:      00000000000000000000000000000000
                                00000000000000000000000000000000
        Assigned Hash Info:     00000000000000000000000000000000
                                FFFFFFFFFFFFFFFFFFFFFF80000000000
        Hash Allotment:         85 (33.20%)
        Packets s/w Redirected: 0
        Connect Time:           00:01:55
        Bypassed Packets
          Process:              0
          Fast:                 0
          CEF:                  0
        WCCP Client ID:         10.88.80.137
        Protocol Version:       2.0
        State:                  Usable
        Initial Hash Info:      00000000000000000000000000000000
                                00000000000000000000000000000000
        Assigned Hash Info:     0000000000000000000003FFFFFFFFFF
                                0000000000000000000007FFFFFFFFFF
        Hash Allotment:         85 (33.20%)
        Packets s/w Redirected: 0
        Connect Time:           00:00:50
```

continues

Example 6-8 *Data Center WAE Hash Bucket Distribution (Continued)*

```
        Bypassed Packets
            Process:              0
            Fast:                 0
            CEF:                  0
AST6-RTR-02#
```

In the preceding output, each WAE has received roughly 33 percent of the hash buckets in the table. Which data center WAE they will be redirected to can be determined by looking at a small sample of client IP addresses from the branch network. Example 6-9 shows the results of this test.

Example 6-9 *Client Distribution Across Data Center WAEs*

```
AST6-RTR-02# show ip wccp 61 hash 0.0.0.0 10.48.136.10 0 0
WCCP hash information for:
    Primary Hash:   Src IP: 10.48.136.10
        Bucket: 184
    WCCP Client: 10.88.81.2
AST6-RTR-02#
AST6-RTR-02# show ip wccp 61 hash 0.0.0.0 10.48.136.50 0 0
WCCP hash information for:
    Primary Hash:   Src IP: 10.48.136.50
        Bucket: 128
    WCCP Client: 10.88.80.137
AST6-RTR-02# show ip wccp 61 hash 0.0.0.0 10.48.136.200 0 0
WCCP hash information for:
    Primary Hash:   Src IP: 10.48.136.200
        Bucket: 122
    WCCP Client: 10.88.80.138
AST6-RTR-02# show ip wccp 61 hash 0.0.0.0 10.48.137.20 0 0
WCCP hash information for:
    Primary Hash:   Src IP: 10.48.137.20
        Bucket: 167
    WCCP Client: 10.88.80.137
AST6-RTR-02# show ip wccp 61 hash 0.0.0.0 10.48.137.70 0 0
WCCP hash information for:
    Primary Hash:   Src IP: 10.48.137.70
        Bucket: 245
    WCCP Client: 10.88.81.2
AST6-RTR-02# show ip wccp 61 hash 0.0.0.0 10.48.137.222 0 0
WCCP hash information for:
    Primary Hash:   Src IP: 10.48.137.222
        Bucket: 109
    WCCP Client: 10.88.80.138
AST6-RTR-02#
```

You can see from the output that clients from a single branch are redirected to all three WAEs in the data center cluster. This results in a DRE context for the branch office WAE in every data center WAE. While this may not pose a problem for small and medium-sized WAAS deployments, as you start to scale to hundreds or thousands of WAEs, keeping a DRE context for every remote WAE in every data center WAE does not scale. For example, if you have a WAAS deployment made up of 350 remote branch offices, you may choose to deploy three WAE-7341s in the data center to support the fan-out ratio. However, when hash assignment is used, each of the three WAE-7341s will likely have a peer relationship with all 350 remote branch WAEs. Therefore, when the number of remote WAEs in a deployment exceeds the fan-out ratio supported by a single WAE in the data center, hash assignment is not recommended.

With WCCP mask assignment, you can influence the load distribution by adjusting the position of the bit in the mask to take only the network portion of the IP address into consideration. Example 6-10 shows the mask/value set distribution across the three WAEs in the data center.

Example 6-10 *Data Center WAE Mask/Value Distribution*

```
DCN-CAT-8# show ip wccp 61 detail
WCCP Cache-Engine information:
        Web Cache ID:           10.88.81.2
        Protocol Version:       2.0
        State:                  Usable
        Redirection:            GRE
        Packet Return:          GRE
        Packets Redirected:     0
        Connect Time:           00:02:53
        Assignment:             MASK
        Mask   SrcAddr    DstAddr     SrcPort DstPort
        ----   -------    -------     ------- -------
        0000: 0x00001741 0x00000000 0x0000  0x0000
        Value SrcAddr    DstAddr     SrcPort DstPort CE-IP
        ----- -------    -------     ------- ------- -----
        0042: 0x00001240 0x00000000 0x0000  0x0000  0x0A585102 (10.88.81.2)
        0043: 0x00001241 0x00000000 0x0000  0x0000  0x0A585102 (10.88.81.2)
        0044: 0x00001300 0x00000000 0x0000  0x0000  0x0A585102 (10.88.81.2)
        0045: 0x00001301 0x00000000 0x0000  0x0000  0x0A585102 (10.88.81.2)
        0046: 0x00001340 0x00000000 0x0000  0x0000  0x0A585102 (10.88.81.2)
        0047: 0x00001341 0x00000000 0x0000  0x0000  0x0A585102 (10.88.81.2)
        0048: 0x00001400 0x00000000 0x0000  0x0000  0x0A585102 (10.88.81.2)
        0049: 0x00001401 0x00000000 0x0000  0x0000  0x0A585102 (10.88.81.2)
        0050: 0x00001440 0x00000000 0x0000  0x0000  0x0A585102 (10.88.81.2)
        0051: 0x00001441 0x00000000 0x0000  0x0000  0x0A585102 (10.88.81.2)
        0052: 0x00001500 0x00000000 0x0000  0x0000  0x0A585102 (10.88.81.2)
        0053: 0x00001501 0x00000000 0x0000  0x0000  0x0A585102 (10.88.81.2)
        0054: 0x00001540 0x00000000 0x0000  0x0000  0x0A585102 (10.88.81.2)
        0055: 0x00001541 0x00000000 0x0000  0x0000  0x0A585102 (10.88.81.2)
        0056: 0x00001600 0x00000000 0x0000  0x0000  0x0A585102 (10.88.81.2)
```

continues

Example 6-10 *Data Center WAE Mask/Value Distribution (Continued)*

```
0057: 0x00001601 0x00000000 0x0000   0x0000   0x0A585102 (10.88.81.2)
0058: 0x00001640 0x00000000 0x0000   0x0000   0x0A585102 (10.88.81.2)
0059: 0x00001641 0x00000000 0x0000   0x0000   0x0A585102 (10.88.81.2)
0060: 0x00001700 0x00000000 0x0000   0x0000   0x0A585102 (10.88.81.2)
0061: 0x00001701 0x00000000 0x0000   0x0000   0x0A585102 (10.88.81.2)
0062: 0x00001740 0x00000000 0x0000   0x0000   0x0A585102 (10.88.81.2)
0063: 0x00001741 0x00000000 0x0000   0x0000   0x0A585102 (10.88.81.2)

Web Cache ID:           10.88.80.137
Protocol Version:       2.0
State:                  Usable
Redirection:            GRE
Packet Return:          GRE
Packets Redirected:     0
Connect Time:           00:01:44
Assignment:             MASK
Mask   SrcAddr    DstAddr     SrcPort DstPort
....   .......    .......     ....... .......
0000: 0x00001741 0x00000000 0x0000   0x0000
Value SrcAddr    DstAddr     SrcPort DstPort CE-IP
..... .......    .......     ....... ....... .....
0011: 0x00000241 0x00000000 0x0000   0x0000   0x0A585089 (10.88.80.137)
0012: 0x00000300 0x00000000 0x0000   0x0000   0x0A585089 (10.88.80.137)
0013: 0x00000301 0x00000000 0x0000   0x0000   0x0A585089 (10.88.80.137)
0014: 0x00000340 0x00000000 0x0000   0x0000   0x0A585089 (10.88.80.137)
0015: 0x00000341 0x00000000 0x0000   0x0000   0x0A585089 (10.88.80.137)
0016: 0x00000400 0x00000000 0x0000   0x0000   0x0A585089 (10.88.80.137)
0017: 0x00000401 0x00000000 0x0000   0x0000   0x0A585089 (10.88.80.137)
0018: 0x00000440 0x00000000 0x0000   0x0000   0x0A585089 (10.88.80.137)
0019: 0x00000441 0x00000000 0x0000   0x0000   0x0A585089 (10.88.80.137)
0020: 0x00000500 0x00000000 0x0000   0x0000   0x0A585089 (10.88.80.137)
0021: 0x00000501 0x00000000 0x0000   0x0000   0x0A585089 (10.88.80.137)
0022: 0x00000540 0x00000000 0x0000   0x0000   0x0A585089 (10.88.80.137)
0023: 0x00000541 0x00000000 0x0000   0x0000   0x0A585089 (10.88.80.137)
0024: 0x00000600 0x00000000 0x0000   0x0000   0x0A585089 (10.88.80.137)
0025: 0x00000601 0x00000000 0x0000   0x0000   0x0A585089 (10.88.80.137)
0026: 0x00000640 0x00000000 0x0000   0x0000   0x0A585089 (10.88.80.137)
0027: 0x00000641 0x00000000 0x0000   0x0000   0x0A585089 (10.88.80.137)
0028: 0x00000700 0x00000000 0x0000   0x0000   0x0A585089 (10.88.80.137)
0029: 0x00000701 0x00000000 0x0000   0x0000   0x0A585089 (10.88.80.137)
0030: 0x00000740 0x00000000 0x0000   0x0000   0x0A585089 (10.88.80.137)
0031: 0x00000741 0x00000000 0x0000   0x0000   0x0A585089 (10.88.80.137)
Web Cache ID:           10.88.80.138
Protocol Version:       2.0
State:                  Usable
Redirection:            GRE
Packet Return:          GRE
Packets Redirected:     0
Connect Time:           00:00:44
Assignment:             MASK
Mask   SrcAddr    DstAddr     SrcPort DstPort
....   .......    .......     ....... .......
```

Example 6-10   *Data Center WAE Mask/Value Distribution (Continued)*

```
         0000: 0x00001741 0x00000000 0x0000  0x0000
         Value SrcAddr    DstAddr    SrcPort DstPort CE-IP
         ----- -------    -------    ------- ------- -----
         0000: 0x00000000 0x00000000 0x0000  0x0000  0x0A58508A (10.88.80.138)
         0001: 0x00000001 0x00000000 0x0000  0x0000  0x0A58508A (10.88.80.138)
         0002: 0x00000040 0x00000000 0x0000  0x0000  0x0A58508A (10.88.80.138)
         0003: 0x00000041 0x00000000 0x0000  0x0000  0x0A58508A (10.88.80.138)
         0004: 0x00000100 0x00000000 0x0000  0x0000  0x0A58508A (10.88.80.138)
         0005: 0x00000101 0x00000000 0x0000  0x0000  0x0A58508A (10.88.80.138)
         0006: 0x00000140 0x00000000 0x0000  0x0000  0x0A58508A (10.88.80.138)
         0007: 0x00000141 0x00000000 0x0000  0x0000  0x0A58508A (10.88.80.138)
         0008: 0x00000200 0x00000000 0x0000  0x0000  0x0A58508A (10.88.80.138)
         0009: 0x00000201 0x00000000 0x0000  0x0000  0x0A58508A (10.88.80.138)
         0010: 0x00000240 0x00000000 0x0000  0x0000  0x0A58508A (10.88.80.138)
         0032: 0x00001000 0x00000000 0x0000  0x0000  0x0A58508A (10.88.80.138)
         0033: 0x00001001 0x00000000 0x0000  0x0000  0x0A58508A (10.88.80.138)
         0034: 0x00001040 0x00000000 0x0000  0x0000  0x0A58508A (10.88.80.138)
         0035: 0x00001041 0x00000000 0x0000  0x0000  0x0A58508A (10.88.80.138)
         0036: 0x00001100 0x00000000 0x0000  0x0000  0x0A58508A (10.88.80.138)
         0037: 0x00001101 0x00000000 0x0000  0x0000  0x0A58508A (10.88.80.138)
         0038: 0x00001140 0x00000000 0x0000  0x0000  0x0A58508A (10.88.80.138)
         0039: 0x00001141 0x00000000 0x0000  0x0000  0x0A58508A (10.88.80.138)
         0040: 0x00001200 0x00000000 0x0000  0x0000  0x0A58508A (10.88.80.138)
         0041: 0x00001201 0x00000000 0x0000  0x0000  0x0A58508A (10.88.80.138)
DCN-CAT-8#
```

The default mask used for mask assignment is 0x1741. Looking at the same six IP addresses from the branch office, the mask function results in the redirection outlined in Table 6-1.

Table 6-1   *Client Distribution Across Data Center WAEs*

IP Address	Mask	Result	WAE
0xa30880a (10.48.136.10)	0x1741	0x0	10.88.80.138
0xa308832 (10.48.136.50)	0x1741	0x0	10.88.80.138
0xa3088c8 (10.48.136.200)	0x1741	0x40	10.88.80.138
0xa308914 (10.48.138.20)	0x1741	0x100	10.88.80.138
0xa308946 (10.48.137.70)	0x1741	0x140	10.88.80.138
0xa3089de (10.48.137.222)	0x1741	0x140	10.88.80.138

In this case, the default mask is sufficient to redirect all traffic from the remote branch office to a single WAE in the data center cluster. However, if the number of WAEs in the cluster increases to 9, traffic sourced from the 10.48.136.0/23 address space begins getting distributed across multiple WAEs in the cluster. Determining when to change the default mask in data center deployments depends on the number of subnet mask bits used on the IP addressing scheme of the remote branch offices.

For large deployments, the default WCCP mask used in the data center should be changed by shifting to the left by the number of host bits in the IP addressing scheme for the remote branch office. By shifting the default mask to the left by the number of host bits in the addressing scheme, the variations in the host addressing are taken out of the load-distribution calculation. In Table 6-1 there are 9 host bits in a /23 addressing scheme. This results in the following change to the default mask:

```
0x1741 << 9 = 0x2e8200
```

Using a mask of 0x2e8200 in this example pins all traffic from 10.48.136.0/23 to a single data center WAE, regardless of the number of WAEs in the cluster. This provides the optimal balance of load distribution and fan-out control.

Application Control Engine Scalability

Similar logic applies when using ACE for transparent interception with WAAS. The mechanism in ACE that controls the distribution of traffic among WAEs is called the predictor method. When intercepting traffic flowing from clients to servers, a predictor method that hashes on the source IP address is applied.

The predictor method is configured in ACE as part of the server farm configuration. The syntax for CLI command is

predictor hash address [source | destination] [*netmask*]

Other predictor methods are available, but this discussion focuses on the address hashing method. Example 6-11 shows the predictor method CLI configuration within ACE.

Example 6-11   *ACE Predictor Method CLI Command*

```
!
serverfarm
 predictor hash address source 255.255.255.0
!
```

This configuration tells ACE to distribute load across the WAEs based on a hash of the first three octets of the source IP address. As with the WCCP mask, the netmask configured as part of the ACE predictor hash address method should focus on the network portion of the IP address. This has the desired effect of redirecting all traffic from the same source network to the same WAE in the data center.

Firewall Integration

Firewalls are a common component deployed within the data center environment. Cisco provides unique integration capabilities between WAAS and Cisco firewall solutions, specifically IOS FW, PIX/ASA appliances, and the Firewall Switch Module (FWSM). Beginning with FWSM software release 3.2.1, FWSM can recognize WAAS-optimized connections and employ security capabilities against these optimized flows. These capabilities include identifying optimized connections by their auto-discovery TCP option, and adjusting to the TCP sequence number space used by the optimized connection. In addition, deep packet inspection capabilities are dynamically disabled, avoiding unnecessary inspection of packet payloads compressed by WAAS. Example 6-12 shows the output of the command **show conn long** *x*, which displays how the FWSM recognized a WAAS-optimized connection, and the connection flag "W" (indicating a WAAS-optimized flow).

Example 6-12 *FWSM Connection Display Output*

```
FWSM# sh conn long 5
0 in use, 3 most used
Flags: A - awaiting inside ACK to SYN, a - awaiting outside ACK to SYN,
       B - initial SYN from outside, b - State bypass, C - CTIQBE media,
       D - DNS, d - dump, E - outside back connection, F - outside FIN,
       f - inside FIN, G - group, g - MGCP, H - H.323, h - H.225.0,
       I - inbound data, i - incomplete, J - GTP, j - GTP data, k - Skinny media,
       M - SMTP data, m - SIP media, n - GUP, O - outbound data,
       P - inside back connection, q - SQL*Net data, R - outside acknowledged FIN,
       R - UDP SUNRPC, r - inside acknowledged FIN, S - awaiting inside SYN,
       s - awaiting outside SYN, T - SIP, t - SIP transient, U - up
       X - xlate creation bypassed, W - WAAS Session
Network Processor 1 connections
Network Processor 2 connections
TCP out 10.1.1.1:2671 in 150.1.1.3:20 idle 0:00:00 Bytes 460698 FLAGS - UOIW

 Flags1: 0xd040 Flags2: 0x0071 Pr_tmout: 0x0002 address: 0x024000e0
 Session ID: 0x0d0e0f5d Xlate ID: 0x0205891f DeltaSeq: 0xf845d440 VCID: 0x0000
 Root:   Send Unack: 0x8005fec8 Next: 0x8005fec8 Scale: 0x07
         Win Size: 0xfff0 TCP Delta: 0x45fe
 NonRoot:Send Unack: 0xd3c0d99e Next: 0xd3c0d9bc Scale: 0x07
         Win Size: 0x2000 TCP Delta: 0xba01
 Ch Ptr (Data): 0x00000000 (Ctrl): 0x024000d6 Fn ID: 0x07 TLV List: 0x00
         AAA Delta: 0x00000000 Lu Last Sync: 0x240b571d
 L7:     Fxup Ctr: 0x0000  Flags: 0xcd3412ab
     Send Next (root): 0x00000000 (non root): 0x00000000
 Mac (root): 0x000ccf6cce80 (non root): 0x00c04f0435fd
 Vlan (root): 0150 (non root): 0080 Ifc (root): 0003 (non root): 0001
 MPC_connTimeout: 0000 mins      MPC_embConnTimeout: 0120 secs
 MPC_halfOpenTimeout: 0000 secs  MPC_halfClosedTimeout: 0000 secs
 MPC_leaf_ext_ptr: 0x0
 PC_Inspect_ptr: 0x0
 Appln Extension: 0x0
 System timestamp: 0x240b5cf6 Connection timestamp: 0x240b5cf5
```

Figure 6-13 shows a sample data center topology with an FWSM deployed in the server farm aggregation layer.

Figure 6-13 *Server Farm Aggregation with FWSM*

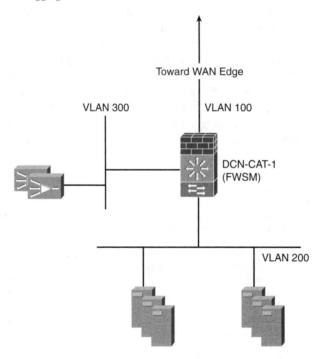

Example 6-13 shows the FWSM configuration for this deployment model.

Example 6-13 *FWSM Configuration with WAAS Interoperability*

```
!
hostname FWSM
enable password 8Ry2YjIyt7RRXU24 encrypted
names
!
interface Vlan200
 nameif server
 security-level 99
 ip address 160.1.1.2 255.255.255.0
!
interface Vlan100
 nameif client
 security-level 10
 ip address 80.1.1.1 255.255.255.0
!
passwd 2KFQnbNIdI.2KYOU encrypted
```

Example 6-13 *FWSM Configuration with WAAS Interoperability (Continued)*

```
ftp mode passive
access-list out2 extended permit tcp any any
access-list out1 extended permit icmp any any echo
access-list out1 extended permit tcp any any eq https
access-list out1 extended permit tcp any any eq 8443
access-list out1 extended permit tcp any any eq www
access-list out1 extended permit tcp any any eq ftp
access-list out1 extended permit tcp any any eq telnet
access-list out1 extended permit tcp any any eq 4050
access-list out1 extended permit tcp any any eq 445
access-list ftp-cap extended permit tcp any any eq ftp
!
<output omitted>
!
icmp permit any server
icmp permit any echo server
icmp permit any client
icmp permit any inside
icmp permit any echo inside
no asdm history enable
arp timeout 14400
nat (inside) 1 0.0.0.0 0.0.0.0
!
static (server,client) 80.1.1.5 150.1.1.3 netmask 255.255.255.255
access-group out1 in interface server
access-group out1 in interface client
access-group out1 in interface inside
route server 170.1.1.0 255.255.255.0 160.1.1.1 1
route server 150.1.1.0 255.255.255.0 160.1.1.1 1
route server 190.1.1.0 255.255.255.0 160.1.1.1 1
route server 80.1.1.5 255.255.255.255 160.1.1.1 1
route client 0.0.0.0 0.0.0.0 70.1.1.2 1
!
<output omitted>
!
class-map inspection_default
 match default-inspection-traffic
!
policy-map global_policy
 class inspection_default
  inspect dns maximum-length 512
  inspect ftp
  inspect h323 h225
  inspect h323 ras
  inspect rsh
  inspect smtp
  inspect sqlnet
  inspect skinny
  inspect sunrpc
  inspect xdmcp
```

continues

Example 6-13 *FWSM Configuration with WAAS Interoperability (Continued)*

```
  inspect sip
  inspect netbios
  inspect tftp
  inspect waas
  inspect icmp
  inspect http
!
service-policy global_policy global
prompt hostname context
!
```

Example 6-13 shows the use of the CLI command **inspect waas**, which enables interoperability between FWSM and WAAS. This command is available in all modes, and can be enabled per context.

Cisco PIX/ASA is also commonly used in data center environments. Like FWSM, PIX/ASA provides interoperability with WAAS beginning in software version 7.2.3. Example 6-14 shows a sample ASA configuration for providing interoperability with WAAS.

Example 6-14 *PIX/ASA Configuration with WAAS Interoperability*

```
!
hostname ASA
domain-name default.domain.invalid
enable password 8Ry2YjIyt7RRXU24 encrypted
names
!
interface GigabitEthernet0/0
 nameif inside
 security-level 100
 ip address 10.30.3.2 255.255.255.0
!
interface GigabitEthernet0/1
 nameif outside
 security-level 0
 ip address 10.30.2.3 255.255.255.0
!
interface GigabitEthernet0/2
 shutdown
 no nameif
 no security-level
 no ip address
!
interface GigabitEthernet0/3
 shutdown
 no nameif
 no security-level
 no ip address
!
interface Management0/0
```

Example 6-14   *PIX/ASA Configuration with WAAS Interoperability (Continued)*

```
nameif management
security-level 100
ip address 171.68.96.120 255.255.255.0
management-only
!
passwd 2KFQnbNIdI.2KYOU encrypted
boot system disk0:/asa722-33-k8.bin
ftp mode passive
dns server-group DefaultDNS
 domain-name default.domain.invalid
same-security-traffic permit intra-interface
access-list outside_access_in extended permit tcp 10.3.0.0 255.255.255.0 any eq
https
access-list outside_access_in extended permit tcp 10.3.0.0 255.255.255.0 any eq 8443
access-list outside_access_in extended permit tcp 10.3.0.0 255.255.255.0 any eq 4050
access-list outside_access_in extended permit tcp 10.3.0.0 255.255.255.0 any eq www
access-list outside_access_in extended permit tcp host 10.0.2.4 any eq 8443
access-list inside_access_in extended permit ip any any
pager lines 24
logging enable
logging console debugging
logging asdm informational
mtu inside 1500
mtu outside 1500
mtu management 1500
no failover
icmp unreachable rate-limit 1 burst-size 1
icmp permit any inside
icmp permit any outside
asdm image disk0:/asdm-522.bin
no asdm history enable
arp timeout 14400
access-group inside_access_in in interface inside
access-group outside_access_in in interface outside
route inside 10.30.0.0 255.255.255.0 10.30.3.1 1
route inside 10.30.1.0 255.255.255.0 10.30.3.1 1
route outside 10.0.2.0 255.255.254.0 10.30.2.1 1
route outside 10.0.254.0 255.255.254.0 10.30.2.1 1
route outside 10.3.0.0 255.255.255.0 10.30.2.1 1
route outside 10.30.4.0 255.255.255.0 10.30.2.1 1
route management 0.0.0.0 0.0.0.0 171.68.96.1 1
timeout xlate 3:00:00
timeout conn 1:00:00 half-closed 0:10:00 udp 0:02:00 icmp 0:00:02
timeout sunrpc 0:10:00 h323 0:05:00 h225 1:00:00 mgcp 0:05:00 mgcp-pat 0:05:00
timeout sip 0:30:00 sip_media 0:02:00 sip-invite 0:03:00 sip-disconnect 0:02:00
timeout uauth 0:05:00 absolute
http server enable
http 0.0.0.0 0.0.0.0 management
no snmp-server location
no snmp-server contact
```

continues

Example 6-14 *PIX/ASA Configuration with WAAS Interoperability (Continued)*

```
snmp-server enable traps snmp authentication linkup linkdown coldstart
telnet 0.0.0.0 0.0.0.0 management
telnet timeout 180
ssh scopy enable
ssh 0.0.0.0 0.0.0.0 management
ssh timeout 5
console timeout 0
!
class-map inspection_default
 match default-inspection-traffic
!
!
policy-map type inspect dns preset_dns_map

 parameters
  message-length maximum 512
policy-map global_policy
  class inspection_default
  inspect dns preset_dns_map
  inspect ftp
  inspect h323 h225
  inspect h323 ras
  inspect netbios
  inspect rsh
  inspect rtsp
  inspect skinny
  inspect esmtp
  inspect sqlnet
  inspect sunrpc
  inspect tftp
  inspect sip
  inspect xdmcp
  inspect waas
!
service-policy global_policy global
prompt hostname context
Cryptochecksum:c11b71317b49a3b461a8a3d7c19e47d1
: end
```

Summary

This chapter looked at the design considerations that are key to a successful WAAS deployment in the data center environment. It looked at different placement and configuration options for transparent interception, and discussed methods to scale transparent interception in the data center to hundreds or thousands of locations. Finally, this chapter looked at the configuration options available for integration between WAAS and popular Cisco firewall solutions, such as PIX/ASA and FWSM. At this point, you should have a solid understanding of the design and network integration options available with Cisco WAAS. Subsequent chapters dive into the deployment and configuration details for the different WAAS components and features.

CHAPTER 7

System and Device Management

The previous chapters have introduced the capabilities of the Cisco WAAS solution and described how the WAE appliances and network modules are integrated into the network. This chapter focuses on how the Cisco WAE devices are initially deployed in the network and then managed centrally by the Cisco WAAS Central Manager.

This chapter provides an overview of Cisco WAE device management and system management, including the capabilities of each. The chapter then focuses on the installation and configuration of each of the components. Device groups, which help minimize ongoing configuration and management overhead, are discussed and examined. Provisioned management capabilities, enabled through role-based access control (RBAC), are discussed and a focus is provided on integrating with external authentication systems. The chapter concludes with a discussion focusing on integration of Cisco WAAS into third-party management and monitoring systems using SNMP and syslog.

It should be noted that this chapter does not provide an exhaustive review of everything that can be configured within Cisco WAAS. Rather, it examines the items necessary to get a system of devices functionally available and ready for central management. Other chapters in this book focus on the details of configuring specific components on a device or within the system. Thus, this chapter lays the management framework foundation that other chapters build upon.

System and Device Management Overview

Each Cisco WAE device can be managed through one of two primary interfaces: the command-line interface (CLI) or the Central Manager (CM) GUI. Deploying a Cisco WAE device requires that you connect to the device through a serial connection to run a CLI initial setup script, which is able to apply the appropriate configuration to the device to make it reachable on the network. Once the WAE device is reachable on the network, you can then connect it to the CM, through the Central Management Subsystem (CMS) service discussed later in this section, or configure it further from the CLI. Use of the CM is recommended, because it is designed to simplify management of each device and the system as a whole while also providing individual device reports and aggregate reports.

This section examines the Cisco WAE setup script and CLI, and provides an overview of the CM and CMS service that runs on each Cisco WAE. This section provides a foundation for future sections in the chapter.

Initial Setup Script and Device Setup

Cisco WAE devices are configured to automatically run the setup script when the device boots for the first time and the administrator is connected to the WAE via a serial connection (9600 baud, 8 data bits, 1 stop bit, no parity bits). The setup script walks you through a series of questions to define the initial configuration of key device settings, including:

- Network interface speed and duplex (or auto-negotiate)
- Network layer configuration (DHCP or static configuration with IP address, subnet mask, default gateway, DNS server, and domain name)

At the end of the initial setup script, you are prompted to save the configuration defined by the responses provided to the script. An example of the initial setup script is shown in Example 7-1.

NOTE   Cisco WAE devices use the startup-config and running-config files in an identical manner to Cisco IOS devices. The setup script ultimately populates these files with the relevant configuration components based on the responses supplied by you.

Example 7-1 *Initial Setup Script*

```
WARNING: Changing any of the network settings from a
telnet session may render the device inaccessible on
the network. Therefore it is suggested that you have
access to the console before modifying the network settings.
Please choose an interface to configure from the following list:
1: GigabitEthernet 1/0
2: GigabitEthernet 2/0
Enter choice: 1
Do you want to configure speed and duplex mode of this interface (y/n) [y]: y
Please enter the speed of this interface (10/100/1000) [100]: 100
Please enter duplex mode (half/full) [full]: full
Do you want to enable DHCP on this interface (y/n) [n]: n
Please enter the IP address of this interface: 10.10.10.10
Please enter the netmask of this interface: 255.255.255.0
Please enter the default gateway: 10.10.10.1
Please enter the domain name server ip: 10.10.10.100
Please enter the domain name: cisco.com
Please enter the hostname: WAE
Based on the following input, the following CLIs will be configured:
    interface GigabitEthernet 1/0
```

Example 7-1   *Initial Setup Script (Continued)*

```
        ip address 10.10.10.10 255.255.255.0
        no autosense
        bandwidth 100
        full-duplex
        exit
      ip default-gateway 10.10.10.1
      ip name-server 10.10.10.100
      ip domain-name cisco.com
      hostname WAE
Do you want to apply the configurations (y/n) [y]: y
```

NOTE   When using auto-negotiate on the WAE, ensure that the adjacent device switchport (for instance, on the switch) is configured as auto-negotiate or full-duplex. Always verify that the connection between the WAE and the adjacent device uses full-duplex operation by using the relevant **show interface** commands on both the switch and the WAE. Use of half duplex will result in lower performance than what is possible when using full duplex.

It is recommended that duplex be hard-coded when working with interface speeds other than Gigabit. Gigabit configurations are automatically full duplex.

This setup script is available upon subsequent boot operations by interrupting the boot sequence by pressing Enter when prompted by the CLI and setting boot flags. Alternatively, you can execute the command **setup** to run the setup script again in the future. Example 7-2 shows where the boot sequence is interrupted, and what prompts are provided.

Example 7-2   *Interrupting the WAE Boot Sequence*

```
Cisco WAAS boot:hit RETURN to set boot flags:0009
Available boot flags (enter the sum of the desired flags):
0x4000 - bypass nvram config
0x8000 - disable login security
[CE boot - enter bootflags]:0x8000
You have entered boot flags = 0x8000
Boot with these flags? [yes]:yes
Setting the configuration flags to 0x8000 lets you into the system, bypassing all
security. Setting the configuration flags field to 0x4000 lets you bypass the NVRAM
configuration.
```

Although the setup script will get the Cisco WAE onto the network, further configuration is necessary to leverage the full acceleration capabilities of Cisco WAAS and centralized management. Along with supplying the basic network information, you must also set the primary interface, define the device mode, define the CM (when configuring an accelerator), enable CMS, and finally save the configuration.

The primary interface of the WAE is used to determine which interface will be used for CM registration, status and health message exchange, and CIFS acceleration transport binding. The primary interface must be assigned prior to enabling CMS, and is performed through the command shown in Example 7-3.

Example 7-3 *Defining the WAE Primary Interface*

```
WAE1# config term
WAE1(config)# primary-interface gigabitEthernet 1/0
```

It is important to ensure that the WAE is able to reach any management-related peers (CM, syslog servers, SNMP servers). Always ensure that the primary interface defined is either on the same subnet as the default gateway or that the appropriate static routes are defined. In most deployments, the primary interface is adjacent to the default gateway, but in situations where multiple addressable WAE interfaces are configured, there may be situations where the default gateway is adjacent to an interface that is not the primary interface. In such deployments, static routes must be defined that point to the next-hop router for the interface that is not the primary interface.

The next step after defining the primary interface is to specify the device mode. The device mode dictates the "personality" of the WAE. For WAEs that are being deployed as a CM (whether it is primary or standby), the "central-manager" device mode would be applied, whereas for WAEs that are being deployed in the network for the purposes of acceleration, the "application-accelerator" device mode would be used (a detailed examination of Central Manager is provided later in the chapter). A Cisco WAE can run only one device mode at a time and cannot run both device modes concurrently. Example 7-4 shows how to specify the device mode for a Cisco WAE.

Example 7-4 *Defining the WAE Device Mode*

```
WAE1(config)# device mode central-manager
```

NOTE Cisco WAEs default to the "application-accelerator" device mode. When configuring a Cisco WAE with the "central-manager" device mode for the first time, you need to reboot the WAE. The console session will notify you of this requirement. Be sure to save your configuration prior to rebooting the WAE. This step can be skipped when deploying devices that will participate in acceleration services, because the configuration will default to the appropriate device mode.

When configuring a Cisco WAE as a CM, it is important to also specify the role (either a primary or standby CM). Configuring a Cisco WAE as a "primary" makes it the active CM in the deployment. Configuring a Cisco WAE as a "standby" makes it a backup for the primary. Standby CM WAEs will, like WAEs configured as accelerators, continually synchronize with the primary CM, including all configuration and reporting data for the entire WAAS network. WAEs configured as standby CMs may be configured *before* the primary CM has been configured; however, CMS cannot be enabled on a standby CM until the primary CM is configured, operational, and reachable on the network. Example 7-5 shows the command syntax for specifying a CM role.

Example 7-5 *Configuring Central Manager Role*

```
WAE1(config)# central-manager role ?
  primary  Set Central Manager role to primary
  standby  Set Central Manager role to standby
WAE1(config)# central-manager role primary
```

NOTE   Cisco WAEs that have been configured as CMs through the device mode command default to a CM role of primary. To configure a CM as a standby, be sure to use the command shown in Example 7-5.

The next configuration step for each Cisco WAE *other* than the primary CM is to specify who the CM is (WAEs that are defined as a primary CM use themselves as the primary CM). This step tells the WAE either the IP address or the hostname of the primary CM WAE. If you are using a hostname for the CM address definition, ensure that DNS is configured and working properly. Use of a hostname for the CM address definition is recommended, because it provides IP address portability for the CM WAE. Should you need to change the IP address of the CM, and each managed WAE uses the DNS name of the CM WAE in its configuration, no change is needed to all of the WAEs in the network. If managed WAEs in the network use the IP address of the CM in their configuration and you need to change the IP of the CM, you would need to change the definition on *each* managed WAE in the network. Example 7-6 shows how to point a WAE to the CM.

Example 7-6 *Specifying the Central Manager*

```
WAE1(config)# central-manager address cm1.cisco.com
```

Once the CM has been defined, and you have verified that the CM is reachable through the network (by ping or other mechanism), you can then enable CMS on each of the WAEs in the network. CMS is a service that runs locally on each WAE that allows it to remain loosely synchronized with the current primary CM based on a scheduled defined within the CM itself. The CMS service allows you to employ configuration changes from the CM GUI and have those changes propagate to the relevant WAEs managed by that CM. Additionally, the

CM continuously collects health, monitoring, and reporting data from each of the managed WAEs and provides visualization and reports for you. You must enable CMS not only on the CM WAEs but also on all accelerator WAEs in the network. Example 7-7 shows how to enable CMS services on a WAE.

Example 7-7 *Enabling Centralized Management Services*

```
WAE1(config)# cms enable
Generating new RPC certificate/key pair
Restarting RPC services
Registering WAAS Central Manager...
Please wait, initializing CMS tables
Successfully initialized CMS tables
Registration complete.
Please preserve running configuration using 'copy running-config startup-config'.
Otherwise management service will not be started on reload and node will be shown
'offline' in WAAS Central Manager UI.
management services enabled
```

NOTE This command must be completed after the definition of the primary interface, device mode and role, and specifying the IP or hostname of the CM. Always use the IP or hostname of the primary CM and not the standby. CMS must be enabled on every WAE in the network.

Finally, it is best practice to save your configuration often. As with other Cisco devices, using the trusted **write mem** or **copy run start** command will suffice.

Command-Line Interface

As demonstrated in the previous section, each WAE is equipped with a fully functional Cisco IOS–like CLI. This CLI is available through a serial connection, Telnet, or SSH. By default, Telnet is enabled and SSH is disabled. Example 7-8 shows how to disable Telnet and enable SSH if so desired.

Example 7-8 *Controlling Console Access to the WAE*

```
WAE1(config)# no telnet enable
WAE1(config)# ssh-key-generate key-length 1024
WAE1(config)# sshd version 2
WAE1(config)# sshd enable
```

NOTE   The **ssh-key-generate** command supports key lengths between 512 and 1024 bytes. The key length should not be less than 768 bytes due to compatibility problems with most modern SSH clients.

The WAE CLI enables you to adjust every aspect of the WAE configuration that is isolated to that particular WAE. This includes network integration, network interception, and local optimization policies. Functions that are implemented at a system level that involve interaction between multiple WAEs, such as CIFS acceleration, must be configured from the CM GUI. It is recommended that, due to its simplicity, you use the CM for all aspects of device configuration when possible. This also helps ensure configuration and policy consistency across a global network of devices, which will minimize ongoing administration and troubleshooting.

The WAE CLI also provides you with insight into detailed statistics about the WAE. Such statistics include network statistics, optimization statistics (including compression ratios and connections optimized), and hardware utilization (CPU, disk, memory). This data is also captured during the CMS synchronization process and is sent to the CM for reporting and monitoring. An examination of key statistics and reports is provided in Chapter 8, "Configuring WAN Optimization," and Chapter 9, "Configuring Application Acceleration."

Central Manager Overview

The Cisco WAAS Central Manager is a secure, scalable, and simple management system built on a distributed computing architecture that is designed to simplify the deployment, management, and monitoring of a large-scale Cisco WAAS network. Central Manager is a device mode that is configured on a WAE in the network. After services have been initialized and activated, this WAE then provides a web GUI for management users, while also communicating directly with each Cisco WAE in the network for the purposes of

- Synchronizing device configuration
- Gathering health and liveliness information
- Retrieving monitoring and statistics data

Central Manager is *secure* in that it uses HTTP over Secure Sockets Layer (HTTPS using TCP port 8443) for management GUI access. Users must authenticate to the CM either using a preconfigured local user account or through integration with a back-end authentication provider such as RADIUS, TACACS, or Active Directory. Furthermore, all data exchange between the CM and managed WAE accelerators is done using HTTPS over TCP port 443. Key management is simplified with Cisco WAAS in that keys are self-signed and generated by the CM and the managed nodes.

NOTE   If firewalls exist in your environment, be sure to allow TCP ports 443 and 8443 to pass through. These ports are used for management and CMS services. It is also recommended that ports for Telnet (TCP 23), SSH (TCP 22), SNMP (UDP 161, 162) and syslog (UDP 514) be permitted. NetBIOS (TCP 135, 137, 138, 139) should be enabled if registering a WAE into a domain when a firewall is deployed between the WAE and the domain controller. CIFS ports should be enabled when using WAE print services where users are connecting through a firewall (TCP 139, 445, 50139). DNS ports should be enabled when performing name resolution on a WAE through a firewall (UDP 53).

Central Manager is *scalable* in that up to 2500 nodes can be managed under a single CM. The number of nodes that can be managed by a single CM is based on which hardware platform is selected. Sizing for CM was discussed in detail in Chapter 2, "Cisco Wide Area Application Engine (WAE) Family." Additionally, a standby CM can be deployed to ensure high availability. Because the standby CM WAE synchronizes its local CMS database with the primary CM (including configuration, monitoring data, reporting data, and more), if the primary fails, the standby can take over operation. Deploying a standby CM provides only high availability and does nothing to increase the number of nodes that can be managed. For deployments larger than 2500 nodes, multiple autonomous (independent) CMs will be necessary.

Central Manager is *simple* in that it provides a powerful yet easy-to-use interface for managing a large WAAS deployment and powerful reporting capabilities. CM has the ability to logically group WAE devices into device groups, which allows you to apply a configuration change to a single entity. Changes applied to a device group are automatically propagated to the managed WAEs within that device group by the CM. With device groups, you can apply a configuration change across the entire WAAS network with a few clicks, and the CM handles the distribution of the configuration change automatically to all WAE devices in the device group.

Figure 7-1 shows the CM GUI login page, which is accessible by browsing to the IP address or DNS name of the CM WAE using HTTPS and specifying port 8443 (that is, https://ip_address_of_cm_wae:8443). The default administrator account is **admin** and the default password for this account is **default**.

Figure 7-1   *Central Manager Login Page*

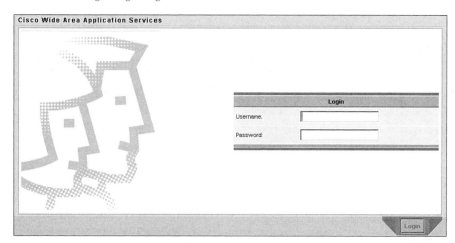

Figure 7-2 shows the CM homepage that is displayed after login. Notice that the CM homepage provides the following information and functions:

- **System Status:** Health indicator showing whether or not any alarms have been triggered and their severity. System status is displayed as a series of lights of different colors (including green, amber, yellow, and red).

- **Devices:** Displays the number of WAE devices in the Cisco WAAS network, and the number of WAE devices configured as core or edge CIFS acceleration devices.

- **Software Version(s):** Displays the software versions installed on the WAE devices in the Cisco WAAS network. If disparate software versions are detected, each is listed.

- **Reports:** Include the application traffic mix for the last week, and the top 10 applications by percent reduction for the last week.

- **Active Alarms and Acknowledged Alarms:** Provide details of the alarms that have been triggered, the associated device, severity, and additional data.

The CM allows you to configure virtually every aspect of the Cisco WAAS network, including device configuration, network configuration, network interception, domain integration, optimization policies, and local services (such as print services). Instead of providing an exhaustive examination of each here, details about each are provided in the appropriate sections for each of these topic areas.

Figure 7-2 *Central Manager Homepage*

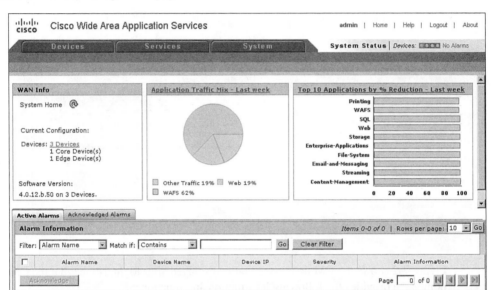

As shown in Figure 7-2, the CM has a hierarchical table of contents; that is, task items are nested within three major tabs, or groupings:

- **Devices:** All configuration aspects of devices and device groups within the Cisco WAAS network, WAN optimization policies, device activation, network interception, and location groups

- **Services:** Configuration of system-wide acceleration services, including CIFS acceleration, print services configuration, application groups, and optimization topology

- **System:** Configuration of system-wide management-related parameters, including CMS intervals, software upgrade and rollback, AAA (authentication, authorization, and accounting), and system logs

Centralized Management System Service

The Centralized Management System (CMS) service is the heart of the management and monitoring framework for Cisco WAAS. CMS is the process that runs on each WAE in the network—whether it is a CM WAE or an accelerator—and ensures that configuration and statistical information remain synchronized between the CM WAE and each managed WAE. CMS uses self-signed and self-generated certificates to encrypt communications between the CM WAE and each managed WAE, and all transmission occurs over TCP port 443. The certificates that are used by CMS are generated when CMS is initialized for the first time, as shown in Example 7-7 earlier in the chapter.

The CMS processes on the CM and on managed WAEs synchronize on a schedule known as the Local Central Management (LCM) cycle. The LCM cycle triggers the synchronization of the CMS processes on a schedule that is configured within the CM GUI itself. A series of variables and their associated parameters dictate the rate of synchronization between the CM and managed WAEs:

- **Data Feed Poll Rate:** Defines the rate at which configuration data is synchronized between the CM and managed WAEs. The configuration synchronization is bidirectional, meaning a configuration change applied on the CM will propagate to a managed WAE. Conversely, a configuration change applied on a managed WAE itself (for instance, via the CLI) will propagate back to the CM. The default value for this parameter is 300 seconds.

- **Health Monitor Collect Rate:** Defines the rate at which the CM examines the health of each managed WAE. This includes service status, load conditions, and subsystem status. Alarms displayed in the CM GUI are based on information gathered during the collection of health monitoring information. The default value for this parameter is 120 seconds.

- **Monitoring Collect Rate:** Defines the rate at which the CM gathers statistics about the optimization components from the WAEs it is managing. This includes information about optimized connections, compression ratios, byte count, traffic mix, and other acceleration data. Graphs displayed in the CM GUI that visualize how the system or an individual WAE is optimizing are based on data collected on this interval. The default value for this parameter is 60 seconds.

NOTE   The preceding variables are configurable within the CM GUI under System > Configuration. Along with these variables, this page allows you to configure other system-wide parameters, including CM GUI session timeout, device recovery key, data retention monitoring, and whether or not overlapping device groups are permitted. Additionally, this page allows you to globally enable or disable monitoring from the CM.

The default values provided by the CM for each of the preceding parameters allow the CM to scale to a level where it can manage the number of WAEs specified in Chapter 2. For smaller deployments, these timers can be decreased to allow for more frequent updating of configuration, health, and monitoring data. Changing these numbers is not recommended unless the number of devices being managed by a CM WAE is less than one-half the supported maximum for that device. Figure 7-3 shows the CM GUI page where the timers can be found.

Figure 7-3 *Central Manager System Timers*

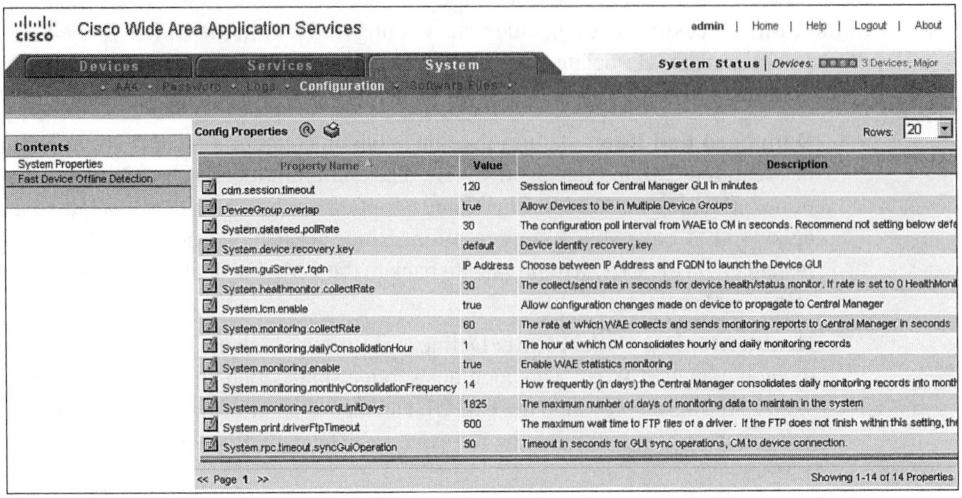

The state of the CMS service can be verified from the CLI of the WAE. The **show cms info** command can be executed on a CM WAE or a managed WAE. This command shows the following:

- Device registration information, including device mode and role. Role is displayed only if the WAE is configured as a CM.

- CMS service information, including the state of the CMS service (shown as cms_cdm in the command output) and management GUI service (shown as cms_httpd in the command output).

Example 7-9 demonstrates the output of this command. In this example, the service is not running, as evidenced in the output of the first execution of **sh cms info**. The example then shows the service being enabled, and then the output of **sh cms info** with the services running correctly.

Example 7-9 *Viewing CMS Registration and Service Status*

```
CM1# sh cms info
Device registration information :
Device registered as              = WAAS Central Manager
Current WAAS Central Manager role = Primary
CMS services information :
Service cms_httpd is not running
Service cms_cdm is not running
CM1# conf t
CM1(config)# cms enable
Please preserve running configuration using 'copy running-config startup-config'.
Otherwise management service will not be started on reload and node will be shown
```

Example 7-9 *Viewing CMS Registration and Service Status (Continued)*

```
'offline' in WAAS Central Manager UI.
CM1(config)# exit
CM1# copy running-config startup-config
CM1# sh cms info
Device registration information :
Device registered as                = WAAS Central Manager
Current WAAS Central Manager role   = Primary
CMS services information :
Service cms_httpd is running
Service cms_cdm is running
```

NOTE   If the cms_cdm service is not running, the device cannot be managed centrally (if configured as an accelerator) or cannot manage WAEs (if configured as a CM). If the cms_httpd service is not running, the management GUI will not be accessible. In situations where the CMS service is disabled on a WAE, it will report as Offline in the CM GUI.

Device Registration and Groups

The previous sections provided details on establishing basic network connectivity to each WAE in the network, defining the CM, and enabling CMS services. During the process of enabling CMS services, a WAE device will "register" with the CM WAE. That is, the WAE will contact the CM and announce that it is interested in associating itself with the CM. In doing so, the WAE can then be managed by the CM, and report monitoring and statistical information back to the CM for visualization. Because the exchange of information between the CM and its managed WAE devices is encrypted, the first step of the process is for the WAE that is attempting to register to generate a self-signed certificate. This certificate, along with the CM WAE certificate, is used to encrypt information exchanged between the CM and the managed WAE.

When a WAE registers with the CM, the CM creates an entry in the CMS database for the registering WAE. This entry is linked to the WAE hostname to provide a simplified means of recovering device identity and configuration if a WAE needs to be replaced. If an entry with that name already exists, the registration of the new WAE fails. In such cases, the existing entry needs to be deleted from the CM GUI, or in the case of device replacement, the identity should be recovered onto the new WAE from the entry that exists in the CM database.

To recover a device identity from the CM database onto a new WAE that is replacing a failed WAE, use the **cms recover identity** command. This command takes an additional argument—the global device identity recovery password—which is set in the CM GUI on the same page as the system timers. For instance, if the global device identity recovery password is **default**, the command shown in Example 7-10 could be used to recover the identity from the CM.

Example 7-10 *Recovering Device Identity*

```
WAE1# cms recover identity default
Registering WAAS Application Engine...
Sending identity recovery request with key default
Registration complete.
```

After executing the device identity recovery process shown in Example 7-10, the WAE device, in terms of its relationship with the CM, is left in a state of "inactive." This is identical to the state that a newly configured WAE device is in after having executed **cms enable** to register with the CM, as shown in Example 7-7. While a WAE is in a state of inactive, either immediately after registration or after identity recovery, it is unable to establish a connection with the CM to synchronize configuration data, reporting information, or health and liveliness information. In this way, it is *registered* with the CM but not *manageable*. Taking a newly registered WAE and enabling it for active participation in the WAAS network through the CM is called *device activation*.

Device Activation

Device activation is a function performed on the CM that can take one or all inactive WAE devices and enable them for active participation within the Cisco WAAS network. Activation is a process that can be done only through the CM GUI and cannot be done through the device CLI. Activation takes a few simple clicks within the CM GUI, and then up to three iterations of the LCM cycle. Therefore, device activation can take up to three times the time interval configured for the CM system data feed poll rate, which is shown in Figure 7-3. Device activation can be performed from one of two locations:

- On the Devices tab homepage, against any and all inactive devices that have registered with the CM
- On the device homepage, for that particular device

When activating all devices from the CM GUI, also known as *global activation*, any devices in an inactive state are changed to active. The icon for this operation is found in the toolbar on the devices homepage at Devices > Device, and is also shown in Figure 7-4. Figure 7-4 also shows the device list homepage.

Figure 7-4   *Device Homepage and Global Activation*

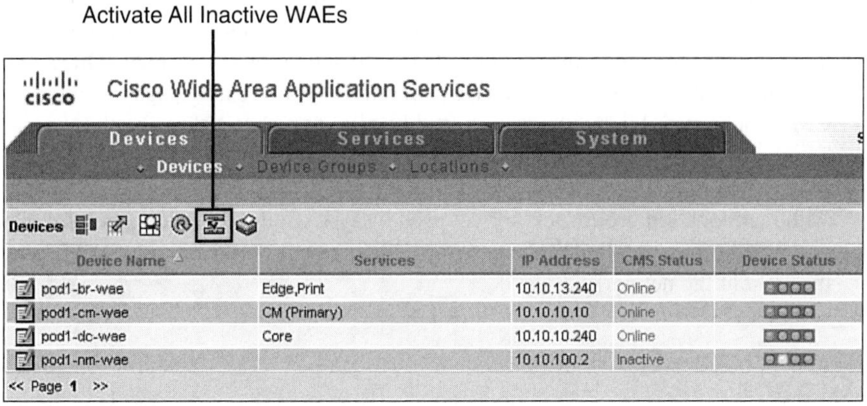

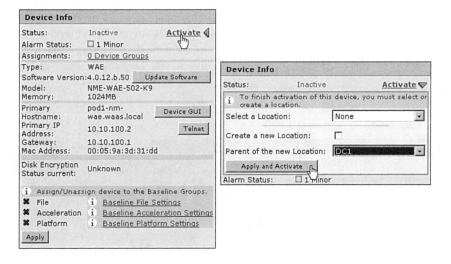

Although it is certainly possible to activate all inactive devices from the device list home-page, it is more common to activate devices as each is registered to the CM. The primary reason that you may want to activate WAE devices individually is that individual activation allows you to define the location group of each WAE (as opposed to putting them all in a single location group or creating a new location group for each). Location groups are not used as of this writing, but will play an integral part in WAAS network design in future releases. Figure 7-5 shows the activation link on the homepage of the inactive WAE device (left) and the activation window (right).

Figure 7-5   *Device Activation*

After a device has been activated, it goes through a state called *Pending* where the initial configuration is being propagated to the device and synchronization is being performed. As mentioned earlier, it generally takes three LCM iterations for the activation to finalize, and the WAE will remain in the *Pending* state until activation is complete. Once activation is completed, the WAE device will have generated keys and established a secure session to the CM, synchronized its configuration, and had its state changed to *Online*.

NOTE   Although location groups are not yet used by WAAS, they provide a helpful means of grasping large-scale deployments by providing visual organization of WAEs deployed throughout the network.

Device Groups

One of the most powerful usability features of the CM is the ability to logically group devices into single configuration containers. These containers, called *device groups*, allow you to rapidly apply a configuration change across multiple WAEs simultaneously. With device groups, the daunting tasks of implementing a seemingly simple configuration change across a large number of devices becomes a painless click of the mouse button.

The CM provides a configuration facility for you to create up to 256 device groups. The configuration page for device groups can be found in the CM GUI at Devices > Device Groups. Devices are added to device groups either during the creation of the device group or by going directly to the device homepage and assigning the WAE to a series of groups. Once a device group has one or more members, configuration changes applied to the device group in the CM GUI are automatically distributed to each of the WAEs that are members of the device group. This distribution of configuration changes happens behind the scenes and without user intervention, which can significantly streamline management. An example of assigning WAE devices to a device group, from the device group configuration page at Devices > Device Groups > (Device Group) > Assign Devices, is shown in Figure 7-6.

Figure 7-6   *Assigning WAEs to a Device Group*

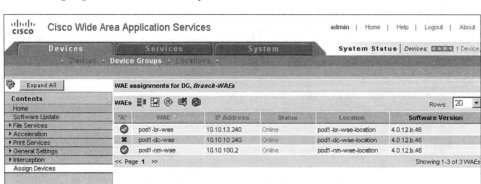

The CM provides a default device group, called *AllDevicesGroup*, which all Cisco WAE devices are automatically joined to upon creation within the CM database. Although the *AllDevicesGroup* device group is commonly used for smaller deployments, it is recommended that you take the small amount of time necessary to think through which device groups are relevant to your organization and minimize use of the AllDevicesGroup device group for anything other than configuration items that are absolutely necessary across the entire infrastructure and will not vary from device to device. Some functional uses of the device grouping capabilities of Cisco WAAS CM include the following:

- **Device group by time zone:** Allows you to employ a common time, date, timezone, and NTP configuration for each device within the same timezone. Also, this allows you to isolate configuration changes to all devices within a specific timezone when necessary.

- **Device group by location type:** Allows you to group devices by classification of the type of location they are deployed in. For instance, you may choose to create a group for all devices that are deployed in data center locations, or create a device group for all devices deployed as router modules. This allows you to apply common configuration settings across all devices in similar location types.

- **Device group by WAN link capacity:** Allows you to group devices by the WAN link type that the device supports. For instance, you may define a "T1" device group, or an "LFN" device group for WAEs that are supporting high-BDP networks. This enables you to apply a common configuration across all devices that are supporting similar link speeds, distances, or other similar characteristics.

- **Device group by services configured:** Allows you to group devices by the types of services configured. For instance, you may have specific devices that perform TCP optimization only, whereas some devices perform full optimization. Alternatively, you may bundle a series of neighboring CIFS core devices together to act as a CIFS core cluster (this is examined in more detail in Chapter 9).

As outlined in the preceding list, there are countless uses for device groups. Device groups can be created to serve just about any configuration purpose. Keep in mind that a device group allows an administrator to configure nearly anything that can be configured directly against an individual WAE, thereby enabling the administrator to "scale themselves", that is, minimize their administrative burden. Also note that changes made to a device group are synchronized with managed WAE devices within that device group on the same schedule that configuration changes applied directly to a managed WAE are made—the LCM cycle. If a WAE is a member of two or more device groups such that configuration conflicts exist, the configuration contained in the last modified device group is applied. Therefore, try to define your device groups and assign devices in such a way that there is very little, if any, overlap.

NOTE   Central Manager WAEs cannot belong to a device group.

Provisioned Management

The CM is also designed to allow multiple discontiguous departments within the same organization to have provisioned management authority. In many environments, it is necessary to allow different teams with different responsibilities—potentially even in different parts of the company—to have some level of administrative privilege over a portion of the infrastructure. Furthermore, many organizations prefer to leverage a centralized, unified platform for authenticating and authorizing users that attempt to access enterprise infrastructure resources. The CM integrates cleanly into environments that have requirements such as these by providing:

- **Role-based access control (RBAC):** Allows for the definition of users, roles, and domains to segregate management responsibility and user privilege across devices in the Cisco WAAS network

- **Integration with authentication providers:** Allows for delegation of authentication functions for users accessing a WAE or the CM to a trusted third party such as TACACS, RADIUS, or Microsoft Active Directory

By providing these two capabilities, the Cisco WAAS CM allows IT organizations with disparate management teams and centralized authentication providers to streamline integration of Cisco WAAS management into their existing IT fabric. The following sections examine each of these systems in detail, along with their configuration.

Role-Based Access Control

RBAC is a feature within the Cisco WAAS CM that provides a flexible means of creating management and administrative domains. With RBAC, the network team can have the appropriate permissions within the CM to adjust the networking parameters on all or specific devices (or groups of devices) within the Cisco WAAS network, while the desktop team is provided access to only configuring CIFS acceleration services or print services.

RBAC is built upon three fundamental components:

- **User:** The entity that is attempting to authenticate with the CM

- **Role:** A template that identifies which pages and functions within the CM that an associated user is able to access

- **Domain:** A template that identifies either a specific set of devices or a specific set of device groups that an associated user is able to access

With the combination of users, roles, and domains, the system-wide administrator for WAAS can, in a very granular fashion, allocate a specific set of configuration pages to all users associated with a particular role. The administrator can then filter the area within the WAAS network from which those configuration pages can be used by applying a domain. In this way, a user, once authenticated, is associated with one or more roles, which determine the pages within the CM the user is allowed to access and functions that the user is able to perform. The user is then associated with a domain, which identifies which devices or device groups a user is able to perform those functions against.

NOTE   Domains can be defined only as a series of unique devices or as a series of device groups. You cannot configure a single domain that contains a list of unique devices along with a list of specific device groups. In such cases, two domains would be necessary.

Users can be assigned to multiple roles and also to multiple domains. Permissions provided to a user in the CM are additive; that is, the sum of all permissions provided to the user by all associated roles is the net effective set of operations the user is allowed to perform. Similarly with domains, the sum of all devices and device groups listed in all domains assigned to the user is the net effective domain of control the user is allowed to impact.

Figure 7-7 shows the configuration page for roles and domains. Note that these pages can be accessed in the CM GUI by going to System > AAA > Roles and System > AAA > Domains.

Figure 7-7   *Roles and Domains Configuration Pages*

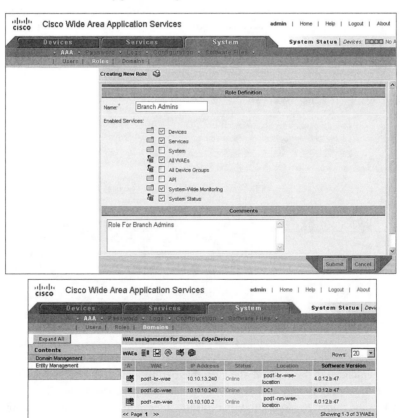

Consider the following example. Zach is a Cisco WAAS administrator and hires Joel to manage his U.S. Cisco WAAS network. Zach also hires Baruch to manage his Cisco WAAS network in Israel. Zach does not want Joel to be able to apply any configuration changes to Baruch's devices in Israel, and he does not want Baruch to be able to change any of Joel's devices in the United States. Zach also has a location in Switzerland where there are two WAEs deployed. Rather than hire an administrator in Switzerland, Zach decides to assign one WAE each to Joel and Baruch, thus dividing management responsibilities for Switzerland between the two.

Using a combination of device groups, users, roles, and domains, Zach's job provisioning Cisco WAAS management is simplified. A single device group for all WAEs in the United States is created, and all WAEs in the United States are assigned to this device group. Similarly, a device group is created for all WAEs in Israel. Joel and Baruch are each assigned to two domains: Joel to a U.S. domain, which calls out the device group for the WAEs in the United States, and another domain that identifies one of the WAEs in Switzerland. Baruch is assigned to the domain that represents the Israel WAEs, and another domain that identifies the other WAE in Switzerland.

Figure 7-8 shows the configuration page for assigning roles and domains to a particular user. Note that this page can be accessed in the CM GUI by going to System > AAA > Users.

Figure 7-8 *Assigning Roles and Domains to a User*

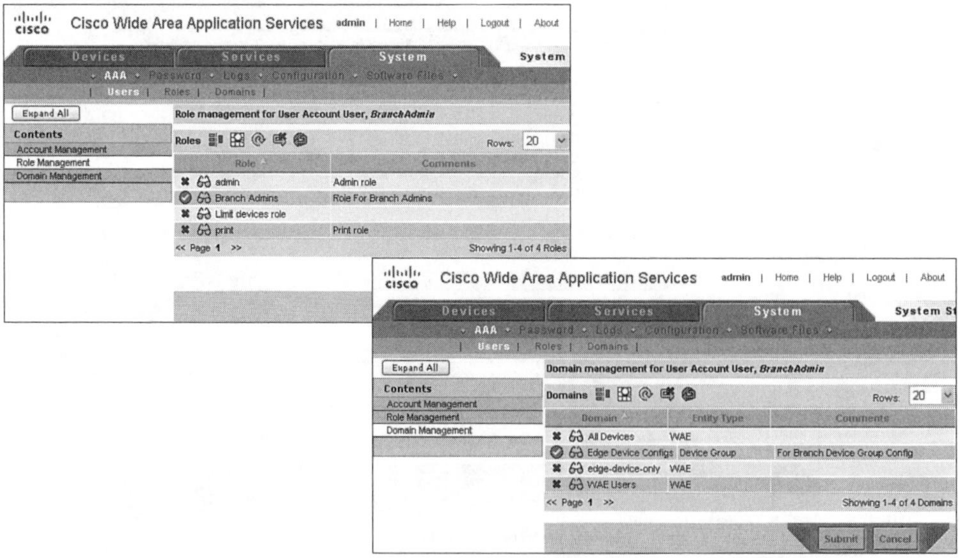

As evidenced in this section, the available permissions and devices against which a user is able to employ change is the sum of the available permissions provided by the assigned roles and domains. Configuration of users, roles, and domains can all be found under System > AAA.

Integration with Centralized Authentication

Authentication for users attempting to access the CM is, by default, performed against a local database stored in the CM WAE itself. Users that are created in the CM are automatically synchronized to each of the WAEs that are managed by that CM. In some deployments, it may be desirable to allow the CM to leverage a third-party centralized authentication provider, such as TACACS, RADIUS, or Active Directory, to manage user accounts and passwords. Cisco WAAS can leverage these third-party providers to authenticate users, which allows you to avoid having to manage user credentials on yet another system deployed within the infrastructure.

While integration with third-party authentication providers does not require that the users be explicitly defined within the CM or within each device, it is recommended that the users be defined. By defining the users (even without supplying the credentials), you can specify either:

- Role assignment within the CM, which dictates the permissions provided to the user upon successful login. Although users can authenticate with the third-party systems, authorization (that is, permission) is still determined by the CM. Thus, roles and domains should be configured, and users should be assigned to roles and domains to specify privilege.

- Privilege level within the device CLI, which dictates the commands that can be executed by the user upon successful login.

In short, a user can log into the system if it is configured for third-party authentication, and will be assigned the default role or permissions upon successful authentication. It is recommended as a best practice that you undertake the following steps to ensure successful integration and security:

- When using third-party authentication, create a series of new roles based on the permissions that authenticated users should have per user type.

- Define all administrative users and assign them to the appropriate groups.

- Minimize the permissions available in the default roles such that any undefined user will have little or no privileges on the system.

- Specify secondary and tertiary servers as needed, with a failover to the local user database. This ensures availability of management access if third-party authentication providers all are unavailable.

Example 7-11 shows how to configure primary and secondary authentication servers as needed, with failover to the local user database. Note that the CLI also allows for the definition of tertiary and quaternary servers as well. Be sure to use the **authentication fail-over server-unreachable** command shown below to only allow login authentication to fail over to the next service in the configuration should the current login server service be unavailable or unreachable. It is best practice to have **local** authentication at the end of the list as an authentication provider of last resort.

Example 7-11 *Configuring Primary and Secondary Servers, and Authentication Failover*

```
WAE# config
WAE(config)# authentication login tacacs enable primary
WAE(config)# authentication configuration tacacs enable primary
WAE(config)# authentication login local enable secondary
WAE(config)# authentication configuration local enable secondary
WAE(config)# authentication fail-over server-unreachable
```

NOTE   **authentication login** commands determine what authentication provider to consult to see if the user has permission to log into the WAE. **authentication configuration** commands determine what authentication provider to consult to see what configuration access privileges the user has on the WAE should he or she authenticate successfully.

Figure 7-9 shows the configuration page for defining an authentication provider. Note that this page can be accessed in the CM GUI by going to Devices > (Devices or device groups) > (device or device group homepage) > General Settings > Authentication. In this example, the WAE will use a Windows Domain for authentication.

Figure 7-9 *Configuring a Third-Party Authentication Provider*

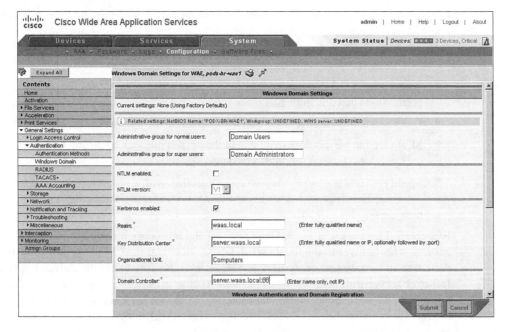

NOTE   When using Windows Domains as third-party authentication providers, it is necessary to join the WAE to the domain. This can be accomplished on the Windows Domain page shown in Figure 7-9. A test tool is supplied on this page to notify you of any issues preventing you from joining the WAE into the domain. Joining the domain requires that the following hold true:

- The domain name must be correctly configured on the WAE, or on a device group that the WAE is a member of.

- The WAE can resolve, using either DNS or explicit configuration, and identify the IP address of a domain controller.

- The WAE has the appropriate authentication protocol enabled (either NTLM or Kerberos) based on the domain type. NTLM should be used only for legacy Windows NT domains, and Kerberos should be used for Windows 2000 and newer domains (mixed mode or native mode).

- System time must be synchronized to the Windows Domain using NTP or static time configuration. The time variance must be less than 5 minutes, and this variance must also account for the date on the system.

Cisco WAAS also provides support for AAA accounting using TACACS, and also honors privilege levels 0 and 15 as supplied by TACACS.

Device Configuration, Monitoring, and Management

The past sections have focused primarily on initial configuration, system management, and integration. This section, in contrast, focuses on the device-specific configuration and management capabilities of the CM, particularly from a device perspective and not from an optimization or service perspective. Chapters 8 and 9 include an examination of using CM to configure and monitor optimization services. Thus, this chapter focuses on configuration and reporting aspects that are not related to the optimization capabilities of Cisco WAAS. This section examines the device homepage, device reports, configurable items, status and health monitoring, and software upgrade and rollback.

Device Homepage

The CM provides you with a tabular list of all the registered WAEs. This tabular list is found on the Devices tab, as shown in Figure 7-10. The device list table provides the following columns, which are helpful in understanding what devices are registered and their status within the system:

- **Device Name:** The name provided using the **hostname** command on the device CLI.

- **Services:** The services that are running on the system beyond basic Layer 4 optimization services. This includes CIFS acceleration services (either Edge, Core, or both), local services, and CM services (either primary or secondary).

- **IP Address:** The IP address on the device.

- **CMS Status:** The status of the CMS services on the device, which can also be representative of status of connectivity from the device to the CM itself. Status will always be one of the following:

  — **Online:** The device is online, healthy, and exchanging information with the CM on the configured schedule.

  — **Offline:** The device is either offline or the network connectivity between the device and the CM has been severed for two or more successive LCM cycles.

  — **Inactive:** The device has registered with the CM but the administrator has yet to activate the device.

  — **Pending:** The device has registered with the CM and the administrator has activated the device, but the CM and the device have not yet finished synchronizing configuration data with one another.

- **Device Status:** The status of the device and its services, visualized in a colorful tree display. The colors displayed include:

  — **Green:** The device is healthy and all configured services are operational.

  — **Yellow:** A warning is present; for instance, a load threshold has been exceeded or an interface is operating in half duplex.

  — **Amber:** An error is present; for instance, an inline group has gone into bypass, a service is down, or a device requires a reboot.

  — **Red:** The device is offline or unavailable and requires attention.

- **Location:** The location that the device is associated with.

- **Software Version:** The version of software that is installed on the device. If a software upgrade is in place, this column also displays details about the software installation.

Figure 7-10 *Device List*

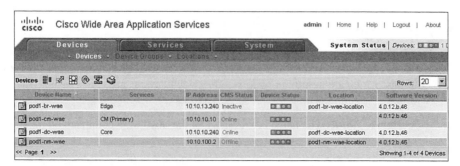

You can select a specific device from the tabular device view by clicking the edit icon shown on the left of each device name in the table. Clicking this icon takes you to the device homepage. Figure 7-11 shows an example of the device homepage.

Figure 7-11   *Device Homepage*

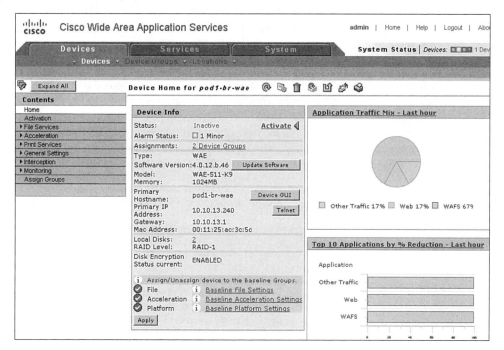

The device homepage provides an immediate status and configuration summary of the device, and a configurable dashboard of reports. The Contents pane on the left side lists the areas in which you can configure the device from the GUI; each configuration change is automatically propagated to the WAE during the LCM cycle:

- **Activation:** Control the activation status of the device, which is useful when first activating a device, or when deactivating a device and making it recoverable during a device recovery scenario

- **File Services:** Configure the CIFS acceleration components of the system, including edge and core services

- **Acceleration:** Configure WAN optimization policies, including enabled features, buffer settings, and classifiers

- **Print Services:** Configure local print services, which allows the WAE to act as a print server in the remote office

- **General Settings:** Configure basic network configuration and integration parameters

- **Interception:** Configure network interception, including WCCPv2 and inline interception
- **Monitoring:** Gather reports from the device for optimization and acceleration services
- **Assign Groups:** Manipulate the group membership of the WAE device

In the middle of the page, the Device Info pane provides a snapshot of the device configuration, including status, alarms, number of device groups, hardware model, memory, software version, network configuration, and disk configuration.

The right side of the screen presents up to four reports as determined by the dashboard configuration. These reports, which primarily deal with WAN optimization and application acceleration services as opposed to device services, can be configured using the "configure dashboard" icon in the toolbar to the right of the text that says "Device Home for *xyz*." The dashboard configuration, which is shown in Figure 7-12, allows you to select up to four reports to visualize on the device homepage. These reports are discussed in detail in Chapters 8 and 9.

Figure 7-12 *Configurable Report Dashboard*

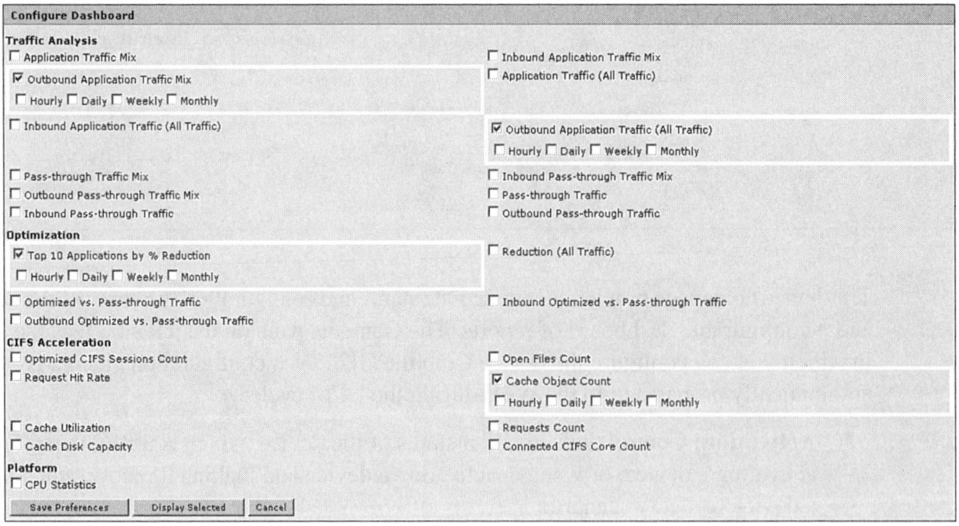

Status and Health Monitoring

Of particular interest on the device homepage, which is also present in the tabular device view and system status view, is the "tree of lights," which is a series of four "bulbs." One or more bulbs are "lit" to reflect the status of the system as an entity (for instance, the bulb for one WAE may be red and the bulb for another may be orange). In the case of a device-specific tree of lights, a single bulb is lit. The tree of lights is displayed not only on the device homepage, which specifies the condition of that particular device, but another tree of lights that represents the system as a whole is presented in the toolbar of every GUI page. Figure 7-13 calls out the locations of the device-specific status indicator and the system-wide status indicator.

Figure 7-13   *Status Indicator Locations*

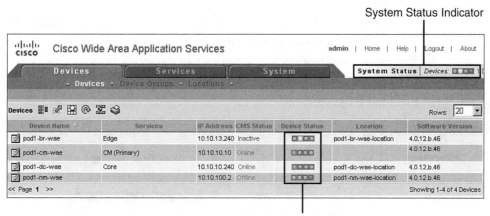

By clicking this status indicator (whether from the system homepage or the device homepage), you are presented with a tabular view of all the alarms and notifications that caused the indicator to be lit. These alarms and notifications could include a variety of situations, such as duplex mismatch, service overload, service failed, reboot required, and so on. When you click the system status indicator, you see an aggregate list of all alarms causing the status indicator color to change—from any device in the system—on a page called Troubleshooting Devices (see Figure 7-14, which shows an example of the window with alarms on two devices). When you click the device status indicator, you see only the list of alarms causing the status indicator color to change relative to that particular device.

The tabular list view on the Troubleshooting Devices page includes all the relevant information needed to appropriately respond to the alarm condition:

- **Device Name:** The name of the device experiencing the alarm condition
- **IP Address:** The IP address of the device experiencing the alarm condition
- **Status:** The status of the device experiencing the alarm condition
- **Severity:** The severity of the alarm represented on that particular row within the tabular list view
- **Alarm Information:** The severity and description of the alarm that caused the status indicator to change

By clicking the alarm information, you are presented with a series of options for resolving the issue:

- **Edit/Monitor Device:** Click to go to the device homepage to examine configuration details and relevant log or statistical data

- **Telnet to Device:** Click to open a Telnet window to allow CLI access to the device in question

- **View Device Log:** Click to examine the log entries that have been generated by the device that has experienced an alarm condition

- **Run Show Commands:** Click to execute CLI commands from the GUI in an effort to troubleshoot or resolve the alarm condition

Figure 7-14 *Troubleshooting Devices Window*

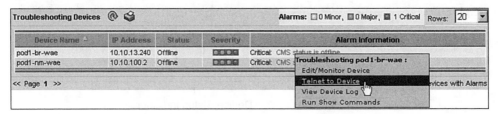

The homepage for the CM, which is presented to the user immediately after login or by clicking the Home link in the upper-right corner, also presents an alarm window. The primary difference between the alarm window on the CM homepage and on the Troubleshooting Devices page is that the alarm window on the CM homepage allows you to filter alarm names and even acknowledge alarms without actually resolving the condition that caused the alarm to be triggered. For instance, if a condition continues to surface, and the appropriate support team has plans to resolve the alarm, you can "acknowledge" the alarm. Acknowledging an alarm does not resolve the issue, but rather keeps the alarm from continuing to display in the alarm list, and from continuing to cause the system status bar to light up.

Figure 7-15 shows the alarm window on the CM homepage, along with the acknowledged alarms.

The Acknowledged Alarms tab provides you with a means of "unacknowledging" alarms as well. That is, if an alarm is accidentally acknowledged, and you want the alarm to continue to be displayed in the alarm list and impact the system status indicator, you can select and unacknowledge that alarm. This returns the alarm to the alarm list.

Figure 7-15   *Alarm Window and Acknowledged Alarms*

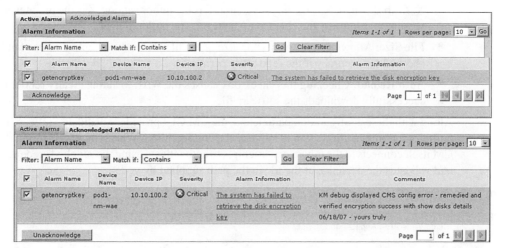

Software Upgrade and Downgrade

The CM provides facilities that enable you to upgrade or downgrade the software version installed on a WAE within the WAAS network seamlessly. From within the CM itself, you can define a software image and all related parameters. This entry, called a software file entry, is nothing more than a link to the actual binary file used to install the software onto the WAE. When a software file entry is applied to a WAE, the details of the entry are sent to that WAE, which causes it to initiate a connection to the download location to begin downloading. If the WAE is successful in its connection attempt, it downloads the file referenced in the link provided to it by the CM. If the download succeeds, the WAE attempts to install the software, and then reboots if the Reboot flag was specified in the software file entry.

The configuration page for defining a software file entry can be found in the CM GUI at System > Software Files, and is shown in Figure 7-16. The parameters associated with a software file entry include:

- **Software File URL:** Includes HTTP and FTP.
- **URL path:** Path and filename for the software image file.
- **Username:** The username that should be supplied by the system (if prompted) to authenticate in order to download the software file.
- **Password:** The password that should be supplied by the system (if prompted) to authenticate in order to download the software file.

- **Software Version:** The version of the software that the file contains, in the format X.Y.Z.b.B, where X is the major version, Y is the minor version, Z is the maintenance version, b is literally the character *b*, and B is the build number.

- **File Size:** Allows you to specify the size of the file. The value supplied in this field is checked for accuracy if the repository permits it.

- **Auto Reload:** Checking this check box causes the WAE to automatically reboot if it successfully downloads the software file.

Along with these configuration parameters, the CM GUI provides a Validate Software File Settings button that allows you to validate the configuration. When you use this tool, the CM itself connects to the repository, attempts to authenticate using the supplied credentials, and validates the presence of the file in the path supplied by you.

Figure 7-16 *Software File Entry Definition Page*

Any time a software upgrade or downgrade is applied to a WAE, that WAE must be rebooted for the new version to take effect. It is important to note that when applying a software image to a CM WAE, if the software image contains an earlier version than the previously installed image, it may be necessary to downgrade the CMS database to support the schema used by the newly installed version.

Example 7-12 shows the output of **show cms info** and **cms database downgrade**, which are used, respectively, to verify that a database downgrade is required and to perform a downgrade of the database. Be sure to disable CMS services prior to the downgrade, and enable CMS services after the downgrade.

Example 7-12   *Downgrading the CMS Database*

```
CM1# sh cms info
DOWNGRADE REQUIRED
------------------
A database downgrade is required to enable CMS services. Please use
the 'cms database downgrade' command to perform the database downgrade.
Device registration information :
Device Id                          = 142
Device registered as               = WAAS Central Manager
Current WAAS Central Manager role   = Primary
CMS services information :
Service cms_httpd is not running
Service cms_cdm is not running
CM1# cms database downgrade

The system will perform a database downgrade without applying a downgrade script.
Please refer to product documentation to confirm that the previously-installed
software release does not require a downgrade script for this release.
Proceed with database downgrade [no]? yes
Creating database backup file cms-db-01-05-2007-03-32.dump
Database downgrade succeeded.
CM1# sh cms info
Device registration information :
Device Id                          = 142
Device registered as               = WAAS Central Manager
Current WAAS Central Manager role   = Primary
CMS services information :
Service cms_httpd is not running
Service cms_cdm is not running
CM1# config term
CM1(config)# cms enable
```

When upgrading a CM to a newer software version, the software installation automatically adjusts the schema of the CMS database if necessary during the reboot. All of the information necessary about prior version database schemas is retained in the CM; thus, when performing an upgrade, the system can automatically identify what version was installed prior and make the appropriate changes to the database to support the new version's schema. However, older versions have no way of knowing what schema a future version will use. As such, a database downgrade may be necessary if downgrading software versions on the CM itself.

An issue related to software upgrade is the recommended order of upgrade. The CM is capable of managing any device that has an equal or newer version of software installed upon it. That is, the CM makes the assumption that any item configurable on the CM GUI can be successfully applied on any WAE managed by that CM. Thus, if the CM is of a newer version than the WAEs that it is managing, it may attempt to configure a feature that the currently installed WAE software is not able to implement or even recognize. Thus, it is required that the CM be the last device in the Cisco WAAS topology to receive a software upgrade.

Software upgrades can be applied directly to a device or to an entire device group. Software upgrades can be done from one of three places:

- **Device homepage:** Click the Update Software button in the Device Info pane (refer to Figure 7-11 earlier in the chapter)

- **Device group homepage:** Click the Software Update link in the Contents menu, as shown in Figure 7-17

- **Device CLI:** Use the **copy** command as shown in Example 7-13

Figure 7-17 shows the Software Update link on the Device Group homepage. Notice that you can choose a particular software file, and that a hyperlink is provided to modify the software file definitions if necessary.

Figure 7-17 *Device Group Software Update*

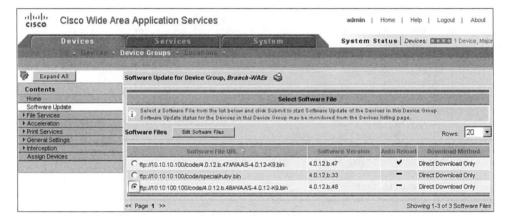

It is important to reiterate that if the Auto Reload check box is not checked during the definition of the software image (see Figure 7-16), the WAE must be rebooted in order to apply the new software version. Also, the CM GUI homepage provides details on what software versions are installed within the WAAS network and on how many WAE devices. This provides you with a quick glimpse of any software version conflicts that may be present.

Software upgrade can also be performed manually from the CLI of a WAE by using the **cop** command. Example 7-13 shows the use of the **copy** command to install a software version from an FTP server.

Example 7-13 *Software Install Using WAE CLI*

```
WAE# copy ftp install 10.10.10.100 /sw-install WAAS-4.0.13-K9.bin
```

Reporting and Logging

Cisco WAAS supports internal and external reporting and logging mechanisms. As mentioned earlier in the chapter, alarms that are generated on a particular WAE will cause a light to be lit in the CM system status or device status tree of lights. The CM also provides robust audit logging for any configuration changes that were made while a user was logged into the CM. These audit trails are enabled automatically and require no additional user configuration. An example audit trail is shown in Figure 7-18.

Figure 7-18   *Central Manager Audit Trail Logs*

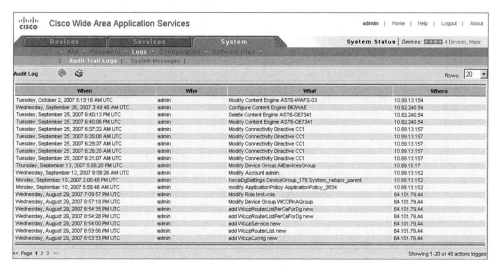

The internal audit trail logs can be found at System > Logs > Audit Trail Logs. The logs contain the following information:

- **When:** When the action was taken
- **Who:** Which user performed an action on the system
- **What:** What action the user performed on the system
- **Where:** What IP address the action came from

Similarly, system messages, which include alarm data, can be viewed from the CM UI at System > Logs > System Messages. The system message repository contains all of the system messages that have been sent to the CM from the managed WAEs and generated locally on the CM itself. Figure 7-19 shows an example of the CM system messages table.

Figure 7-19 *Central Manager System Messages Table*

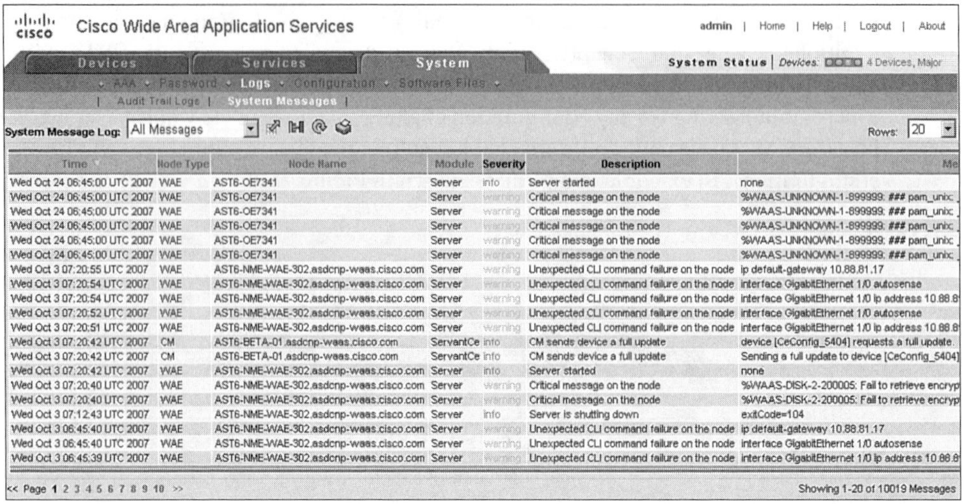

Whereas the audit trail shows what function was performed by a particular user, the system messages table contains information about alarms and events that have been generated on the CM or managed nodes. The system messages table also includes a Severity column to identify how critical the message is and an icon that allows you to export the table for offline viewing and analysis.

The CM, as well as any WAE device, also supports definition of up to four syslog servers and SNMP configuration. Syslog is configured from the device or device group homepage under General Settings > Notification and Tracking > System Logs. From the CLI, syslog servers are defined using the global configuration command shown in Example 7-14.

Example 7-14 *Defining Syslog Servers in the CLI*

```
WAE# config term
WAE(config)# logging host 10.10.10.100
```

NOTE   Similar to when using the GUI, from the CLI you can configure additional syslog parameters such as port, default priority level, and a rate limit on the number of messages that can be sent per second. These items are all configured under the **logging host** global configuration mode command.

Messages sent to external syslog servers are sourced from the local syslog.txt file found on the WAE in the /local/local1 directory.

Similarly, SNMP can be configured from within the device or device group homepage under General Settings > Notification and Tracking > SNMP. A number of subitems exist under SNMP, each of which provides a separate configuration area. SNMP settings can be configured from the device CLI using the global configuration mode command **snmp-server**.

Cisco WAAS provides support for the MIBs listed and described in Table 7-1.

Table 7-1   *SNMP MIBs Supported by Cisco WAAS*

MIB	Description
MIB-II	Published in RFC-1213, also known as the "Internet Standard MIB," and is used for network management protocols in IP networks
HOST-RESOURCES-MIB	Published in RFC-1514, provides information about hardware resources in the WAE device
EVENT-MIB	Published in RFC-2981, defines event triggers and actions for network management purposes
ACTONA-ACTASTOR-MIB	Provides CIFS acceleration statistics, print services statistics, and service liveliness and statistics information
CISCO-CDP-MIB	Provides interface information and CDP-related information
CISCO-CONTENT-ENGINE-MIB	Provides platform-level statistics for the Cisco WAE hardware platform, which are shared with the legacy Cisco Content Engine
CISCO-CONFIG-MAN-MIB	Provides configuration manager data, including information on data existing in memory (running configuration), hardware, local (NVRAM or flash memory), and remote network locations
CISCO-ENTITY-ASSET-MIB	Provides data about installed items with orderable part numbers that comprise the system; includes information about part number, serial number, hardware revision, and more

Backup and Restore of Central Manager

The previous sections in this chapter have provided details on connecting WAE devices to the network, registering them with the CM, and organizing them into device groups. The previous sections have also examined other integration aspects, including provisioned management, reporting, and logging.

Although some level of availability can be provided by deploying a primary and a standby CM, it is best practice to keep up-to-date backups of the CM database on hand in case of a system-wide outage or other disaster scenario.

The CMS database can be backed up and restored in a manner similar to performing a configuration file backup or restore on any other Cisco device. The only caveats associated with these procedures are the following:

- A CMS database restore must be performed on a WAE running the same version of the WAAS software that the backup was taken from.

- Prior to restoring a CMS database, the CMS service must first be disabled.

When creating a backup of the CMS database, the WAAS software automatically drops the backup file into the directory /local/local1 filesystem. The way in which you navigate a filesystem on a WAE device is identical to how you navigate a Linux server.

Example 7-15 shows how to make a backup of the CMS database, and then copy the backup to an FTP server.

Example 7-15 *Backup of the CMS Database*

```
waas-cm# cms database backup
Creating database backup file cms-db-09-13-2007-05-07.dump
Backup file local1/cms-db-09-13-2007-05-07.dump is ready.
Please use `copy' commands to move the backup file to a remote host.
waas-cm# pwd
/local
waas-cm# cd /local/local1
waas-cm# ls
cms-db-09-13-2007-05-07.dump
waas-cm# copy disk ftp 10.10.10.100 / cms-db-09-13-2007-05-07.dump
Enter username for remote ftp server: administrator
Enter password for remote ftp server:
Initiating FTP upload...
Sending: USER administrator
Microsoft FTP Service
Password required for administrator.
Sending: PASS ***********
User administrator logged in.
Sending: TYPE I
Type set to I.
Sending: PASV
Entering Passive Mode (10,10,10,100,128,149).
Sending: CWD /
CWD command successful.
Sending PASV
Entering Passive Mode (10,10,10,100,128,150).
Sending: STOR cms-db-09-13-2007-05-07.dump
Data connection already open; Transfer starting.
Transfer complete.
Sent 146747 bytes
```

The process of restoring a CMS database is similar to the process of backing up the CMS database. To restore the CMS database, you must first copy the CMS database files to the local filesystem. Then, you must disable CMS services. You should then issue the **cms database restore** command and, upon successful restore, re-enable CMS services.

Example 7-16 shows how to perform a CMS database restore.

Example 7-16   *Restore of the CMS Database*

```
waas-cm# copy ftp disk 10.10.10.100 / cms-db-09-13-2007-05-07.dump /local/local1/
  cms-db-09-13-2007-05-07.dump
Enter username for remote ftp server: administrator
Enter password for remote ftp server:
Initiating FTP upload...
Sending: USER administrator
Microsoft FTP Service
Password required for administrator.
Sending: PASS ***********
User administrator logged in.
Sending: TYPE I
Type set to I.
Sending: PASV
Entering Passive Mode (10,10,10,100,128,149).
Sending: CWD /
CWD command successful.
Sending PASV
Entering Passive Mode (10,10,10,100,128,150).
Receiving: STOR cms-db-09-13-2007-05-07.dump
Data connection already open; Transfer starting.
Transfer complete.
Received 146747 bytes
waas-cm# pwd
/local
waas-cm# cd /local/local1
waas-cm# ls
cms-db-09-13-2007-05-07.dump
waas-cm# config term
waas-cm(config)# no cms enable
waas-cm(config)# exit
waas-cm# cms database restore /local/local1/cms-db-09-13-2007-05-07.dump
```

Summary

This chapter provided a detailed examination of how to move from unconfigured WAE devices to registered, grouped, and upgraded devices that are integrated into the enterprise framework. An intuitive and easy-to-use setup script is provided that walks you through basic network configuration. From there, you can register and activate devices within the CM, which provides a scalable, secure, and simple means of centralized system administration and monitoring. The CM and the managed WAEs remain in constant communication through the CMS service and the frequent synchronization of configuration, monitoring, and reporting data based on the configured LCM cycle. The CM provides powerful and flexible capabilities for centralized system management, including device groups, which help automate the distribution of configuration to its managed devices. The CM also provides facilities for centralized software upgrade and rollback using a scalable architecture that allows the managed nodes to directly download software images, thereby eliminating the CM as a bottleneck in the download and upgrade.

The CM provides intuitive alarm visualization mechanisms that alert you when a threshold has been exceeded. You can act upon an alarm or, if you do not want to be notified of that particular alarm again in the future, acknowledge the alarm. The CM and each of the managed WAEs can be integrated into existing monitoring architectures that leverage syslog and SNMP. Protection of the CM database is simple and straightforward, similar to protecting the running-configuration and startup-configuration files on a router.

With the power to configure nearly every aspect of a WAE and in a scalable manner, most enterprise organizations will find that their day-to-day administration, management, and monitoring tasks will be performed through the CM's easy-to-use interface. Having a scalable, secure, and simple architecture for centralized management of a large fabric of distributed nodes is essential for controlling operational costs associated with IT systems, which is exactly what the CM affords organizations that have deployed Cisco WAAS.

CHAPTER 8

Configuring WAN Optimization

The capabilities of Cisco WAAS are commonly associated with the terms WAN optimization and application acceleration. On the surface, these two terms seem similar, but in fact they are fundamentally different. WAN optimization refers to a set of capabilities that operates in an application-agnostic manner, either at the transport or network layer, making the transfer of information over the WAN more efficient. In the case of Cisco WAAS, WAN optimization is implemented in the transport layer. Application acceleration, on the other hand, refers to a set of capabilities that operates in an application-specific manner, and interacts at the application protocol layer to improve performance. This chapter briefly revisits the WAN optimization capabilities of Cisco WAAS, and provides an in-depth examination of WAN optimization configuration and monitoring. Application acceleration capabilities of Cisco WAAS are examined in the next chapter.

Cisco WAAS WAN Optimization Capabilities

Cisco WAAS provides transparent, network-integrated WAN optimization capabilities that improve efficiency and performance for almost any TCP-based application operating in a WAN environment. The Cisco WAAS WAN optimization components include Transport Flow Optimization (TFO), Data Redundancy Elimination (DRE), and Persistent LZ Compression (PLZ). All of these features are configurable from either the CLI or from the Central Manager (CM) GUI. As a refresher, this section provides a review of the WAN optimization components.

Transport Flow Optimization

TFO is the foundational optimization layer of Cisco WAAS. TFO in itself provides optimizations to TCP to improve efficiency and mitigate performance limitations caused by latency and packet loss. Along with providing these optimizations, TFO acts as the data path for all the other optimizations for Cisco WAAS. That is, other optimizations that are being employed are called after being handled by TFO.

At its lowest layer, TFO provides a TCP proxy for connections that are being optimized by the WAE devices in the network. That is, connections from the source to the adjacent WAE are terminated locally by the WAE, new connections are managed over the WAN between WAEs, and new connections are generated on the remote LAN between the remote WAE and the destination. Connections between the source and the adjacent WAE, or between the destination and the adjacent WAE, are called *original connections*. Connections between the WAEs themselves are called *optimized connections*. It is important to note that the TCP proxy provided by Cisco WAAS is transparent, and that the original and optimized connections are dispersed physical segments of the same logical end-to-end TCP connection.

The WAE, and more specifically the TCP proxy, manages the exchange of information from an original connection to an optimized connection and visa versa. For example, assume a user has a connection that is being optimized by WAAS. This user is downloading an object via HTTP from a web server. As the server is sending data in response to the user's HTTP GET request, the data is received by the WAE adjacent to the server as part of the original connection. The data is then buffered in the TCP receive buffer on the WAE optimized connection. Based on the configured policy, discussed later in the chapter, the WAE may pass this buffered data to other optimization services, such as DRE or PLZ, for encoding. TFO then manages the drainage of the optimized data from the optimization services to the optimized connection TCP transmit buffer, and the data is subsequently transmitted. The optimized data is then received by the WAE adjacent to the user (through network interception) and is placed in the TCP receive buffer for the optimized connection. TFO then passes the data to the appropriate optimization services for decoding. TFO then manages the drainage of the unoptimized data from the optimization services to the original connection TCP transmit buffer, and the data is subsequently transmitted to the recipient.

Figure 8-1 shows an example of how the TCP proxy interacts with data from optimized and original connections. The first example shows the HTTP GET request from the user going to the server.

Figure 8-1 *TCP Proxy Interacting with Original and Optimized Connections*

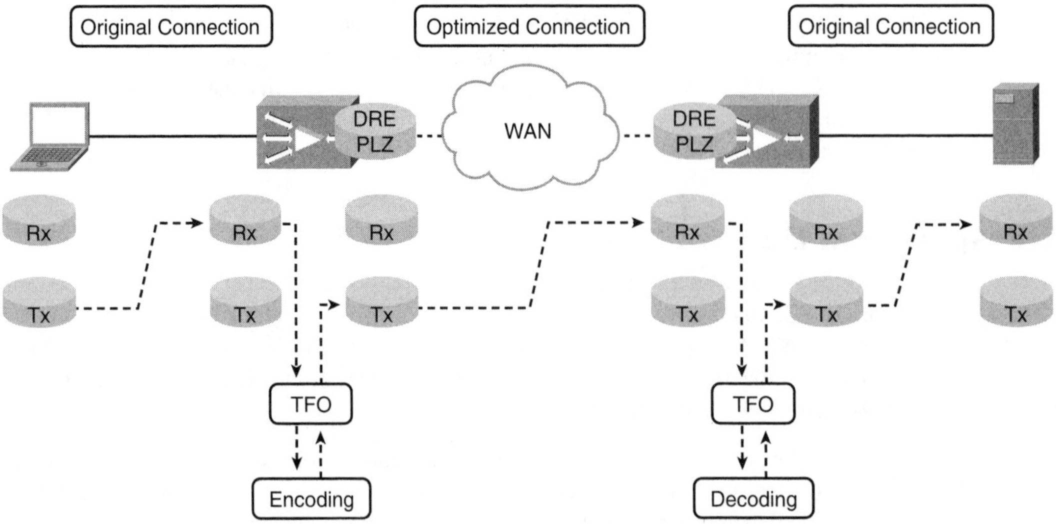

The optimization capabilities that are enacted by TFO, listed as encoding and decoding in Figure 8-1, are determined by the policy applied to the connection. The policy that is applied to the connection, and how this is determined beyond a cursory examination of the configuration of the two WAEs, is discussed later in the chapter. TFO, on its own, provides a series of optimizations as well, which help improve performance for TCP-based applications:

- **Loss mitigation:** With a TCP proxy, packet loss encountered in the WAN is managed by the sending WAE. Thus, the TCP stack for the original sender (for instance, the user or the server) never notices the packet loss, and therefore the TCP stack on the original sender is not impacted. In short, a TCP proxy shields the communicating nodes from packet loss encountered in the WAN. Furthermore, the WAEs employ selective acknowledgment (SACK) and extensions to minimize the amount of data that must be retransmitted when a segment has been lost in the WAN.

- **Latency mitigation:** With a TCP proxy, impact from latency encountered in the WAN is minimized, as the adjacent WAEs manage TCP for each original connection. That is, the WAEs locally acknowledge TCP segments for the original senders, which provides the sender a LAN-like TCP experience. This allows the sending nodes to put more data on the network more quickly, as they do not have to wait from acknowledgments from nodes that are across the high-latency WAN.

- **Slow-start mitigation:** TFO employs large initial windows (see RFC 3390), which doubles the original segment size for new connections. By increasing the original segment size, connections exit slow-start more quickly, allowing them to more rapidly enter congestion avoidance where bandwidth scalability techniques are employed that can improve throughput.

- **Bandwidth scalability:** TFO uses window scaling, large buffers, and Binary Increase Congestion avoidance to allow certain applications to better utilize available bandwidth capacity. This is particularly important for high-bandwidth or high-delay networks, which are generally difficult for a sender to fully capitalize on with a legacy TCP implementation.

- **Fairness:** The Binary Increase Congestion avoidance algorithm used by TFO ensures fairness across optimized and unoptimized connections. That is, optimized connections compete fairly with unoptimized connections for available WAN bandwidth regardless of the round-trip time of any connection. In this way, an optimized connection will not starve an unoptimized connection of available network bandwidth, thus ensuring performance consistency.

Data Redundancy Elimination

Data Redundancy Elimination (DRE) is another optimization component provided by Cisco WAAS. DRE leverages both disk and memory as a history from which data from an original connection can be compared to identify and remove redundancy from the transmission. If redundant data patterns are identified, DRE can replace the redundant pattern with a reference that the peer WAE understands, which is much smaller in size. This allows the WAE to provide potentially very high levels of compression, particularly when managing the transmission of content that has been transmitted previously in its entirety or partially.

DRE is effectively a database containing chunks of data from previous exchanges on optimized connections with an index designed for fast lookup and retrieval. The DRE index is stored on disk, which ensures persistence if the WAE is rebooted. The WAE memory is provisioned to allow the index to remain fully in memory, ensuring high performance and low latency during run-time operation. Additionally, WAE memory is optimized using an extended buffer cache to minimize the impact of flushing of DRE chunk data from main memory to disk. These system adjustments help minimize the amount of operational latency incurred when leveraging DRE against an optimized connection. By optimizing access to the DRE database index and data, encode and decode operations can be performed against optimized connections without adding substantial latency to the connection or the operations it carries.

DRE leverages a per-peer context architecture, meaning that entries in the DRE index and database are specific to a particular peer. This means that if a WAE peers with ten other WAEs that are identified during automatic discovery, the DRE database on that WAE will have entries specific to each of the ten peers. Although the use of a per-peer context architecture is less efficient in terms of storage utilization (a chunk of data may be stored once for each peer that it is transferred to), it provides tremendous advantages in terms of the following:

- **Operational latency:** Connections can be quickly associated with the appropriate DRE database and index. Lookup operations are performed against a smaller, isolated database, and fewer I/O operations are required to extract data or write data to the database.

- **Compression scalability:** By using a per-peer architecture with higher efficiency and lower latency, much more data can be processed by the system with less overhead. This allows the WAEs to reach higher levels of throughput. Compression scalability refers to the maximum application layer throughput that the system can sustain with heavily compressed content. A system with a high degree of compression scalability is one in which the compression itself does not impede the performance of the applications being compressed.

- **Latency mitigation:** By potentially replacing a large amount of data with a few small references, the WAEs can minimize the number of packets that must be exchanged over the WAN to complete an operation. Thus, the amount of latency perceived by the application may be reduced.

Persistent LZ Compression

Persistent LZ Compression (PLZ) is another WAN optimization component provided by WAAS. Similar to DRE, PLZ leverages a history of previously seen information to reduce redundancy. Whereas DRE provides a WAE-to-WAE compression history, PLZ provides a connection-oriented compression history; that is, PLZ leverages information found within a single connection to employ compression. PLZ is applied in memory only and thus provides high levels of throughput and minimal operational latency. PLZ is effective at compressing not only content that has never been seen by DRE before, but also DRE reference information. Unlike other compression technologies, PLZ implements a persistent connection history (hence the name persistent) that allocates a larger amount of memory than a standard LZ or DEFLATE algorithm would provide. With a larger history, PLZ is capable of generally providing higher levels of compression.

PLZ is also applied adaptively. In certain circumstances, PLZ might not be effective. The WAE analyzes connection data in real time using entropy calculations to determine if PLZ will have a positive effect on the data. If the WAE determines that the data is not compressible, PLZ is not employed for that portion of the data. Furthermore, if DRE compression achieves high compression ratios (above 90 percent), PLZ will not be employed for that portion of the data.

Automatic Discovery

Cisco WAAS uses an automatic discovery mechanism to intelligently determine which two WAEs are closest to the two nodes involved in a connection. The automatic discovery process, which is a component of TFO, is commonly referred to as TFO automatic discovery, or TFO AD. TFO AD operates by adding a small 12-byte reference to the options field of TCP connection setup packets received by a WAE through interception when an optimization policy is configured for that connection or connection type. This 12-byte option, which is listed as TCP option 33 (or as hex 0x21 in packet capture applications), contains the following information:

- A command that informs other WAEs that this particular WAE would like to optimize this connection.

- A device identifier of the local WAE. WAEs use the MAC address of the primary interface as their device ID to ensure global uniqueness.

- Optimization capabilities. Define which optimizations the WAE would like to apply to this connection.

The TFO AD option is applied only to TCP SYN (synchronize), SYN/ACK (synchronize and acknowledge), and ACK messages used for the connection setup, and is not applied to TCP data segments. As such, WAE devices must see the full three-way handshake of the TCP connection to discover one another. In situations where WAEs do not see the full three-way handshake, they cannot automatically discover one another, and cannot optimize that particular connection.

Upon receipt of an unmarked TCP SYN packet, the first WAE adds the TFO AD option to the packet, containing the information in the preceding list, and forwards the packet assuming a peer WAE will see the marked packet. If any additional WAEs along the path see the marked TCP SYN packet, they make a note of the device ID found in the marked TCP SYN packet. Once the marked TCP SYN packet reaches its intended destination, the first WAE in the path will have marked the TCP SYN packet, and each additional WAE in the path will have taken note of the device ID of the WAE that marked the packet.

When the destination node receives the TCP SYN packet, it generally responds with a TCP SYN/ACK packet to begin the second part of the three-way handshake (to establish the TCP connection). Similar to the manner in which WAEs react to the TCP SYN packet, the first WAE to see the SYN/ACK packet, which is generally at the other end of the network from the WAE that marked the SYN packet, applies the TFO AD option. At this point, the WAE marking the SYN/ACK packet knows information about the WAE that marked the SYN packet, including its device ID, intention to optimize, and desired policy. The marked SYN/ACK packet is then sent through the network toward the connection requestor. Any intermediary WAEs between the WAE that marked the SYN packet and the WAE that marked the SYN/ACK packet now know that they are not the outermost WAEs for this connection (that is, closest to the two endpoints of the TCP connection), and thus do not participate in optimization.

When the WAE closest to the connection requestor receives the marked TCP SYN/ACK packet, containing information about the WAE closest to the connection recipient, it examines the contents of the TFO AD option. The option, similar to the TFO AD option used on the TCP SYN packet, contains the device ID, intention to optimize, and optimization capabilities. An ACK packet containing a TFO AD option that acknowledges successful completion of automatic discovery is then generated by the WAE that marked the SYN packet, which notifies the WAE that marked the SYN/ACK packet that optimization can commence.

At this time, the connection is intercepted by the TCP proxy service (TFO) of both WAEs, and connection data is routed through the appropriate optimization components. Each WAE then generates and sends a TCP acknowledgment to the adjacent node participating in the connection, to complete the three-way handshake. The WAE that marked the TCP SYN packet acknowledges the node that created the TCP SYN packet, and the WAE that marked the TCP SYN/ACK packet acknowledges the node that created the TCP SYN/ACK packet. As discussed earlier in the chapter, the connection between the TCP endpoint and the WAE is considered an *original connection*, and the connection between the two WAEs is considered an *optimized connection*. Figure 8-2 illustrates the full automatic discovery process.

Figure 8-2 *TFO Automatic Discovery*

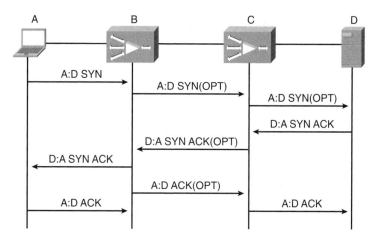

TFO AD natively supports hierarchical networks where multiple WAEs may exist in the path between two TCP endpoints. The operation of TFO AD automatically identifies the outermost WAEs for optimization—that is, the WAEs closest to the TCP endpoints. Any intermediary WAEs—that is, the WAEs in between the outermost WAEs—simply treat the connection as pass-through and allow the outermost WAEs to apply optimization. Pass-through connections on intermediary WAEs do not impact the number of connections that can be optimized by an intermediary WAE.

NOTE   When a WAE has reached its connection limit, or has gone into overload due to system load conditions, it does not participate in automatic discovery and, as such, cannot accept new connections to optimize. Connections encountered during this time are handled pass-through, which allows the communication to continue. If the network design, traffic flow, and placement of the WAEs permit, another pair of WAEs may be deployed in the network in such a way that allows them to optimize the connection, even if one of the WAEs is in an overload state or unavailable.

Enabling and Disabling Features

All of the WAN optimization features of the WAE can be enabled or disabled via the CLI or from the CM GUI. Because TFO acts as the data path for all optimization services of Cisco WAAS, it must be enabled for any other optimization capabilities to be employed. That is, you cannot leverage DRE or PLZ without using TFO. All WAN optimization features of the WAE are enabled by default. Generally, it is not necessary to disable any of these features unless you are operating in an environment where only TCP optimization is required. This is common in cases where bandwidth is not a performance-limiting factor, but latency or loss may be impacting application throughput. For instance, in an implementation where multiple gigabit links between data centers are in place, DRE and PLZ can be disabled, and Cisco WAAS will leverage TFO to help applications "fill-the-pipe." In these scenarios, the WAEs help the applications better utilize available link capacity by overcoming latency and loss limitations.

Example 8-1 shows how to enable and disable each optimization service.

Example 8-1 *Enabling and Disabling WAN Optimization Features in the WAE CLI*

```
WAE# config
WAE(config)# no tfo optimize
! disables all optimization
WAE(config)# tfo optimize DRE yes compression none
! disables LZ only
WAE(config)# tfo optimize DRE no compression LZ
! disables DRE only
WAE(config)# tfo optimize full
! enables all optimization
WAE(config)# end
WAE# show tfo status
  Optimization Status:
     Configured: optimize full
     Current: optimize full
  This device's ID: 00:14:5e:41:eb:78
  TFO is up since Sat Sep 29 14:35:59 2007
  TFO is functioning normally.
```

As shown in Figure 8-3, these same features can be enabled or disabled in the CM GUI. In most cases, these features are enabled or disabled on a device group containing multiple devices throughout the network that require only a specific set of services. As an example, WAE devices that need to perform only TCP optimization can be added to a device group, and the appropriate configuration can be applied against the device group. For reference, these features can be enabled or disabled from the CM GUI by visiting **Devices** > *Device or Device Group* > **Acceleration** > **Enabled Features**.

NOTE   EndPoint Mapper (EPM) Classification, one of the features listed in Figure 8-3, is discussed later in the chapter.

Automatic discovery is a core component of the Cisco WAAS architecture and cannot be enabled or disabled.

Figure 8-3 *Enabling and Disabling WAN Optimization Features in the CM GUI*

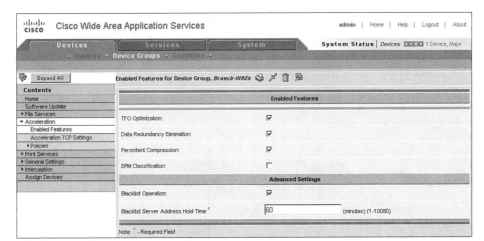

TFO Blacklist Operation

Another setting found in Figure 8-3 is Blacklist Operation and its associated Blacklist Server Address Hold Time field. As discussed earlier, TFO AD leverages TCP options during connection establishment to identify the outermost WAEs in the traffic path between two TCP endpoints. Once the WAEs have automatically discovered one another, they can begin optimizing the connection. In some situations, network components along the path may be configured to drop packets that contain unknown TCP options. TFO blacklist operation, upon receipt of a subsequent SYN from the TCP originator, will send the SYN packet to that destination without the TFO AD option. This allows the WAEs to automatically discover one another up to the point in the network where the device dropping marked packets is deployed.

As an example, assume that a WAE is deployed in a branch office with a user, and another WAE is deployed at the WAN boundary of the corporate campus network. Within the data center, which is well behind the WAN boundary of the corporate network, a firewall is deployed, which is dropping packets that contain unknown TCP options. When the user in the branch attempts to access a server in the data center behind this firewall, the TCP SYN packet containing TFO AD options is dropped by the firewall.

The WAEs deployed in the network detect the loss of the marked TCP SYN packet, and add the destination IP address to the TFO blacklist for a period of 60 seconds (or the value configured for the Blacklist Server Address Hold Time). Any connections going to that IP passing through the pair of WAEs going toward the destination server will not have the TFO AD options appended to them. However, if a SYN/ACK packet from the server, sent in response to an unmarked SYN (with no TFO AD options), is received, the WAE at the WAN boundary learns that the destination server cannot receive marked packets but can receive unmarked packets.

To notify the peer WAE that the connection can be optimized, the campus WAE appends the TFO AD options to the SYN/ACK packet, which was originally sent by the server. The branch WAE, when in receipt of the SYN/ACK packet with the TFO AD option set, then learns that the destination server cannot receive options but can be optimized. This allows the two WAEs to continue to discover one another and apply optimization to the connections going to that server (or any server behind that firewall).

Figure 8-4 shows an example of the TFO blacklist operation.

Figure 8-4 *TFO Blacklist Operation*

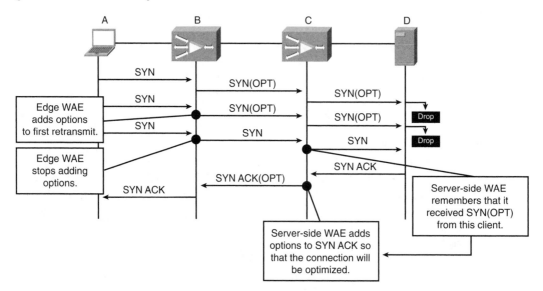

TFO blacklist operation is helpful in environments where a device that dropped marked packets is not deployed between WAE devices. In environments where firewalls are deployed between WAE devices, one of the following conditions must be met to ensure interoperability with Cisco WAAS:

- **Cisco firewalls:** All Cisco firewall products, including the Cisco PIX/ASA (Adaptive Security Appliance), IOS Firewall, and Firewall Services Module (FWSM), have software versions and configurations that provide full transparent interoperability with Cisco WAAS. A host of whitepapers and configuration guides for Cisco firewalls, including references that outline software version requirements, is available on Cisco.com.

- **Non-Cisco firewalls:** TCP option 33 (hex 0x21) must be permitted and stateful inspection of TCP packets needs to be disabled. WAE devices initially shift the sequence number of optimized connections by 2 GB to ensure that optimized packets are discarded if they are received by a TCP endpoint. WAE devices perform verification of sequence numbers for optimized connections to ensure that sequence numbers are within the expected range. This provides protection against attacks that use out-of-sequence segments and is similar to the sequence number protection provided by firewalls.

Tuning TFO Buffers

TCP provides connection-oriented, guaranteed delivery of information between two endpoints. To ensure guaranteed delivery, TCP employs end-to-end acknowledgments of delivered segments and timers to detect when segments may have become lost. When an acknowledgment is received from a peer, TCP understands that it no longer needs to retain a copy of that particular segment, and can free that portion of its memory to accept new data. When an acknowledgment is not received, it is up to TCP to retrieve a copy of that segment from memory and retransmit the segment. In short, TCP makes extensive use of memory to ensure guaranteed delivery.

Similarly, TCP uses memory to pipeline the transmission of data. By leveraging a sliding window protocol and memory, TCP can continue to "flush" data, that is, transmit data, while also receiving an equal amount of data from an application process that is attempting to transmit. In this way, TCP acts as an intermediary between the application and the network, acting as a traffic cop and making sure that there are no accidents.

One of the most significant challenges associated with TCP is its inherent inability to fill a network link that is *long* in terms of distance (latency) and *fat* in terms of capacity (bandwidth). Hence, the term *long fat network* (LFN) came into existence. The challenge with filling LFNs is that the amount of memory allocated to TCP is less than the capacity of the network multiplied by the distance. In short, TCP cannot receive enough data from the application to adequately saturate the network with data.

Figure 8-5 shows an example of the performance challenges associated with having limited memory for TCP, especially when dealing with LFNs. In this example, notice the percentage of the cylinder representing the network that is occupied by the squares (which represent packets).

Figure 8-5 *TCP Challenges with LFNs*

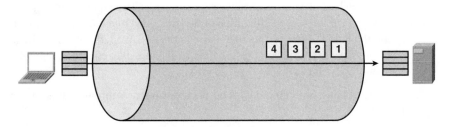

TFO, which uses an optimized implementation of TCP based on Binary Increase Congestion TCP (BIC-TCP), also uses memory for the purposes of guaranteed delivery and pipelining. TFO also leverages other TCP optimizations, including window scaling, selective acknowledgment, and large initial windows, to improve TCP performance. However, all the optimization in the world will not improve performance if buffer capacity is simply too small to fill the available network link. In such cases, the buffer capacity may need to be increased to accommodate the WAN link separating two or more locations.

Figure 8-6 shows how throughput can be improved for LFNs when allocating a larger amount of memory to TCP. In this example, notice that WAEs are deployed, which can be configured to provide extremely large buffers. Adjusting buffer sizes on the WAEs can provide immediate performance improvement without having to make configuration changes to workstations and servers.

Figure 8-6   *Adding Memory to Improve TCP Performance over LFNs*

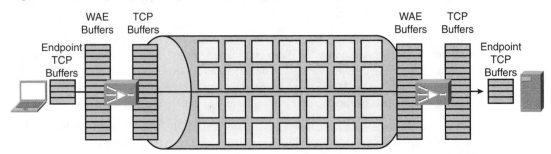

The example in Figure 8-6 shows only the benefit of providing increased memory capacity and does not show the benefit of coupling the increased memory capacity with other optimizations, including compression. Increasing the memory allocated to TCP connections, which in the case of WAEs is called adjusting TFO buffers, allows more data to be in flight between two nodes at a given time. This is also referred to as "keeping the pipe full", because it can allow communicating nodes to fully leverage the available bandwidth of the network. When coupling other optimizations, such as DRE or PLZ, the performance improvement can be exponentially higher as "keeping the pipe full" becomes "keeping the pipe full of compressed data." Consider a scenario where a T3 link connects a campus to a remote data center over very long distance. Although an increase to TCP memory (adjusting TFO buffers) may allow for near line-speed utilization of this link, how much more throughput could be realized if the link was full of data that was compressed at a ratio of 5:1? With a 45-Mbps link carrying streams of 5:1 compressed data at line rate, that equates to application throughput of 225 Mbps.

An example of how combining these optimizations impacts throughput is shown in Figure 8-7.

Figure 8-7 *Combining TCP Optimization with Compression*

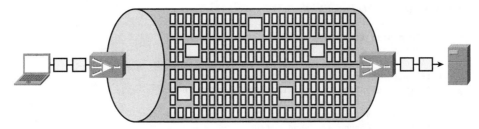

Increasing the memory allocated to TCP generally is only necessary in situations where LFNs are encountered. By default, the WAEs are preconfigured with TFO buffer settings that allow the WAE to fill a link of capacity equal to the WAE rated capacity at a fair distance. The default TFO buffer settings are as follows:

- **NME-WAE models 302, 502, 522, and WAE-512 appliance:** 32 KB send and receive for both original connection and optimized connection

- **WAE-612 appliance:** 32 KB send and receive for original side connection and 512 KB for send and receive on the optimized connection

- **WAE-7326, 7341, 7371 appliances:** 32 KB send and receive for original connection and 2048 KB for send and receive on the optimized connection

Although these values may be adequate for almost all deployments, they may require adjustment when deploying in environments with high bandwidth and high latency. WAE buffer settings should be configured based on the following guidelines:

- Original connections should not be adjusted unless the LAN throughput has become a bottleneck for WAN throughput (which is rare). This is typically only common in scenarios where WAN bandwidth is in excess of 45 Mbps or the network latency is in excess of 200 ms.

- Optimized connections should be set to four times the BDP of the network. The BDP of the network is equal to the bandwidth of the network (in bits) multiplied by the latency of the network (in seconds) and divided by eight (to end at a result in bytes).

For example, consider a network link that is an OC3 (155 Mbps) with 100 ms of latency. This equates to a BDP of $((155 \text{ Mbps} \times .1) / 8) = 1.94$ MB. Given the preceding guidelines, the optimized side TFO buffers would need to be adjusted to at least 4×1.94 MB, or roughly 8192 KB.

Like other configuration aspects of the system, TFO buffer settings can be configured from either the CLI or the GUI. Changes made from the GUI are applied based on the LCM cycle, and it is recommended that these changes be applied against device groups rather than against devices directly. In any case, the configuration change would be required on both ends of the WAN link, so it makes sense to use a device group as opposed to making the configuration changes discretely on each device.

Example 8-2 shows how to configure TFO buffer settings from the CLI.

Example 8-2 *Configuring TFO Buffer Settings*

```
WAE# config term
! optimized connection receive buffer:
WAE(config)# tfo tcp optimized-receive-buffer 2048
! optimized connection send buffer:
WAE(config)# tfo tcp optimized-send-buffer 2048
! original connection receive buffer:
WAE(config)# tfo tcp original-receive-buffer 512
! original connection send buffer:
WAE(config)# tfo tcp original-send-buffer 512
```

You can also configure TFO buffer settings from the CM GUI by going to **Devices >** *Device or Device Group* **> Acceleration > Acceleration TCP Settings**, as shown in Figure 8-8. Changes to the buffer settings of a WAE take effect only for new connections that are established after the configuration change. Connections that were established prior to the configuration change are not impacted.

Figure 8-8 *Configuring TFO Buffer Settings from the CM GUI*

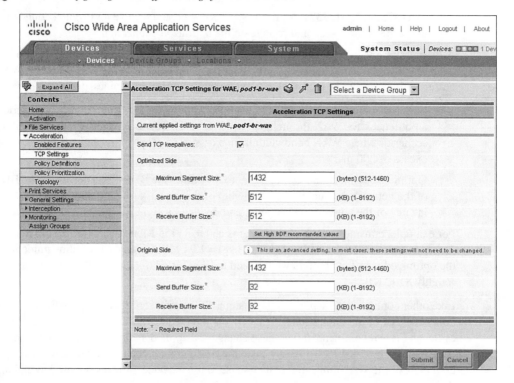

If a WAE encounters a situation where the system memory is oversubscribed based on the TFO buffer configuration and the number of connections to optimize, it will begin reassigning memory from existing connections to support new connections. In this way, the WAE can adapt to changes in load, even if it is configured to allocate large amounts of memory to connections.

NOTE	Additional TFO settings include TFO keepalives and MSS values. TFO keepalives, enabled by default, help the WAEs track connection status. If a keepalive fails after three attempts, the connection is automatically torn down. MSS settings are used to adjust the MSS used on the original and optimized connections. It may be necessary to shrink the MSS values on the optimized connection (optimized-mss) if encapsulation or Virtual Private Network (VPN) is present in the network between the WAEs to ensure that fragmentation is not encountered, which can significantly impact performance. Both of these settings can be configured from the CLI or CM GUI.

Application Traffic Policy

When a WAE receives a packet, it first examines the IP Protocol to identify if it should be sent to the optimization system. Any packets that are non-TCP, such as UDP, ICMP, or other packets, are not sent to the optimization subsystems. For WAE devices deployed in-path, any non-TCP packets are sent to the inlinegroup interface that is paired with the interface that the packet was initially received on. This is done to ensure that the packet is routed appropriately to its destination. Packets that are TCP are routed to the WAE Application Traffic Policy, or ATP, to determine how they should be handled.

The ATP is the lowest layer of the optimization system itself, and acts as the "traffic director" that defines the path through the optimization system that a flow will take. The ATP effectively determines whether a WAE will apply some optimization to a flow and, if so, what level of optimization is applied. The ATP is built from three key components:

- **A**pplication groups
- **T**raffic classifiers
- **P**olicy maps

While the ATP can be configured directly on the WAE CLI, it is recommended that the ATP be configured from the CM GUI. Using the CM GUI for ATP configuration ensures consistent configuration across all WAEs in the network, which can effectively eliminate policy configuration overlap or underlap as a component that requires troubleshooting when something is not working correctly.

Figure 8-9 illustrates the placement of the ATP in the WAE architecture.

Figure 8-9 *WAE Architecture and the Application Traffic Policy*

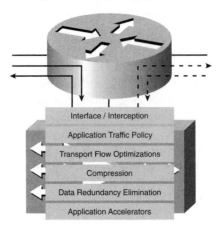

Application Groups

Application groups are containers for policies and traffic classifiers. Application groups are also used as a point of correlation for all statistics related to optimization that the WAE has applied to TCP connections. Applications can be defined on the WAE directly through the CLI, or configured through the CM GUI. The application group itself has only two parameters: a Comments field (for free text), and enable statistics check box. Comments can be supplied only via the CM GUI. The Enable Statistics check box in the CM GUI has no effect on the behavior of the WAE, as all statistics for all applications are recorded on the WAE. Rather, the Enable Statistics check box is used to indicate which application groups the CM requests from each of the managed WAEs.

Example 8-3 demonstrates how to configure an application group from the WAE CLI.

Example 8-3 *Defining and Removing an Application Group from the WAE CLI*

```
WAE# config
WAE(config)# policy-engine application name application_name
WAE(config)# no policy-engine application name application_name
! or:
WAE(config)# policy-engine application
WAE(config-pol-eng-app)# name application_name
WAE(config-pol-eng-app)# no name application_name
WAE(config-pol-eng-app)# end
WAE# show running-config
… portions removed …
!
policy-engine application
  name application_name
```

Figure 8-10 shows how to configure an application group from the CM GUI. Application groups can be found by going to **Services > Acceleration > Applications**. Cisco WAAS provides over 20 application groups by default.

Figure 8-10   *Configuring an Application Group in the CM GUI*

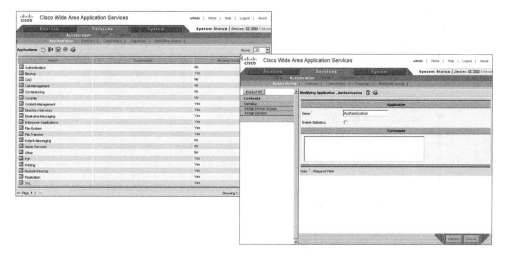

After you configure an application group in the CM GUI, you must then assign it to managed WAEs. From the **Services > Acceleration > Applications > Edit** page, you can choose a series of devices, a series of device groups, or a combination thereof. By selecting devices or device groups, the configuration on the respective devices is updated through the LCM cycle. Figure 8-11 shows the assignment status of an application group to a device group.

Figure 8-11   *Assigning an Application Group to a Device Group*

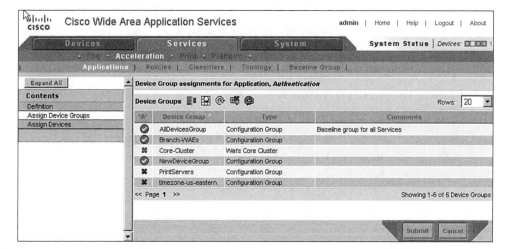

Traffic Classifiers

A traffic classifier is the component of the ATP that is responsible for defining the criteria that a flow is evaluated against to determine if it is a match for the policy. That is, the traffic classifier defines the flow characteristics that, when matched with a flow in question, would engage the configured optimization policy action.

Traffic classifiers can be configured from the CM GUI or from the WAE CLI. Much like other configuration items, it is recommended that the CM GUI be used for classifier configuration to ensure consistency throughout the network. Match conditions within traffic classifiers can be defined using any of the following parameters:

- Source IP Address
- Source IP Wildcard
- Source TCP Port
- Source TCP Port Range
- Destination IP Address
- Destination IP Wildcard
- Destination TCP Port
- Destination TCP Port Range

Example 8-4 shows how to configure a traffic classifier from within the WAE CLI.

Example 8-4 *Defining, Viewing, and Removing a Traffic Classifier from the WAE CLI*

```
WAE# config
WAE(config)# policy-engine application classifier classifier_name
!… or:
WAE(config)# policy-engine application
WAE(config-pol-eng-app)# classifier classifier_name
WAE(config-app-cls)# match (all | dst | src) (host | ip | port)
WAE(config-app-cls)# match src ip 10.10.10.0 0.0.0.255
WAE(config-app-cls)# match dst ip 10.10.9.2 0.0.0.0
WAE(config-app-cls)# match dst port eq 80
WAE(config-app-cls)# match dst port range 83 85
WAE(config-app-cls)# list
match src ip 10.10.10.0 0.0.0.255
match dst ip 10.10.9.2 0.0.0.0
match dst port eq 809
match dst port range 83 85
```

NOTE	Use of **match all** in the CM GUI or WAE CLI automatically disables all other options for that particular classifier, and all traffic will be matched.
	When **match all** is not specified, all items defined within the classifier must be matched in order for the policy to be invoked against the flow.

Alternatively, all of the match conditions can be defined on a single line with the definition of the classifier, as shown in Example 8-5. Example 8-5 shows the same classifier definition as shown in Example 8-4, but using a single command.

Example 8-5 *Single Command Defines Classifier and Match Conditions*

```
WAE(config)# policy-engine application classifier classifier_name match conditions
WAE(config)# policy-engine application classifier classifier_name match src ip
  10.10.10.0 0.0.0.255 dst ip 10.10.9.2 0.0.0.0 dst port eq 80 dst port range 83 85
WAE(config)# policy-engine application classifier classifier_name list
match src ip 10.10.10.0 0.0.0.255
match dst ip 10.10.9.2 0.0.0.0
match dst port eq 809
match dst port range 83 85
```

You configure traffic classifiers within the CM GUI under the policy definitions page at **Devices** > *Device or Device Group* > **Acceleration** > **Policies** > **Definitions**. Then, open the policy associated with the classifier to edit, and click **Edit Classifier**. You can then edit match conditions by clicking the **New** icon or the **Edit** icon. Figure 8-12 shows the application classifier definition page, along with the match conditions configuration page.

Figure 8-12 *Modifying Classifiers and Match Conditions from CM GUI*

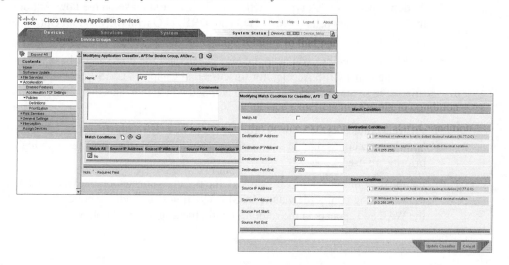

Policy Maps

Policy maps are the final piece of the ATP and perform two critical tasks: associate classifiers with application groups, and assign actions to matched flows. The definition of a policy map contains the application name, classifier name, and action to be applied. Policies are listed in priority order in both the running-config file of the WAE CLI and the CM GUI. That is, when a WAE is making a determination on how to optimize a flow, it processes the policy list serially and leverages the first policy based on a match of the classifier. If there are overlapping policies, the policy that appears first in the WAE running-config file or is of higher priority in the CM GUI will be applied.

NOTE   You can configure policy prioritization in the CM GUI by going to **Devices >** *Devices or Device Groups* **> Acceleration > Policies > Prioritization**. Policy prioritization can also be configured from the CLI, as discussed later in this section.

The definition of a policy map includes the following parameters:

- **Type:** Defines the type of policy map. Options include Basic, which is a normal optimization policy; WAFS Transport, which is used for CIFS acceleration and discussed in Chapter 9; and EPM, which is discussed in the next section.

- **Application:** Defines the application group that the policy is associated with. Any statistics gathered against flows optimized by this policy are rolled into the application group statistics.

- **Application Classifier:** Defines the traffic classifier that specifies match conditions that activate the policy against the flow.

- **Action:** Specifies what type of action (optimization) to take on the flow. Actions include Passthrough, TFO Only, TFO with DRE, TFO with LZ, and Full Optimization (TFO with DRE and LZ).

- **Accelerate:** Specifies which application accelerator the flow should be passed to, including either CIFS Accelerator (discussed in Chapter 9), MS Port Mapper (discussed in the next section), or Do Not Set, which indicates that no application accelerator should be used.

- **Position:** Indicates the priority order of the policy. The priority can be set to First, Last, or a specific value. In situations where policies overlap, policies with higher priority are used.

- **Enabled:** If this check box is checked, the policy is enacted on the WAE and added to the running-config file via the LCM cycle. If not enabled, the policy is enacted on the WAE and appears in the running-config file as a disabled policy.

You configure policies in the CM GUI under **Devices** > *Devices or Device Groups* > **Acceleration** > **Policies** > **Definition**. Figure 8-13 shows the policy list page, and the policy definition page.

Figure 8-13 *Policy List Page and Editing Policies*

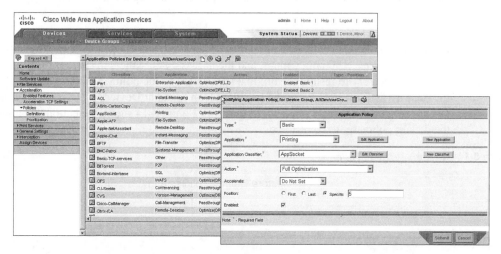

You can also define policies on the WAE CLI, as shown in Example 8-6.

Example 8-6 *Configuring Policies from WAE CLI*

```
WAE# config
WAE(config)# policy-engine application
WAE(config-pol-eng-app)# map basic name application-name classifier classifier-name
  action pass-through
WAE(config-pol-eng-app)# map basic name application-name classifier classifier-name
  action optimize DRE (no¦yes) compression (LZ¦none)
WAE(config-pol-eng-app)# map basic name application-name classifier classifier-name
  action optimize full
```

Additionally, you can combine the definition of the maps with the **policy-engine application** command to allow for definition of a policy map on a single line. Additional commands found under **policy-engine application** include:

- **map basic list:** Displays the list of all policies and the optimization associated with the policy

- **map basic disable (#):** Specifies a policy to disable

- **map basic insert (first|last|pos):** Allows you to insert a policy at the beginning, end, or in a specific location within the policy list

- **map basic move from (#) to (#):** Allows you to move a policy at a specific position to another position

NOTE	Policy engine commands are hierarchical and can be simplified by first using **policy-engine application map basic**. This takes you to a section of the CLI where you can enter commands such as **list**, **disable**, **insert**, and so on individually rather than having to enter the entire string of items such as **policy-engine application map basic** *command*.

Each Cisco WAE ships with a default policy set enabled, which includes approximately 25 application groups, 150 policy maps, and the necessary classifiers to support them. If it becomes necessary to restore the original application traffic policy settings, you can click the **Restore Default Policies and Classifiers** icon found at **Devices** > *Devices or Device Groups* > **Acceleration** > **Policies** > **Definitions**. Figure 8-14 shows the button that allows the default policy set to be restored.

Figure 8-14 *Restoring Default Policy Set*

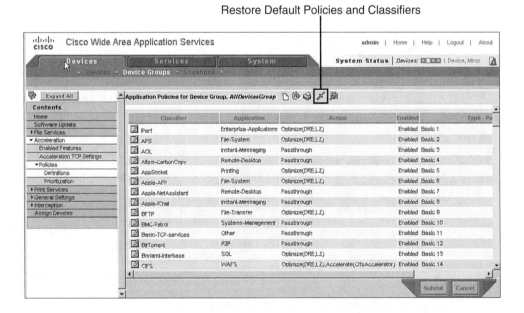

You can also restore the default policy set from the WAE CLI by using the command shown in Example 8-7. Note that this command does not ask for confirmation before executing, so use this command only when you are certain that you want to restore the default policy set.

Example 8-7 *Restoring Default Policies from WAE CLI*

```
WAE# config
WAE(config)# policy-engine application config restore-predefined
```

A special policy, called the *other* policy, is found at the bottom of the priority list. This is a required policy that acts as a catch-all and defines what the behavior of the WAE should be in situations where no configured policies are matched. In essence, if a flow cannot be classified, it is caught by the *other* policy, and the optimizations configured in this policy are applied to the flow. The *other* policy, like normal policies, can be configured from the CM GUI or the WAE CLI in an identical manner to that shown in the figures and examples presented in this chapter. Two primary schools of thought exist with regard to the *other* policy:

- **Optimize full (default):** The default option is to optimize everything full if it cannot be classified. The benefit of this option is that all traffic will be optimized if it cannot be classified. The downside to this option is that traffic will fall into the "other" category in reports (reports are discussed later in this chapter) and the number of connections that can be optimized will be impacted when a connection is identified that cannot be classified, as it will be optimized.

- **Pass-through:** Configuring the *other* policy with pass-through causes the WAE to not optimize traffic that it cannot classify. The benefit of this option is that traffic that cannot be classified will not consume system resources. The downside to this option is that traffic that cannot be classified will not be optimized.

Adapter policies are discussed later in this chapter, as well as in Chapter 9.

Negotiating Policies

Although it is certainly possible that WAEs deployed in the same network may have disparate policy configurations, it is recommended that variations in policy configurations be minimized throughout the network to ensure consistency, ease of management, and simplified trouble-shooting. Even in instances where a consistent policy is employed throughout the entire network, situations exist that may cause the configured policy to not be used. Policy configurations are enforced in a best-effort manner; that is, if the WAE has adequate resources to perform the configured optimization, it will attempt to do so.

This behavior is especially important when examining the TFO AD process. During this process, WAEs announce themselves in order to identify a peer, and advertise what optimization policy they would like to employ for the connection. In situations where the WAE is heavily loaded and has exhausted its optimized connection pool, it will stop participation in TFO AD altogether for new connections. Thus, these connections will go into pass-through, and this behavior will continue until the number of optimized connections falls to a number lower than the maximum capacity of the WAE.

Additionally, if optimization services are unable to perform the action advertised during TFO AD, in-band messages between WAEs will negotiate to a policy that both WAEs can accommodate. This allows the WAE to perform some level of optimization even if certain services are impaired. Naturally, the intent is to minimize such situations, and the WAE has numerous software watchdogs in place that can self-repair degraded services or even restart them when they cannot be repaired.

When the configured policies do not match, the least common denominator will be selected. For instance, if the configured policy on two WAEs is Full Optimization, yet one of them advertises TFO only, the applied policy between the two WAEs will be TFO only. Additionally, the optimization policies are consulted on each new connection encountered by a WAE, thus allowing policy changes to be implemented immediately for new connections. Changes made to policy configuration do not impact the level of optimization applied to connections that are already established and optimized.

EndPoint Mapper Classification

EndPoint Mapper (EPM) is one of two types of accelerators available in WAAS as of this writing. The second is CIFS acceleration, which is discussed in detail in Chapter 9. The purpose of the EPM classification system is to allow WAAS to accurately classify MS-RPC traffic flows that use dynamic ports assigned by a *port mapper*, also known as a *dispatcher*, which is an application that provides a port number to use upon receipt of application-specific information.

In the case of EPM, the application-specific information that is shared from one node to another is a universally unique identifier (UUID). In essence, when a client connects to a server for a particular application, it establishes a TCP connection on the dispatcher port and provides the UUID. The server then examines the UUID and provides a response with the TCP port number that should be used for the message exchange for that application. The EPM classification system in WAAS provides classification support for common Microsoft applications including Active Directory (MS-AD) Replication, Remote-Procedure-Call applications (MS-RPC), Exchange (MS-Exchange), and File Replication Service (MS-FRS). For Microsoft applications, this service runs on TCP 135 on the server. Clients connecting to this port that supply a UUID are assigned a dynamic destination port to connect to for their particular application. The server, once this port is assigned, then opens the port locally, and associates the port with the upper-layer application.

Figure 8-15 shows the interaction between the client and server in an environment where port mappers are used.

WAAS relies on the EPM classification system to learn what dynamic ports are being used by a particular application. As a WAE is either physically or virtually inline to all communication entering or leaving an interception point, connections established to port mapper ports and exchanges of UUID information to receive a dynamic port assignment will also be intercepted. With the EPM service, WAAS can listen to this conversation and learn what application the user is trying to use, and what port the server instructs the user to connect on.

Figure 8-15 *Port Mappers and Dynamic Port Assignment*

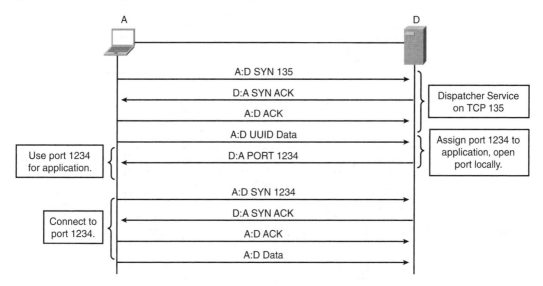

Figure 8-16 shows the same interaction between the client and the server in a WAAS environment, and how WAAS uses this information to understand what applications and ports are being used.

EPM classification can be enabled or disabled through the Enabled Features page, as shown earlier in Figure 8-3. Policies exist within the default policy set to account for applications that use EPM and can be found at the bottom of the policy list (see Figure 8-13 for the location of the policy list).

Figure 8-17 shows the construction of the EPM policy, which is very similar to basic policies. The primary difference is the presence of the UUID field, which includes a default set of UUIDs including MAPI (MS-Exchange), MS-SQL-RPC, MS-AD-Replication, MS-FRS, and Custom. Choosing **Custom UUID** allows you to specify UUIDs unique to your particular application. Also, note that for an EPM policy, the Application Classifier drop-down list box should be set to **Match All Traffic** because the EPM classifier will be used rather than the regular Layer 3 (IP) and Layer 4 (TCP) classification fields provided by the traffic classification system.

Figure 8-16 *Port Mappers and Dynamic Port Assignment with WAAS*

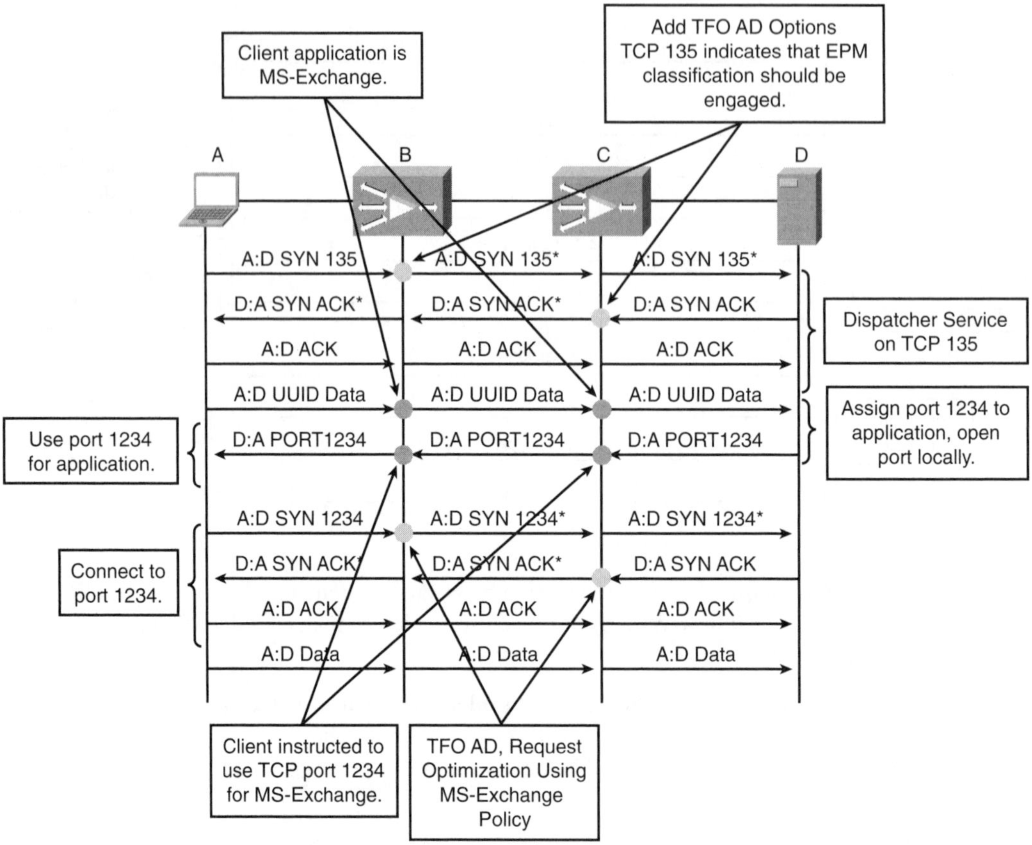

Example 8-8 shows how to enable or disable EPM classification on a WAE using the CLI.

Example 8-8 *Enabling or Disabling EPM Classification from WAE CLI*

```
WAE# config
WAE(config)# adapter epm enable
WAE(config)# no adapter epm enable
```

Figure 8-17   *EPM Policy Configuration in CM GUI*

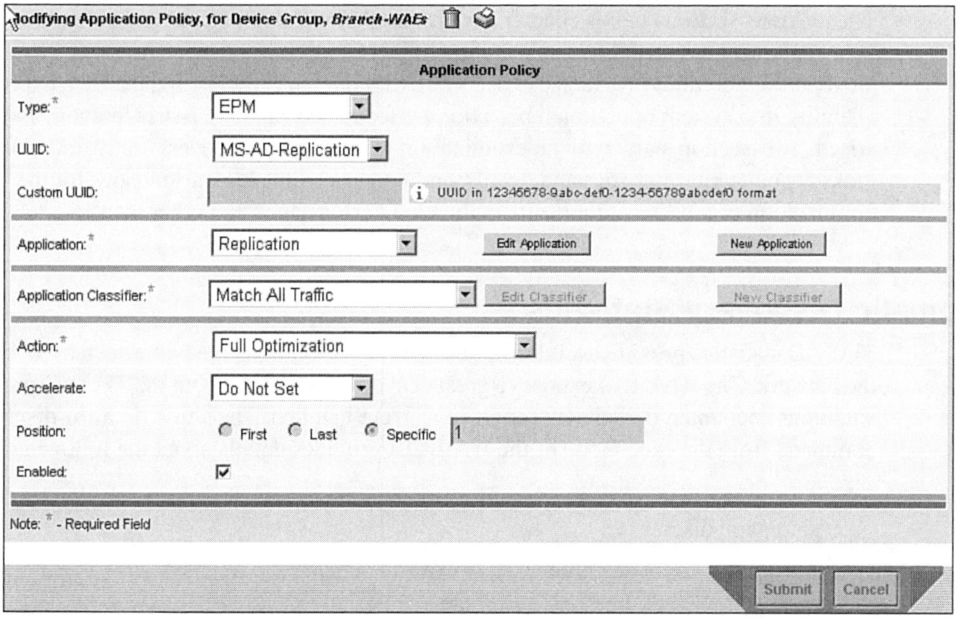

EPM classification can also be configured from the WAE CLI in a similar manner to how basic policies are configured. Example 8-9 shows the configuration of an EPM policy from the WAE CLI.

Example 8-9   *Configuring an EPM Policy from WAE CLI*

```
WAE# config
WAE(config)# policy-engine application
WAE(config-pol-eng-app)# map adaptor EPM (UUID)
! … or:
WAE(config-pol-eng-app)# map adaptor EPM (ms-sql-rpc | mapi | ms-ad-replication |
  ms-frs)
WAE(config-app-adv)# name (application group name) all action (optimize | pass-
  through)
```

NOTE   EPM classification is currently disabled by default in WAAS. Before enabling EPM classification, ensure that there is no asymmetric routing in your network, because asymmetric routing may cause complications with EPM classification and application connectivity.

Reporting

The previous sections in this chapter have focused on the deployment and configuration of WAN optimization capabilities and building application traffic policies. This section examines the reporting facilities provided by Cisco WAAS, both the CM GUI and the CLI, to provide visibility into system operational behavior, performance, and any issues that may have arisen. This section starts with an examination of automatic discovery statistics, and then looks at connection statistics and details, and finishes with a look at statistics for the WAN optimization capabilities relative to application performance and other metrics.

Automatic Discovery Statistics

TFO AD statistics provide useful insight into how connections are being seen by WAEs in the network. The WAE CLI exposes a great deal of information about the TFO AD process, situations encountered, and how connections were handled. The **show tfo auto-discovery** command from the exec mode of the WAE CLI provides details about the following:

- **Automatic discovery success:** How many connections have successfully completed automatic discovery

- **Automatic discovery failure:** How many connections have failed automatic discovery, and what were the reasons for failure

Example 8-10 shows an annotated output of this command. An explanation is provided for each of the key output fields. Some text has been removed from the command output to eliminate less-commonly used information and to allow focus on the most important pieces of output data from this command.

Example 8-10 *CLI Automatic Discovery Statistics*

```
WAE# show tfo auto-discovery
Auto discovery structure:
        Allocation Failure:                     0
        Allocation Success:                     52
        Deallocations:                          52
        Timed Out:                              3

! Allocation failure and allocation success indicate whether or not a connection

! was successfully allocated space in the TFO AD table. Each closed connection that

! had successfully been allocated to the TFO AD table should have a deallocation

! as well. Allocation failures could be caused by timeout, network connectivity

! issues, or overload conditions on the WAE itself.
```

Example 8-10   *CLI Automatic Discovery Statistics (Continued)*

```
… portions removed …
Auto discovery failure:
        No peer or asymmetric route:            26
        Insufficient option space:              0
        Invalid option content:                 0
        Invalid connection state:               0
        Missing Ack conf:                       0
! The auto discovery failure section provides helpful guidance on why TFO AD may
! have encountered failure conditions. This includes scenarios where a peer WAE
! could not be identified, asymmetric routing was present, insufficient option
! space in the TCP options field (if other options were present), and corrupt
! option content. Option content should not be corrupt unless  bits on the
! network were flipped, which is a condition commonly corrected by examination
! of packet header checksums and CRCs.
Auto discovery success TO:
        Internal server:                        8
        External server:                        44
! Internal servers include any process on the WAE that is explicitly listening
! for traffic, such as a management service or CIFS acceleration service.
! External servers are any nodes other than WAEs that other nodes are
! attempting to connect to, i.e. the recipient endpoint in the TCP connection.
Auto discovery success FOR:
        Internal client:                        0
        External client:                        29
! Internal clients include any process on the WAE that is explicitly generating
! connections to! another node on the network and can include management services
! or the CIFS acceleration service. External clients are any nodes other than WAEs
! that are attempting to connect to other nodes on the network, i.e. the sender
! endpoint in the TCP connection.
Auto discovery Miscellaneous:
        Intermediate device:                    12
        RST received:                           0
        SYNs found with our device id:          3
        SYN retransmit count resets:            0
! The miscellaneous fields provide insight into additional conditions that
! may be encountered, such as when the WAE is an intermediate WAE and not an
! outermost WAE in the network path between two TCP endpoints. "SYNs found
! with our device ID" could represent routing loops in the network topology,
! that is, a SYN packet marked with a TFO AD option was re-routed after
! marking back through the WAE that added the TCP option.
```

Additional automatic discovery statistics can be gathered through the following commands:

- **show tfo auto-discovery blacklist entries:** Displays a table containing a list of the TCP endpoints that have been added to the TFO AD blacklist due to options propagation failure.

- **show tfo auto-discovery list:** Displays a table containing a list of the TCP connections that are presently in the automatic-discovery state, and what their status is. As connections are generally built quickly, execution of this command will provide an immediate point-in-time snapshot.

Connection Statistics and Details

Along with providing visibility into the automatic discovery process, the WAE CLI provides details about the connections that are being optimized by the WAE. The CM GUI also provides these details in an easy-to-use connection table, which also allows you to zoom into a specific connection to watch its behavior in near real time.

Two ways exist to examine the list of optimized and pass-through connections on the WAE. The first is from the WAE CLI through the use of the **show tfo connection summary** command. This command provides a tabular list of all connections (optimized and pass-through) along with the four-tuple (source IP, destination IP, source port, destination port), internal connection ID, peer ID, and policy. The policy portion of the table is broken into four columns:

- **Local Configured Policy:** Specifies what policy was defined in the local WAE application traffic policy.

- **Peer Configured Policy:** Specifies what policy was defined in the peer WAE application traffic policy.

- **Negotiated Policy:** Specifies the least common denominator between the policy configured locally and the policy configured on the peer WAE.

- **Applied Policy:** Specifies the policy applied to the connection. This should generally be the same as the negotiated policy unless load conditions prevent one of the WAEs from applying a capability in the negotiated policy.

The policy portion of the table contains a single character for each of the four policy columns:

- **F (Full optimization):** TFO, DRE, and LZ are applied to this connection.

- **D (TFO+DRE):** Only TFO and DRE are applied to this connection.

- **L (TFO+LZ):** Only TFO and LZ are applied to this connection.

- **T (TFO Only):** Only TFO is applied to this connection.

Example 8-11 shows sample output from the **show tfo connection summary** command.

Example 8-11 *Display Connections from WAE CLI*

```
WAE# show tfo connection summary
Optimized Connection List
Policy summary order: Our's, Peer's, Negotiated, Applied
F: Full optimization, D: DRE only, L: LZ Compression, T: TCP Optimization
Local-IP:Port          Remote-IP:Port        ConId   PeerId               Policy
10.10.100.2:10386      10.10.10.240:4050     12      00:05:9a:3d:31:dd F,F,F,F
10.10.100.2:10387      10.10.10.240:4050     13      00:05:9a:3d:31:dd F,F,F,F
10.10.100.2:10388      10.10.10.240:4050     14      00:05:9a:3d:31:dd F,F,F,F
10.10.13.240:37849     10.10.10.240:4050     2       00:11:25:ac:3c:5c F,F,F,F
10.10.13.240:37850     10.10.10.240:4050     3       00:11:25:ac:3c:5c F,F,F,F
10.10.13.240:37851     10.10.10.240:4050     4       00:11:25:ac:3c:5c F,F,F,F
10.10.13.100:2847      10.10.10.100:80       5       00:11:25:ac:3c:5c F,F,F,F
10.10.10.100:48329     10.10.13.100:3389     99321   00:11:25:ac:3c:5c T,T,T,T
```

You can find this same information in the CM GUI by going to the device homepage at **Devices > Device > Monitoring > Connection Statistics,** as shown in Figure 8-18.

Figure 8-18   *Display Connections from CM GUI*

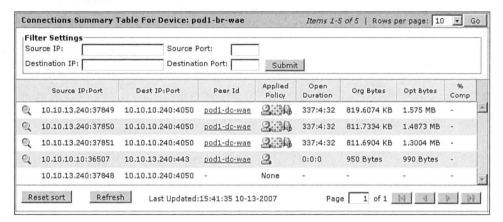

The magnifying glass icon next to each of the connection entries provides a simplified means of drilling into the details for a specific connection. By clicking this icon, a pop-up window appears, which is automatically refreshed every three seconds. This pop-up window provides the following details about the connection:

- **Connection Traffic Statistics:** The amount of traffic found in the connection graphed over time

- **Percentage Compression:** The amount of compression applied to the connection graphed over time

- **Connection Details:** Including four-tuple, duration (length of the connection), and device ID of the peer WAE used to optimize the connection

- **Policy:** Including the locally configured policy, configured policy on the peer, negotiated policy, and applied policy

- **Traffic Statistics:** Original connection and optimized connection statistics, including bytes read, bytes written, total bytes, percentage compression, and effective capacity gain through optimization

The information found in the Connection Details pane continues to refresh throughout the life of the connection. Graphs and statistics are continually updated. This information is especially helpful to track the progress and performance of long-lived connections.

Figure 8-19 shows an example of the detailed connection statistics that are provided when opening the details of an optimized connection from the CM GUI.

Figure 8-19 *Detailed Connection Statistics from CM GUI*

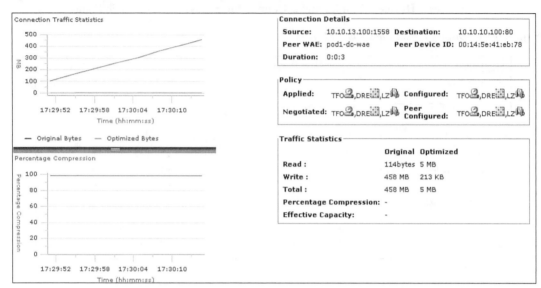

The same level of detail about a connection can be gathered from the WAE CLI using a series of commands:

- **show tfo connection:** Provides connection details, policy details, state, and processing latency for a particular connection.

- **show stat dre connection:** Provides compression details for all optimized connections or a specific connection. Details include four-tuple, open and close timestamps, duration, encode statistics (bytes in vs. bytes out), decode statistics (bytes in vs. bytes out), processing latency caused by compression, and message size distribution.

Example 8-12 demonstrates sample output from the **show statistics dre connection** command, along with the same command applied to a single connection.

Example 8-12 *Examining Compression Statistics from WAE CLI*

```
WAE# show statistics dre connection
Conn   Peer      Client-ip:port       Server-ip:port     Encode-in/  Status
  Id   No                                                 Decode-in   (A-Active)
                                                                      (C-Closed)

99674   1     10.10.13.100:1559    10.10.10.100:445      737B/ 1KB   C(6m46s)
99673   1     10.10.13.100:1560    10.10.10.100:139        0B/  0B   C(6m57s)
99645   1     10.10.13.100:1558    10.10.10.100:80       487MB/  0B   C(7m49s)
WAE# show statistics dre connection id 99645
```

Example 8-12 *Examining Compression Statistics from WAE CLI (Continued)*

```
Conn-ID: 99645 10.10.13.100:1558 -- 10.10.10.100:80  Peer No:  1 Status: Closed
-------------------------------------------------------------------------
Open at 10/20/2007 17:37:52, Close at 10/20/2007 17:38:32, Duration: 40 secs
Encode:
   Overall: msg:      15427, in:    487 MB, out:   5416 KB, ratio:  98.92%
       DRE: msg:      15427, in:    487 MB, out:   5691 KB, ratio:  98.86%
DRE Bypass: msg:          0, in:      0 B
        LZ: msg:       1562, in:    932 KB, out:    657 KB, ratio:  29.49%
 LZ Bypass: msg:      13865, in:   4759 KB
   Avg latency:      1.405 ms
  Message size distribution:
    0-1K=1%  1K-5K=4%  5K-15K=13%  15K-25K=16%  25K-40K=30%  >40K=33%
Decode:
   Overall: msg:          0, in:      0 B, out:      0 B, ratio:   0.00%
       DRE: msg:          0, in:      0 B, out:      0 B, ratio:   0.00%
DRE Bypass: msg:          0, in:      0 B
        LZ: msg:          0, in:      0 B, out:      0 B, ratio:   0.00%
 LZ Bypass: msg:          0, in:      0 B
   Avg latency:      0.000 ms
  Message size distribution:
    0-1K=0%  1K-5K=0%  5K-15K=0%  15K-25K=0%  25K-40K=0%  >40K=0%
```

Many of the optimization statistics commands that produce tabular output on the WAE CLI can be filtered by a variety of parameters, including client IP address, client TCP port, server IP address, server TCP port, peer ID, connection ID, or a combination of these parameters.

WAN Optimization Statistics

The commands and GUI locations found in the previous sections allow you to identify how WAEs are automatically discovering one another, issues encountered during TFO AD, identify the policies applied to connections, and examine connection statistics. This section focuses on the impact of these optimizations on the connections that are traversing the network.

Both the WAE CLI and the CM GUI provide powerful reporting tools that provide visibility into what the traffic distribution seen by the WAEs is, as well as what impact optimization services are having on the connections. One of the most important questions that demands an answer is, "How much bandwidth am I saving?" The WAE CLI includes a command that provides this information, **show statistics tfo saving**, which is shown in Example 8-13.

Example 8-13 *Examining Bandwidth Savings from WAE CLI*

```
WAE# sh statistics tfo saving
Application              Inbound                 Outbound
-------------------- ---------------------- ----------------------
… portions removed …
WAFS
    Bytes Savings                  118348                60877374
    Packets Savings                     0                   35815
    Compression Ratio                 1.1:1                 18.5:1
Web
    Bytes Savings                 4886829              1037171275
    Packets Savings                154295                  693334
    Compression Ratio                 1.3:1                 39.0:1
WAE# sh statistics tfo saving Web
Application              Inbound                 Outbound
-------------------- ---------------------- ----------------------
Web
    Bytes Savings                 4886829              1037171275
    Packets Savings                154295                  693334
    Compression Ratio                 1.3:1                 39.0:1
```

As Example 8-13 demonstrates, this command can also be filtered to show the output from a single application group as well, by simply appending the name of the application group to the end of the command. It is important to note that the application group aggregates the bandwidth savings statistics. Thus, the amount of savings reported includes statistics from all traffic classifiers associated with that application group. Another important item to note is that the command displays the packet savings associated with use of optimization. In most cases, the number of packets that must be transmitted decreases as compression increases. This not only helps to save bandwidth, but also mitigates the impact of latency, as fewer round trips must be made across the WAN.

The CM GUI also provides a tremendous amount of useful information about the performance of the system and bandwidth savings. You can find the majority of these reports on the device homepage, or view them in aggregate form by visiting the device group homepage or system homepage. Using statistics from a single device as an example, a tabular view of application groups, the percentage of overall traffic consumed by each application group, effective capacity, and compression statistics can be found by going to **Devices > Device > Monitoring > Optimization Statistics**. Figure 8-20 shows the tabular view from this page.

Figure 8-20 *Application Group Statistics for a WAE in CM GUI*

Application Traffic Statistics Report for WAE *pod1-br-wae*			
☐ Backup	0	1X	0	0
☐ Content-Management	0	1X	0	0
☐ Directory-Services	0	1.1X	8	8
☐ Email-and-Messaging	0	1X	0	0
☐ Enterprise-Applications	0	1X	0	0
☐ File-System	0	1X	0	0
☐ File-Transfer	0	1X	0	0
☐ Other Traffic	0	1X	0	0
☐ P2P	0	1X	0	0
☐ Printing	0	1X	0	0
☐ Remote-Desktop	2	1X	0	0
☐ Replication	0	1X	0	0
☐ SQL	0	1X	0	0
☐ Storage	0	1X	0	0
☐ Streaming	0	1X	0	0
☐ Systems-Management	0	1X	0	0
☐ Version-Management	0	1X	0	0
☐ WAFS	11	1X	0	0
☐ Web	87	33.3X	97	97
☑ All Traffic	100	5.9X	83	83

Along with providing per-application statistics, you can view additional reports that
provide visibility and system performance information, including the following:

- **Application Traffic Mix:** A pie chart that visualizes the breakdown of traffic
  identified by application group.

- **Application Traffic:** A line graph that displays the amount of traffic from each
  application group over a period of time.

- **Pass-Through Traffic Mix:** A pie chart that visualizes the breakdown of why
  traffic was handled in pass-through.

- **Pass-Through Traffic:** A line graph that displays the amount of pass-through
  traffic that has been handled by the WAE over a period of time.

- **Optimized vs. Pass-Through Traffic:** A line graph that displays the amount of
  optimized traffic and pass-through traffic together, which helps you understand
  how much of your network utilization is being optimized by WAAS.

- **Reduction:** A line graph that displays the percentage reduction over a period of
  time. This graph can be shown including or excluding pass-through traffic, and is
  helpful in determining what level of compression has been applied to traffic.

All of the graphs can be configured with a specific time interval, including last hour, last day, last week, and last month. A custom date range can be supplied if you require that the report span a specific set of days. The line graphs produced by this page can also be filtered to include all traffic or specific application groups, and can include a specific direction of traffic flow or both directions of traffic flow. Figure 8-21 shows an example of one of the many reports. In this figure, compression ratios applied across four application groups and *other* traffic are displayed for a custom time period.

Figure 8-21 *Examining Optimization Statistics in the CM GUI*

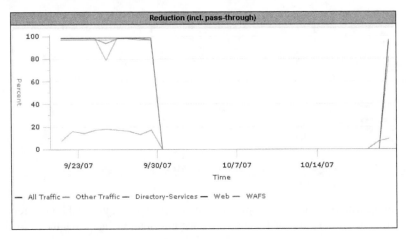

The CM GUI also provides a useful application traffic statistics detail report at **Devices > Device > Monitoring > Optimization Statistics Details**. This report, much like the reports mentioned before, can be filtered based on specific application groups or over time. The statistics detail report provides the following information:

- **Traffic:** Total number of bytes processed and average number of bytes processed per hour.

- **Savings:** Total number of bytes saved, percentage reduction including and excluding pass-through, and effective capacity provided.

- **Pass-Through Traffic:** Total number of bytes handled pass-through, amount of traffic handled pass-through because no peer device was identified, amount of traffic handled pass-through due to configured policy, amount of pass-through traffic due to being an intermediate device, and all other pass-through traffic.

Figure 8-22 shows an example of this report.

Figure 8-22 *Statistics Detail Report in CM GUI*

Statistics report for - Application: **All Traffic** Direction: **Bi-directional** Time Frame: **Last Week**	
Traffic	
Total bytes :	593250 KB
Average number of bytes processed per hour:	4237 KB
Savings	
Total bytes saved:	491157 KB
Percent reduction (incl. pass-through) provided by this device:	83 %
Percent reduction (excl. pass-through) provided by this device:	83 %
Effective capacity provided by this device:	5.9 X
Pass-through Traffic	
Total pass-through traffic :	65 KB
Pass-through traffic due to no peer:	47 KB
Pass-through traffic due to configured policy:	5 KB
Pass-through traffic due to this device being an intermediate device:	0 KB
All other pass-through traffic:	13 KB

Summary

Cisco WAAS provides powerful WAN optimization capabilities, including TFO, DRE, and PLZ, to minimize bandwidth consumption, minimize the impact of latency, and improve overall application performance. WAE devices automatically discover one another during the establishment of TCP connections, and advertise their availability and policy that they would like to employ. The ATP is the component of the WAE in which policies are configured (either through the CLI or CM GUI) that dictate what policy a WAE will attempt to apply to a specific type of connection. These policies are negotiated during the automatic discovery phase to the least common denominator of the two configured policies, unless load conditions prevent a specific policy from being used. Once a policy has been negotiated, WAE devices begin applying optimization to the connection based on the configured policy, and collecting statistics against the connection and the optimization used. These statistics are made available to the user both in the WAE CLI and in the CM GUI, which provide helpful insight into how the system is performing and what conditions are being encountered by the WAEs.

CHAPTER 9

Configuring Application Acceleration

Previous chapters have examined a number of aspects of Cisco WAAS, ranging from network integration to management to configuring WAN optimization policies. This chapter focuses on the application acceleration components of Cisco WAAS, which help enable IT organizations to

- Consolidate server and storage infrastructure
- Improve performance of accessing file servers over the WAN

This chapter provides a technical overview and architectural examination of the application acceleration capabilities provided by Cisco WAAS. This chapter also provides a detailed explanation of how to configure and integrate Cisco WAAS application acceleration into a network. Along with providing an examination of how Cisco WAAS accelerates the Common Internet File System (CIFS) protocol, which is commonly used in Microsoft Windows environments for accessing files stored on file server shares, this chapter explores the details and configuration aspects of two other value-added Cisco WAAS capabilities that are directly related to application acceleration—CIFS prepositioning and disconnected mode of operation.

Application Acceleration Overview

As discussed earlier in the book, WAN optimization refers to techniques that are employed to overcome WAN conditions, making the WAN more tolerable from an application performance perspective. Whereas WAN optimization focuses specifically on application-agnostic techniques to accomplish this lofty goal, application acceleration focuses on specific applications to improve performance. To compare and contrast, WAN optimization helps improve transport characteristics, efficiency, and performance, whereas application acceleration interacts with the application protocols themselves to overcome these limitations. Employing both of these techniques to flows traversing the WAN provides the powerful framework for ensuring that distributed users can interact with applications and collaborate with other users at performance levels similar to those enjoyed by users in the corporate campus, near the application servers themselves.

Application acceleration, especially when deployed in conjunction with WAN optimization, bridges the divide between two opposing forces. The first force is the drive to consolidate costly infrastructure for the obvious operational and capital savings (management, utilization, efficiency, data protection, recovery, hardware, and more). The challenge with consolidation is that a large portion of enterprise users would then be separated by the WAN from the resources they need to be productive, which significantly impedes performance (as discussed earlier in the book). The second force is the drive to empower remote users to increase productivity and efficiency. This force is in stark contrast to consolidation, because a foundational concept of empowering users to increase efficiency and performance is that they have application infrastructure readily available with high performance. This force tends to dictate the need to distribute application infrastructure.

Application acceleration helps bridge this divide by providing the best of both worlds—infrastructure consolidation and application acceleration—and provides the user with near-LAN response time in an environment where infrastructure is consolidated. Application acceleration, like WAN optimization, generally relies on a device deployed on both sides of a WAN link (such as a Cisco WAAS appliance or network module). These devices interact with application protocols to minimize the impact of latency, loss, and bandwidth limitations by acting as a transparent or nontransparent application layer proxy. The device closest to the user acts like the server to the user, whereas the device closest to the server acts like the user to the server. This architecture is similar to the TCP proxy architecture presented in Chapter 8, "Configuring WAN Optimization," but rather than interacting at the transport layer, application acceleration operates at the session layer or above.

Figure 9-1 shows an example of how application acceleration in a CIFS environment looks from a user and server perspective.

Figure 9-1 *Integration of Application Acceleration*

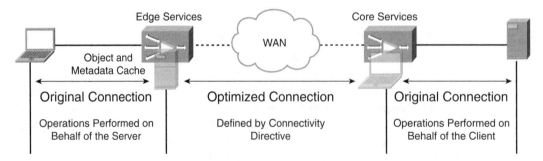

As mentioned in Chapter 1, "Introduction to Cisco Wide Area Application Services (WAAS)," the CIFS acceleration architecture of Cisco WAAS uses a number of acceleration techniques, including caching, read-ahead, write-behind, pipelining, and multiplexing, to improve performance while enabling centralization.

CIFS is a stateful client/server protocol; that is, a long-lived session is established between two nodes—a client and a server. Although CIFS can be used between two servers, one will be acting as a client (mounting a shared resource and using the resource) and the other will be acting as a server (making a shared resource available). Given that CIFS is stateful, it is important to note that the client/server session may not be interrupted even in the face of a broken transport layer connection, because session management is employed above the transport layer. That is, a CIFS session remains active on the client and server until closed at the session layer, even if the underlying transport layer connection is terminated. It is also important to note that application layer acceleration for the CIFS protocol requires that Cisco WAAS see the application layer session be established, along with the establishment of the TCP connection itself.

CIFS acceleration is employed within Cisco WAAS through a dual-sided application proxy. WAAS devices deployed throughout the network perform a particular set of tasks for CIFS sessions based on the proximity to a CIFS endpoint, which determines the services that should be enabled on that WAAS device. For frame of reference, CIFS uses TCP as a transport over TCP ports 139 (CIFS over NetBIOS over TCP) or 445 (CIFS natively over TCP). Legacy Microsoft environments (for instance, Windows for Workgroups) could leverage CIFS over NetBEUI, which provided its own transport mechanism. However, these environments are rare, and it is highly unlikely that any organizations still leverage NetBEUI.

To perform CIFS acceleration, Cisco WAAS leverages three foundational components: core services, edge services, and connectivity directives. The following sections detail each of these.

Core Services

Core services are the data center component of CIFS acceleration and should be enabled on WAAS devices that are deployed near file servers. In any-to-any sharing environments, where workstations are acting as servers (which is less likely), the WAAS devices deployed next to those workstations should also be configured with core services. Core services act as aggregation points for WAAS devices that are configured with edge services (discussed in the next section) and act as *virtual clients* to the servers that users are attempting to connect to. That is, when a user's session is accelerated through WAAS, the edge device acts on behalf of the server to that user, and the core device acts on behalf of the client to the server that is being accessed.

Along with providing the server-side proxy functionality necessary for accelerating CIFS, the core services also provide termination of the CIFS proxy connections that are established between edge and core WAAS devices. These proxy connections, which run over TCP port 4050, are used to transport accelerated CIFS requests between WAAS devices. Two or more of these connections are established between edge and core WAAS devices, as described later in the chapter in the section "Connectivity Directives."

WAAS devices configured with core services must be added to a "core cluster," which is a logical grouping of adjacent WAAS devices, each of which has been configured as a core device. Edge devices are mapped to core clusters to ensure high availability.

NOTE   Core services requires a WAE with a minimum of 2 GB of RAM.

Edge Services

Edge services are the remote office component of CIFS acceleration and should be enabled on WAAS devices that are deployed near users. Edge service WAAS devices establish CIFS proxy connections to a unique core service WAAS device within a configured core cluster based on the connectivity directive (discussed later in the section "Connectivity Directives"). WAAS devices configured with edge services act as "virtual servers" to the clients that are attempting to establish a session to a server in the data center.

Along with providing the user-side proxy functionality necessary for accelerating CIFS, the edge services also provide termination of the CIFS proxy connections that are established between edge and core WAAS devices. WAAS devices configured with edge services provide a client-side object cache and metadata cache for CIFS, which is independent of the DRE compression history. By keeping the application cache independent of the compression history, application performance can be maintained even in the event of massive compression history eviction, which could happen if a user were to, for instance, back up their entire home movie or music library over the WAN. Furthermore, having a separate application cache ensures that failures and cache-clearing events are isolated from one another. As an example, an application cache may be used to hold numerous gigabytes of distributed software or patches, which, if evicted, may need to be transferred over the WAN again. Keeping the cache and compression history isolated from one another provides numerous benefits in terms of operational efficiency.

In the case of both core and edge services, acceleration of the CIFS protocol is employed only when it is safe to do so. By monitoring connection state, and the interactive messages exchanged between client and server, WAAS can adjust its level of optimization to employ only those optimizations that are acceptable at that time. For instance, in the case of multiple users interacting with the same file on the server, WAAS can detect this situation and temporarily disable caching for this object. Furthermore, WAAS does not proxy (that is, respond to locally) application layer messages that could impact correctness or data integrity. As an example, a lock message, which indicates that a portion of a file needs to be locked for a particular user, is never handled locally by WAAS, and is always sent synchronously to the server for server-side processing. Safety mechanisms such as these are built into WAAS and require no user configuration.

NOTE   Edge services requires a WAE with a minimum of 1 GB of RAM.

Connectivity Directives

The connectivity directive is the component that interlinks edge and core WAAS devices, and is necessary to enable CIFS acceleration. The connectivity directive definition identifies the network capacity to be consumed by CIFS acceleration, and determines the number of proxy connections that are established between edge and core devices. The proxy connections that are established are then used as the transport by which accelerated messages are exchanged between edge and core, either toward the server or toward the client. One connection is always established pass-through, and is used for messages that are synchronous and highly sensitive to latency. Such messages are generally control messages and contain little to no payload, and simply require the fastest possible delivery to their intended destination. Additional connections, which are configured to leverage the underlying WAN optimization components, are established for every 64 KB of BDP as determined by the connectivity directive definition.

NOTE   BDP is calculated by converting the network data rate to bytes, by dividing by 8, and then multiplying by the network latency in seconds. For example, a T1 (1.544 Mbps) equates to 193 kBps. With 100 ms of latency, the BDP of the network would be 19.3 KB. In this example, two proxy connections would be established, one as pass-through for synchronous control messages and the other for data.

As another example, assume a T3 (45 Mbps, equates to 5.625 MBps) with 200 ms of latency yields a BDP of 1.125 MB. One pass-through connection would be established for synchronous control messages, and 16 data connections would be established.

Up to 20 proxy connections can be established for each connectivity directive.

Core and edge devices can establish from 2 to 20 proxy connections between one another. This number is determined based on the bandwidth and latency parameters configured against the connectivity directive, and is discussed later in the chapter. The connectivity directive definition identifies one or more edge devices or groups, and one core cluster. In situations where a WAAS device is configured as both edge and core, a connectivity directive is required for both directions of CIFS acceleration. As an example, consider a scenario where WAAS devices are installed in two geographically separated campus locations. Each campus has users and servers, and users in each campus need to access servers locally and in the other campus. In this scenario, the WAAS devices in each location would be configured as both core and edge devices, and a connectivity directive would need to be defined for each direction.

Interaction with WAN Optimization

With the exception of latency-sensitive synchronous signaling messages, all exchanges between edge and core for acceleration CIFS sessions leverage the underlying WAN optimization framework of Cisco WAAS. The Wide Area File Services (WAFS) policy determines the level of optimization applied between proxy connections established between edge and core. By leveraging the WAN optimization components of Cisco WAAS, not only are CIFS sessions accelerated, but the transfer of messages across the WAN is highly optimized. By coupling a user-side object and metadata cache (and other optimizations) with WAN optimization, the following benefits are realized:

- **Increase in application throughput:** Higher data rates through local object delivery (full or partial) and minimized WAN bandwidth consumption (through compression and DRE).

- **Decrease in perceived latency:** Faster delivery of partial or full objects (through user-side cache) and optimized transfer over the WAN.

- **Decrease in server load:** Message processing by the user-side object and metadata cache when safe minimizes the number of messages that must traverse the WAN and be processed by the server, resulting in a decrease in server workload and utilization.

Figure 9-2 visualizes the application acceleration components of Cisco WAAS, and their interaction with underlying WAN optimization techniques.

Figure 9-2   *Visualization of Application Acceleration Components*

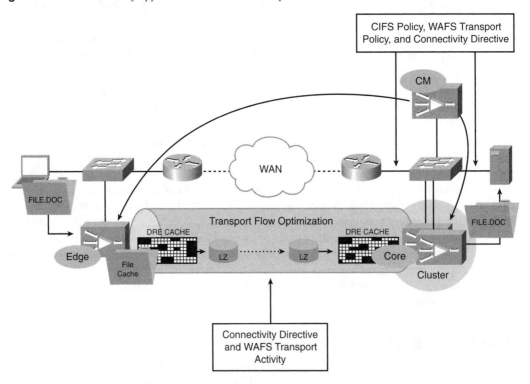

Configuring CIFS Acceleration

This section examines the configuration and validation of all of the necessary CIFS acceleration components, including core services and clusters, edge services, connectivity directives, and the relevant application traffic policies. Configuration of CIFS acceleration must be performed from the Central Manager. Verification can be done in numerous locations, including the Central Manager, device GUI, and device CLI.

Configuring Core Services

The first step in configuring CIFS acceleration is to identify which WAAS devices will be configured with core services. Any WAAS device that is deployed near file servers that will be accessed in an accelerated fashion through a distant WAAS device should be configured with core services. Configuration of core services involves two steps: defining one or more WAFS core clusters, and enabling and starting core services on the WAAS devices themselves.

Creating a WAFS Core Cluster

A WAFS core cluster is a type of device group that identifies WAAS devices that are deployed within the same location that should act as aggregation points for WAAS devices configured with edge services performing CIFS acceleration. A WAFS core cluster should be configured for each location, and only in certain corner cases should multiple WAFS core clusters be required within a single location. Given that the vast majority of deployments do not require multiple core clusters in a given location, this text will not focus on such a deployment.

The WAFS core cluster is the entity that edge devices are mapped to through connectivity directives. When the connectivity directive information is propagated to edge WAAS devices, the information about each of the WAFS core cluster members is also sent. When the edge device receives this information, it retains it in memory to allow identification of an alternate cluster member should the member it is connected to fail. The edge device chooses the WAFS core cluster member to connect to by randomizing the list of devices contained in the cluster, and attempting connection sequentially through the list until the connection is accepted. If a connection from the edge to the core fails after it is already established, the edge assumes responsibility for attempting reconnection to a member of the WAFS core cluster. If all members of the WAFS core cluster are offline, the edge continuously attempts reconnection in 90-second intervals.

To configure the WAFS core cluster device group from the CM, choose **Devices > Device Groups** and click the **Create New Device Group** icon. Additionally, you can edit existing WAFS core cluster device groups from this page by clicking the **Edit** icon next to the device group entry. When you are defining or editing the device group, ensure that the Type field is set to **WAFS Core Cluster**.

The WAFS core cluster takes the following parameters, which you should consider prior to configuring the group:

- **Name:** The name of the device group. Generally, it is best practice to include the name of the location where the WAAS devices are deployed, to simplify management.

- **File server credentials:** The username and password that should be used by the core WAAS devices for preposition. Note that credentials are not required for accelerating interactive user sessions.

- **QoS configuration:** DSCP values can be assigned to high-priority accelerated CIFS messages, which can help improve performance, assuming QoS is configured in the network to handle these messages in a high-priority manner. An explicit value can be supplied, or the core cluster can be configured to match the settings configured on the edge devices connected to it.

- **Members:** WAAS devices that are already configured with core services can be assigned to the group.

Figure 9-3 shows the configuration page for defining or editing a WAFS core device group.

Figure 9-3 *Configuring WAFS Core Device Group*

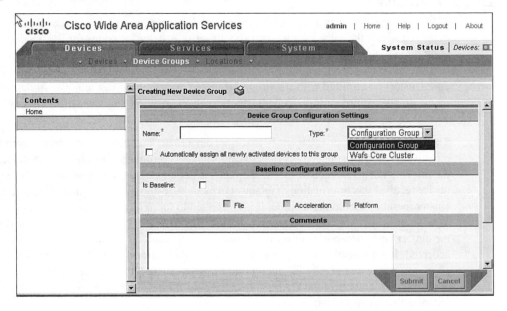

Enabling Core Services

The next step is to enable core services on each of the WAAS devices that are deployed near the file servers. Enabling core services starts the upper-layer process (ULP) on the WAAS devices, allowing them to listen for incoming proxy connections from edge services running on remote WAAS devices. To enable core services on the WAAS devices through the Central Manager, choose **Devices > Devices >** *WAE* **> File Services > Core Configuration**. From there, check the **Enable Core Server** check box and choose the core cluster to assign the WAAS device to.

Figure 9-4 shows the configuration page for enabling core services on the WAAS device. Note that enabling core services on a WAAS device requires that the device be rebooted before the service can be started.

Figure 9-4   *Enabling Core Services*

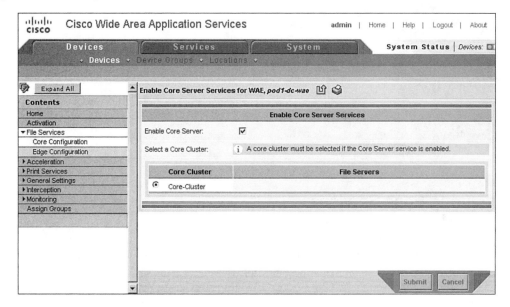

After you have enabled core services on the device, you can control and verify the status of the core services from the device GUI, which you can access in one of two ways:

- From the CM homepage of the device, click the Device GUI button.
- In your browser, browse directly to https://(ipaddress):8443/mgr, and then authenticate using the appropriate username and password.

Within the device GUI, navigate to **Cisco WAE > Control > Components**. The configured CIFS acceleration services (WAFS Core, WAFS Edge) are listed, with either a green check mark or a red X in the Status column. Ensure that the core service is started. You can control services by clicking the service name and then clicking **Start**, **Stop**, or **Restart**.

Figure 9-5 shows the device GUI homepage, where you can control and verify the status of CIFS acceleration services.

Figure 9-5 *Controlling CIFS Acceleration Services*

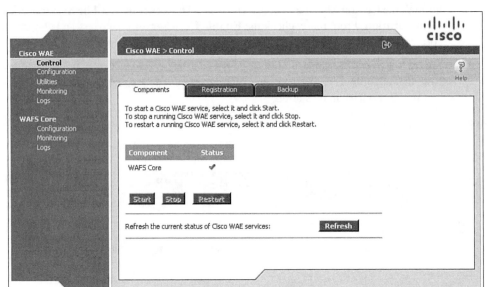

Configuring Edge Services

The next step in configuring CIFS acceleration is to configure edge services. Edge services should be enabled on WAAS devices that are deployed near users that are accessing remote file servers, when the remote file servers have adjacent WAAS devices configured with core services. Similar to configuring core services and core clusters, edge services must be configured through the CM. Choose **Devices > Devices >** *WAE* **> File Services > Edge Configuration**.

The Edge Configuration page, shown in Figure 9-6, takes the following parameters:

- **Enable Edge Server:** Checking this box enables edge CIFS acceleration services on the WAE. Enabling edge services requires a reboot of the WAE.

- **Enable Transparent Mode:** Ensure that this box is checked. Transparent mode allows the WAE to intercept CIFS messages destined to the origin server name for acceleration. Nontransparent mode, which requires the user map to a server name published by the WAE, is being phased out.

- **Active Directory Site Name:** Applicable only to nontransparent mode (which should not be used), this name allows the WAE to understand where in the Active Directory topology it is deployed to ensure that, should DFS referrals be encountered, the user can be routed to the appropriate link target. Again, ensure that **Enable Transparent Mode** is checked, and this parameter is not required.

- **Enable CIFS over NetBIOS Connections:** Checking this box allows the WAE to intercept CIFS requests on TCP port 139, which is used for CIFS messages transmitted over the NetBIOS session protocol. CIFS over NetBIOS is commonly used for legacy Windows releases (those released prior to Windows 2000). It is recommended that you check this box, to ensure legacy clients receive the benefits of acceleration.

- **Enable CIFS over TCP/IP Connections:** Checking this box allows the WAE to intercept CIFS requests on TCP port 445, which is used for CIFS messages transmitted natively over TCP. CIFS over TCP/IP is commonly used for newer Windows releases (from Windows 2000 on). Ensure that this box is checked.

- **Enable Double-Byte Language Support:** Checking this box allows the WAE to support double-byte characters, which is required for foreign language support and for optimizing Windows 98 clients. It is recommended that you check this box.

- **Set DSCP Value for High Priority Messages:** Checking this box allows the WAE to apply a configured DSCP value to high-priority CIFS messages that must be transferred over the WAN. Check this box if you are using QoS in the network, and supply a DSCP value that represents high-priority interactive traffic that aligns with your QoS strategy.

NOTE   As mentioned earlier, you can configure the core service to apply a DSCP setting to high-priority CIFS messages. You can also configure the core service to use the configuration settings applied to the connected edge WAE with which it is communicating.

Figure 9-6   *Enabling Edge Services*

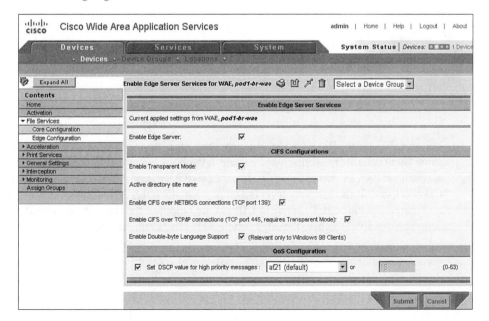

After you have configured edge services, you must reboot the WAE before the services can be utilized. This is due to the reprovisioning of the file system that must take place to allocate capacity for the CIFS object and metadata cache. You can reboot the system by using the **reload** CLI command, or by clicking the Reload WAE icon on the device homepage in the Central Manager.

Similar to core services, edge services can be verified and controlled from the device GUI. Figure 9-7 shows the device GUI with edge services enabled.

Figure 9-7 *Device GUI with Edge Services*

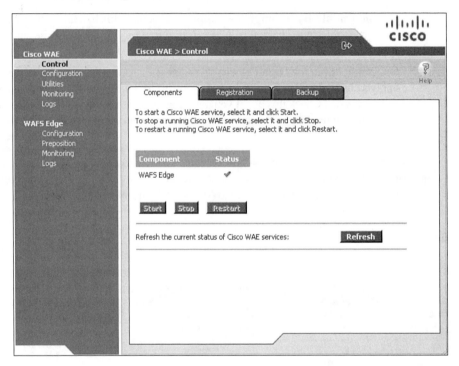

You can also use the WAE CLI to verify that the edge services are running. The command **show tfo accelerators**, as discussed earlier in the book, shows the status of each of the acceleration components of the WAE. In the case of edge services, a TFO accelerator named **CIFS** is listed. If the handling level is 100 percent, the CIFS edge services are properly configured and enabled. Example 9-1 shows the output of the **show tfo accelerators** command on a WAE where the edge services are functioning normally.

Example 9-1   *Verifying Edge Services Status from WAE CLI*

```
WAE# show tfo accelerators
Name: TFO                    State: Registered,  Handling Level: 100%
   Keepalive timeout: 3.0 seconds,  Session timeouts: 0,  Total timeouts: 0
   Last keepalive received 00.6 Secs ago
   Last registration occurred 48:13:14:05.4 Days:Hours:Mins:Secs ago
Name: EPM                    State: Not Registered,  Handling Level: 100%
   Keepalive timeout: 5.0 seconds,  Session timeouts: 0,  Total timeouts: 0
   Last keepalive received 48:13:14:19.0 Days:Hours:Mins:Secs ago
   Last registration occurred 48:13:14:21.0 Days:Hours:Mins:Secs ago
Name: CIFS                   State: Registered,  Handling Level: 100%
   Keepalive timeout: 4.0 seconds,  Session timeouts: 0,  Total timeouts: 0
   Last keepalive received 00.5 Secs ago
   Last registration occurred 48:13:13:09.9 Days:Hours:Mins:Secs ago
```

Configuring Connectivity Directives

Connectivity directives interlink WAE devices configured with edge services to those that are configured with core services for the purposes of CIFS acceleration. The connectivity directive defines the configuration for the transport over which CIFS proxy connections are established between edge and core WAE devices using TCP port 4050. CIFS-related messages that are exchanged between edge and core WAEs use this transport, which includes control and data exchanges.

To configure connectivity directives from the Central Manager, choose **Services > File > Connectivity** and specify the following parameters:

- **Name:** Provide a name for the connectivity directive. Connectivity directives are commonly named using a convention involving the core cluster name and the edge device or edge group name or location, such as BostonCore-SeattleEdge or simply Boston-Seattle.

- **Core Cluster:** Specify the core cluster that should provide one end of termination for this connectivity directive. All core cluster members will participate in this connectivity directive.

- **File Server Settings tab:** Defines how file server names are exported, which is only necessary for nontransparent CIFS deployments. Using nontransparent CIFS deployments is not recommended, so do not apply any changes to this tab.

- **Edge Devices or Groups:** Specify which edge devices or edge device groups should provide the opposite end of termination for this connectivity directive. All items defined must be of the same type; that is, there cannot be a mix of edge devices and edge groups in the connectivity directive definition.

- **WAN Utilization:** Defines the WAN bandwidth and latency characteristics of the link connecting the edge and core devices. This allows the edge WAE to calculate the number of proxy connections that must be established between edge and core to ensure that the link capacity can be fully leveraged.

NOTE	Cisco WAAS automatically detects CIFS servers and does not require that you manually define each of them. You can define CIFS servers manually (at **Services > File > File Servers**) if you want to, but there is no benefit in doing so. This text focuses solely on deployment scenarios where WAAS is allowed to automatically detect CIFS servers and does not cover deployment scenarios where CIFS servers are explicitly configured.
	Additionally, Cisco WAAS will bypass acceleration in very low-latency environments to eliminate resource consumption. This is manifested when users connect to file servers through WAAS devices over a LAN.

Because WAN utilization is configured as part of the connectivity directive, sharing a connectivity directive across a group of edge devices is recommended only if the WAN bandwidth and latency between the core devices and all of the edge devices is very similar. The edge device calculates the BDP of the network, and determines the number of proxy connections to establish to the selected core cluster member from the connectivity directive. As described in a note earlier in the chapter, the edge can establish up to 20 proxy connections to the core for a given connectivity directive.

The proxy connections that are established between edge and core devices use the underlying WAN optimization framework provided by WAAS, including TFO. TFO helps to ensure fairness among optimized and unoptimized connections by using an adaptive congestion avoidance mechanism. The congestion avoidance mechanism in TFO aggressively increases the available window capacity in scenarios where packet loss is absent, and reverts to a less aggressive behavior that closely resembles TCP when packet loss is frequent.

This is important for ensuring that proxy connections—even in networks without QoS—do not compromise on all of the available WAN bandwidth. If the proxy connections begin consuming a significant portion of WAN bandwidth—to the point that it causes congestion—the proxy connections will be throttled due to the adaptive congestion avoidance of TFO. To summarize this concept, configuring the actual link speed and WAN latency in the connectivity directive will not cause accelerated CIFS traffic over the proxied connections from starving other accelerated or pass-through connections from being able to leverage their fair share of network capacity. In situations where the bandwidth is freely available without contention, the proxy connections will be able to leverage a generous portion of the link capacity.

After you define the connectivity directive, you can use the WAE CLI to validate the presence of proxy connections. Additionally, you can use the WAE device GUI to validate connectivity between edge and core.

Example 9-2 shows how to verify the presence of CIFS acceleration proxy connections from the WAE CLI.

Example 9-2 *Verifying CIFS Acceleration Proxy Connections*

```
WAE# show tfo connection summary server-port 4050
Optimized Connection List
Policy summary order: Our's, Peer's, Negotiated, Applied
F: Full optimization, D: DRE only, L: LZ Compression, T: TCP Optimization
Local-IP:Port        Remote-IP:Port       ConId   PeerId            Policy
10.10.100.2:13512    10.10.10.240:4050    119815  00:05:9a:3d:31:dd F,F,F,F
10.10.100.2:13513    10.10.10.240:4050    119816  00:05:9a:3d:31:dd F,F,F,F
10.10.100.2:13514    10.10.10.240:4050    119817  00:05:9a:3d:31:dd F,F,F,F
10.10.13.240:37849   10.10.10.240:4050    2       00:11:25:ac:3c:5c F,F,F,F
10.10.13.240:37850   10.10.10.240:4050    3       00:11:25:ac:3c:5c F,F,F,F
10.10.13.240:37851   10.10.10.240:4050    4       00:11:25:ac:3c:5c F,F,F,F
```

You can also use the WAE device GUI to validate the presence of CIFS acceleration proxy connections. On the edge WAE, choose **WAFS Edge > Monitoring > Connectivity**. On the core WAE, choose **WAFS Core > Monitoring > Connectivity**. Figure 9-8 shows an example of using the device GUI to validate connectivity between edge and core, as shown from the edge device GUI.

Figure 9-8 *Validating CIFS Proxy Connections Using Edge Device GUI*

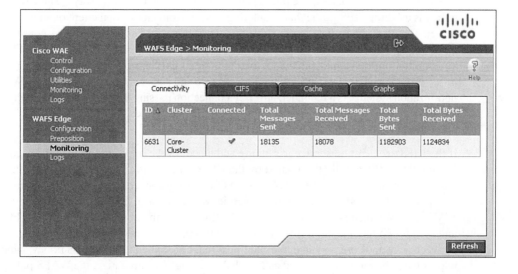

Examining CIFS Acceleration Traffic Policies

The final piece in verifying the configuration of CIFS acceleration is to examine the configuration of the CIFS acceleration traffic policies. These policies are configured by default and should require no modification. However, an examination of each of the policies is provided here to enable you to understand the reason for the policies and, if you ever need to change them, give you a reference for how to ensure they are configured correctly.

Like other application traffic policies, as discussed in Chapter 8, the CIFS acceleration policies are constructed using the ATP, and can be defined explicitly against a device or a device group. For the purposes of ensuring consistent configuration, it is recommended that these policies be configured against a device group. The CIFS acceleration policies are included in the default policy that is, by default, applied to the AllDevicesGroup.

CIFS acceleration relies on two policies:

- **CIFS policy:** A basic policy that defines the application as "WAFS" using traffic classifier CIFS, and specifies that the flow should be handled by the CIFS Accelerator. An optimization of Full Optimization is specified, in case any of the messages require transmission over the WAN.

- **WAFS policy:** A WAFS transport policy that defines the application as "WAFS" using traffic classifier Match All Traffic, and specifies that the flow should leverage the optimization of Full Optimization.

The CIFS accelerator uses these policies individually in the following ways. The CIFS policy is used for CIFS traffic that is entering a WAE from an external client or an external server. That is, when a client issues a CIFS request, or a server issues a CIFS response, the CIFS policy is used to classify the traffic as CIFS and direct the traffic first to the CIFS acceleration service running on that particular node. If CIFS acceleration is not configured, traffic is not passed to the CIFS acceleration service and is instead passed through the WAN optimization system. As a reminder, any TCP connection passing through WAN optimization must complete automatic discovery for any policy to be applied, and CIFS is not an exception.

If the CIFS acceleration service is running and a peer of the opposite service type is connected, the traffic is fully terminated by the CIFS acceleration service. Any traffic that requires transmission over the WAN uses the CIFS proxy connections, which are internally generated by the local CIFS acceleration service (edge or core). This traffic is caught by the WAFS policy, which is configured for Full Optimization, thereby leveraging DRE, TFO, and PLZ for communications over the WAN. CIFS proxy connections that are established between edge and core populate internal filters that are applied to the WAFS policy, which allows the policy to be configured as Match All Traffic. To summarize, the WAFS policy, even though it is configured as Match All Traffic, will be applied only to CIFS proxy connections.

Figure 9-9 shows the configuration pages for the CIFS traffic policy and the WAFS traffic policy.

Figure 9-9   *CIFS Acceleration Policies*

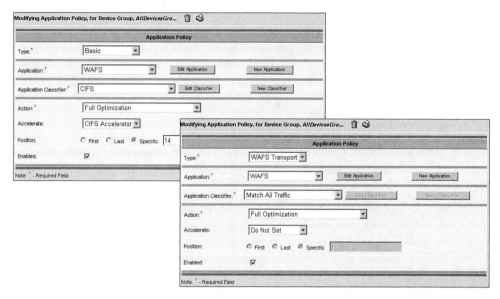

CIFS acceleration policies, like other application traffic policies, appear in the running-config file of the WAEs themselves. Thus, you can use the CLI to validate that the policies are configured correctly. Example 9-3 shows the output of the **show running-config** command with the CIFS acceleration policies displayed.

Example 9-3   *Verifying CIFS Acceleration Policies*

```
WAE# show running-config
… portions removed …
policy-engine application
   name WAFS
   classifier CIFS
      match dst port eq 139
      match dst port eq 445
   map basic
      name WAFS classifier CIFS action optimize full accelerate CIFS-adaptor
   map adaptor WAFS transport
      name WAFS All action optimize full
```

Verifying CIFS Acceleration

With services configured, connectivity directives defined, and policies in place, WAAS can move beyond basic WAN optimization of CIFS traffic and into the realm of accelerating CIFS traffic. The difference between the two is that WAN optimization primarily minimizes bandwidth consumption for CIFS traffic, whereas acceleration of CIFS traffic mitigates latency and can tremendously improve the user experience. As discussed earlier, because CIFS is a chatty protocol, WAN optimization alone might not improve the user experience in latency-bound environments.

WAAS provides numerous facilities for verifying that CIFS acceleration is occurring. These facilities exist in the device CLI and the device GUI. An examination of these facilities is provided in this section. Before proceeding, it is important to note again that CIFS is a session-oriented protocol, and CIFS sessions tend to be very long-lived—even if the underlying transport connection is broken and reestablished. The CIFS acceleration capabilities provided in WAAS rely on the presence of two important situations before CIFS can be accelerated:

- **Full visibility to the establishment of the TCP connection:** WAAS must see the TCP connection from the beginning in order to complete the TFO AD process described in Chapter 8.

- **Full visibility to the establishment of the CIFS session:** WAAS must see the establishment of the CIFS session between the client and server in order to begin applying CIFS acceleration to the session.

If WAAS does not have visibility to the establishment of the TCP connection, WAE devices will be unable to automatically discover one another. In this scenario, the connection will be treated as pass-through and neither optimization nor acceleration will be applied. If WAAS does not have visibility to the establishment of the CIFS session, WAE devices will be unable to discern the state of the user to server connection, nor will WAE devices be able to discern whether or not the user has successfully authenticated, whether or not the user has become authorized, or what share or file is being used by that particular user. In this scenario, the session will be treated as pass-through by the CIFS acceleration system, even if it is optimized by the WAN optimization layer beneath it.

Put simply, if connections or user sessions were established prior to enabling CIFS acceleration, you must break these connections and reestablish them for WAAS to be able to optimize and accelerate them. Multiple means of forcing reestablishment of the CIFS session and underlying TCP connection exist, including:

- Reboot the client machine
- Disable and enable the client network adapter
- Log out and log back into the client machine
- From the server, disconnect the user session

NOTE   One of the biggest challenges faced by those implementing CIFS acceleration is long-lived user sessions. Be sure to pay careful attention to this seemingly trivial detail when implementing CIFS acceleration.

The following device CLI commands, executed on the edge, can help validate the presence of CIFS acceleration. You should execute these commands only after user sessions have been established through a properly configured WAAS network in which CIFS acceleration is configured correctly.

Example 9-4 shows the use of the **show cifs connectivity peers** command, which validates that peer devices running the opposite CIFS acceleration services are connected. This command can be executed on either edge or core devices.

Example 9-4   *Verifying Presence of CIFS Peers*

```
WAE# show cifs connectivity peers
In_1219580214_10.10.100.2
In_1003195315_10.10.13.240
```

Example 9-5 shows the use of the **show cifs session count** and **show cifs session list** commands, which, respectively, identify the number of accelerated CIFS sessions and identify each of the accelerated CIFS sessions. These commands can be executed from the edge only, and will return an error message if executed from the core.

Example 9-5   *Verifying Accelerated CIFS Sessions*

```
WAE# show cifs session count
1
WAE# show cifs session list
Accelerated CIFS Sessions
Client                  Server              State   Idle(s)  Resolved
10.10.13.100:2593       10.10.10.100:445    active  38       server.peap.local
```

You can also use the device GUI to validate the presence of accelerated CIFS connections. From the device GUI, choose **WAFS Edge > Monitoring > CIFS**, and examine the field **Connected Sessions Count**. Figure 9-10 shows sample output from this page.

This page also provides other valuable information, including the amount of time saved by using CIFS acceleration, the number of locally served requests as compared to the number of requests that needed to traverse the WAN, and the number of files that are open through accelerated CIFS sessions.

Figure 9-10 *Verifying Accelerated CIFS Sessions from Edge Device GUI*

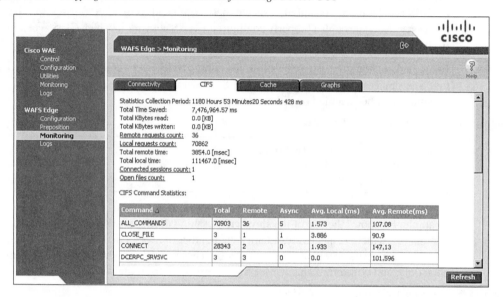

CIFS Preposition

The CIFS acceleration capability of WAAS includes a feature that allows you to schedule the delivery of selected pieces of information to a specific WAE device. This feature, called CIFS preposition (or just preposition), populates the CIFS cache in the target WAE (running edge services) and the DRE compression history. The use cases for CIFS preposition are significant, including:

- **Software distribution:** Improve the performance and delivery of applications, software updates, and service packs to remote offices

- **Prime the compression history:** Prepopulate the compression history on multiple devices with data that may be used interactively by users

- **Enable disconnected operations:** Ensure specific content is available in the cache when transitioning into disconnected mode of operation (discussed later, in the section "Disconnected Mode of Operation"

- **Ensure highest performance for first open:** Prepopulating data to the edge cache, which also populates the compression history, improves the performance for the first user accessing the content

CIFS Preposition Architecture

CIFS preposition is a component of CIFS acceleration. Thus, CIFS acceleration must be configured and operational before preposition can be configured. Preposition is configured from the Central Manager and cannot be configured from the CLI. Architecturally, preposition is a capability that leverages the following pieces in the manner described:

- **Central Manager:** Used to define the preposition task, origin server, destination (WAEs running edge services), job details, and schedule

- **Core WAE:** Fetches a manifest (list of contents) from the origin server based on the job configuration and sends that manifest to the edge. The Edge WAE then proactively fetches content that is new or has changed based on the status of the edge cache

- **Edge WAE:** Receives the manifest from the core WAE, and then begins requesting objects from the core based on the difference between the current cache state and manifest that was received from the core

In essence, the core acts as a "staging area," because it is unaware of the status of the edge cache. The core, once it receives the manifest from the origin server (based on the job configuration), passes the manifest to the edge. Then, the core begins fetching files from the origin server based on the manifest. These files are then stored in a temporary staging area, which is ~1 GB in capacity. As the edge fetches files, they are removed from the staging area and the core continues to fetch additional files from the origin server. If the staging area becomes full of files, and the edge requests a file that is not in the staging area, the core will know that the edge does not need any of the files found in the staging area. In such a case, the core will empty its staging area and begin fetching files from the origin server starting with the file requested by the edge. Because the core and edge are working from the same manifest, the core can adapt and evict files from the staging area based on the requests coming from the edge.

Preposition tasks have a number of configurable parameters that allow you to specify content, origin server, size parameters, and time parameters. For instance, you can specify that a preposition job should run for no more than 1 hour, and copy all *.msi files that are at least 1 MB from a particular server to all of the edge WAEs. The parameters that you can configure on a preposition task include:

- **Name:** Name of the preposition task. It is recommended that the type of content being prepositioned be referenced in the name (for instance, InstallerFiles or ServicePacks).

- **Status:** A preposition task can either be "enabled" or "disabled."

- **File Server:** Prepositioning requires that the origin server be defined under the System > File > File Servers tab. This is the origin server that the content will be fetched from, as well as the root share, directories, and filename patterns.

- **Cache Parameters:** Specify the percentage of cache capacity that can be consumed before the edge is instructed to stop fetching new files. This allows you to impose a capacity limit around the preposition task itself.

- **File Parameters:** Specify the minimum file size, maximum file size, and type of preposition task (all files, changed since last preposition, or changed in the last specified interval).

- **Edge Devices:** Defines the target devices or device groups that should be populated with the content referenced in the task. Note that devices or device groups can be defined.

- **Schedule:** Defines when the preposition job should run, including now (immediate), daily (including a start time), date (specify a date), weekly (specify a day of week), monthly (specify one or more days of the month), or monthly weekdays (specify, for instance, the third Sunday of each week).

Figure 9-11 shows the architecture of preposition, along with the interaction of the edge, core, and origin server.

Figure 9-11 *CIFS Preposition Architecture*

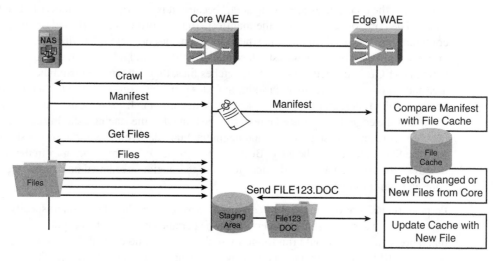

NOTE   CIFS preposition uses the underlying CIFS proxy connections for transfer, which leverage DRE, TFO, and persistent LZ. Files transferred through preposition will also populate the DRE compression history, which can provide substantial performance improvement if the data is written back by a remote user to a server in the data center.

Configuring CIFS Preposition

The first step in configuring CIFS preposition is to define the origin server from which you wish to fetch content. In the Central Manager, choose **Services > File > File Servers**, click the **Create New File Server** icon, and then define the following parameters (see Figure 9-12):

- **File Server Name:** Supply either the NetBIOS name, fully qualified domain name (FQDN), or IP address of the file server that you wish to distribute content from.

- **Allow Access on WAN Failure:** This item is used by disconnected mode of operation, discussed in the next section. Check this box if you are using disconnected mode of operation.

Then, click **Assign Core Clusters** in the left to specify a core cluster that is near the file server. One member of the core cluster will be responsible for fetching files and acting as a staging area for the content during the execution of the preposition task.

Figure 9-12 *Defining a File Server*

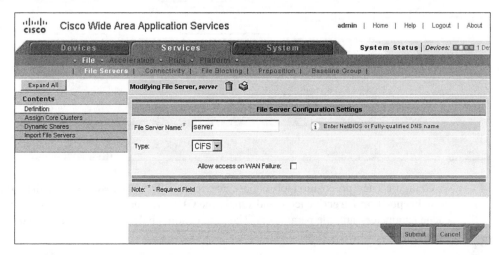

It is important to note that the core cluster you select should be configured with the appropriate credentials for accessing the file server. To configure the credentials for a core cluster, choose **Devices > Device Groups > ** *<devicegroupname>* **> Core Server Settings**. The credentials configured on this page are used only during preposition tasks, and are not required for accelerating interactive CIFS sessions from a user to a server.

Figure 9-13 shows the Central Manager configuration page for defining the credentials used by a core cluster when connecting to a file server for the purposes of prepositioning. The credentials supplied need only read access to the share and its contents; it is not necessary to supply read/write access. You should always follow the principle of least privilege when distributing permissions to network devices.

The next step in configuring preposition is to create the preposition job. Before continuing, be sure you have a solid understanding of what it is you want to preposition, where you want to preposition it to, and where the content should be fetched from. A good list to examine before defining a preposition job is the second list in the previous section ("CIFS Preposition Architecture"), which outlines the configuration items associated with a preposition job.

Figure 9-13 *Core Cluster Credentials*

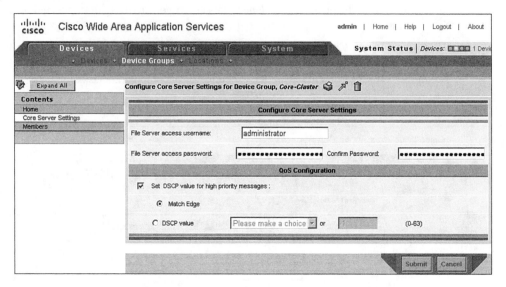

To configure a new preposition job, choose **Services > File > Preposition**, click the **Create New Preposition Directive** icon, and supply the GUI with the name, status, file server, cache parameters, and file parameters. The preposition job definition page is shown in Figure 9-14.

Figure 9-14 *Preposition Directive Configuration*

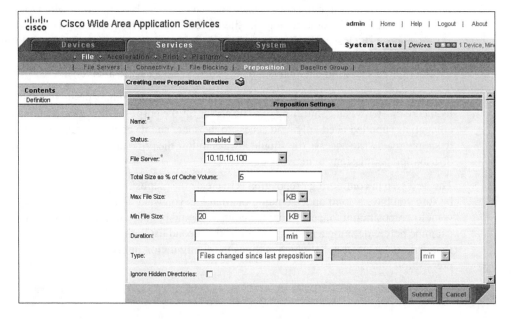

Of particular interest on the preposition job configuration page is the Browse button that appears after you have specified the file server. Clicking this button enables you to interactively select shares and folders contained within those shares in a similar manner to using a file browser. Using this tool simplifies the definition of the source location that content should be distributed from.

Figure 9-15 shows an example of the interactive browser provided within the preposition job configuration page. When navigating the preposition browser, be sure not to use the browser's Back button. Instead, use the navigation options such as the "move up to parent folder" icon, which is represented as a blue arrow.

Figure 9-15   *Preposition Directive Browser*

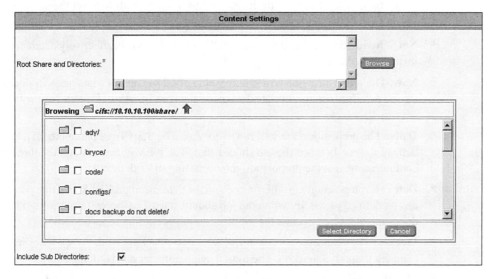

After you have specified the initial preposition job parameters, click the **Submit** button to save the configuration. Upon saving the parameters, the table of contents in the left pane will adjust to show the remainder of the preposition configuration items, which include edge device/group assignment and schedule. Similar to other configuration items, edge devices and edge groups can be configured by simply clicking the blue X next to the device or group name, and this configuration can be saved by clicking **Submit**.

Figure 9-16 shows an example of the appearance of the edge group configuration page. Notice that the Branch-WAEs group is already configured as a target for this preposition job, and the AllDevicesGroup has been selected but the update has not yet been submitted. It should be noted that the configuration page for selecting one or more edge devices individually is very similar, but shows the list of unique devices as opposed to the list of groups.

Figure 9-16 *Defining Preposition Job Edge Groups*

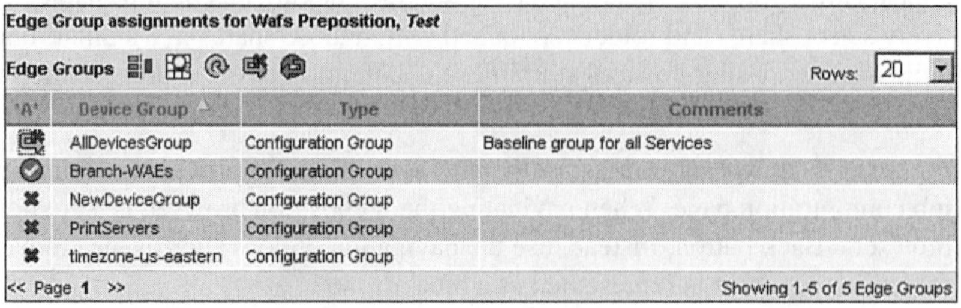

After selecting the target devices or device groups, click **Schedule** to set the schedule for the preposition job. Preposition jobs can be assigned one of the following schedules:

- **Not Scheduled:** The preposition job will not run. The job is effectively disabled when it is not scheduled.

- **Now:** The preposition job will run immediately. The Central Manager will distribute the job details to the appropriate devices on the next LCM cycle interaction with those devices.

- **Daily:** The preposition job will run every day. The Start Time parameter can be defined to specify when the job should start. The job will run through the duration configured against the preposition job according to its definition.

- **Date:** The preposition job will run once on the date specified. The Start Time parameter can be defined to specify when the job should start. The job will run through the duration configured against the preposition job according to its definition.

- **Weekly:** The preposition job will run weekly on the days of the week specified (Sunday through Saturday). The Start Time parameter can be defined.

- **Monthly Days:** The preposition job will run monthly on the individual days selected (1 through 31). The Start Time parameter can be defined. If the defined days do not exist in a particular month (for instance, if you check 30 and enter the month of February), the job will not run. As such, it is best to configure preposition jobs to run earlier in the month as opposed to later.

- **Monthly Weekdays:** The preposition job will run upon encountering the specific occurrence of a particular weekday. For instance, the third Thursday of every month. The Start Time parameter can be defined.

Figure 9-17 shows an example of the configuration page for defining the schedule of a preposition job.

After you have defined the preposition job, it appears in the Preposition Status window. This window shows the target edge devices and groups, and identifies the start time, duration, amount copied, status, and any reason associated with the job status.

Figure 9-17 *Configuring Preposition Job Schedule*

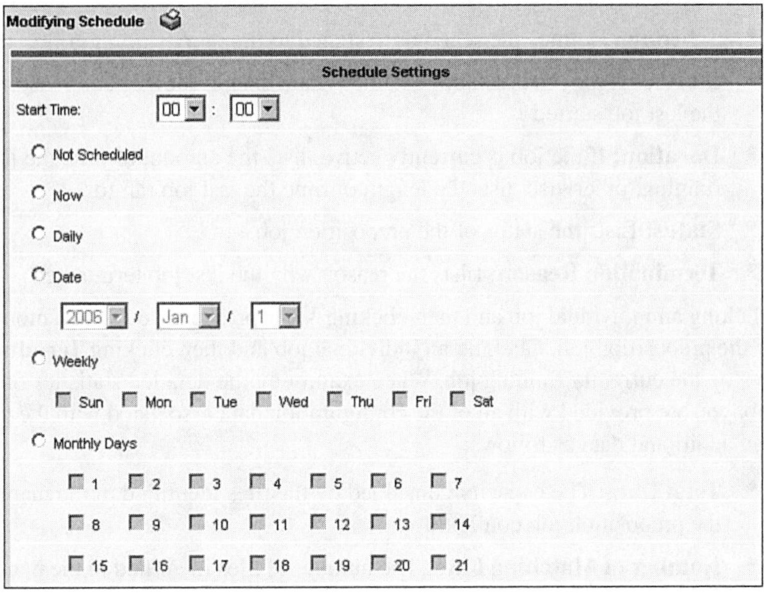

Modifying Schedule

Schedule Settings

Start Time: 00 ▼ : 00 ▼

○ Not Scheduled

○ Now

○ Daily

○ Date

    2006 ▼ / Jan ▼ / 1 ▼

○ Weekly

    ☐ Sun ☐ Mon ☐ Tue ☐ Wed ☐ Thu ☐ Fri ☐ Sat

○ Monthly Days

    ☐ 1   ☐ 2   ☐ 3   ☐ 4   ☐ 5   ☐ 6   ☐ 7

    ☐ 8   ☐ 9   ☐ 10 ☐ 11 ☐ 12 ☐ 13 ☐ 14

    ☐ 15 ☐ 16 ☐ 17 ☐ 18 ☐ 19 ☐ 20 ☐ 21

Examining Preposition Statistics

As mentioned in the previous section, you can examine the status of a preposition job on the Preposition Status page in the Central Manager (choose **Services > File > Preposition > Preposition Job > Preposition Status**). Figure 9-18 shows an example of the preposition status.

Figure 9-18 *Preposition Status in Central Manager*

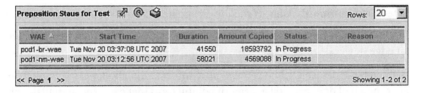

WAE	Start Time	Duration	Amount Copied	Status	Reason
pod1-br-wae	Tue Nov 20 03:37:08 UTC 2007	41550	18593792	In Progress	
pod1-nm-wae	Tue Nov 20 03:12:56 UTC 2007	58021	4569088	In Progress	

<< Page **1** >>   Showing 1-2 of 2

The Central Manager is not the only place that you can check the preposition status. You can examine the device GUI for the edge devices to see the status and statistics for each of the preposition jobs. Open the device GUI for the edge and choose **WAFS Edge > Preposition** to see a tabular view containing the following information:

- **Job ID:** A unique identifier, created by WAAS, that identifies the preposition job
- **Description:** The name of the preposition job

- **Root Directory:** Defines the listing of servers, shares, and folders that are included in the preposition job

- **Schedule:** Defines the schedule assigned to the preposition job

- **Started:** If the job is running, defines when the job started; otherwise, identifies when the last job started

- **Duration:** If the job is currently active, lists the amount of time the job has been running; otherwise, lists the length of time the last job ran for

- **Status:** Lists the status of the preposition job

- **Termination Reason:** Lists the reason why the last job terminated

Clicking an individual job and then clicking **View** provides you with a more detailed view of the preposition job. Clicking an individual job and then clicking **Terminate** allows you to stop the currently running job. When examining the detailed statistics of a preposition job, you are provided with all of the configuration data associated with the preposition job, and additional data as follows:

- **Total Data:** The capacity consumed by the files identified in the manifest as per the preposition job configuration.

- **Number of Matching Files:** The number of files identified in the manifest as per the preposition job configuration.

- **Amount Copied:** The amount of data that has been copied up to this point as a result of running the preposition job.

- **Number of Files Copied:** The number of files copied up to this point as a result of running the preposition job.

- **Throughput:** The average rate of transmission of the preposition job. Note that throughput is listed in kBps, as opposed to kbps or Mbps.

- **Status:** The status of the current job.

- **Termination Reason:** If the job terminated, the reason why the job terminated.

Figure 9-19 shows the status page from a preposition job as seen from the device GUI of an edge device.

Although the device CLI does not expose information about specific preposition jobs that are running, it does provide a series of helpful tools that can expose statistics about the edge cache. For instance, you can examine the disk capacity consumed by the CIFS cache from the device CLI, and identify the number of objects stored in the CIFS cache. During a preposition job, if there are any changed files or new files, these counters will increment as the files are fetched. Neither the device CLI nor the device GUI exposes the list of files that are cached in the device itself. This is done to ensure the security of the contents of the WAE disk contents.

Figure 9-19 *Preposition Status from Edge Device GUI*

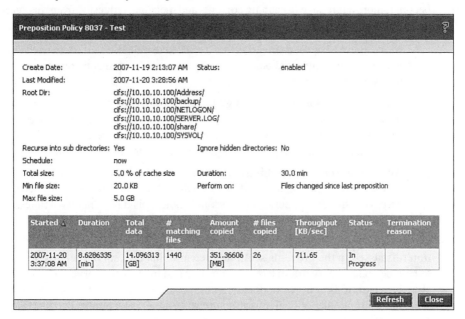

Example 9-6 shows the output of the commands that can be executed from the WAE CLI
to examine cache disk capacity consumption and the number of cached objects.

Example 9-6 *Examining Cache Consumption and Number of Objects*

```
WAE# show cifs cache entry-count
86
WAE# show cifs cache disk-use
513667072
```

Disconnected Mode of Operation

The last capability of the CIFS acceleration component of Cisco WAAS covered in this
chapter is disconnected mode of operation. Disconnected mode of operation, also called
disconnected mode, is a caching model that, when implemented on the edge, allows the
edge WAE to provide read-only service to remote users in the event of a network or service
disconnection. Disconnected mode is a configurable parameter and is applied to a server
that has been defined in the Central Manager. When this setting is applied (by checking the

Allow Access on WAN Failure check box, shown earlier in Figure 9-12), the edge device becomes more aggressive in caching contents and metadata requested from this server. This behavior can be characterized as follows:

- **More aggressive read-ahead requests:** The edge device will try to cache larger portions of the requested objects to improve probability that an object is available in the event of a WAN disconnection.

- **Directory and metadata caching:** The edge device normally caches directory metadata for a short period of time (5 seconds) to optimize interactive user operations such as folder browsing. With disconnected mode, the edge device caches directory metadata persistently, until evicted due to change or capacity constraints.

- **Access control entry caching:** The edge device, which normally does not cache access control information, will begin caching this data, and use it for determining access control during periods of disconnection. This data is not used unless the network is in a disconnected state.

It is recommended that disconnected mode be used in conjunction with CIFS preposition (discussed in the previous section) to ensure that contents of interest are available during periods of network disconnection. For instance, if the server being made available during periods of network disconnection is used to provide application installation files, hotfixes, or other critical infrastructure software, it is recommended that one or more preposition jobs be configured to run periodically to ensure that these objects are cached. Using preposition helps to improve the likelihood that the objects are available during periods of disconnection. In reality, it is not the *server* that needs to be available during periods of disconnection, but rather the *information* stored on that server.

Disconnected mode of operation requires that a local Active Directory domain controller be reachable on the network to successfully transition into disconnected mode. That is, if the network becomes severed, a domain controller must be reachable to authenticate users. For remote offices in which a domain controller is installed, or in cases where the connection to the data center is severed but a domain controller can be reached elsewhere, the edge device can transition into disconnected mode without an issue. Given that the edge device never locally authenticates a user (it relies on the authentication provided within CIFS at the beginning of each session), the edge device cannot provide value in disconnected mode if a domain controller is not available to authenticate users.

Domain Integration

Disconnected mode requires that edge devices be joined to the Active Directory domain. By joining the edge device into the domain, it can then forward authentication requests to a domain controller for the purpose of authenticating users. If a user is *authenticated* successfully by a domain controller (that is, the user's identity is verified through the request that was forwarded by the edge device to the domain controller), the edge device can then *authorize* the user based on cached access control entries for the object in question. If the edge device cannot reach a domain controller, or does not have cached the access control entry information about the object being requested, then the object will not be made available.

Domain integration can be configured from the Central Manager, device GUI, or device CLI. For purposes of ensuring simplicity, this chapter covers integration of the WAE into the domain using the Central Manager or the device CLI.

Configuring System Time

The first step in ensuring integration into the domain is to set the correct time zone and time on each WAE. Domain integration requires that each domain member, including WAEs, be no more than 5 minutes askew from the relative time on the domain controller. That is, the time difference on the WAE, after accounting for time zone differences, must be within 5 minutes of the relative time on the domain controller.

The simplest way to align time on the WAE device with the domain is to first set the time zone on each WAE and then configure each WAE to use a Network Time Protocol (NTP) server. Although this can be easily accomplished through the device CLI, as you can see in Example 9-7, recommended practice dictates that you create unique device groups, where each device group represents a separate time zone. After you add the appropriate WAE devices into each timezone-based device group, you can apply the NTP server settings to the device group.

Example 9-7 *Configuring Time Zone and Time on Device CLI*

```
WAE# show clock
Local time: Wed Nov 21 23:09:49 UTC 2007
WAE# clock set 23:49:00 21 Nov 2007
WAE# configure
WAE(config)# clock timezone PST8PDT -8 0
WAE(config)# ntp server 10.10.10.100
```

Figure 9-20 shows how to configure NTP server settings from the Central Manager against a device group. To reach this page, choose **Devices > Device Groups >** *Device Group* > **General Settings > Miscellaneous > Date/Time > Time Zone**.

Figure 9-20 *Configuring NTP Server Settings in Central Manager*

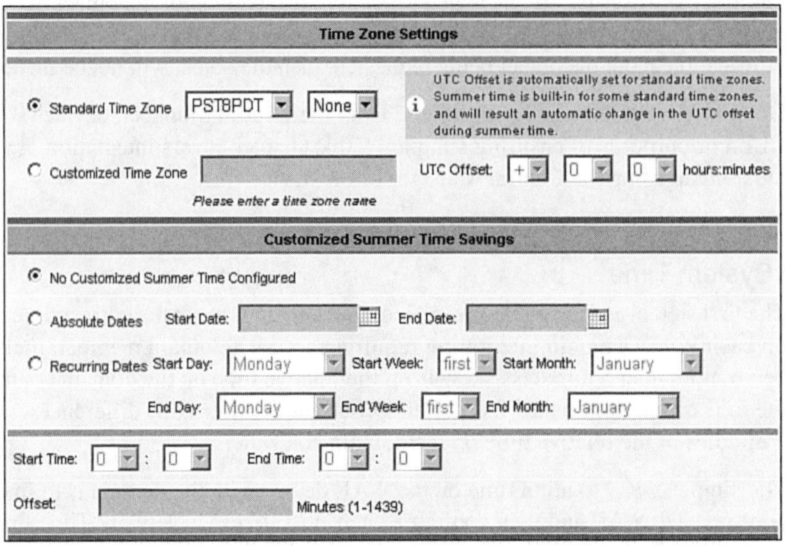

Once the system time between the WAE and the domain has been aligned, and is within a 5-minute skew, the next step is to ensure each WAE device has an assigned NetBIOS name. You can configure the NetBIOS name from either the device CLI or the Central Manager. Example 9-8 shows how to configure the WAE NetBIOS name from the device CLI.

Example 9-8 *Configuring WAE NetBIOS Name from Device CLI*

```
WAE# configure
WAE(config)# windows-domain netbios-name POD1-BR-WAE
```

Figure 9-21 shows how to configure the WAE NetBIOS name from the Central Manager using the activation page found at Devices > Devices > *WAE Device Name* > Activation. Note that device groups cannot be used for configuring NetBIOS names, because each NetBIOS name within the domain must be unique. Thus, a NetBIOS name cannot be shared among WAEs; each must be unique.

Figure 9-21 *Configuring WAE NetBIOS Name from Central Manager*

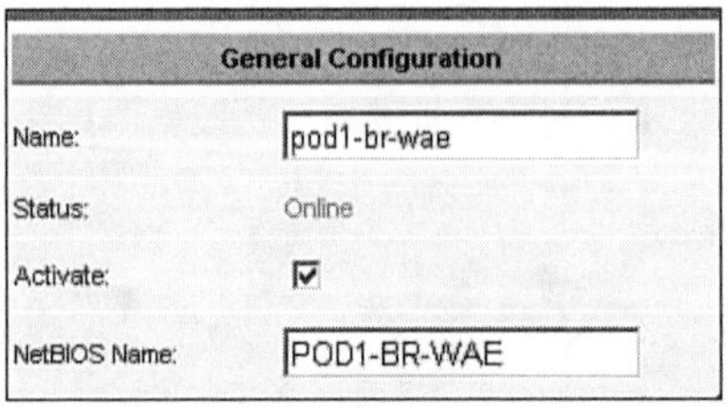

Defining Domain-Related Parameters

The next step in domain integration is to define domain-related parameters within each WAE device or against a common device group. If WAEs are to be registered against multiple autonomous domains, it is recommended that you either apply the domain settings individually to each WAE or configure separate device groups to represent each possible configuration. If WAEs are to be registered against a single domain using common, shared parameters, it is recommended that you apply these settings against the AllDevicesGroup device group. Domain-related parameters include the following, which much be configured:

- **Domain Name Server (DNS) addresses:** Used for name resolution.

- **Windows Internet Name Service (WINS) Server addresses:** Used if DNS is not available. WINS may not be necessary, as many customers have migrated to DNS-based Active Directory and phased WINS out of their environments.

- **Domain Name:** The domain name that the WAE will be integrated into.

- **Domain Controller IP or Fully Qualified Domain Name (FQDN):** The IP address or FQDN on the domain controller that the WAE should attempt to register itself with.

- **Authentication Protocol Specific Options:** Parameters related to the authentication protocol being used. Because Kerberos is the most commonly encountered, this chapter focuses on Kerberos specifically. Note that NTLMv1 and v2 are also supported.

Example 9-9 shows how to configure the DNS and WINS server entries from the device CLI.

Example 9-9   *Configuring DNS and WINS Settings from Device CLI*

```
WAE# configure
WAE(config)# ip domain-name company.com
WAE(config)# ip name-server 10.10.10.100
WAE(config)# windows-domain wins-server 10.10.10.100
WAE(config)# windows-domain workgroup "PEAP"
```

You can also configure the DNS and WINS settings from the Central Manager using the following pages, which you access from the device homepage:

- **Domain Name:** General Settings > Network > DNS

- **DNS Server Addresses:** General Settings > Network > DNS

- **Windows Domain Name:** General Settings > Network > Windows Name Services

- **WINS Server Addresses:** General Settings > Network > Windows Name Services

The next step is to define the domain controller either by its IP address or its FQDN. Example 9-10 shows how to define the domain controller in the device CLI. Kerberos is shown in this example.

Example 9-10 *Defining Domain Controller Using Device CLI*

```
WAE# configure
WAE(config)# kerberos local-realm COMPANY.COM
WAE(config)# kerberos realm company.com COMPANY.COM
WAE(config)# kerberos server COMPANY.COM 10.10.10.100 port 88
WAE(config)# windows-domain password-server "company.com"
WAE(config)# windows-domain security ADS
WAE(config)# windows-domain realm "COMPANY.COM"
```

From the Central Manager GUI, you can configure these same settings by choosing **Devices > Devices >** *WAE Device Name* **> General Settings > Authentication > Windows Domain**. If the WAE or WAEs are to be integrated into a Windows domain where Windows 2000 Server Service Pack 4 or newer or Windows 2003 Server Service Pack 1 or newer is being used, it is recommended that you also add the command shown in Example 9-11.

Example 9-11 *Additional Command to Support Newer Windows Domains*

```
WAE# configure
WAE(config)# smb-conf section global name "client schannel" value "no"
```

Joining an Active Directory Domain

After you have applied the configuration, the next step is to instruct the WAE to join the Windows domain, which you can do from either the device CLI or the Central Manager. The Central Manager provides a status screen that automates verification of all of the domain integration components. The CLI, on the other hand, does not, but commands are available to validate successful integration and, more importantly, why an attempt to join the Windows domain failed.

To join a Windows domain using Kerberos from the device CLI, execute the command shown in Example 9-12. When executing this command, be sure to include the quotes, but do not use the brackets, which are only there to show you the value that needs to be supplied. It is important to note that the credentials supplied (username and password) must have the appropriate permissions within the Windows domain to add new computer accounts. It is generally recommended that the domain administrator credentials be used.

Example 9-12 *Joining a Windows Domain from the Device CLI*

```
WAE# windows-domain diag net "ads join -S servername -U username%password"
Using short domain name -- PEAP
Joined 'POD1-BR-WAE' to realm 'PEAP.LOCAL'
```

If you encounter an issue, use the following commands to troubleshoot issues with joining the domain:

- To check the trust secret between the Windows domain and the WAE, use **windows-domain diagnostics wbinfo –t**.

- To check the domain sequence number, use **windows-domain diagnostics wbinfo -- sequence**.

- To verify accessibility of domain information, use **windows-domain diagnostics wbinfo –D** *domainname*.

Joining the Windows domain from the Central Manager can be done from a single page in the GUI, and thus it is the recommended interface for this task. To join the WAE into the Windows domain, ensure that the settings defined in the last section are configured, and then choose **Devices > Devices >** *WAE Device Name* **> Authentication > Windows Domain**. All relevant parameters configured in the previous section should appear in the appropriate location. Near the bottom of the page, as shown in Figure 9-22, are fields that allow you to specify the domain administrator username and domain administrator password. It is again important to note that the credentials supplied here must have the appropriate permissions within the domain to join a new computer into the domain.

Figure 9-22 *Joining a Windows Domain from Central Manager*

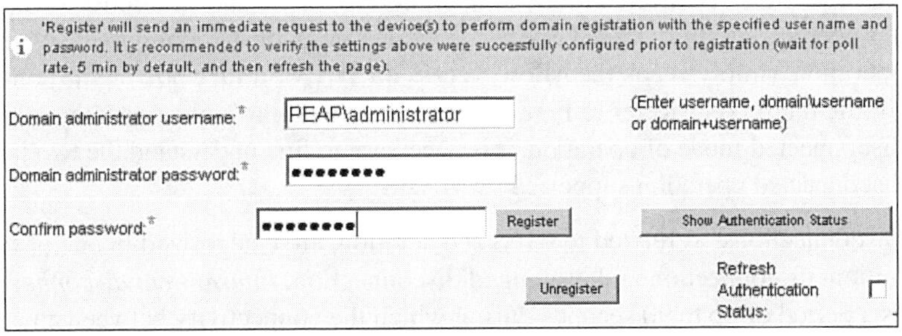

After supplying the credentials, click the **Register** button. This causes the WAE to attempt to join the Windows domain. Then, click **Show Authentication Status** to view the status of integration. Figure 9-23 shows the Authentication Status window. If there is an issue with joining the WAE into the domain, this window provides troubleshooting tips on what is not configured correctly or what failed when attempting to join the domain.

Figure 9-23 *Authentication Status from Central Manager*

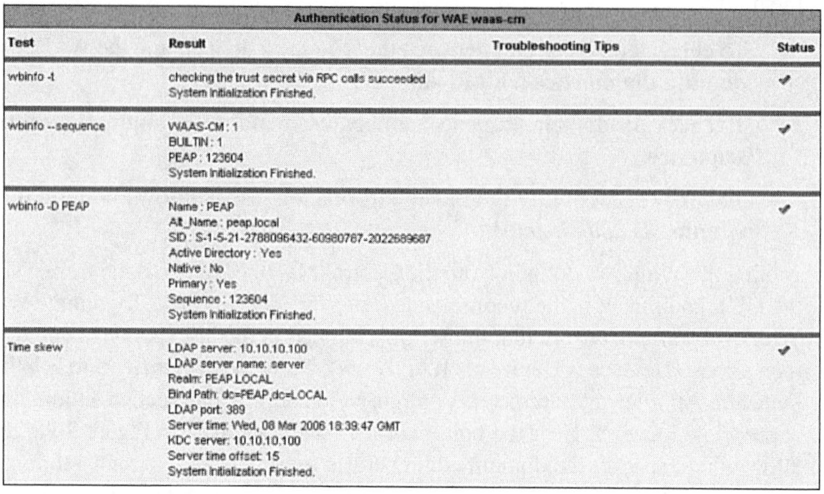

Authentication Status for WAE waas-cm			
Test	**Result**	**Troubleshooting Tips**	**Status**
wbinfo -t	checking the trust secret via RPC calls succeeded System Initialization Finished.		✔
wbinfo --sequence	WAAS-CM : 1 BUILTIN : 1 PEAP : 123604 System Initialization Finished.		✔
wbinfo -D PEAP	Name : PEAP Alt_Name : peap.local SID : S-1-5-21-2788096432-60960767-2022689687 Active Directory : Yes Native : No Primary : Yes Sequence : 123604 System Initialization Finished.		✔
Time skew	LDAP server: 10.10.10.100 LDAP server name: server Realm: PEAP.LOCAL Bind Path: dc=PEAP,dc=LOCAL LDAP port: 389 Server time: Wed, 08 Mar 2006 18:39:47 GMT KDC server: 10.10.10.100 Server time offset: 15 System Initialization Finished.		✔

Configuring Disconnected Mode of Operation

Configuring disconnected mode of operation is simple and straightforward, once the WAE has been successfully joined into the Windows domain. To configure disconnected mode of operation, simply check the **Allow Access on WAN Failure** box on the configuration page for the file server. (Refer to Figure 9-12.) Before taking a closer examination of the disconnected mode of operation, it is necessary to first understand the two types of disconnected operation supported by WAAS.

Disconnections, as related to CIFS acceleration, are categorized in one of two ways: inter- mittent disconnection and prolonged disconnection. *Intermittent disconnection* is defined as a period of up to 90 seconds during which the connectivity between an edge device and a core device is severed. During this period of time, the user might not notice a disturbance, because WAAS masks intermittent disconnection by temporarily queuing requests until the connection between edge and core is restored. If the client submits an interactive request, which demands a server response (such as a file save operation), the operation will hang and the application may become temporarily unresponsive until either connectivity is either restored or the system enters into prolonged disconnected mode. During this initial 90-second period, the edge WAE begins testing connectivity to additional devices that are members of the peer core cluster. If a new peer is identified, all CIFS sessions are destroyed, causing the client redirector to automatically reestablish the session. From a user perspective, this is disruptive only in cases where interactive requests are present.

Prolonged disconnected mode is any disconnection scenario that extends beyond the 90-second window. In this mode, the edge device destroys any active CIFS sessions, which forces the sessions to be re-created. At this point, the edge device begins publishing the name of the disconnected server on the network, and intercepts all requests going to that server to be handled locally. When the new CIFS session requests inevitably come in from the users that were active during the disconnection (or new user sessions), the WAE forwards the authentication request to the domain controller. If the domain controller deems the user authentic, the WAE begins to provide that user access to cached metadata and data based on the cached authorization information (access control entries). If a file is not fully cached, or certain metadata is not cached, the file is not made available to the user even if they are authorized, because the WAE does not have the information in the first place.

If the connection between the edge and core is restored, which is checked every 90 seconds once prolonged disconnected mode has been entered, CIFS sessions are once again torn down. New sessions, which are typically re-created automatically by the user, will be accelerated as normal.

Figure 9-24 shows the transition into prolonged disconnected mode of operation.

Figure 9-24   *Transition into Prolonged Disconnected Mode*

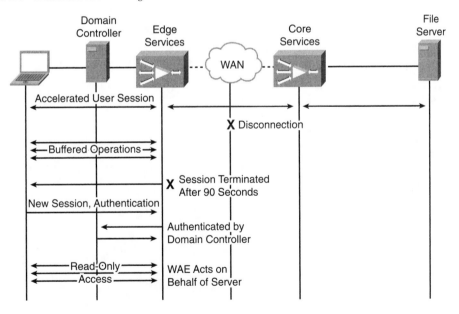

Summary

Cisco WAAS provides a powerful suite of CIFS acceleration components that complement the underlying WAN optimization framework to help enable infrastructure consolidation and improve the user experience. CIFS acceleration couples a number of application layer optimization techniques, including edge-side caching, multiplexing, and read-ahead to dramatically improve CIFS throughput and response times, thereby providing remote users with the impression that they are working with local servers. CIFS acceleration depends upon the configuration of the edge service, core service, core cluster, and connectivity directives, each of which plays a vital role in improving performance and availability. Additionally, WAAS provides value-added features for CIFS acceleration such as preposition and disconnected mode of operation. Preposition improves probability that a set of files will be cached and data from those files will be present in the compression history, which helps to improve the performance for the first user access to the object. By using preposition, organizations can confidently consolidate additional infrastructure components such as software distribution servers while continuing to provide similar levels of performance and service. With disconnected mode of operation, organizations can provide nearly uninterrupted read-only access to cached contents if a network disconnection event occurs.

CHAPTER 10

Case Studies

The previous chapters provided you with the knowledge to successfully design, integrate, and deploy Cisco WAAS. This chapter applies that knowledge to different deployment scenarios in a multisite WAAS design. Each site in the example design is treated like a mini case study, where a set of site-specific requirements is presented, potential design/ configuration options are discussed, and the final solution is described. The full device configurations are presented for each location in the design.

Common Requirements

For this design, a set of common requirements exists that applies to every location or the solution as a whole. The common requirements for this case study are defined as follows:

- No significant changes should be made to the existing network topology or routing policy.

- All TCP traffic (excluding VoIP) destined for the WAN should be intercepted and redirected to WAAS.

- VoIP control traffic should not be intercepted.

- Traffic on TCP ports 3250–3255 should not be optimized by WAAS.

- No WAE redundancy is required in the remote office deployments.

Existing WAN Topology

The existing WAN is built on an MPLS-based service from a national service provider. The WAN service provides any-to-any connectivity for remote-to-remote and remote-to-data–center connectivity. WAN bandwidth ranges from 1.5 Mbps at the smallest remote sites up to 180 Mbps (aggregate) at the data center. A single data center is included in this design, supporting 250 domestic remote offices. Figure 10-1 shows a high-level overview of the existing WAN topology.

Figure 10-1 *High-Level WAN Topology*

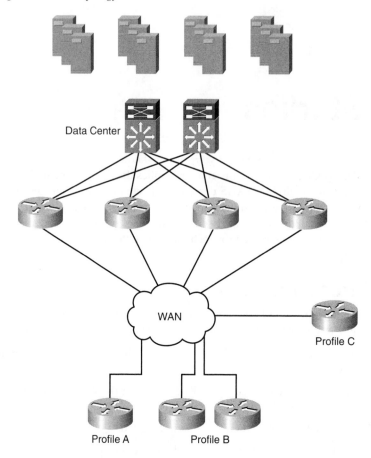

You need to consider the following key aspects of the WAN topology for the design:

- Remote offices should be grouped based on common characteristics, such as business function, topology, user community characteristics, and so forth.

- The MPLS-based WAN service provides any-to-any connectivity. The location of client/server resources, and the traffic flow impact of fan-out, should be taken into consideration for WAE sizing.

- Some remote sites and the data center have multiple connections to the WAN. The routing policy and path preference need to be understood and accounted for in the design.

Remote Site Profile A

To simplify the design and provide a consistent deployment across the enterprise, the remote sites in this design have been grouped into three "profiles." Remote site Profile A is reviewed first.

Profile A Site Requirements

The following site-specific requirements exist for remote offices grouped in Profile A:

- Field sales offices have between 25 and 40 users.
- A single 1.5-Mbps connection to the WAN exists.
- WAN transport terminates on Cisco 3600 Series router.
- All L3 services (routing and so forth) are provided by the WAN router.
- The link between the router and primary LAN switch is an 802.1Q trunk.
- VoIP traffic is isolated to a separate VLAN.

Site Network Topology

Figure 10-2 shows the topology for remote offices in Profile A.

Figure 10-2   *Profile A Remote Office Topology*

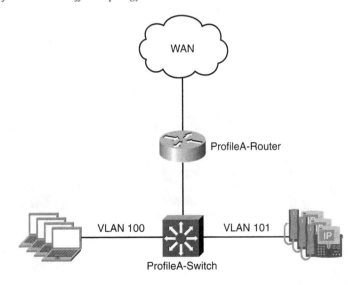

WAE Placement and Interception

One of the first design decisions is to determine the options for WAE placement and the interception method that will be used. Recall from Chapter 5 that the two most common interception methods for branch office deployments are WCCP and inline. In this case, the inline interception method is used to avoid any potential performance issues on the 3600 Series routers caused by the increased throughput from the WAE. Based on the number of users at the site, the WAE-512 is the WAE model that will be deployed. The WAE is placed physically inline between the WAN routers and the LAN switch. A single InlineGroup is used, because no redundant connections exist between the WAN router and LAN switch. No configuration changes are required on the WAN router or LAN switches.

To meet the common requirement that VoIP control traffic is not intercepted, the dedicated VoIP VLAN (VLAN 101) will be explicitly excluded as part of the InlineGroup configuration. To simplify the deployment, the management IP address of the WAE is configured on InlineGroup 1/0. This prevents the need for a separate physical connection for management. The IP address assigned to the WAE is allocated from one of the existing IP address ranges assigned to the site.

Figure 10-3 shows the Profile A site topology with the WAE deployed.

Figure 10-3 *Profile A Final Topology*

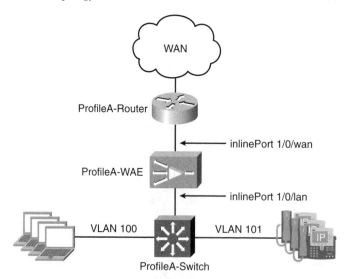

WAE Configuration Details

Example 10-1 shows the WAE configuration for Profile A sites.

Example 10-1 *Profile A Site WAE Configuration*

```
ProfileA-WAE# show running-config
! WAAS version 4.0.15 (build b6 Dec 13 2007)
!
device mode application-accelerator
!
hostname ProfileA-WAE
!
exec-timeout 5
!
primary-interface InlineGroup 1/0
!
interface GigabitEthernet 1/0
 shutdown
 exit
interface GigabitEthernet 2/0
 shutdown
 exit
!
interface InlineGroup 1/0
 ip address 10.10.10.5 255.255.255.0
 inline vlan all
 no inline vlan 101
 exit
interface InlineGroup 1/1
 inline vlan all
 shutdown
 exit
!
ip default-gateway 10.10.10.1
!
no auto-register enable
!
! ip path-mtu-discovery is disabled in WAAS by default
!
username admin password 1 bVmDmMMmZAPjY
username admin privilege 15
!
authentication login local enable primary
authentication configuration local enable primary
!
no telnet enable
!
no sshd version 1
sshd enable
```

continues

Example 10-1 *Profile A Site WAE Configuration (Continued)*

```
!
central-manager address 10.88.80.132
cms enable
!
<default ATP configuration removed>
!
! End of WAAS configuration
ProfileA-WAE#
```

WAN Router Configuration Details

Example 10-2 shows the WAN router configuration for Profile A sites.

Example 10-2 *Profile A Site WAN Router Configuration*

```
ProfileA-Router# show running-config
Building configuration...

Current configuration : 979 bytes
!
version 12.3
service timestamps debug datetime msec
service timestamps log datetime msec
no service password-encryption
!
hostname ProfileA-Router
!
boot-start-marker
boot-end-marker
!
logging buffered 163843 debugging
no logging console
enable secret 5 $1$jq0n$Cr5PxpMX8IJ/eJan1hmQS/
!
no aaa new-model
ip subnet-zero
!
ip cef
no ip domain lookup
!
interface FastEthernet0/0
 no ip address
 duplex auto
 speed auto
!
interface FastEthernet0/0.100
 description ** User Data VLAN **
 encapsulation dot1Q 100
 ip address 10.10.10.1 255.255.255.0
```

Example 10-2 *Profile A Site WAN Router Configuration (Continued)*

```
!
interface FastEthernet0/0.101
 description ** Dedicated VoIP VLAN **
 encapsulation dot1Q 34
 ip address 10.10.11.1 255.255.255.0
!
interface Serial0/0
 description ** MPLS WAN Service **
 ip address 10.88.80.253 255.255.255.252
!
router ospf 100
 log-adjacency-changes
 passive-interface default
 no passive-interface Serial0/0
 network 10.88.80.252 0.0.0.3 area 0
 network 10.10.10.0 0.0.0.255 area 0
 network 10.10.11.0 0.0.0.255 area 0
!
no ip http server
ip classless
!
line con 0
 password cisco
line aux 0
line vty 0 4
 password cisco
 login
!
end
ProfileA-Router#
```

LAN Switch Configuration Details

Example 10-3 shows the LAN switch configuration for Profile A sites.

Example 10-3 *Profile A Site LAN Switch Configuration*

```
ProfileA-Switch# show running-config
Building configuration...

Current configuration : 7537 bytes
!
upgrade fpd auto
version 12.2
service timestamps debug uptime
service timestamps log datetime msec localtime show-timezone
service password-encryption
service internal
service counters max age 5
```

continues

Example 10-3 *Profile A Site LAN Switch Configuration (Continued)*

```
!
hostname ProfileA-Switch
!
boot-start-marker
boot-end-marker
!
logging buffered 16384 debugging
no logging console
enable secret 5 $1$Yw6R$/H/1bMJdjEkKhjh8wkbZE0
!
no aaa new-model
!
no ip domain-lookup
vtp mode transparent
!
vlan internal allocation policy ascending
vlan access-log ratelimit 2000
!
vlan 100
 name USER-DATA
!
vlan 101
 name DEDICATED-VOICE
!
interface GigabitEthernet1/16
 description ** ProfileA-WAE, interface LAN0 **
 switchport
 switchport trunk encapsulation dot1q
 switchport trunk allowed vlan 100,101
 switchport mode trunk
!
interface Vlan100
 ip address 10.10.10.2 255.255.255.0
!
ip default-gateway 10.10.10.1
!
no ip http server
no ip http secure-server
!
control-plane
!
dial-peer cor custom
!
line con 0
 password 7 140005
line vty 0 4
 password 7 140005
 login
 transport input lat pad udptn telnet rlogin ssh
line vty 5 15
 password 7 120E12
 login
```

Example 10-3 *Profile A Site LAN Switch Configuration (Continued)*

```
 transport input lat pad udptn telnet rlogin ssh
!
scheduler runtime netinput 300
!
end
ProfileA-Switch#
```

Remote Site Profile B

Profile B encompasses the second type of remote sites. Sites in this profile are unique in that they are small kiosk locations within other businesses. In addition to being space constrained, kiosks are commonly shutting down and reopening in different locations based on business demands. This section looks at how these types of sites are addressed from a design perspective.

Profile B Site Requirements

The following site-specific requirements exist for remote offices grouped in Profile B:

- Kiosk structures are within rented space on other businesses' property.
- Each kiosk is staffed with one or two users.
- A single 1.5-Mbps connection to the WAN exists.
- WAN transport terminates on Cisco 2800 Series router.
- All L3 services (routing and so forth) are provided by the WAN router.
- Physical space consumption for IT hardware should be kept to a minimum.

Site Network Topology

Figure 10-4 shows the topology for remote offices in Profile B.

Figure 10-4 *Profile B Remote Office Topology*

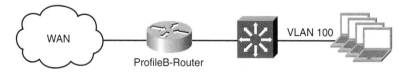

WAE Placement and Interception

Given the physical space challenges at Profile B locations and a desire to minimize the amount of infrastructure that has to be moved when a kiosk is closed and relocated, the NME-WAE-502 is the WAE model that will be deployed. The NME-WAE is physically installed in the existing 2800 Series router, thus eliminating the need for any additional rack space. WCCP will be used as the interception method, transparently redirecting all TCP traffic across the internal interface to the NME-WAE.

To meet the common requirement that VoIP control traffic is not intercepted, traffic to and from the dedicated VoIP VLAN (VLAN 101) will be excluded from interception using a WCCP redirect list. Because the internal connection between the WAN router and NME-WAE functions like a point-to-point link, a /30 network will be allocated to each Profile B site. The two usable IP addresses in this network will be used for the router IntergratedServicesEngine interface IP address and WAE IP address.

Figure 10-5 shows the final topology for remote offices in Profile B.

Figure 10-5 *Profile B Final Topology*

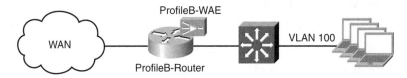

WAE Configuration Details

Example 10-4 shows the WAE configuration for Profile B sites.

Example 10-4 *Profile B Site WAE Configuration*

```
ProfileB-WAE# show running-config
! WAAS version 4.0.15 (build b6 Dec 13 2007)
!
device mode application-accelerator
!
hostname ProfileB-WAE
!
clock timezone CST6CDT -6 0
!
ip domain-name asdcnp-waas.cisco.com
!
exec-timeout 5
!
primary-interface GigabitEthernet 1/0
```

Example 10-4 *Profile B Site WAE Configuration (Continued)*

```
!
interface GigabitEthernet 1/0
 ip address 10.88.80.222 255.255.255.252
 no autosense
 bandwidth 1000
 full-duplex
 exit
interface GigabitEthernet 2/0
 shutdown
 exit
!
ip default-gateway 10.88.80.221
!
no auto-register enable
!
! ip path-mtu-discovery is disabled in WAAS by default
!
ip name-server 10.88.80.53
!
ntp server 10.88.80.132
!
wccp router-list 1 10.88.80.221
wccp tcp-promiscuous router-list-num 1
wccp version 2
!
username admin password 1 1Kat1k753Qknw
username admin privilege 15
username admin print-admin-password 1 CEC32C13191F9B56AAD3B435B51404EE
6E73ED22ADDAFAA4FACD2513341E6B7C
!
windows-domain netbios-name "PROFILEB-WAE"
!
authentication login local enable primary
authentication configuration local enable primary
!
no telnet enable
!
no sshd version 1
sshd enable
!
central-manager address 10.88.80.132
cms enable
!
! End of WAAS configuration
ProfileB-WAE#
```

WAN Router Configuration Details

Example 10-5 shows the WAN router configuration for Profile B sites.

Example 10-5 *Profile B Site WAN Router Configuration*

```
ProfileB-Router# show running-config
Building configuration...

Current configuration : 1935 bytes
!
version 12.4
service timestamps debug datetime msec
service timestamps log datetime msec
no service password-encryption
!
hostname ProfileB-Router
!
boot-start-marker
boot-end-marker
!
no logging console
enable secret 5 $1$Ox0L$yBovhDx4AYaumzLBVVNOT0
!
no aaa new-model
ip wccp 61
ip wccp 62 redirect-list PT-VOICE-CONTROL
!
ip cef
!
no ip domain lookup
!
multilink bundle-name authenticated
!
voice-card 0
 no dspfarm
!
interface FastEthernet0/0
 no ip address
 duplex auto
 speed auto
!
interface FastEthernet0/0.100
 description ** User Data VLAN **
 encapsulation dot1Q 100
 ip address 10.10.20.1 255.255.255.0
 ip wccp 61 redirect in
!
interface FastEthernet0/0.101
 description ** Dedicated VoIP VLAN **
 encapsulation dot1Q 101
 ip address 10.10.21.1 255.255.255.0
!
interface Serial0/0
```

Example 10-5 *Profile B Site WAN Router Configuration*

```
 description ** MPLS WAN Service **
 ip address 10.88.80.249 255.255.255.252
 ip wccp 62 redirect in
!
interface Integrated-Service-Engine1/0
 ip address 10.88.80.221 255.255.255.252
 service-module ip address 10.88.80.222 255.255.255.252
 service-module ip default-gateway 10.88.80.221
 no keepalive
!
router ospf 100
 log-adjacency-changes
 passive-interface default
 no passive-interface Serial0/0
 network 10.10.20.0 0.0.0.255 area 0
 network 10.10.21.0 0.0.0.255 area 0
 network 10.88.80.220 0.0.0.3 area 0
!
no ip http server
no ip http secure-server
!
ip access-list extended PT-VOICE-CONTROL
 deny    ip any 10.10.21.0 0.0.0.255
 deny    ip 10.10.21.0 0.0.0.255 any
 permit ip any any
!
control-plane
!
line con 0
 password cisco
line aux 0
line vty 0 4
 password cisco
 login
!
scheduler allocate 20000 1000
!
end
ProfileB-Router#
```

Remote Site Profile C

The final remote office profile is Profile C. Profile C sites are some of the largest remote offices in the enterprise, and have redundant network infrastructure for increased availability. Recall that preservation of the existing topology as routing policy was an important common requirement. This section addresses both these requirements and the site-specific requirements.

Profile C Site Requirements

The following site-specific requirements exist for remote offices grouped in Profile C:

- Large admin and engineering offices have between 125 and 500 users.
- Multiple multi-Mbps connections to the WAN exist.
- WAN transport terminates on Cisco 3800 or 7200 Series routers.
- All L3 services (routing and so forth) are provided by the WAN routers.
- The links between the routers and LAN switches are 802.1Q trunks.
- VoIP traffic is isolated to a separate VLAN.
- Gateway Load Balancing Protocol (GLBP) is used for default gateway redundancy and outbound distribution of client load across both WAN routers.

Site Network Topology

Figure 10-6 shows the topology for remote offices in Profile C.

Figure 10-6   *Profile C Remote Office Topology*

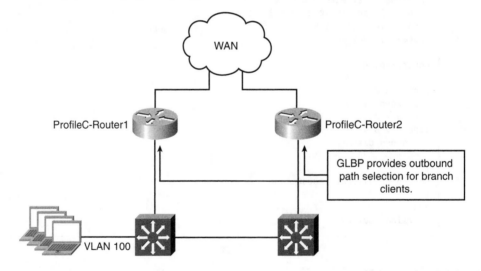

WAE Placement and Interception

Both WAN routers at Profile C locations are connected to both LAN switches; therefore, there are too many connections for inline interception to be an option. WCCP will be used as the interception method at Profile C locations. Based on the sizing requirement for the site, the WAE-7341 is the WAE model that will be deployed. A separate VLAN will be created for the WAE, which will allow for HSRP to be used as the default gateway redundancy mechanism. In addition, during a review of the WAN router configurations, it was discovered that the customer had Unicast Reverse Path Forwarding (uRPF) configured on the client LAN interfaces.

For information regarding Unicast Reverse Path Forwarding, see http://tools.ietf.org/html/rfc3704.

Because WAAS is functioning as a transparent proxy, traffic from the WAE can appear to uRPF as entering the router on the incorrect interface. By placing the WAEs in a separate, dedicated segment, the uRPF feature can be left off of that router interface.

To preserve the default gateway selection (via GLBP) made by the client, the egress method for Profile C sites will be set to negotiated-return. This will cause the WAE to send traffic back to the intercepting router that redirected the traffic to it, as opposed to using the configured default gateway. As an additional optimization, the WAE will be configured with a static route for each intercepting router's WCCP router ID. The next hop of each static route will be the directly connected IP address of the intercepting router that router ID belongs to. This allows the WAE to return the traffic directly back to the intercepting router, as opposed to forwarding the traffic to its configured default gateway when the router ID is not directly connected.

To meet the common requirement that VoIP control traffic is not intercepted, traffic to and from the dedicated VoIP VLAN (VLAN 101) will be excluded from interception using a WCCP redirect list.

Figure 10-7 shows the final topology for remote offices in Profile C.

Figure 10-7   *Profile C Final Topology*

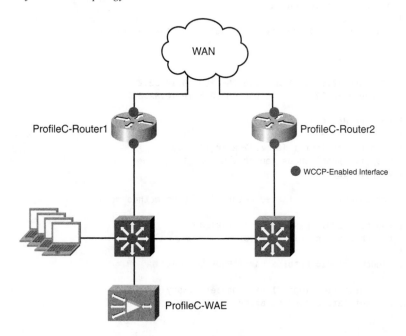

WAE Configuration Details

Example 10-6 shows the WAE configuration for Profile C sites.

Example 10-6 *Profile C Site WAE Configuration*

```
ProfileC-WAE# show running-config
! WAAS version 4.0.15 (build b6 Dec 13 2007)
!
device mode application-accelerator
!
hostname ProfileC-WAE
!
clock timezone CST6CDT -6 0
!
ip domain-name asdcnp-waas.cisco.com
!
exec-timeout 5
!
primary-interface GigabitEthernet 1/0
!
interface GigabitEthernet 1/0
 ip address 10.10.32.5 255.255.255.0
 exit
interface GigabitEthernet 2/0
 shutdown
 exit
!
ip default-gateway 10.10.32.1
!
no auto-register enable
!
! ip path-mtu-discovery is disabled in WAAS by default
!
ip name-server 10.88.80.53
!
ip route 10.99.99.1 255.255.255.255 10.10.32.2
ip route 10.99.99.2 255.255.255.255 10.10.32.3
!
ntp server 10.88.80.132
!
wccp router-list 1 10.10.32.2 10.10.32.3
wccp tcp-promiscuous router-list-num 1
wccp version 2
!
egress-method negotiated-return intercept-method wccp
!
username admin password 1 1Kat1k753Qknw
username admin privilege 15
!
windows-domain netbios-name "PROFILEC-WAE"
!
authentication login local enable primary
authentication configuration local enable primary
```

Example 10-6   *Profile C Site WAE Configuration (Continued)*

```
!
no telnet enable
!
no sshd version 1
sshd enable
!
central-manager address 10.88.80.132
cms enable
!
no adapter epm enable
!
! End of WAAS configuration
ProfileC-WAE#
```

WAN Router 1 Configuration Details

Example 10-7 shows the WAN router 1 configuration for Profile C sites.

Example 10-7   *Profile C Site WAN Router 1 Configuration*

```
ProfileC-Router1# show running-config
Building configuration...

Current configuration : 979 bytes
!
version 12.4
service timestamps debug datetime msec
service timestamps log datetime msec
no service password-encryption
!
hostname ProfileC-Router1
!
boot-start-marker
boot-end-marker
!
logging buffered 163843 debugging
no logging console
enable secret 5 $1$jq0n$Cr5PxpMX8IJ/eJan1hmQS/
!
no aaa new-model
ip wccp 61
ip wccp 62 redirect-list PT-VOICE-CONTROL
ip subnet-zero
!
ip cef
no ip domain lookup
!
interface Loopback0
 ip address 10.99.99.1 255.255.255.255
```

continues

Example 10-7 *Profile C Site WAN Router 1 Configuration (Continued)*

```
!
interface FastEthernet0/0
 no ip address
 duplex auto
 speed auto
!
interface FastEthernet0/0.100
 description ** User Data VLAN **
 encapsulation dot1Q 100
 ip address 10.10.30.2 255.255.255.0
 ip verify unicast reverse-path
 ip wccp 61 redirect in
 glbp 1 ip 10.10.30.1
 glbp 1 priority 110
 glbp load-balancing host-dependent
!
interface FastEthernet0/0.101
 description ** Dedicated VoIP VLAN **
 encapsulation dot1Q 101
 ip address 10.10.31.2 255.255.255.0
 ip verify unicast reverse-path
 glbp 2 ip 10.10.31.1
 glbp 2 priority 110
 glbp load-balancing host-dependent
!
interface FastEthernet0/0.300
 description ** WAE Service VLAN **
 encapsulation dot1q 300
 ip address 10.10.32.2 255.255.255.0
 standby 1 ip 10.10.33.1
 standby 1 priority 105
!
interface Serial0/0
 description ** MPLS WAN Service **
 ip address 10.88.80.241 255.255.255.252
 ip wccp 62 redirect in
!
router ospf 100
 log-adjacency-changes
 passive-interface default
 no passive-interface Serial0/0
 network 10.10.30.0 0.0.0.255 area 0
 network 10.10.31.0 0.0.0.255 area 0
 network 10.10.32.0 0.0.0.255 area 0
!
no ip http server
!
ip access-list extended PT-VOICE-CONTROL
 deny   ip any 10.10.31.0 0.0.0.255
 deny   ip 10.10.31.0 0.0.0.255 any
 permit ip any any
```

Example 10-7   *Profile C Site WAN Router 1 Configuration (Continued)*

```
!
ip classless
!
line con 0
 password cisco
line aux 0
line vty 0 4
 password cisco
 login
!
end
ProfileC-Router1#
```

WAN Router 2 Configuration Details

Example 10-8 shows the WAN router 2 configuration for Profile C sites.

Example 10-8   *Profile C Site WAN Router 2 Configuration*

```
ProfileC-Router2# show running-config
Building configuration...

Current configuration : 979 bytes
!
version 12.4
service timestamps debug datetime msec
service timestamps log datetime msec
no service password-encryption
!
hostname ProfileC-Router2
!
boot-start-marker
boot-end-marker
!
logging buffered 163843 debugging
no logging console
enable secret 5 $1$jq0n$Cr5PxpMX8IJ/eJan1hmQS/
!
no aaa new-model
ip wccp 61
ip wccp 62 redirect-list PT-VOICE-CONTROL
ip subnet-zero
!
ip cef
no ip domain lookup
!
interface Loopback0
 ip address 10.99.99.2 255.255.255.255
```

continues

Example 10-8 *Profile C Site WAN Router 2 Configuration (Continued)*

```
!
interface FastEthernet0/0
 no ip address
 duplex auto
 speed auto
!
interface FastEthernet0/0.100
 description ** User Data VLAN **
 encapsulation dot1Q 100
 ip address 10.10.30.3 255.255.255.0
 ip verify unicast reverse-path
 ip wccp 61 redirect in
 glbp 1 ip 10.10.30.1
 glbp load-balancing host-dependent
!
interface FastEthernet0/0.101
 description ** Dedicated VoIP VLAN **
 encapsulation dot1Q 101
 ip address 10.10.31.3 255.255.255.0
 ip verify unicast reverse-path
 glbp 2 ip 10.10.31.1
 glbp load-balancing host-dependent
!
interface FastEthernet0/0.300
 description ** WAE Service VLAN **
 encapsulation dot1q 300
 ip address 10.10.32.3 255.255.255.0
 standby 1 ip 10.10.33.1
!
interface Serial0/0
 description ** MPLS WAN Service **
 ip address 10.88.80.245 255.255.255.252
 ip wccp 62 redirect in
!
router ospf 100
 log-adjacency-changes
 passive-interface default
 no passive-interface Serial0/0
 network 10.10.30.0 0.0.0.255 area 0
 network 10.10.31.0 0.0.0.255 area 0
 network 10.10.32.0 0.0.0.255 area 0
!
no ip http server
!
ip access-list extended PT-VOICE-CONTROL
 deny    ip any 10.10.31.0 0.0.0.255
 deny    ip 10.10.31.0 0.0.0.255 any
 permit ip any any
```

Example 10-8   *Profile C Site WAN Router 2 Configuration (Continued)*

```
!
ip classless
!
line con 0
 password cisco
line aux 0
line vty 0 4
 password cisco
 login
!
end
ProfileC-Router2#
```

Data Center Profile

Now that all of the remote office profiles have been addressed, this section takes a closer look at the WAAS deployment in the data center. It is usually recommended to evaluate each data center on its own, as opposed to trying to group them into common profiles.

Data Center Site Requirements

The following site-specific requirements exist for the data center:

- Hosts resources are accessed by all remote offices with WAAS deployed.
- Multiple 45-Mbps connections to the WAN exist.
- WAN transport terminates on multiple Cisco 7200 Series routers.
- Traffic to and from remote offices is divided between the available WAN routers based on route metrics advertised to the MPLS cloud.
- All WAN routers aggregate into a single pair of Cisco Catalyst 6500 Series switches.
- Access to other data centers is also provided through the same MPLS cloud used by remote offices.
- Data center-to-data center traffic should be excluded from interception.

Site Network Topology

Figure 10-8 shows the topology for the data center.

Figure 10-8 *Data Center Topology*

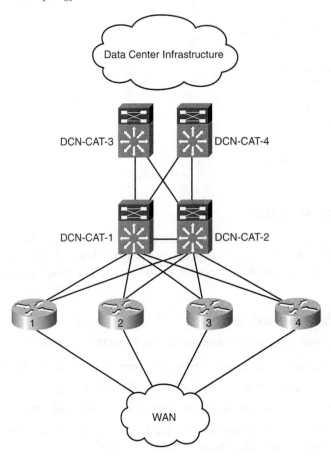

WAE Placement and Interception

The first preference for the interception method in the data center is WCCP. The Cisco 7200 Series routers terminating the WAN transport are a potential location to enable WCCP, but the customer is concerned about the potential performance impact due to the high volume of traffic flowing between the data center and WAN. The pair of Catalyst 6500 switches where all of the WAN routers aggregate is another possibility. The benefit of configuring WCCP on the 6500 is that all of the interception can be handled in hardware. Another benefit is that the 6500s have a full view of the routing table from the WAN access routers, allowing them to make the optimum forward decision for optimized traffic from the WAEs destined to the WAN. Based on the sizing requirements of the deployment, two WAE-7371s are required. To provide N+1 redundancy for the WAEs in the data center, a third WAE will be deployed. Each WAE-7371 will be connected to both 6500 switches using the standby interface feature. This provides an additional level of redundancy in the event of a switch or interface failure. A separate VLAN will be created and trunked between the Catalyst 6500 switches. HSRP will be used on the WAE VLAN to provide default gateway redundancy.

To meet the requirement that data center-to-data center traffic is not intercepted, a WCCP redirect list will be used. The egress method configured on the WAEs will be IP forwarding. The **l2-redirect** and **mask-assign** options are used to ensure complete WCCP redirection in hardware on the Catalyst 6500 switches, as opposed to the hash assignment method, which might cause an increase in MSFC CPU utilization.

Figure 10-9 shows the final topology for the data center.

Figure 10-9   *Data Center Final Topology*

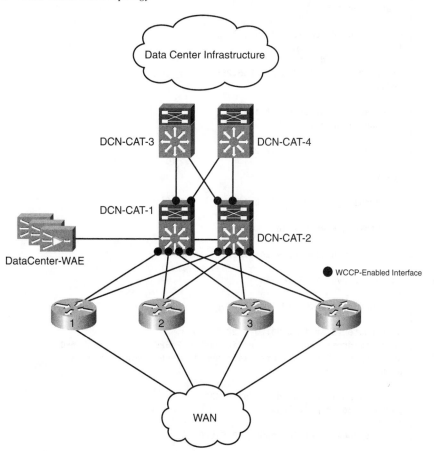

WAE Configuration Details

Example 10-9 shows the WAE configuration for the data center.

Example 10-9 *Data Center WAE Configuration*

```
DataCenter-WAE# show running-config
! WAAS version 4.0.15 (build b6 Dec 13 2007)
!
device mode application-accelerator
!
hostname DataCenter-WAE
!
clock timezone CST6CDT -6 0
!
ip domain-name asdcnp-waas.cisco.com
!
exec-timeout 5
!
primary-interface Standby 1
!
interface Standby 1
 ip address 20.20.20.5 255.255.255.0
 exit
!
interface GigabitEthernet 1/0
 standby 1 priority 110
 exit
interface GigabitEthernet 2/0
 standby 1
 exit
!
ip default-gateway 20.20.20.1
!
no auto-register enable
!
! ip path-mtu-discovery is disabled in WAAS by default
!
ip name-server 10.88.80.53
!
ntp server 10.88.80.132
!
wccp router-list 1 20.20.20.2 20.20.20.3
wccp tcp-promiscuous mask src-ip-mask 0x2e8200 dst-ip-mask 0x0
wccp tcp-promiscuous router-list-num 1 l2-redirect mask-assign
wccp version 2
!
username admin password 1 1Kat1k753Qknw
username admin privilege 15
!
windows-domain netbios-name "PROFILEC-WAE"
!
authentication login local enable primary
authentication configuration local enable primary
```

Example 10-9   *Data Center WAE Configuration (Continued)*

```
!
no telnet enable
!
no sshd version 1
sshd enable
!
central-manager address 10.88.80.132
cms enable
!
no adapter epm enable
!
<default ATP removed>
!
! End of WAAS configuration
DataCenter-WAE#
```

Data Center Switch 1 Configuration Details

Example 10-10 shows the data center switch 1 configuration for the data center.

Example 10-10   *Data Center Switch 1 Configuration*

```
DCN-CAT-1# show running-config
Building configuration...

Current configuration : 7537 bytes
!
upgrade fpd auto
version 12.2
service timestamps debug uptime
service timestamps log datetime msec localtime show-timezone
service password-encryption
service internal
service counters max age 5
!
hostname DCN-CAT-1
!
boot-start-marker
boot-end-marker
!
logging buffered 16384 debugging
no logging console
enable secret 5 $1$Yw6R$/H/1bMJdjEkKhjh8wkbZE0
!
no aaa new-model
ip subnet-zero
ip wccp 61 redirect-list PT-DC-TO-DC
ip wccp 62 redirect-list PT-DC-TO-DC
```

continues

Example 10-10   *Data Center Switch 1 Configuration (Continued)*

```
!
no ip domain-lookup
vtp mode transparent
mls netflow interface
no mls flow ip
mls cef error action reset
!
redundancy
 keepalive-enable
 mode sso
 main-cpu
  auto-sync running-config
spanning-tree mode pvst
diagnostic cns publish cisco.cns.device.diag_results
diagnostic cns subscribe cisco.cns.device.diag_commands
!
vlan internal allocation policy ascending
vlan access-log ratelimit 2000
!
vlan 300
 name WAE-SERVICE-VLAN
!
interface Port-channel1
 description ** Trunk to DCN-CAT-2 **
 switchport
 switchport trunk encapsulation dot1q
 switchport mode trunk
!
interface GigabitEthernet1/1
 description ** Link to DCN-WAN-RTR-1 **
 ip address 10.88.80.225 255.255.255.252
 ip wccp 61 redirect in
!
interface GigabitEthernet1/2
 description ** Link to DCN-WAN-RTR-2 **
 ip address 10.88.80.229 255.255.255.252
 ip wccp 61 redirect in
!
interface GigabitEthernet1/3
 description ** Link to DCN-WAN-RTR-3 **
 ip address 10.88.80.233 255.255.255.252
 ip wccp 61 redirect in
!
interface GigabitEthernet1/4
 description ** Link to DCN-WAN-RTR-4 **
 ip address 10.88.80.237 255.255.255.252
 ip wccp 61 redirect in
!
interface GigabitEthernet1/5
 switchport
 switchport mode trunk
 channel-group 1 mode desirable
```

Example 10-10   *Data Center Switch 1 Configuration (Continued)*

```
!
interface GigabitEthernet1/6
 switchport
 switchport mode trunk
 channel-group 1 mode desirable
!
interface GigabitEthernet1/7
 switchport
 switchport mode trunk
 channel-group 1 mode desirable
!
interface GigabitEthernet1/8
 switchport
 switchport mode trunk
 channel-group 1 mode desirable
!
interface GigabitEthernet1/9
 description ** Link to DCN-CAT-3 **
 ip address 10.88.80.209 255.255.255.252
 ip wccp 62 redirect in
!
interface GigabitEthernet1/10
 description ** Link to DCN-CAT-4 **
 ip address 10.88.80.213 255.255.255.252
 ip wccp 62 redirect in
!
interface Vlan300
 description ** WAE Service VLAN **
 ip address 20.20.30.2 255.255.255.0
 standby 1 ip 20.20.20.1
 standby 1 priority 105
!
router ospf 100
 log-adjacency-changes
 passive-interface default
 no passive-interface Vlan300
 network 10.88.80.0 0.0.1.255 area 0
 network 20.20.30.0 0.0.0.255 area 0
 default-information originate always
!
ip classless
ip route 0.0.0.0 0.0.0.0 Null0
!
no ip http server
no ip http secure-server
!
ip access-list extended PT-DC-TO-DC
 deny   ip 10.10.10.0 0.0.0.255 10.10.20.0 0.0.0.255
 deny   ip 10.10.20.0 0.0.0.255 10.10.10.0 0.0.0.255
 permit ip any any
```

continues

Example 10-10   *Data Center Switch 1 Configuration (Continued)*

```
!
control-plane
!
dial-peer cor custom
!
line con 0
 password 7 140005
line vty 0 4
 password 7 140005
 login
 transport input lat pad udptn telnet rlogin ssh
line vty 5 15
 password 7 120E12
 login
 transport input lat pad udptn telnet rlogin ssh
!
scheduler runtime netinput 300
!
end
DCN-CAT-1#
```

Data Center Switch 2 Configuration Details

Example 10-11 shows the data center switch 2 configuration for the data center.

Example 10-11   *Data Center Switch 2 Configuration*

```
DCN-CAT-2# show running-config
Building configuration...

Current configuration : 7537 bytes
!
upgrade fpd auto
version 12.2
service timestamps debug uptime
service timestamps log datetime msec localtime show-timezone
service password-encryption
service internal
service counters max age 5
!
hostname DCN-CAT-2
!
boot-start-marker
boot-end-marker
!
logging buffered 16384 debugging
no logging console
enable secret 5 $1$Yw6R$/H/1bMJdjEkKhjh8wkbZE0
!
no aaa new-model
```

Example 10-11 *Data Center Switch 2 Configuration (Continued)*

```
ip subnet-zero
ip wccp 61 redirect-list PT-DC-TO-DC
ip wccp 62 redirect-list PT-DC-TO-DC
!
no ip domain-lookup
vtp mode transparent
mls netflow interface
no mls flow ip
mls cef error action reset
!
redundancy
 keepalive-enable
 mode sso
 main-cpu
  auto-sync running-config
spanning-tree mode pvst
diagnostic cns publish cisco.cns.device.diag_results
diagnostic cns subscribe cisco.cns.device.diag_commands
!
vlan internal allocation policy ascending
vlan access-log ratelimit 2000
!
vlan 300
 name WAE-SERVICE-VLAN
!
interface Port-channel1
 description ** Trunk to DCN-CAT-1 **
 switchport
 switchport trunk encapsulation dot1q
 switchport mode trunk
!
interface GigabitEthernet1/1
 description ** Link to DCN-WAN-RTR-1 **
 ip address 10.88.80.193 255.255.255.252
 ip wccp 61 redirect in
!
interface GigabitEthernet1/2
 description ** Link to DCN-WAN-RTR-2 **
 ip address 10.88.80.197 255.255.255.252
 ip wccp 61 redirect in
!
interface GigabitEthernet1/3
 description ** Link to DCN-WAN-RTR-3 **
 ip address 10.88.80.201 255.255.255.252
 ip wccp 61 redirect in
!
interface GigabitEthernet1/4
 description ** Link to DCN-WAN-RTR-4 **
 ip address 10.88.80.205 255.255.255.252
 ip wccp 61 redirect in
```

continues

Example 10-11 *Data Center Switch 2 Configuration (Continued)*

```
!
interface GigabitEthernet1/5
 switchport
 switchport mode trunk
 channel-group 1 mode desirable
!
interface GigabitEthernet1/6
 switchport
 switchport mode trunk
 channel-group 1 mode desirable
!
interface GigabitEthernet1/7
 switchport
 switchport mode trunk
 channel-group 1 mode desirable
!
interface GigabitEthernet1/8
 switchport
 switchport mode trunk
 channel-group 1 mode desirable
!
interface GigabitEthernet1/9
 description ** Link to DCN-CAT-3 **
 ip address 10.88.80.217 255.255.255.252
 ip wccp 62 redirect in
!
interface GigabitEthernet1/10
 description ** Link to DCN-CAT-4 **
 ip address 10.88.80.221 255.255.255.252
 ip wccp 62 redirect in
!
interface Vlan300
 description ** WAE Service VLAN **
 ip address 20.20.30.3 255.255.255.0
 standby 1 ip 20.20.20.1
!
router ospf 100
 log-adjacency-changes
 passive-interface default
 no passive-interface Vlan300
 network 10.88.80.0 0.0.1.255 area 0
 network 20.20.30.0 0.0.0.255 area 0
 default-information originate always
!
ip classless
ip route 0.0.0.0 0.0.0.0 Null0
!
no ip http server
no ip http secure-server
```

Example 10-11 *Data Center Switch 2 Configuration (Continued)*

```
!
ip access-list extended PT-DC-TO-DC
 deny    ip 10.10.10.0 0.0.0.255 10.10.20.0 0.0.0.255
 deny    ip 10.10.20.0 0.0.0.255 10.10.10.0 0.0.0.255
 permit ip any any
!
control-plane
!
dial-peer cor custom
!
line con 0
 password 7 140005
line vty 0 4
 password 7 140005
 login
 transport input lat pad udptn telnet rlogin ssh
line vty 5 15
 password 7 120E12
 login
 transport input lat pad udptn telnet rlogin ssh
!
scheduler runtime netinput 300
!
end
DCN-CAT-2#
```

Application Traffic Policy

To handle the requirement that traffic on TCP ports 3250–3255 should not be optimized by WAAS, you need to create a custom policy-map entry. The best place to do this is in the Central Manager AllDevicesGroup, which will ensure that the policy is applied consistently to all WAEs in the deployment. To better traffic this type of application traffic, a new application named CustomAppTraffic is also created. This allows you to collect statistics and assess the amount of traffic volume for this application.

Figures 10-10 and 10-11 show the Central Manager configuration screens for the custom policy.

Figure 10-10 *Custom Application Traffic Classifier*

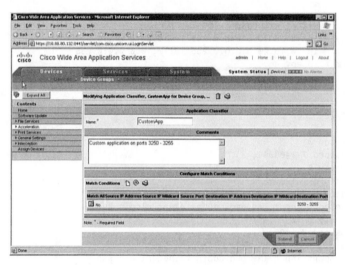

Figure 10-11 *Custom Application Traffic Policy-Map*

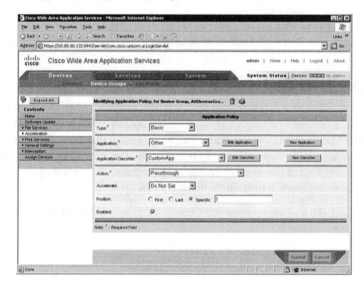

Example 10-12 shows the resulting ATP CLI configuration.

Example 10-12   *Custom Application Traffic Policy CLI*

```
!
policy-engine application
name CustomAppTraffic
classifier CustomApp
      match dst port range 3250 3255
   exit
   map basic
      name Other classifier CustomApp action pass-through
exit
!
```

Summary

This chapter showed the practical application of the knowledge gained throughout this book. Several different types of site deployment were analyzed, with slightly varying implementation solutions chosen at each site. The example design in this chapter highlights the use of various different interception methods in the same overall deployment. Detailed example configurations were provided for all of the key components in the design.

INDEX

Numbers

7 services, 5–8
   application performance barriers, 5–8
   bandwidth inefficiencies, 7–8
   latency, 6
   performance, 6

A

ABE (Access-Based Enumeration), 66
access
   controlling, 71
   RBAC, 224–226
accounts (user), 71
ACE (Application Control Engine), 109–110
   data center deployment, 186–192
      bridged mode, 187–189
      routed mode configuration, 190–192
   data center scalability, 198
activating devices, 220–222
active directory domains, joining, 318–319
addresses
   IP next hop, 159
   VIP, 112
aggregation of links, 78–79
Alarm Book website, 70
alarms
   conditions, 233
   window, 234
AllDevicesGroup device group, 223
appliances (WAE), 40
   physical requirements website, 56
   WAE models, 41–42
application acceleration, 16, 23–25
   CIFS preposition
      architecture, 304–306
      configuring, 306–310
      statistics, 311–313
   configuring
      connectivity directives, 297–299
      core services, 291–293
      edge services, 294–297
      traffic policies, 300–301
   connectivity directives, 289
   core services, 287–288
   disconnected mode, 313–314
      configuring, 320–321
      domain integration, 314–319
   edge services, 288
   local response handling, 24
   long-lived user sessions, 302
   multiplexing, 25, 29
   object caching, 24–27
   overview, 285–287
   prepositioning, 24, 27
   read-aheads, 24, 27
   verifying, 301–303
   WAN optimization, 289–290
   write-behinds, 25, 28
Application Control Engine. *See* **ACE**
application performance barriers, 3
   application layer, 4
   Layer 4, 5–8
   network infrastructure, 8
      bandwidth, 9–11
      latency, 11–13
      packet loss and congestion, 14–15
   presentation layer, 4
   session layer, 4
   solutions, 15–16
   transport protocols, 4
Application Traffic Policy. *See* **ATP**
applications
   groups, 262–263, 280
   layers
      application performance barriers, 4
      latency, 6
   requirements, 64–65
architecture
   CIFS preposition, 304–306
   network modules, 38
   n-tier, 4
   WAE, 33
      ATP engine, 36–37
      CMS, 35
      disk encryption, 34–35
      interface manager, 35
      network interception and bypass manager, 36
      reporting interface, 35

ATP (Application Traffic Policy), 17, 261–262
    application groups, 262–263
    custom policy-map, 355–357
    engine, 36–37
    policy consistency, 269–270
    policy maps, 266–269
        default policies, 268
        parameters, 266
        policies, configuring, 267
    traffic classifiers, 264–265
    WAN optimization, 17
audit trail logs, 239
authentication
    failover, 227
    third-party, 227–229
authentication configuration command, 228
authentication fail-over server-unreachable command, 227
authentication login command, 228
automatic discovery, 30, 251–253, 274–275
availability requirements, 68

B

backing up CM, 242
bandwidth
    BDP, 12
    LANs, 9
    Layer 4, 7–8
    network performance, 9–11
    savings statistics, 279
    WAE interfaces, increasing, 78–82
    WANs, 9, 46–47
bandwidth command, 77
BDP (bandwidth delay product), 12
best practices of network integration, 114–115
blacklist operation (TFO), 255–257
branch office network integration
    in-path deployment, 117–118
        nonredundant branch office, 118–122
        redundant branch office, 122–125
        serial clustering, 125
    off-path deployment, 127
        IOS FW, 161–162
        large nonredundant branch offices, 134–140
        large redundant branch offices, 142, 149–157
        NME-WAE, 131–132
        PBR, 158–161
        redundant branch offices, 141
        small to medium-sized nonredundant branch offices, 127–130
        small to medium-sized redundant branch offices, 141–149
        two-arm deployment, 132–134
buffers (TFO), 22, 257–261

C

caching
    CLI consumption, 312
    objects, 24–27
        benefits, 26
        first-user penalty, 27
        hit/miss scenarios, 26
capacity (disks), 44–45
case studies
    ATP custom policy-map, 355–357
    common requirements, 325
    data centers
        requirements, 345
        switch 1 configuration, 349–352
        switch 2 configuration, 352–355
        topology, 345
        WAE configuration, 348–349
        WAE placement/interception, 346–347
    existing WAN topology, 325–326
    remote site Profile A, 327
        LAN switch configuration, 331–333
        requirements, 327
        topology, 327
        WAE configuration, 329–330
        WAE placement/interception, 328
        WAN router configuration, 330–331
    remote site Profile B
        requirements, 333
        topology, 333
        WAE configuration, 334–335
        WAE placement/interception, 334
        WAN router configuration, 336–337

remote site Profile C
 requirements, 338
 topology, 338
 WAE configuration, 340–341
 WAE placement/interception, 338–339
 WAN router 1 configuration, 341–343
 WAN router 2 configuration, 343–345
Catalyst 6500
 ACE bridged mode configuration, 188–189
 ACE routed mode configuration, 190–192
Central Manager. *See* **CM**
Centralized Management System. *See* **CMS**
characteristics of traffic flows, 62
checklists
 network infrastructure, 64
 planning overview, 52
 requirements
  application, 65
  availability, 68
  management, 70
  platform, 67
  scalability, 67
  security, 72
  WAFS AO, 67
 site information, 56
CIFS (Common Internet File System)
 peers, 303
 policies, 300
 preposition, 304
  architecture, 304–306
  configuring, 306–310
  statistics, 311–313
 proxy connections, verifying, 298–299
 traffic policies, 300–301
 servers, 298
CIFS acceleration, 287
 CIFS preposition, 304
  architecture, 304–306
  configuring, 306–310
  statistics, 311–313
 configuring
  connectivity directives, 297–299
  core services, 291–293
  edge services, 294–297
  traffic policies, 300–301
 connectivity directives, 289
 core services, 287–288

disconnected mode, 313–314
 configuring, 320–321
 domain integration, 314–319
edge services, 288
long-lived user sessions, 302
verifying, 301–303
WAN optimization, 289–290
Cisco Integrated Services Router (ISR), 29
CLI (command-line interface), 212
 automatic discovery statistics, 274–275
 cache consumption, 312
 connection statistics, 276–279
  compression statistics, 278
  details, 277
  viewing from CM, 277
  viewing from WAE, 276
 device management, 212–213
 syslog servers, defining, 240
client-to-client traffic, 62
client-to-server traffic, 62
CM (Central Manager), 30
 application group statistics, 280
 backing up, 242
 CIFS preposition status, 311
 connections, viewing, 277
 core cluster credentials, 307
 defining, 211
 devices
  activation, 220–222
  grouping, 222–223
  homepage, 229–232
  identities, recovering, 219
  registration, 219
 domains, 72
 file servers, defining, 307
 homepage, 215
 licenses, 42
 login page, 214
 overview, 213–216
 provisioned management, 224
  RBAC, 224–226
  third-party authentication, 227–229
 reporting/logging, 239–241
  audit trail logs example, 239
  syslog servers, defining, 240
  system messages table, 239
 restoring, 242–243
 roles, 71–72, 211

scalability, 214
security, 213
software upgrade/downgrade, 235–238
status/health monitoring, 232–234
system messages table, 239
table of contents, 216
TFO buffer settings, configuring, 260
WAE, 48–49
WAN optimization statistics, 282
**CMS (Centralized Management System),
216–219**
downgrading, 236
enabling, 212
LCM cycle, 217
overview, 216–219
registration and service status, 218
state, 218
timers, 217
cms database downgrade command, 236
cms database restore command, 243
cms recover identity command, 219
collecting requirements, 52–53
applications, 64–65
availability, 68
management, 68–70
platform, 67
scalability, 67
security, 70–72
WAFS AO, 65–67
command-line interface. *See* **CLI**
commands
authentication configuration, 228
authentication fail-over server-unreachable,
227
authentication login, 228
bandwidth, 77
cms database downgrade, 236
cms database restore, 243
cms recover identity, 219
inline vlan all, 124
inspect waas, 202
ip wccp redirect exclude in, 100, 132
logging host, 240
no normalization, 190
no wccp ver 2, 95
policy-engine application, 267
set ip next-hop, 105

set ip next-hop verify-availability, 159
setup, 209
show cifs connectivity peers, 303
show cifs session count, 303
show cifs session list, 303
show cms info, 218
show conn long, 199
show interface, 77
show interface PortChannel, 80
show interface Standby, 85
show stat der connection, 278
show statistics tfo saving, 279
show tfo accelerators, 296
show tfo auto-discovery, 274
show tfo connection, 276–278
snmp-server, 241
ssh-key-generate, 213
standby, 77
Common Internet File System. *See* **CIFS**
common requirements (case studies), 325
compact flash cards, 33
compression
history, 44
statistics, 278
configuring
ACE
bridged mode, 188–189
routed mode, 190–192
authentication failover, 227
Central Manager roles, 71
CIFS acceleration
connectivity directives, 297–299
core services, 291–293
edge services, 294–297
traffic policies, 300–301
CIFS preposition, 306–310
browser, 309
core cluster credentials, 307
edge groups, 309
file servers, defining, 307
preposition jobs, 307
saving, 309
scheduling preposition jobs, 310
CM roles, 211
connectivity directives, 297–299
parameters, 297
proxy connection verification, 298–299

core services, 291
  enabling core services, 292–293
  WAFS core clusters, creating, 291–292
disconnected mode, 320–321
DNS servers, 317
domain-related parameters, 317–318
edge services, 294–297
  device GUI, 296
  enabling edge services, 295
  verification, 296
EPM policies, 271–273
EtherChannel, 79–82
FWSM, 200–202
LAN switches, 331–333
NTP servers, 315
PBR, 104
PIX/ASA, 202–204
policies, 267
primary servers, 227
secondary servers, 227
standby interface feature, 84–86
switches, 349–355
system time, 315–316
TFO buffer settings, 260
third-party authentication provider, 228
time zones, 315
traffic classifiers, 264
WAE
  data centers, 348–349
  interfaces, 76
  with MHSRP, 156–157
  NetBIOS names, 316
  Profile A sites, 329–330
  Profile B sites, 334–335
  Profile C sites, 340–341
WAN distribution switches, 180–184
WAN routers
  Profile A site, 330–331
  Profile B sites, 336–337
  Profile C sites, 341–345
  WAE, 178–179
  WCCP, 176–178
WCCP, 98–102
  IOS, 100–102
  router lists, 99
WINS servers, 317

congestion
  avoidance, 14
  packets, 14–15
  TFO congestion avoidance, 22
connections
  directives, 289, 297–299
  EMIC, 111–113
  EtherChannel configuration, 79–82
  link aggregation, 78–79
  optimized, 248
  original, 248
  standby interface feature, 82–86
  statistics, 276–279
    compression statistics, 278
    details, 277
    viewing from CM, 277
    viewing from WAE, 276
  TCP optimized, 46
  viewing
    CM, 277
    WAE, 276
  WAE interfaces, 75–78
content-based chunking, 19–20
content switching, 109
  ACE, 109–110
  data center deployment, 186–192
    bridged mode configuration, 187–189
    routed mode configuration, 190–192
core cluster credentials, 307
core services, 287–288
  configuring, 291
    enabling core services, 292–293
    WAFS core clusters, creating, 291–292
  enabling, 292–293

D

data centers
  ACE scalability, 198
  content switch deployment, 186–192
    bridged mode configuration, 187–189
    routed mode configuration, 190–192
  firewalls, 199–204
    FWSM, 199–202
    PIX/ASA configuration, 202–204
    server farm aggregation with FWSM, 200

placement, 165, 168, 171–173
  dual data center with symmetric routing,
    168
  multiple centers reference topology, 168
  multiple WAAS clusters, 173
  reference topology, 165
  server farm distribution, 172
  WAN edge WAAS placement, 167
  WAN failure, 169
  WCCP service groups, 171
requirements, 345
switch 1 configuration, 349–352
switch 2 configuration, 352–355
topology, 60–61, 345
WAE
  configuration, 348–349
  placement/interception, 346–347
WCCP deployment, 175–186
  dual data centers, 185–186
  WAN distribution switch configuration,
    180–184
  WAN edge router configuration, 176–179
  WCCP enabled on WAN distribution
    switches, 179
  WCCP enabled on WAN edge routers, 175
WCCP scalability, 192–198
  client distribution, 194–195
  WAE hash bucket distribution, 193–194
  WAE mask/value distribution, 195–197
data encryption, 70
Data Redundancy Elimination. *See* **DRE**
default policies, 268
deleting traffic classifiers, 264
deployment
  data centers with content switching, 186–192
    bridged mode configuration, 187–189
    routed mode configuration, 190–192
  data centers with WCCP, 175–186
    dual data centers, 185–186
    WAN distribution switch configuration,
      180–184
    WAN edge router configuration, 176–179
    WCCP enabled on WAN distribution
      switches, 179
    WCCP enabled on WAN edge routers, 175

in-path, 117–118
  nonredundant branch office, 118–122
  redundant branch office, 122–125
  serial clustering, 125
off-path, 127
  IOS FW, 161–162
  large nonredundant branch offices,
    134–140
  large redundant branch offices, 142,
    149–157
  NME-WAE, 131–132
  PBR, 158–161
  redundant branch offices, 141
  small to medium-sized nonredundant
    branch offices, 127–130
  small to medium-sized redundant branch
    offices, 141–149
  two-arm deployment, 132–134
planning, 51–52
requirements collection, 52–53
sites, 54
  checklist, 56
  physical environments, 55–56
  types, 54–55
  user community, 55
devices
activation, 220–222
CLI, 212–213
CM
  backing up, 242
  device homepage, 229–232
  overview, 213–216
  reporting/logging, 239–241
  restoring, 242–243
  security, 213
  software upgrade/downgrade, 235–238
  status/health monitoring, 232–234
CMS
  enabling, 212
  overview, 216–219
grouping, 222–223, 238
homepage, 229–232
identities, recovering, 219
managing, 207
modes, defining, 210
pending state, 222
registration, 219

setup script, 208–212

  boot sequence interruption, 209

  CM, 211

  device mode, defining, 210

  primary interface, 210

  running, 209

troubleshooting, 233

WAE

  Central Manager, 48–49

  compression history, 44

  disk capacity, 44–45

  LAN throughput, 46–47

  memory, 43

  optimized TCP connections, 46

  peers, 47–48

  WAN bandwidth, 46–47

digital signatures, 66

disconnected mode, domain integration, 314

  active directory domains, joining, 318– 319

  configuring, 320–321

  domain-related parameters, 317–318

  system time configuration, 315–316

discovery, 30

disks

  capacity, 44–45

  encryption, 34–35

distribution switches (WAN)

  WAE configuration, 184

  WCCP

    configuration, 180–183

    enabling on, 179

DNS servers, configuring, 317

domains

  active directory, joining, 318–319

  Central Manager, 72

  controllers, defining, 318

  defining, 225

  integration, disconnected mode, 314

    active directory domains, joining, 318– 319

    domain-related parameters, 317–318

    system time configuration, 315–316

  parameters, configuring, 317–318

downgrading software, 235–238

DRE (Data Redundancy Elimination), 17–19, 249

  content-based chunking, 19–20

  encoding, 20

  message validation, 21

  pattern matching, 20

WAN optimization, 249–250

dual data centers

  asymmetric routing, 185

  WAE configuration, 185–186

dynamic ports, assigning, 270–271

dynamic services, 88

dynamic shares, 66

E

edge devices, 312

edge groups, 309

edge services, 288

  configuring, 294–297

  enabling, 295

  verifying, 296

egress traffic, 111–113

EMIC (Egress Methods for Intercepted Connections), 111–113

encryption

  data, 70

  disks, 34–35

  DRE, 20

enterprise-class scalability, 30

enterprise licenses, 42

EPM (EndPoint Mapper), 270–273

  enabling/disabling, 272

  policy configuration, 271–273

  port mappers, 270–271

Error Message Book website, 70

EtherChannel, 78–82

existing WAN topology case study, 325–326

extensions (TFO), 22

F

failover, 227

failure detection, 94

file servers, defining, 307

Firewall Switch Module. *See* **FWSM**

firewalls, 199–204

  allowed ports, 214

  FWSM

    configuration, 200–202

    connection display, 199

    server farm aggregation, 200

  PIX/ASA configuration, 202–204

first-user penalty (caching), 27
flow protection (WCCP), 95
forwarding methods, 90–92
FWSM (Firewall Switch Module), 199
    configuring, 200–202
    connection display, 199
    server farm aggregation, 200

G

GLBP (Gateway Load Balancing Protocol), 112
graceful shutdown (WCCP), 95
GRE forwarding, 90
groups
    application, 262–263, 280
    devices, 222–223, 238
    edge, 309
    service
        placement, 97–98
        WCCP, 87–90, 171

H

hardware
    platforms, 102–103
    WAE, 38
        appliances, 40–42
        router-integrated network modules, 38–40
hash assignments, 92
health/status monitoring, 232–234
homepage (CM), 215
HTTPS (HTTP over Secure Sockets Layer), 213

I

identities of devices, 219
infrastructure of networks
    checklist, 64
    data center topology, 60–61
    remote office topology, 59–60
    traffic flows, 62–63
    WAN topology, 56–58
inline interception, 105–108
    cabling guidelines, 108

InlineGroup configuration, 108
    multiple routers, 106
    one-armed routing, 107
    operating modes, 106
inline vlan all command, 124
in-path deployment, 117–118
    nonredundant branch office, 118–122
        management IP address on inlineGroup,
            121
        reference topology, 118
        WAE configuration, 120
        WAE inlineGroup configuration, 119
    redundant branch office, 122–125
        reference topology, 122
        WAE configuration, 124
        WAE inlineGroup configuration, 124
    serial clustering, 125
inspect waas command, 202
Integrated Services Router (ISR), 29
integration
    best practices, 114–115
    branch office networks
        in-path deployment. See in-path
            deployment
        IOS FW, 161–162
        NME-WAE, 131–132
        off-path deployment. See off-path
            deployment
        PBR, 158–160
        two-arm deployment, 132–134
    data centers, 165, 168, 171–173
interception
    content switching, 109–110
    data centers. *See* data centers
    inline, 105–108
        cabling guidelines, 108
        InlineGroup configuration, 108
        multiple routers, 106
        one-armed routing, 107
        operating modes, 106
    policy-based routing, 103–105
    redirection
        failure detection, 94
        flow protection, 95
        forwarding/return methods, 90–92
        graceful shutdown, 95
        load distribution, 92

redirect lists, 96–97
scalability, 95–96
service group placement, 97–98
WAE
  data centers, 346–347
  Profile A sites, 328
  Profile B sites, 334
  Profile C sites, 338–339
WCCP, 86
  configuration, 98–102
  hardware-based platforms, 102–103
  overview, 87
  service groups, 87–90
interfaces (WAE)
  bandwidth, increasing, 78–82
  configuring, 76
  connectivity, 75–78
  managing, 35
  names, 77
  reporting, 35
  standby interface feature, 82–86
intermittent disconnection, 320
IOS FW (IOS Firewall), 161–162
IOS WCCP global configuration, 100
**IOS WCCP inbound redirection configuration,
   101–102**
IP forwarding, 111–112
IP next hop addresses, 159
ip wccp redirect exclude in command, 132
ip wccp redirect exclude in commands, 100
ISR (Integrated Services Router), 29

J – K

joining active directory domains, 318–319

keepalives (TFO), 261

L

L2 forwarding, 90
LACP (Link Aggregation Control Protocol), 79
LANs (local-area networks)
  bandwidth, 9
  latency, 11

switches, 331–333
throughput, 46–47
**large nonredundant branch offices, off-path
   deployment, 134–140**
  LAN switch configuration, 137
  reference topology, 135
  WAE configuration, 137, 140
  WAN router configuration, 136
  WCCP
    interception, 138
    LAN switch configuration, 139
**large redundant branch offices, off-path
   deployment, 142, 149–157**
  LAN switch configuration, 151–153
  MHSRP configuration on WAE VLAN, 155
  reference topology, 141, 149
  WAE configuration, 154–157
latency
  application layers, 6
  LANs, 11
  Layer 4, 6
  networks, 11–13
  WANs, 11
layers
  application
    application performance barriers, 4
    latency, 6
  Layer 4, 5–8
  presentation, 4
  session, 4
LCM (Local Central Management), 35, 217
LFNs (long fat networks), 257–258
licensing, 42
link aggregation, 78–79
Link Aggregation Control Protocol (LACP), 79
Linux platform, 33
load distribution (WCCP), 92
local-area networks. *See* **LANs**
Local Central Management (LCM), 35, 217
local response handling, 24
locations. *See* **sites**
logging, 239–241
  audit trail logs example, 239
  syslog servers, defining, 240
  system messages table, 239
logging host command, 240

login page (CM), 214
long fat networks (LFNs), 257–258
long-lived user sessions, 302
loss (packets), 14–15

M

management
   Central Manager, 30
     application group statistics, 280
     backing up, 242
     CIFS preposition status, 311
     connections, viewing, 277
     core cluster credentials, 307
     defining, 211
     devices. See CM, devices
     domains, 72
     file servers, defining, 307
     homepage, 215
     licenses, 42
     login page, 214
     overview, 213–216
     provisioned management, 224–229
     reporting/logging, 239–241
     restoring, 242–243
     roles, 71–72, 211
     scalability, 214
     security, 213
     software upgrade/downgrade, 235–238
     status/health monitoring, 232–234
     system messages table, 239
     table of contents, 216
     TFO buffer settings, configuring, 260
     WAE, 48–49
     WAN optimization statistics, 282
   CMS, 216–219
     downgrading, 236
     enabling, 212
     LCM cycle, 217
     overview, 216–219
     registration and service status, 218
     state, 218
     timers, 217
   devices, 207
     CLI, 212–213
     setup script, 208–212

   network interception and bypass, 36
   provisioned, 224
     RBAC, 224–226
     third-party authentication, 227–229
   requirements, 68
     checklist, 70
     SNMP community strings, 69–70
     SNMP traps/inform routing, 69
     syslog servers, 70
   WAE interface, 35
mask assignments, 92, 195–197
memory (WAE devices), 43
messages
   DRE validation, 21
   local response handling, 24
metadata, caching, 25–27
MIB (SNMP supported), 241
Microsoft Access-Based Enumeration (ABE), 66
Microsoft Volume Shadow Copy Services (VSS), 66
modules, router-Integrated network modules (WAE), 38
   NME-WAE model 302, 39
   NME-WAE model 502, 39
   NME-WAE model 522, 40
monitoring, status/health with CM, 232–234
   status indicator locations, 233
   Troubleshooting Devices window, 234
MSS settings (TFO), 261
multiplexing, 25, 29

N

names (WAE)
   interfaces, 77
   NetBIOS, 316
NetQos SuperAgent website, 59
Network Module Enhanced (NME), 38
Network Module Enhanced WAE. See NME-WAE
networks
   application performance barriers, 8
     application layer, 4
     bandwidth, 9–11
     latency, 11–13
     Layer 4, 5–8
     packet loss and congestion, 14–15

infrastructure
  checklist, 64
  data center topology, 60–61
  remote office topology, 59–60
  traffic flows, 62–63
  WAN topology, 56, 58
integration, 114–115
interception
  content switching, 109–110
  failure detection, 94
  flow protection, 95
  forwarding/return methods, 90–92
  graceful shutdown, 95
  inline, 105–108
  load distribution, 92
  policy-based routing, 103–105
  redirect lists, 96–97
  scalability, 95–96
  service group placement, 97–98
  WCCP, 86–90
  WCCP configuration, 98–102
  WCCP hardware-based platforms,
    102–103
latency, 11–13
transparency, 29
WAN oversubscription, 9
NME (Network Module Enhanced), 38
**NME-WAE (Network Module Enhanced WAE),
  131–132**
interface connectivity, 75
models
  302, 39
  502, 39
  522, 40
no normalization command, 190
no wccp ver 2 command, 95
nonredundant branch offices
in-path deployment, 118–122
  management IP address on inlineGroup,
    121
  reference topology, 118
  WAE configuration, 119–120
off-path deployment for large, 134–140
  LAN switch configuration, 137
  reference topology, 135
  WAE configuration, 137, 140

  WAN router configuration, 136
  WCCP interception, 138
  WCCP on LAN switch configuration, 139
off-path deployment for small to medium-sized,
  127–130
  reference topology, 127
  WAE configuration, 129
  WCCP configuration, 129
  WCCP GRE return traffic flow, 128
n-tier architecture, 4
NTP servers, configuring, 315

O

objects, caching, 24–27
benefits, 26
first-user penalty, 27
hit/miss scenarios, 26
off-path deployment, 127
IOS FW, 161–162
large nonredundant branch offices, 134–140
  LAN switch configuration, 137
  reference topology, 135
  WAE configuration, 137, 140
  WAN router configuration, 136
  WCCP interception, 138
  WCCP on LAN switch configuration, 139
large redundant branch offices, 142, 149–157
  LAN switch configuration, 151–153
  MHSRP configuration on WAE VLAN, 155
  reference topology, 141, 149
  WAE configuration, 154–157
PBR, 158–161
  IP next hop address verification, 159
  multiple IP next hop addresses, 159
  traffic distribution, 160
redundant branch offices, 141
small to medium-sized nonredundant branch
  offices, 127–130
  NME-WAE, 131–132
  reference topology, 127
  two-arm deployment, 132–134
  WAE configuration, 129
  WCCP configuration, 129
  WCCP GRE return traffic flow, 128

small to medium-sized redundant branch
offices, 141–149
redirection loop, 145
WAE configuration, 144, 148
WAE subnet as transit path, 145
WAN router configuration, 143, 146
Open Systems Interconnection. *See* **OSI model**
optimization
connections, 248
TCP connections, 46
WANs, 16–18, 247
application acceleration, 289–290
ATP, 261–269
automatic discovery, 251–253
DRE, 17–21, 249–250
enabling/disabling features, 253–254
EPM, 270–273
PLZ, 17, 21, 251
policy consistency, 269–270
statistics, 279–282
TFO, 17, 22, 247–249
TFO blacklist operation, 255–257
TFO buffers, tuning, 257–261
trusted, 30
original connections, 248
OSI (Open Systems Interconnection) model, 4
application layer
application performance barriers, 4
latency, 6
presentation layers, 4
session layers, 4
other policy, 269
oversubscription (WANs), 9

P

packet loss and congestion, 14–15
parameters
CIFS preposition, 305
connectivity directives, 297
domain-related, 317–318
edge services, 294
policy maps, 266
WAFS core cluster, 292
PBR (policy-based routing), 103–105, 158–161

peers
CIFS, 303
WAE, 47–48
pending states (devices), 222
performance
application performance barriers, 3
application layer, 4
Layer 4, 5–8
network infrastructure, 8–15
presentation layer, 4
session layer, 4
solutions, 15–16
transport protocols, 4
WAE system limits, 43
Central Manager, 48–49
device memory, 43
disk capacity, 44–45
LAN throughput, 46–47
optimized TCP connections, 46
peers, 47–48
WAN bandwidth, 46–47
WAFS AO, 66
Persistent LZ Compression (PLZ), 17, 21, 251
physical environments, 55–56
PIX/ASA, 202–204
placement
data centers, 165, 168, 171–173
dual data center with symmetric routing, 168
multiple centers reference topology, 168
multiple WAAS clusters, 173
reference topology, 165
server farm distribution, 172
WAN edge WAAS placement, 167
WAN failure, 169
WCCP service groups, 171
service groups, 97–98
WAE
data centers, 346–347
Profile A site, 328
Profile B sites, 334
Profile C sites, 338–339
planning deployment, 51–52
platforms
requirements, 67
WCCP hardware-based, 102–103

PLZ (Persistent LZ Compression), 17, 21, 251
policies
    CIFS, 300–301
    configuring, 267
    consistency, 269–270
    default policies, 268
    EPM, 271–273
    other policy, 269
    WAFS transport, 300
policy-based routing (PBR), 103–105, 158–161
policy-engine application command, 267
policy maps, 266–269
    custom, creating, 355–357
    default policies, 268
    parameters, 266
    policies, configuring, 267
ports
    allowing through firewall, 214
    dynamic, 270–271
    mappers, 270–271
preposition jobs
    configuring, 307
    scheduling, 310
prepositioning, 24, 27
presentation layers, 4
primary interface, defining, 210
primary servers, configuring, 227
Profile A sites, 327
    LAN switch configuration, 331–333
    requirements, 327
    topology, 327
    WAE
        configuration, 329–330
        placement/interception, 328
    WAN router configuration, 330–331
Profile B sites
    requirements, 333
    topology, 333
    WAE
        configuration, 334–335
        placement/interception, 334
    WAN router configuration, 336–337
Profile C sites
    requirements, 338
    topology, 338
    WAE
        configuration, 340–341
        placement/interception, 338–339

WANs
    router 1 configuration, 341–343
    router 2 configuration, 343–345
prolonged disconnected mode, 321
protocols
    LACP, 79
    TCP
        optimization with compression, 258
        optimized connections, 46
        over LFNs, 258
        packet loss and congestion, 14–15
        TFO, compared, 22
        WAN optimization, 17
    transport, 4
    SNMP
        community strings, 69–70
        MIBs supported, 241
        traps/inform routing, 69
    WCCP, 86
        configuring, 98–102
        failure detection, 94
        flow protection, 95
        forwarding/return methods, 90–92
        graceful shutdown, 95
        hardware-based platforms, 102–103
        load distribution, 92
        overview, 87
        redirect lists, 96–97
        scalability, 95–96
        service group placement, 97–98
        service groups, 87–90
        small to medium-sized nonredundant
            branch office configuration, 129
    WCCPv2, 36
provisioned management, 224
    RBAC, 224–226
    third-party authentication, 227–229

R

RBAC (role-based access control), 224–226
read-aheads, 24, 27
recovering device identities, 219
redirect lists (WCCP), 96–97
redirection
    traffic, 90–92

WCCP
  failure detection, 94
  flow protection, 95
  forwarding/return methods, 90–92
  graceful shutdown, 95
  load distribution, 92
  redirect lists, 96–97
  scalability, 95–96
  service group placement, 97–98
redundant branch offices
  in-path deployment, 122–125
    reference topology, 122
    WAE configuration, 124
    WAE inlineGroup configuration, 124
  large off-path deployment, 142, 149–157
    LAN switch configuration, 151–153
    MHSRP configuration on WAE VLAN, 155
    reference topology, 141, 149
    WAE configuration, 154–157
  off-path deployment, 141
  small to medium-sized off-path deployment,
    141–149
    redirection loop, 145
    WAE configuration, 144, 148
    WAE subnet as transit path, 145
    WAN router configuration, 143, 146
registration of devices, 219
remote office topology, 59–60
remote site case studies
  Profile A, 327
    LAN switch configuration, 331–333
    requirements, 327
    topology, 327
    WAE configuration, 329–330
    WAE placement/interception, 328
    WAN router configuration, 330–331
  Profile B
    requirements, 333
    topology, 333
    WAE configuration, 334–335
    WAE placement/interception, 334
    WAN router configuration, 336–337
  Profile C
    requirements, 338
    topology, 338
    WAE configuration, 340–341
    WAE placement/interception, 338–339

    WAN router 1 configuration, 341–343
    WAN router 2 configuration, 343–345
reporting, 239–241
  audit trail logs example, 239
  automatic discovery statistics, 274–275
  connection statistics, 276–279
    compression statistics, 278
    details, 277
    viewing from CM, 277
    viewing from WAE, 276
  syslog servers, defining, 240
  system messages table, 239
  WAE interface, 35
  WAN optimization statistics, 279–282
    application group statistics, 280
    bandwidth savings, 279
    examining, 282
    traffic details, 282
requirements
  applications, 64–65
  availability, 68
  case studies, 325
  collecting, 52–53
  data centers, 345
  management, 68
    checklist, 70
    SNMP community strings, 69–70
    SNMP traps/inform routing, 69
    syslog servers, 70
  platform, 67
  Profile A sites, 327
  Profile B sites, 333
  Profile C sites, 338
  scalability, 67
  security, 70–72
    access control, 71
    Central Manager, 71–72
    checklist, 72
    data encryption, 70
  WAFS AO, 65–67
restoring
  CM, 242–243
  default policies, 268
return methods, 90–92
role-based access control (RBAC), 224–226
roles (CM), 71–72, 211

router-integrated network modules (NME-WAE), 38
model 302, 39
model 502, 39
model 522, 40
routers
lists (WCCP), 99
ISR, 29
WAN edge
WAE configuration, 178–179
WCCP configuration, 176–178
WAN configurations
Profile A sites, 330–331
Profile B sites, 336–337
Profile C sites, 341–345

S

SACK (selective acknowledgment), 22
saving
CIFS preposition configuration, 309
bandwidth statistics, 279
scalability
CM, 214
data centers
ACE, 198
WCCP, 192–198
enterprise-class, 30
requirements, 67
WAE system limits, 43
Central Manager, 48–49
device memory, 43
disk capacity, 44–45
LAN throughput, 46–47
optimized TCP connections, 46
peers, 47–48
WAN bandwidth, 46–47
WCCP, 95–96
scheduling preposition jobs, 310
secondary servers, configuring, 227
security
CM, 213
firewalls, 199–204
allowed ports, 214
FWSM configuration, 200–202
FWSM connection display, 199

FWSM server farm aggregation, 200
PIX/ASA configuration, 202–204
requirements, 70–72
access control, 71
Central Manager, 71–72
checklist, 72
data encryption, 70
selective acknowledgment (SACK), 22
serial clustering, 125
servers
CIFS, 298
DNS, 317
file, 307
NTP, 315
primary, 227
secondary, 227
syslog, 70, 240
WINS, 317
server-to-server traffic, 62
services
CMS, 212
core, 287–288
configuring, 291–292
enabling, 292–293
edge, 288
configuring, 294–297
device GUI, 296
enabling, 295
verifying, 296
groups
placement, 97–98
WCCP, 87–90, 171
Layer 4, 5–8
VSS, 66
sessions
CIFS, 303
layers, 4
set ip next-hop command, 105
set ip next-hop verify-availability command, 159
setup command, 209
setup script, 208–212
boot sequence interruption, 209
CM, 211
CMS, enabling, 212
device mode, defining, 210
primary interface, 210
running, 209

shares (dynamic), **66**
show cifs connectivity peers command, **303**
show cifs session count command, **303**
show cifs session list command, **303**
show cms info command, **218**
show conn long command, **199**
show interface command, **77**
show interface PortChannel command, **80**
show interface Standby command, **85**
show stat der connection command, **278**
show statistics tfo saving command, **279**
show tfo accelerators command, **296**
show tfo auto-discovery command, **274**
show tfo connection command, **278**
show tfo connection summary command, **276**
signatures (digital), **66**
Simple Network Management Protocol. *See* SNMP
sites, **54**
    checklist, 56
    physical environments, 55–56
    Profile A sites, 327
        LAN switch configuration, 331–333
        requirements, 327
        topology, 327
        WAE, 328–330
        WAN router configuration, 330–331
    Profile B sites
        requirements, 333
        topology, 333
        WAE, 334–335
        WAN router configuration, 336–337
    Profile C sites
        requirements, 338
        topology, 338
        WAE configuration, 340–341
        WAE placement/interception, 338–339
        WAN router 1 configuration, 341–343
        WAN router 2 configuration, 343–345
    types, 54–55
    user community, 55
small to medium-sized nonredundant branch
  offices, off-path deployment, **127–130**
    reference topology, 127
    WAE configuration, 129
    WCCP
        configuration, 129
        GRE return traffic flow, 128

small to medium-sized redundant branch offices,
  off-path deployment, **141–149**
    redirection loop, 145
    WAE
        configuration, 144, 148
        subnet as transit path, 145
    WAN router configuration, 143, 146
SNMP (Simple Network Management Protocol)
    community strings, 69–70
    MIBs supported, 241
    traps/inform routing, 69
snmp-server command, **241**
software
    file entries, 235
    upgrades/downgrades, 235–238
ssh-key-generate command, **213**
standby command, **77**
standby interface feature, **82–86**
states
    CMS, 218
    devices, 222
status
    CIFS preposition, 311–312
    indicator, 233
    status/health monitoring, 232–234
        status indicator locations, 233
        Troubleshooting Devices window, 234
switches
    data centers, 349–355
    LANs, 331–333
    WAN distribution
        WAE configuration, 184
        WCCP configuration, 180–183
        WCCP enabled on, 179
syslog servers, **70, 240**
system messages table (CM), **239**
system time, configuring, **315–316**

T

table of contents (CM), **216**
TCP (Transmission Control Protocol), **14**
    optimization
        compression, 258
        connections, 46
        WANs, 17

over LFNs, 258
packet loss and congestion, 14–15
TFO, compared, 22
TFO (Transport Flow Optimization), 17, 22, 247
AD, 251–253, 274–275
blacklist operation, 255–257
buffers, 22, 257–261
congestion avoidance, 22
extensions, 22
keepalives, 261
large initial windows, 22
MSS settings, 261
SACK, 22
TCP, compared, 22
WAN optimization, 247–249
window scaling, 22
third-party authentication, 227–229
throughput (LANs), 46–47
time zones, configuring, 315
timers (CMS), 217
topologies
data center, 60–61
remote office, 59–60
WAN, 56–58
traffic
classifiers, 264–265
distribution, 160
egress, 111–113
forwarding/return methods, 90–92
flows, 62–63
policies (CIFS), 300–301
statistics detail report, 282
Transmission Control Protocol. *See* **TCP**
transparency, 29
Transport Flow Optimization. *See* **TFO**
transport licenses (WAE), 42
transport protocols, 4
tree of lights, 233
troubleshooting devices, 233–234
trusted WAN optimization, 30
two-arm deployment, branch office networks, 132–134
traffic flow, 132
WAE configuration, 134
WAN router configuration, 133
types
sites, 54–55
traffic flows, 62

U

Unicast Reverse Path Forwarding, 339
upgrading software, 235–238
users
accounts, 71
RBAC, 225–226
site community information, 55
UUIDs (universally unique identifiers), 270

V

validating messages, 21
verifying
CIFS acceleration, 301–303
policies, 301
proxy connections, 298–299
edge services, 296
IP next hop addresses, 159
viewing
CMS registration and service status, 218
connections
CM, 277
WAE, 276
traffic classifiers, 264
VIP (virtual IP) addresses, 112
VSS (Volume Shadow Copy Services), 66

W

WAAS (Wide Area Application Services), 3
WAE (Wide Area Application Engine), 33
appliances, 40
physical requirements website, 56
WAE model 512, 41
WAE model 612, 41
WAE model 7326, 41
WAE model 7341, 41
WAE model 7371, 42
architecture, 33
ATP engine, 36–37
CMS, 35
disk encryption, 34–35
interface manager, 35
network interception and bypass manager, 36
reporting interface, 35

compact flash cards, 33
compression statistics, 278
configuring
    data centers, 348–349
    with MHSRP, 156–157
    Profile A site, 329–330
    Profile B sites, 334–335
    Profile C sites, 340–341
connections, viewing, 276
content switching, 109–110
dual data center configuration, 185–186
EtherChannel, 78–82
hardware, 38
inline interception, 105–108
    cabling guidelines, 108
    InlineGroup configuration, 108
    multiple routers, 106
    one-armed routing, 107
    operating modes, 106
interception
    data centers, 346–347
    Profile A site, 328
    Profile B sites, 334
    Profile C sites, 338–339
interfaces
    bandwidth, increasing, 78–82
    configuring, 76
    connectivity, 75–78
    names, 77
    standby interface feature, 82–86
large nonredundant branch office deployment
    configuration, 137
large redundant branch office off-path
    deployment, 154
licensing, 42
Linux platform, 33
mask/value distribution (data centers), 195–197
NetBIOS names, 316
Network Module Enhanced (NME-WAE),
    131–132
    interface connectivity, 75
    models, 39–40
nonredundant branch office in-path
    deployment, 120
PBR, 103–105
performance and scalability system limits, 43
    Central Manager, 48–49

device memory, 43
disk capacity, 44–45
LAN throughput, 46–47
optimized TCP connections, 46
peers, 47–48
WAN bandwidth, 46–47
placement
    data centers, 346–347
    Profile A site, 328
    Profile B sites, 334
    Profile C sites, 338–339
primary interface, 210
redundant branch office in-path configuration,
    124
router-integrated network modules, 38
    NME-WAE model 302, 39
    NME-WAE model 502, 39
    NME-WAE model 522, 40
setup script, 208–212
    boot sequence interruption, 209
    CM, 211
    CMS, enabling, 212
    device mode, defining, 210
    primary interface, 210
    running, 209
small to medium-sized nonredundant branch
    office configuration, 129
small to medium-sized redundant branch office
    configuration, 148
    deployment, 144
two-arm deployment configuration, 134
WAN
    distribution switch configuration, 184
    router configuration, 178–179
WCCP on LAN switch deployment
    configuration, 140
WAE model 512, 41
WAE model 612, 41
WAE model 7326, 41
WAE model 7341, 41
WAE model 7371, 42
**WAFS AO (Wide Area File Services Application
Optimizer), 65**
    advanced features, 66
    performance, 66
    requirements, 65–67
WAFS core clusters, creating, 291–292

WAFS transport policies, 300
WANs (wide-area networks), 3
  application performance barriers, 3
    application layer, 4
    Layer 4, 5–8
    network infrastructure, 8–15
    presentation layer, 4
    session layer, 4
    solutions, 15–16
    transport protocols, 4
  bandwidth, 9, 46–47
  distribution switches
    WAE configuration, 184
    WCCP configuration, 180–183
    WCCP enabled on, 179
  edges
    data center placement, 166
    routers, 176–179
  existing WAN topology case study, 325–326
  latency, 11
  network oversubscription, 9
  optimization, 16–18, 247
    application acceleration, 289–290
    ATP, 261–269
    automatic discovery, 251–253
    DRE, 17–21, 249–250
    enabling/disabling features, 253–254
    EPM, 270–273
    PLZ, 17, 21, 251
    policy consistency, 269–270
    statistics, 279–282
    TFO,17, 22, 247–249
    TFO blacklist operation, 255–257
    TFO buffers, tuning, 257–261
    trusted, 30
  router configurations
    Profile A sites, 330–331
    Profile B sites, 336–337
    Profile C sites, 341–345
  topology, 56–58
WCCP (Web Cache Communication Protocol), 86
  configuring, 98–102
    IOS, 100–102
    router lists, 99

  data center deployment, 175–186
    dual data centers, 185– 186
    WAN distribution switches, 180–184
    WAN edge routers, 176–179
    WCC, enabling, 175, 179
  data center scalability, 192–198
    client distribution, 194–195
    WAE hash bucket distribution, 193–194
    WAE mask/value distribution, 195–197
  hardware-based platforms, 102–103
  overview, 87
  redirection
    failure detection, 94
    forwarding/return methods, 90–92
    graceful shutdown, 95
    load distribution, 92
    redirect lists, 96–97
    scalability, 95–96
    service group placement, 97–98
  redirection flow protection, 95
  service groups, 87–90
    attributes, 88–90
    data centers, 171
  small to medium-sized nonredundant branch office configuration, 129
WCCPv2 (Web Cache Coordination Protocol version 2), 36, 87
Web Cache Communication Protocol. *See* WCCP
web-cache service, 88
websites
  Alarm Book, 70
  Error Message Book, 70
  NetQos SuperAgent, 59
  Unicast Reverse Path Forwarding, 339
  WAE appliance physical requirements, 56
  WCCPv2 IETF draft, 87
well-known services, 88
Wide Area Application Services (WAAS), 3
Wide Area File Services Application Optimizer. *See* WAFS AO
Wide Area Application Engine. *See* WAE
wide-area networks. *See* WANs
window scaling (TFO), 22
WINS servers, configuring, 317
write-behinds, 25, 28

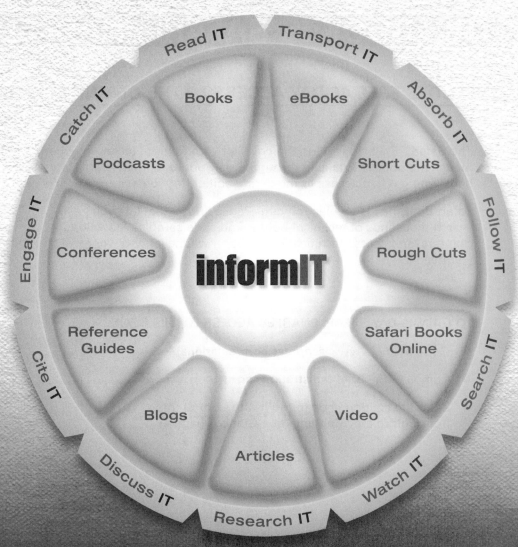

BOOKS ONLINE

ENABLED

THIS BOOK IS SAFARI ENABLED

INCLUDES FREE 45-DAY ACCESS TO THE ONLINE EDITION

The Safari® Enabled icon on the cover of your favorite technology book means the book is available through Safari Bookshelf. When you buy this book, you get free access to the online edition for 45 days.

Safari Bookshelf is an electronic reference library that lets you easily search thousands of technical books, find code samples, download chapters, and access technical information whenever and wherever you need it.

TO GAIN 45-DAY SAFARI ENABLED ACCESS TO THIS BOOK:

● Go to **http://www.ciscopress.com/safarienabled**

● Complete the brief registration form

● Enter the coupon code found in the front of this book before the "Contents at a Glance" page

If you have difficulty registering on Safari Bookshelf or accessing the online edition, please e-mail customer-service@safaribooksonline.com.